ARCO

Everything you need to know to get a civil service job

CIVIL SERVICE HANDBOOK

13th Edition

Edited by
Hy Hammer
Chief of Examining Service Division
New York City Department of Personnel (Retired)

MACMILLAN • USA

Thirteenth Edition

Macmillan Reference USA
A Simon & Schuster Macmillan Company
1633 Broadway
New York, NY 10019-6785

An Arco Book

Manufactured in the United States of America

10 9 8 7 6 5 4 3 2 1

Library of Congress Number 97-80438

ISBN: 0-02-862172-7

CONTENTS

Introduction

There are few occupations or professions in the private sector that are not also represented in the federal, state, or municipal civil service. Doctors, nurses, engineers, physicists are employed by the government along with secretaries, typists, and unskilled laborers. Very few occupations indeed exist only in the private sector. Even job titles like seamstress and tailor exist in the public service although opportunities for these and similar categories may not be as plentiful as many others. If you are seeking a career in government service, you will probably be able to put to use the skills you have acquired at one level of government or another.

The main difference between working for the government and working in the private sector is that civil service appointments usually require the applicant to meet basic requirements as outlined in a published job announcement and then to compete with other aspirants for that position on the basis of an examination. The examination requires that applicants demonstrate that they possess knowledge, skills, and abilities to perform the duties of the position being sought. Those who perform best on the examination will be considered first to fill existing vacancies; those who do not perform well will not be considered at all.

This book is intended to acquaint the civil service job aspirant with just what it takes to obtain a government job. Requirements are listed for a rich variety of jobs at all three levels of government service: federal, state, and municipal. These job announcements list the requirements for filing for each job, typical duties to be performed, and other important facts in which job seekers are likely to be interested. Also included in this book are job opportunities in the U.S. Postal Service. Since the Postal Service is no longer under the direct control of Congress, employment with this agency cannot be construed to be federal service.

You will find that the section "Federal Employment" supplies information about the essential steps leading to federal employment and that these steps are very similar to those that lead to state and municipal employment. Used properly this book will be a ready reference to the many job opportunities that exist in the government sector and will serve as a guide to the most direct approach to obtaining them.

[illegible]

[illegible]

[illegible]

[illegible]

PART ONE

Working for the Federal Government

CONTENTS

FEDERAL EMPLOYMENT

The federal government is the employer of a far greater number of Americans than is any other employer. A large percentage of these government employees are members of the military, but there are also millions of civilian federal employees. Many civilian federal employees are employed through the Legislative Branch—the Congress itself, the General Accounting Office, the Government Printing Office, and the Library of Congress, for example—and through the Judicial Branch—the Supreme Court and the U.S. Court system. But by far the greatest number of federal civilian employees are employees of the Executive Branch, Executive Departments, and Independent Agencies such as the U.S. Postal Service, the General Services Administration, the Smithsonian, the Environmental Protection Agency, and the Office of Personnel Administration itself, to name only a few.

The Executive Branch includes the Office of the President, the departments with cabinet representation, and a number of independent agencies, commissions, and boards. This branch is responsible for such activities as administering federal laws, handling international relations, conserving natural resources, treating and rehabilitating disabled veterans, conducting scientific research, maintaining the flow of supplies to the armed forces, and administering other programs to promote the health and welfare of the people.

The federal government employs about three million white-collar workers. Entrance requirements for white-collar jobs vary widely. Entrants into professional occupations are required to have highly specialized knowledge in a specified field, as evidenced by completion of a prescribed college course of study. Occupations typical of this group are attorney, physicist, and engineer.

Entrants into administrative and managerial occupations usually are not required to have specialized knowledge but rather they must indicate, by graduation from a four-year college or by responsible job experience, that they have the potential for future development. The entrant usually begins at a trainee level and learns the duties of the job after being hired. Typical jobs in this group are budget analyst, claims examiner, purchasing officer, administrative assistant, and personnel officer.

Technician, clerical, and aide-assistant jobs have entry level positions that usually are filled by persons having a high school diploma or the equivalent. For many of these positions, no prior experience or training is required. The entry level position is usually that of trainee, where the duties of the job are learned and skill is improved. Persons with junior college or technical school training or those having specialized skills may enter these occupations at higher levels. Jobs typical of this group are engineering technician, supply clerk, clerk-typist, and nursing assistant.

Blue-collar jobs—service, craft, and manual labor—provide employment to over 600,000 workers. The majority of these workers are in establishments such as naval shipyards, arsenals, air bases, or army depots, or they work on construction, harbor, flood-control, irrigation, or reclamation projects.

The single largest group of blue-collar workers consists of mobile equipment operators and mechanics. Among these jobs are forklift operator, chauffeur, truck driver, and automobile mechanic. The next largest group is general laborers who perform a wide variety of manual jobs.

Many skilled occupations may be entered through apprenticeship programs. Experience normally is not required to qualify, but a test may be given to indicate whether an applicant has an aptitude for the occupation.

Federal employees are stationed in all parts of the United States and its territories and in many foreign countries. (Although most government departments and agencies have their headquarters in the Washington, D.C., metropolitan area, only 1 out of 11 federal workers was employed there at the beginning of this year.)

General Categories of Federal Jobs

Professional occupations are those requiring knowledge in a field, characteristically acquired through education or training equivalent to a bachelor's or higher degree, with major study in or pertinent to the specialized field, e.g., engineer, accountant, biologist, chemist.

Administrative occupations are those which require progressively responsible experience or college level general education, e.g., personnel specialist, administrative officer.

Technical occupations are those involving support of a professional or administrative field which is nonroutine in nature, e.g., computer technician, electronic technician.

Clerical occupations are those involving structured work in support of office, business, or fiscal operations, e.g., clerk-typist, mail and file clerk.

Other occupations are those that do not fall into the above categories, e.g., painters, carpenters, and laborers.

Specific Programs in the Federal Service

Part-time positions—16 to 32 hours per week—are available in agencies throughout the federal government. Flex time, job sharing, and nontraditional configurations of workday and workweek are also available in some positions. Make inquiries at the personnel office of the agency of your choice.

Summer employment opportunities for high school, college, law, medical, and dental students are available in limited numbers throughout the federal government. Applications are accepted for summer employment from December through April 15, and the jobs tend to run from mid-May through September 30. Hiring is done by the individual agencies. There are certain restrictions that limit summer employment in the same department or agency in which a parent is employed.

The student career experience is a work/study program for high school, vocational/technical school, and college students who are enrolled in school at least half time. This program offers employment in positions directly related to the student's course of study. Positions in this program may lead to permanent employment with the agency upon the student's graduation from school. Students who are interested in a career experience should contact their high school counselors, college employment coordinators, or the agency at which they would like to work.

Student temporary employment is part-time employment for students which is not necessarily related to the careers for which they are preparing. This employment must end when the student is no longer enrolled in school at least half time. The procedure for locating and securing this employment is similar to that for the student career experience.

The PMI program for Presidential Management Interns is specifically targeted for graduate students in the last year of their graduate programs. Only graduate students who expect to receive their degrees by the next June should apply. These students enter the two-year PMI program at the GS-9 level and perform high level work in their chosen fields. At the end of the two years, PMIs may continue in regular federal employment at the GS-12 level. Students interested in this program must be nominated by the Dean of the college or university or by the chairman of their department or graduate program. With government cutbacks and downsizing, all student programs are limited.

Veterans are entitled to special consideration in hiring. In some cases, veterans are entitled to positions that are not open to the general public. In other instances, extra points are added to their exam scores, placing them at a competitive advantage. The Veterans Employment Coordinator of the agency can give more information.

Persons with physical disabilities should contact the Selective Placement Coordinator at the agency of interest for special placement assistance.

Alaska, Guam, Hawaii, Puerto Rico, and the Virgin Islands offer very limited federal employment possibilities. Residents of these localities will receive first consideration for employment in these areas. Other candidates will be considered only when there are no qualified residents available.

Postal Service hiring is very localized. Rather than making application to the Postal Service, interested persons should make inquiry and application at the post office branch in which they wish to be employed.

Where and How to Obtain Information

By far the easiest and most efficient way to get information about job openings throughout the country and to get application materials is to call the Career America Connection at (912) 757-3000. This is a toll call, but it is a 24-hour automated service, so you can hold down costs by calling at night or on the weekend. You will need a touch tone telephone to utilize the service. Allow yourself at least one-half hour to search job categories and geographical areas. The system is equipped to record your name and mailing address so that you can be sent announcements and required forms through the mail. If you have a computer with modem, you can access the same information from an OPM electronic bulletin board by dialing (912) 757-3100.

You might also look under the heading "U.S. Government" in the blue pages of your telephone directory for a listing for Office of Personnel Management or Federal Job Information Center. A telephone call to this number may give you automated information pertinent to your own area or may direct you to a location at which you can pick up printed materials or conduct a search on a computer touch screen.

Some state employment services maintain computer touch screens which contain listings of available federal jobs within the state. You might also check with your public library and, for postal employment, on your post office bulletin board. Announcement material should tell you how to proceed with making application for the position.

At one time, federal hiring was a centralized function of the Office of Personnel Management. This is no longer the case. All hiring is done by the individual agencies. If you know which agencies you wish to work for, you may contact them directly to learn what vacancies exist and the application procedures. At some agencies you may prepare an application to be kept on file for future vacancies. Other agencies accept applications only for current or projected openings. If a federal agency has offices in your area, you may find the telephone number under "U.S. Government" in the blue pages. If the agency has no office in your area, you may have to place a call to information in the District of Columbia, (202) 555-1212, to ask for the telephone number of the personnel office or employment office of the agency that you wish to reach. Calls to government offices must be made during business hours, so prepare your questions ahead of time to hold down your phone bill.

How to Apply

The announcement of the position for which you are applying will specify the form of application requested. For most federal jobs, you may submit either the Optional Application for Federal Employment (OF 612) or a resume which fulfills the requirements set forth in the pamphlet, Applying for a Federal Job (OF 510). The essence of each of these publications is reproduced below.

You will note that you are repeatedly cautioned not to send more backup material than is requested on the announcement. By the same token, be sure to include any backup material that is requested. Your application must be complete according to the requirements of the announcement, but must not be overwhelming. You want to command hiring attention by exactly conforming to requirements.

NEW ELECTRONIC OPTIONS

The most recent development in the federal employment picture is the construction of the Office of Personnel Management web site. You can access this site at its URL: www.usajobs.opm.gov/ At this site you can find explanations of federal job categories and specific job descriptions. You can then search geographically and alphabetically to find out which jobs have current openings and exactly where the openings are located. The listings, in turn, refer you to full vacancy announcements, including qualifications requirements and application procedures and deadlines. With adequate equipment you can download the announcement. Or you can then take notes from the information on your screen. Likewise, with sophisticated equipment you can download application forms or even apply electronically using your computer. Or, you can follow instructions for getting the proper forms by telephone or mail.

Optional Application for Federal Employment — OF 612

Form Approved
OMB No. 3206-0219

You may apply for most jobs with a resume, this form, or other written format. If your resume or application does not provide all the information requested on this form and in the job vacancy announcement, you may lose consideration for a job.

1 Job title in announcement		**2** Grade(s) applying for	**3** Announcement number
4 Last name	First and middle names		**5** Social Security Number
6 Mailing address City	State	ZIP Code	**7** Phone numbers (include area code) Daytime ( ) Evening ( )

WORK EXPERIENCE

8 Describe your paid and nonpaid work experience related to the job for which you are applying. Do **not** attach job descriptions.

1) Job title (if Federal, include series and grade)

From (MM/YY)	To (MM/YY)	Salary per $	Hours per week
Employer's name and address			Supervisor's name and phone number ( )

Describe your duties and accomplishments

2) Job title (if Federal, include series and grade)

From (MM/YY)	To (MM/YY)	Salary per $	Hours per week
Employer's name and address			Supervisor's name and phone number ( )

Describe your duties and accomplishments

50612-101 NSN 7540-01-351-9178 Optional Form 612 (September 1994) U.S. Office of Personnel Management

9 May we contact your current supervisor?

YES [ ] **NO** [ ] ➔ If we need to contact your current supervisor before making an offer, we will contact you first.

EDUCATION

10 Mark highest level completed. **Some HS** [ ] **HS/GED** [ ] **Associate** [ ] **Bachelor** [ ] **Master** [ ] **Doctoral** [ ]

11 Last high school (HS) or GED school. Give the school's name, city, State, ZIP Code (if known), and year diploma or GED received.

12 Colleges and universities attended. Do **not** attach a copy of your transcript unless requested.

	Name			Total Credits Earned		Major(s)	Degree (if any) – Year Received
	City	State	ZIP Code	Semester	Quarter		
1)							
2)							
3)							

OTHER QUALIFICATIONS

13 **Job-related** training courses (give title and year). **Job-related** skills (other languages, computer software/hardware, tools, machinery, typing speed, etc.). **Job-related** certificates and licenses (current only). **Job-related** honors, awards, and special accomplishments (publications, memberships in professional/honor societies, leadership activities, public speaking, and performance awards). Give dates, but do **not** send documents unless requested.

GENERAL

14 Are you a U.S. citizen? **YES** [ ] **NO** [ ] ➔ Give the country of your citizenship. ____________

15 Do you claim veteran's preference? **NO** [ ] **YES** [ ] ➔ Mark your claim of 5 or 10 points below.

5 points [ ] ➔ Attach your DD 214 or other proof. **10 points** [ ] ➔ Attach an *Application for 10-Point Veterans' Preference* (SF 15) and proof required.

16 Were you ever a Federal civilian employee?

NO [ ] **YES** [ ] ➔ For highest civilian grade give:

Series	Grade	From (MM/YY)	To (MM/YY)

17 Are you eligible for reinstatement based on career or career-conditional Federal status?

NO [ ] **YES** [ ] ➔ If requested, attach SF 50 proof.

APPLICANT CERTIFICATION

18 I **certify** that, to the best of my knowledge and belief, all of the information on and attached to this application is true, correct, complete and made in good faith. I **understand** that false or fraudulent information on or attached to this application may be grounds for not hiring me or for firing me after I begin work, and may be punishable by fine or imprisonment. **I understand** that any information I give may be investigated.

SIGNATURE **DATE SIGNED**

APPLYING FOR A FEDERAL JOB—OF 510

Here's what your resume or application must contain

(in addition to specific information requested in the job vacancy announcement):

JOB INFORMATION

- ❑ Announcement number, and title and grade(s) of the job for which you are applying

PERSONAL INFORMATION

- ❑ Full name, mailing address *(with ZIP code)* and day and evening phone numbers *(with area code)*
- ❑ Social Security Number
- ❑ Country of citizenship *(Most Federal jobs require United States citizenship.)*
- ❑ Veterans' preference *(See reverse.)*
- ❑ Reinstatement eligibility *(If requested, attach SF 50 proof of your career or career-conditional status.)*
- ❑ Highest Federal civilian grade held *(Also give job series and dates held.)*

EDUCATION

- ❑ High school
  - Name, city, and State *(ZIP Code if known)*
  - Date of diploma or GED
- ❑ Colleges and universities
  - Name, city, and State *(ZIP Code if known)*
  - Majors
  - Type and year of any degrees received *(If no degree, show total credits earned and indicate whether semester or quarter hours.)*
- ❑ Send a copy of your college transcript only if the job vacancy announcement requests it.

WORK EXPERIENCE

- ❑ Give the following information for your paid and nonpaid work experience related to the job for which you are applying *(Do not send job descriptions.)*
  - Job title *(include series and grade if Federal job)*
  - Duties and accomplishments
  - Employer's name and address
  - Supervisor's name and phone number
  - Starting and ending dates *(month and year)*
  - Hours per week
  - Salary
- ❑ Indicate if we may contact your current supervisor

OTHER QUALIFICATIONS

- ❑ **Job-related** training *courses* *(title and year)*
- ❑ **Job-related** skills, for example, other languages, computer software/hardware, tools, machinery, typing speed
- ❑ **Job-related** certificates and licenses *(current only)*
- ❑ **Job-related** honors, awards, and special accomplishments, for example, publications, memberships in professional or honor societies, leadership activities, public speaking, and performance awards *(Give dates but do not send documents unless requested.)*

The Federal Government is an equal opportunity employer

Job Openings

For job information 24 hours a day, 7 days a week, call **912-757-3000**, the U.S. Office of Personnel Management (OPM) automated telephone system. Or, with a computer modem dial **912-757-3100** for job information from an OPM electronic bulletin board. You can also reach the board through the Internet (Telnet only) at FJOB.MAIL.OPM.GOV.

Applicants with Disabilities

You can find out about alternative formats by calling OPM. Select "Federal Employment Topics" and then "People with Disabilities." Or, dial our electronic bulletin board. If you have a hearing disability, call **TDD 912-744-2299**.

How to Apply

Review the list of openings, decide which jobs you are interested in, and follow the instructions given. **You may apply for most jobs with a resume, the *Optional Application for Federal Employment,* or any other written format you choose.** For jobs that are unique or filled through automated procedures, you will be given special forms to complete. (You can get an *Optional Application* by calling OPM or dialing our electronic bulletin board at the numbers given above.)

What to Include

Although the Federal Government does not require a standard application form for most jobs, we do need certain information to evaluate your qualifications and determine if you meet legal requirements for Federal employment. If your resume or application does not provide all the information requested in the job vacancy announcement and in this flyer, you may lose consideration for a job. Help speed the selection process by keeping your resume or application brief and by sending only the requested material. Type or print clearly in dark ink.

Veterans' Preference in Hiring

- ❑ If you served on active duty in the United States Military and were separated under honorable conditions, you may be eligible for veterans' preference. To receive preference if your service began after October 15, 1976, you must have a Campaign Badge, Expeditionary Medal, or a service-connected disability. For further details, call OPM at **912-757-3000**. Select "Federal Employment Topics" and then "Veterans." Or, dial our electronic bulletin board at **912-757-3100**.
- ❑ Veterans' preference is not a factor for Senior Executive Service jobs or when competition is limited to status candidates (current or former Federal career or career-conditional employees).
- ❑ To claim 5-point veterans' preference, attach a copy of your DD-214, *Certificate of Release or Discharge from Active Duty*, or other proof of eligibility.
- ❑ To claim 10-point veterans' preference, attach an SF 15, *Application for 10-Point Veterans' Preference*, plus the proof required by that form.

Other Important Information

- ❑ Before hiring, an agency will ask you to complete a *Declaration for Federal Employment* to determine your suitability for Federal employment and to authorize a background investigation. The agency will also ask you to sign and certify the accuracy of all the information in your application. **If you make a false statement in any part of your application, you may not be hired; you may be fired after you begin work; or you may be fined or jailed.**
- ❑ If you are a male over age 18 who was born after December 31, 1959, you must have registered with the Selective Service System (or have an exemption) to be eligible for a Federal job.
- ❑ The law prohibits public officials from appointing, promoting, or recommending their relatives.
- ❑ Federal annuitants (military and civilian) may have their salaries or annuities reduced. All employees must pay any valid delinquent debts or the agency may garnish their salary.

Working Conditions, Benefits, and Holidays

HOURS OF WORK

The usual government workweek is 40 hours. Most government employees work eight hours, five days a week, Monday through Friday, but, in some cases, the nature of the work may call for a different workweek. As in any other business, employees sometimes have to work overtime. If you are required to work overtime, you will either be paid for overtime or given time off to make up for the extra time you worked.

ADVANCEMENT

Most agencies fill vacancies by promoting their own employees whenever possible.

Federal employees receive on-the-job training. They may also participate in individual career development programs and receive job-related training in their own agency, in other agencies, or outside the government (for example, in industrial plants and universities). It is not always necessary to move to a new job in order to advance in grade. Sometimes an employee's work assignments change a great deal in the ordinary course of business. The job "grows." When that happens, it is time for a position classifier to study the job again. If he or she finds that the job should be put in a higher grade because of increased difficulty or responsibility of the duties, the change is made.

EFFICIENCY COUNTS

At intervals, employees are rated on their job performance. In most agencies, the ratings are "outstanding," "satisfactory," and "unsatisfactory."

Employees with "outstanding" ratings receive extra credit toward retention in case of layoffs. An employee whose rating is "unsatisfactory" may be dismissed or assigned to another position with duties he or she can be expected to learn to do satisfactorily.

INCENTIVE AWARDS

Government agencies encourage their employees to suggest better, simpler, or more economical ways of doing their jobs. They may give a cash award to an employee for a suggestion or invention that results in money savings or improved service. They may also reward outstanding job performance or other acts that are deserving of recognition.

VACATION AND SICK LEAVE

Most federal employees earn annual leave for vacation and other purposes, according to the number of years (civilian plus creditable military service) they have been in the federal service. They earn it at the rate of 13 days a year for the first 3 years of service and 20 days a year for the next 12 years of service. After 15 years, they earn 26 days of annual leave each year.

Sick leave is earned at the rate of 13 days a year. You can use this leave for illnesses serious enough to keep you away from your work and for appointments with a doctor, dentist, or optician. Sick leave that is not used can be saved for future use.

INJURY COMPENSATION

The government provides generous compensation benefits, including medical care, for employees who suffer injuries in the performance of official duty. Death benefits are also provided if an employee dies as a result of such injuries.

GROUP LIFE INSURANCE

As a federal employee, you may have low-cost term life insurance without taking a physical examination. Two kinds of insurance are provided: (1) life insurance, and (2) accidental death and dismemberment insurance.

HEALTH BENEFITS

The government sponsors a voluntary health insurance program for federal employees. The program offers a variety of plans to meet individual needs, including basic coverage and major medical protection against costly illnesses. The government contributes part of the cost of premiums, and the employee pays the balance through payroll deductions.

RETIREMENT

The Federal Employees Retirement System (FERS) offers very favorable terms for retirement. The government's share of the retirement package is generous, and the employee has opportunities to contribute to the program so as to create an even more comfortable retirement. The FERS retirement plan stands on three legs.

The first part of FERS is Social Security. All federal employees are members of the Social Security system. This means that employees pay a portion of each salary check toward social security insurance and another percentage toward Medicare. At retirement at age 62 or later, these employees are entitled to monthly Social Security benefits based upon number of quarters' contribution into the system and the level of those contributions. At age 65, these same employees, retired or not, are eligible for Medicare hospitalization insurance and can pay for low-cost Medicare Part B insurance toward other medical expenses. Employees pay 6.2% of their salaries into the Social Security system and 1.45% into the Medicare fund. The government matches these contributions, just as do all private employers.

The second part of FERS is the Basic Benefit Plan. Employees contribute .8% of their salaries into the retirement fund of the Basic Benefit Plan. An employee who has served for at least five years becomes eligible for retirement; that is, the employee vests in the retirement fund. If the vested employee leaves federal service before the age of 62, the employee has the option of withdrawing retirement funds or of leaving them with the government to be withdrawn as an annuity at retirement after age 62. In general, the basic retirement benefit is based on "high-3 average pay." This means that the highest salary earned in any three consecutive years is averaged; then 1% of this figure is multiplied by the number of years of service. Government retirement annuities are increased by regular Cost-of-Living Adjustments (COLAs). COLAs are based on the increase in the Consumer Price Index (CPI).

The third leg of FERS is the Thrift Savings Plan (TSP). TSP is similar to the 401(k) plans of workers in the private sector and to the 403(b) plans of persons employed by government entities other than the federal government. Under these plans, employees contribute towards their own retirement on a before-tax basis. This means that they do not pay income tax on the money they contribute to the plans. Rather, they pay tax upon the money they withdraw at retirement, at which time they are likely to be in a lower tax bracket. Funds contributed to the TSP are invested in common stock funds, government securities funds, and bond index funds as directed by the employee. These funds all yield dividends which are then reinvested through TSP. The income generated by these funds is also tax deferred until drawn out by the retiree as lump sum or as monthly payments.

Employees are not required to join TSP. Even if an employee chooses not to contribute, the government contributes 1% of the employee's salary toward TSP each pay period. The employee may contribute up to 10%. The government makes TSP contributions even more attractive by a matching program. For the first 3% of the employee's salary which he or she invests in TSP, the government matches dollar for dollar. The next 2% of the employee's investment is matched by the government at the rate of 50 cents on the dollar. No further contribution is matched, but the employee still receives the benefit of deferring tax on the contribution and on the interest earned.

HOLIDAYS

Government workers are entitled to the following ten regular holidays each year.

- New Year's Day, January 1
- Martin Luther King's Birthday, third Monday in January
- Presidents' Day, third Monday in February
- Memorial Day, last Monday in May
- Independence Day, July 4
- Labor Day, first Monday in September
- Columbus Day, second Monday in October
- Veterans Day, November 11
- Thanksgiving Day, fourth Thursday in November
- Christmas Day, December 25

When Inauguration Day falls on a regularly scheduled workday, employees in the Washington metropolitan area get an eleventh holiday.

THE JOB ANNOUNCEMENT

A job announcement or an examination announcement is published when jobs in a specific category are to be filled. It contains the job requirements, the duties of the position, typical tasks, and special requirements. It may also contain the number and location of the vacancies, the type of examination to be given, method of rating, and may even contain the types of questions to be asked. It will also include when and where to file for the examination and the forms to be filled out. Study the job announcement carefully because it will answer many of your questions and will be of invaluable assistance to you in preparing for your examination. Job announcements are issued by the agency administering the examination you are interested in taking.

A Typical Job Announcement

RECRUITMENT BULLETIN
Bureau of Land Management

Bulletin Number: CSO-95-06(DEU)
Open: 02-06
Close: 02-27
Publicity Area: CAL/NEVADA

AN EQUAL OPPORTUNITY EMPLOYER: All candidates will receive consideration without regard to race, color, sex, age, religion, national origin, or other non-merit factors.

Public Affairs Specialist
GS-1035-12
Duty Station: Sacramento, California

Number of Vacancies: One or two positions may be filled

Location: California State Office
External Affairs Staff

Salary: $43,270 per annum

Tour of Duty: Permanent Full-Time

Benefits: Entitled to health insurance, life insurance, retirement coverage and annual (vacation) and sick leave

Description of Duties: The position is on the Public Affairs Staff of the Office of the State Director under the immediate direction of the External Affairs Chief. The incumbent is in the capacity of a principal assistant to the Staff Chief on statewide matters related to contacts with Bureau managers and staff and the news media, interest groups, educational groups, and counterparts in government agencies on the national, state and local levels; also for matters related to the Freedom of Information Act. Incument is assigned highly controversial issues within many major program areas. Advises and counsels the External Affairs Chief, program managers, staff specialist and other Bureau officials on public affairs policies and procedures as they affect Bureau relationships with the public and media. Identifies issues and actions contained in the Bureau policies, plans and program that should receive public affairs emphasis and recommends appropriate course of action.

Qualification Requirements: Candidates must have the following length and type of experience:

One year of specialized experience equivalent to the GS-11 level in the federal service.

Specialized Experience: Experience which is in or directly related to public affairs and which has equipped the candidate with the particular knowledge, skills and abilities to successfully perform the duties of the position.

Basis of Rating: No written test is required. Candidates will be rated on a scale of 70-100 based on the nature, quality and extent of their experience in relation to the duties and requirements of this position and the following ranking factors:

1. Knowledge of issues in ecosystem/multiple-use programs of a natural resource agency.
2. Ability to work with California Congressional delegation and the California legislature.
3. Skill in professional journalistic and public relations in order to prepare all necessary materials and to advise on sensitive issues.
4. Skill in establishing and maintaining effective relations with state and national media, interest groups and other agencies.
5. Ability to organize, plan and conduct a public affairs initiative project on a state level.
6. Ability to operate personal computers and associated software.

Important Notice: On a separate sheet of paper(s), as a supplement to your application, please provide examples of your experience/education which best describe the extent and level of your ability in each of the above areas. Your application cannot receive proper consideration unless you submit this supplemental information.

Who May Apply: All interested U.S. citizens

How to Apply: Submit the following forms:

1. A resume or the Optional Application for Federal Employment (Form number OF 612). Please indicate the number of this Recruitment Bulletin on your application.
2. Written response to ranking factors
3. DI-1935, Application Background Survey Form. Submission of this form is strictly voluntary. It is used for statistical purposes only and is not used in the evaluation process.
4. DD-214, if you are claiming 5-point veteran preference
5. DD-214 and SF-15 if you are claiming 10-point veteran preference. Proof dated within the last 12 months is required to establish 10-point veteran preference.

The required application forms may be obtained by writing or calling the Bureau of Land Management, Branch of Human Resources Management, at the address/phone number given below or by calling the Career America Connection in San Francisco on (415) 744-JOBS (5627) or dialing the electronic bulletin board (912) 757-3100.

Mail completed forms to:

USDI, Bureau of Land Management
Federal Office Building
2800 Cottage Way, Room E-2845
Sacramento, CA 95825
ATTN: Branch of Human Resources Management
(916) 979-2900

Applications must be received or postmarked by: FEBRUARY 27.

Meeting the Requirements

Before you apply, read the announcement carefully. It gives information about the job to be filled and what qualifications you must have to fill it.

If the announcement says that only persons who have one year of experience in certain areas will qualify and you don't have that experience, don't apply. If the announcement says that the jobs to be filled are all in a certain locality and you don't want to work in that locality, don't file. Many disappointed applicants would have saved time and trouble if they had only read the announcement carefully.

Credit may be given for unpaid experience or volunteer work, such as in community, cultural, social service and professional association activities, on the same basis as for paid experience, but it must be of the type and level acceptable under the announcement. Therefore, you may, if you wish, report such experience in one or more of the experience blocks at the end of your personal qualifications statement if you feel that it represents qualifying experience for the positions for which you are applying. To receive proper credit, you must show the actual time, such as the number of hours a week, spent in such activities.

Quality of Experience

For most positions, in order to qualify *on experience* for any grade above the entrance level, an applicant must have either six months or one year of experience at a level comparable in difficulty and responsibility to that of the next lower grade level in the federal service. In some instances for positions at GS-11 and below, experience may have been obtained at two levels below that of the job to be filled.

Depending on the type of position, the next lower level may be either one or two grades lower. If you were applying for a position as a stenographer (single grade interval position), at grade GS-5, you should have at least one year of experience doing work equivalent to that done by a stenographer at the GS-4 level. If you were applying for a two-grade interval position, however, such as computer specialist GS-7, you would need at least one year of experience equivalent to that of a GS-5 computer specialist in Federal Service, or six months equivalent to the GS-6 level. Where necessary, the announcement will provide more specific information about the level of experience needed to qualify.

The Duties

The duties of various positions are quite different even though the positions may bear the same broad title. A public relations *clerk,* for example, does work very different from that of a payroll *clerk,* although both positions are considered to be broadly in the same general area. Every announcement describes the precise duties of the job in detail, usually under the heading: *Description of Work.* Make sure that these duties come within the range of your experience and ability.

Sometimes the words *Optional Fields,* or even just *Options,* may appear on the front page of the announcement. This designation refers to related positions that may be filled through the same announcement. If a particular position in which you are especially interested is listed under this heading, you may apply to it simultaneously with the primary position on the announcement.

Some Things to Watch For

In addition to educational and experience requirements, there are some general requirements.

AGE

"How old are you?" There is no maximum age limit. The usual minimum age limit is 18, but high school graduates may apply at 16 for many jobs.

If you are 16 or 17 and are out of school but not a high school graduate, you may be hired only (1) if you have successfully completed a formal training program preparing you for work, or (2) if you have been out of school for at least three months, not counting summer vacation, and if school authorities sign a form agreeing with your preference for work instead of additional schooling. The form will be given to you by the agency that wants to hire you.

Remember, job opportunities are best for those who graduate. If you can, you should complete your education before you apply for full-time work.

If you are in high school, you may be hired for work during vacation periods if you are 16. (For jobs filled under the Summer Employment Examination, however, you must be 18 if still in high school.) You may be hired for part-time work during the school year if you are 16 and meet the following conditions:

1. your work schedule is set up through agreement with your school
2. your school certifies that you can maintain good standing while working
3. you remain enrolled in high school

Some announcements, specifically those for law enforcement and firefighting positions, may set age limits. Be sure to check the announcement carefully before applying.

PHYSICAL REQUIREMENTS

What is your physical condition? You must be physically able to perform the duties of the position and must be emotionally and mentally stable. This does not mean that a handicap will disqualify an applicant so long as he or she can do the work efficiently without being a hazard to himself/herself or to others.

For most positions, appointees must have good distant vision in one eye and be able to read without strain printed material the size of typewritten characters. They may use glasses to meet these requirements.

Persons appointed are usually required to be able to hear the conversational voice. They may use a hearing aid to meet this requirement. Blind persons and deaf persons may apply and be examined for positions with duties they can perform.

An amputation of an arm, hand, leg, or foot does not bar a person from Federal employment; the test is whether the person can do the duties of the position satisfactorily and without hazard to self or others.

The Federal government is the world's largest employer of handicapped people and has a strong program aimed at their employment. It recognizes that, in almost every kind of work, there are some positions suitable for the blind, the deaf, and others with serious impairments.

Of course, there are some positions—such as border patrol agent, firefighter, and criminal investigator—that can be filled only by people in top-notch physical condition. Whenever this is the case, the physical requirements are described in detail in the announcements.

THE GOVERNMENT TESTS YOU

Most applicants for civil service jobs are worried by that awesome instrument called **the test.** Haunted by schoolday memories, applicants often approach the examination with fear, imagining that someone is going to give them a big list of trick questions, to trap them; or that they will have to sit down and laboriously work out the answers to difficult problems. The only factor that helps many people face the test is the knowledge that they aren't alone, that everybody else competing with them faces the same problems. Those who have had any dealings with civil service applicants never cease to wonder at how widespread this attitude is. If you are one of those who has this concept of a government test, change your opinion. It's all wrong!

You have found the position you'd like, have filled out the application form, and have sent it off to the agency to which you are applying, as specified on the announcement.

What now?

Kinds of Tests

The announcement describes the kind of test given for the particular position. Please pay special attention to this section. It tells what areas are to be covered in the written test and lists the specific subjects on which questions will be asked. Sometimes sample questions are given.

The test questions and review materials in this ARCO book are based on the requirements as given in this section of a variety of announcements as well as on questions that have appeared on actual tests.

If the announcement says that a written test will be given, you will receive a notice through the mail telling you when and where to report for the test.

Special arrangements will be made for blind, deaf, or otherwise handicapped applicants who indicate the nature of their disability according to instructions on the announcement.

The written test will be job-related. It will test your ability to do the job for which you have applied, or it will test your ability to learn the job.

If you fail a written test, you can usually take it again as long as applications are being accepted. If you pass but want to improve your score, you can usually retake the test after a year has passed provided the announcement is open at the time.

Usually the announcement states whether the examination is to be assembled or unassembled. In an *assembled* examination, applicants *assemble* at the same time to take a written or performance test. The *unassembled* examination is one in which an applicant does not take a test; instead the applicant is rated on education and experience and whatever records of past achievement the announcement requests.

If you apply for a position that does not involve a written test, your rating will be assigned on the basis of the experience and training you describe in your statement and on any additional evidence secured by the examiners. Your qualifications may also be verified with your former employers and supervisors.

If your examination is of the *unassembled* variety, you may be asked to submit further evidence of your ability in the form of work accomplished. In the meantime, statements on your application form will be checked. When all this information has been gathered, you will be "rated," and the agency will write to you telling you how your qualifications look to the examiners. That's all there is to it, until you are called to the job.

In announcements that cover several grades or salary levels, you will be rated for those you qualify for, but you will not be rated for any grade if the pay for that grade is less than the minimum pay you state you will accept.

You will be notified whether you passed or failed the examination by the office that announced it. Be sure to notify that office of changes in essential information, such as address, name, availability, etc. When writing, give your full name, your Social Security number, the title of the announcement, and the rating you received.

There are two main types of tests—competitive and noncompetitive.

In a *competitive* examination, all applicants for a position compete with each other; the better the mark, the better the chance of being appointed. In a *noncompetitive* examination, the applicant is tested solely to determine his or her qualification for a given position; he or she need only pass to become eligible for appointment.

The method of rating on all civil service written tests is on a scale of 100, with 70 as the usual passing mark.

Rating Examinations

The rating of the examination is usually done by the office which has issued the announcement.

Written tests are most frequently rated by machine. In some written examinations, and for rating experience and training, two examiners work independently. In case of a protest about the rating, a third examiner will be assigned to rate the exam again. Thus the chances of error, arbitrary grading, or bias are almost completely eliminated.

EVALUATING EDUCATION

In evaluating the candidate's background, credit may be given for appropriate training received in the armed forces. A certificate of completion from an educational institution for a correspondence course is often counted as good background. Courses offered through the Armed Forces Institute are granted credit, too, in rating examinations. The announcement always tells the kind of education needed for the specific job, and the examiners give careful consideration to the entire educational background of the candidate as listed on the application form. Often the examiners classify as helpful for the post courses which the candidate had not considered to be relevant. These courses may raise the candidate's total rating.

EVALUATING EXPERIENCE

When experience is a factor, the examiners give credit for all kinds of valuable background, including experience gained in religious, civic, welfare, service, and organizational activities. Whether the experience was paid or unpaid makes no difference, but its length and quality do.

Veterans obtain special experience credit in one of two ways, whichever would benefit the candidate more:

1. Military service may be considered an extension of the employment in which the applicant was engaged just before entrance into the armed forces.
2. Duties performed while in military service may be considered on the basis of their value to the job for which the veteran is applying.

"SUITABILITY"

Investigations to determine an applicant's "suitability qualifications" with respect to character and loyalty are considered a part of the entire examining process, regardless of whether such investigations are conducted before or after appointment.

When all the parts of an examination have been rated, the applicant is notified of his or her *numerical rating,* or mark.

If he or she has passed, he or she is an *eligible,* that is, his or her name is placed on a list for appointment.

SELECTED JOBS IN THE FEDERAL SERVICE

Clerical Positions

Nearly half the jobs in the federal civil service are clerical, and the government's demand for clerical workers often exceeds the supply. Agencies have not been able to fill all the positions for competent stenographers, typists, office machine operators, and file clerks.

In government the title "clerk" describes more positions than it does in private industry. An editor or a writer may be called a clerk (Editorial Clerk); a purchasing agent with fairly important responsibilities may be a clerk (Purchasing Clerk); or an accountant may be called a clerk (Cost Accounting Clerk).

These are the names of some of the government clerical jobs: Clerk-Stenographer, Clerk-Typist, Correspondence Clerk, Dictating Machine Operator, Shorthand Reporter, Mail Clerk, File Clerk, Record Clerk, and Business Machine Operator.

Clerks perform personnel work, auditing and statistical operations, property and supply work, and proofreading. They make blueprints and photostats, prepare payrolls, supply information, work on traffic plans, operate switchboards, decipher codes, and work in engraving and printing plants.

Clerical salaries have risen sharply in recent years, probably exceeding average salaries for similar jobs in private industry. There are usually good opportunities for advancement, and clerk jobs can be the start of a real career in the government.

Here is a typical job announcement for a clerical position.

CLERK, GS-2, GS-3

Description of Work

A wide variety of clerical positions will be filled from this examination. Among the basic duties to be performed are, for example: searching for and compiling information and data; indexing, filing, and maintaining records; receiving and routing mail; answering inquiries orally or by correspondence; coding information for mechanical tabulation; maintaining time, leave, payroll, personnel, retirement, or other records; and other similar duties.

Basis of Rating

Competitors will be rated on the basis of scores on the verbal abilities and clerical abilities tests. The ratings will be based on a scale of 100. Better performance in the test will be required to establish eligibility at grade GS-3 than at grade GS-2.

Labor and Mechanical Positions

Most citizens do not realize that the United States government is the largest employer of mechanical, manual, and laboring workers in the country.

The government is more than offices: it is factories, shipyards, shops, docks, and power plants. The government makes gimmicks and battleships and runs irrigation systems and a printing office in Washington. There are more than a million mechanical and manual workers in the government.

APPRENTICES

The government hires fully qualified mechanics, craftsmen, and laborers, of course, but several of the agencies conduct their own apprenticeship training programs. A young person who wants to learn a trade may come in under this program and earn his or her way from the very beginning. There are apprenticeship training programs in many occupations, among them carpenter, coppersmith, electrician, electronics mechanic, electroplater, glass apparatus maker, instrument maker, joiner, letterer and grainer, machinist, modelmaker, painter, patternmaker, pipefitter, plumber, refrigeration and air conditioning mechanic, sheetmetal worker, toolmaker, and welder.

Apprentices are employed in navy yards, arsenals, other Department of Defense establishments, and the Government Printing Office. Four classes of apprentices have been established in some of the Navy Yard trades. There is no hard and fast pay scale for all apprentices. The apprentice pay rate is usually set in ratio to the journeyman pay in the trade.

Apprentices must often buy textbooks and certain other equipment.

The minimum age for apprentices is usually eighteen. There is no maximum age limit.

As a beginner in a skilled trade, the apprentice receives instruction through an apprentice school and shop assignments in the rudiments of the trade and in technical subjects such as mechanical drawing, mathematics, and blueprint interpretation. He or she learns to work with the machinery and materials of the trade and does elementary tasks under the supervision of a shop instructor.

Apprenticeships usually last four years, or eight six-month periods, made up of approximately 1,025 shop and school hours. The first year's shop and school work is considered a trial period. Apprenticeships in the Government Printing Office are of longer duration.

There are no educational requirements, but the applicant for an apprenticeship must take a written test.

Advancement comes regularly to the apprentice who completes his or her service satisfactorily; and when he or she has finished the prescribed period of training, he or she is promoted to the status of artisan, regardless of age.

SKILLED AND SEMISKILLED POSITIONS

We must preface our survey of the skilled and semiskilled jobs in the government by reminding the reader that this is only a selection. The full list of such positions includes probably every kind of job in this class. Most, but not all, such positions are paid at hourly rates which may vary somewhat for different sections of the country.

The government usually follows the custom of the trade, paying, in some cases, on a piecework basis. Overtime is on a time-and-a-half basis, rather than, as in jobs of other types, at straight time. The rate of pay in many cases is determined by skill. Some positions are available on both hourly and annual salary. The minimum age limit is usually eighteen; the applicant must be physically able to do the work.

Here are some of the positions found in federal establishments:

Steamfitter, Stationary Boiler Fireman, Auto Equipment Repair Assistant Foreman, Engineer Equipment Repair Foreman, Auto Equipment Repairer, Shoe Repair Foreman, Sheet-Metal Worker, Sheet-Metal and Welding Foreman, Carpenter, Packer and Crater, Engineering Equipment Operator, Plumber, Woodworker, Aircraft Mechanic, Metalsmith (Aviation), Radio Mechanic, Electrician, Upholsterer, Electrotyper (Molder), Electrotyper (Finisher), Stereotyper, Printer (Monotype Keyboard Operator), Printer (Slug Machine Operator), Printer Proofreader, Photoengraver, Carpenter (Junior), Carpenter (Superintendent), Refrigeration and Air-Conditioning Mechanic, Mason (Brick and Stone), Painter, General Helper, Toolmaker, Model Maker, Machinist Helper, Machinist, Aircraft Painter and Doper, Aircraft Parachute and Clothing Repairer, Radio and Electrical Instrument Repairer, Radio and Electronics Mechanic.

Radar Mechanic, Typewriter Cleaner and Case Repairer, Typewriter Repairer, Duplicating Machine Mechanic, Computing Machine Mechanic, Water Plant Operator, Wire Worker (Aviation), Office Appliance Repairer, Aircraft Jet Engine Mechanic, Automotive Mechanic, Aircraft Service Mechanic, Preflight Mechanic, Flight Test Mechanic, Assistant Engineer (Pipeline Dredge-Class), Firefighter (Marine), Leverman, Mate (Pipeline Dredge-Class), Mate (Pipeline Dredge-Class), Operator (Pushboat).

Cook, Locksmith, Gardener, Laborer, Operator (Road-Building Equipment), Butcher, Blacksmith, Box Shop Helper, Laborer (Warehouse), Auto Trade Laborer, Utilities Trades Laborer, Carpenter Shop Laborer, Munitions Handler, Freight Handler, Handyman, Track Worker, Junior Reclamation Worker, Mail Handler (this is an Army, not a Post Office position), Lineman, Groundman, Line Truck Operator, Laundry Helper.

Skilled and semiskilled craft positions are also open on a full-time, annual-salary basis. Here are some typical positions of this kind.

Electrician—Plumber—Carpenter—Painter

Applicants must have completed a four-year apprenticeship or have been in trade at least four years to qualify. Another year's journeyman experience is required for a higher-paid post; and two years' journeyman experience for the top-rated post.

Operating Engineer

Applicants for the job must show two years'or three years' experience and training in operating or installing such equipment as boilers in buildings. And experience is required in steam generation, air conditioning, or refrigeration.

Office Appliance Repairman

Three years of experience are required.

Photographer

One to four years of experience in photography work required. A resident course in photography may be substituted for part of the experience. There is also a photographer position which requires 6 months' experience. The job includes routine photo lab work and aid to photographers. It is a good spot for young people to learn the field.

UNSKILLED POSITIONS

Thousands of positions in the government service are open to persons with no skills or with only a small amount of training. Here are some of them:

Housekeeping Aide

Performs routine manual domestic work such as making beds and cleaning quarters, hallways, bathrooms, etc. Restricted to veterans.

Kitchen Helper

Assists in the preparation of foods for cooking and service. Sets dining room tables, washes dishes, scrubs kitchen. Restricted to veterans.

Janitor

Three months' experience in manual work using physical effort.

Messenger

No experience; restricted to veterans; written examination tests ability to learn.

Elevator Operator

Three months' experience.

Laborer (General)

Three months' experience.

Laborer (Custodial)

These jobs are restricted to veterans and require at least three months' experience in manual work requiring strength and physical effort.

Laundry Worker

From three to six months' experience in laundry operations such as checking, sorting, washing, and ironing.

Mess Attendant

No specific experience of any particular kind is required. This position is open to veterans only.

Storekeeping Clerk

No experience needed for the lowest grade.

Professional and Administrative Positions

The following professional and administrative positions are filled by government agencies that have been delegated the authority to do so by the Office of Personnel Management. Although this list is far from complete, it is a good indication of the many careers available to qualified job seekers in the federal government. The examinations which are administered and the eligible lists which are established by these agencies follow the rules and regulations of the Civil Service Act, thus the eventual appointments are valid civil service appointments.

When assembled or written examinations are given, they usually consist of questions designed to measure a candidate's ability to be trained rather than to evaluate what he or she may already know concerning the duties of the position being sought. This makes it possible for candidates with the proper credentials to compete for a rich variety of positions in:

> Personnel management, computer science, general administration, economics and other social sciences, Social Security administration, management analysis, tax collection, electronic data processing, budget management, park ranger activities, statistics, investigation (including wage and hour), procurement and supply, housing management archival science, adjudication and other quasi-legal work, food and drug inspection, and others.

Some agencies offer a limited number of what are, perhaps, the most coveted assignments. These are known as management internships. Specially planned programs are designed to develop persons with unusual promise as future administrators. Persons considered for these internships will be required to pass additional tests of greater difficulty. Those selected for one of these programs receive specialized instruction, varied work assignments and understudy or other types of training designed to develop managerial skills and knowledge.

Legal Positions

Application for Attorney positions should be made directly to the particular government agency in which employment is desired. The Office of Personnel Management is ordinarily not informed of openings and does not, therefore, maintain or publish lists of federal agencies which may wish to employ Attorneys. Each federal agency is responsible for determining, in accordance with appropriate standards, the qualifications of Attorneys who apply to it for employment as well as for making the appointments.

Attorney positions are filled on a more subjective basis than are most civil service jobs. The standing of the law school from which the attorney received his or her degree and the attorney's standing in that law school are of great importance; the federal application form or scored resume also weigh heavily. Of equal, perhaps even greater, importance is the impression the applicant makes at a series of interviews. And recommendations from politicians, college professors, and other influential persons do help. The attorney who would like to work for the federal government should keep up with news of agencies and bureaus as they are authorized and formed. Getting in at start-up offers the most opportunities for employment and for advancement. Colleagues who are already in federal employment are a great source of information about new openings; regular contact with agencies in which the attorney is interested is also important.

Federal judges are appointed by the President, as are federal district attorneys and assistant district attorneys. Patronage is an important factor in these positions; the advice of senators and representatives and the local party political leaders pretty much decides who gets the job. The political activities of the prospective judge or district attorney are likely to be a telling consideration.

Federal Clerkships are perhaps the most eagerly sought short-term legal positions. All federal judges are allotted at least two law clerks. A clerkship runs from one to two years during which the clerk does legal research and brief writing at the request of the judge and assists at various tasks in the office of the judge. The experience of a clerkship is excellent legal training and offers the clerk an opportunity to make lifelong contacts in both legal and political worlds. Various factors enter into winning a federal clerkship: the prestige of the law school; law school grades, publications, and honors; the desire of the judge for "balance" among the clerks in terms of gender, race, and geography; the interview; and enthusiasm and standing of those who recommend the applicant.

Congressional committees also use lawyers to investigate, question witnesses, gather evidence, and write reports. The lawyer who wants that kind of job should make the acquaintance of political leaders and cultivate the party leaders who are in a position to hand out such posts. Keeping posted on congressional events and following up on the creation of special committees is important, also.

These positions, varying in grade and salary with the duties involved, range from higher-grade legal positions that require full professional legal training to those in the lower grades, requiring legal training but little or no experience.

Investigation and Law Enforcement Positions

The highly publicized Federal Bureau of Investigation is only one of the federal agencies which enforce the law. A dozen government agencies employ "cops" or detectives for jobs ranging from guarding property and patrolling borders to the most highly technical intelligence operations. Agencies which employ investigators or law enforcement personnel include: Department of Justice, State Department, Treasury, Postal Service, Army Department, Navy Department, Office of Personnel Management, Nuclear Regulatory Commission, Food and Drug Administration, Securities and Exchange Commission, and Customs Bureau. Most federal agencies also employ inspectors in various capacities.

The work of law-enforcement officers and investigators is often dramatic, but is often arduous, too, and dangerous. In some of the security positions the training is as tough as that given commando units in the armed forces. The work may be dull for long stretches, but it may become intense and exciting.

Federal law enforcement frequently requires long absence from home and family and operating under trying physical conditions.

Most of the posts naturally have stiff physical requirements, calling for well-proportioned, healthy, agile persons. Eyesight and hearing requirements are higher than for most other federal jobs, and candidates must have full use of arms and legs. Speech defects, scars, blemishes, or other defects which might interfere with the appointee's duties will cause rejection.

The positions mentioned below are representative of the law-enforcement, investigation and inspection positions in the federal service.

SPECIAL AGENT, FBI

The Federal Bureau of Investigation has been delegated the authority to hire its own personnel. In addition to its agents, it also administers examinations that result in the hiring of clerical and specialized personnel. Applications may be filed at any time, and may be obtained from the Director, Federal Bureau of Investigation, Washington, D.C., or from any of the Bureau's offices which are located in most larger cities.

Duties

The special agent is engaged in enforcing federal law, investigating its violations, gathering evidence for prosecution, checking the background of individuals, and tracing criminals. The work extends from enforcing antitrust laws to tracing bribes or uncovering evidence of espionage.

Requirements

The applicant must be a citizen between the ages of twenty-three and thirty-seven and meet high educational requirements. His or her vision must be not less than 20/40 in one eye and 20/50 in the weaker eye without glasses, 20/20 vision is required in each eye corrected, and color blindness will cause rejection. He or she must be able to hear ordinary conversation at least fifteen feet away with each ear. The applicant must be able to perform strenuous physical exertion and have no defects which would interfere with the use of firearms or participation in raids, dangerous assignments, or defensive tactics. He or she must be willing to serve in any part of the United States or its possessions, and must know how to drive a car.

There are five entrance programs under which applicants can qualify for possible appointment to FBI Special Agent. These are Law, Accounting, Language, Modified, and Science. An applicant applying under the Law Program must be a graduate of a state-accredited resident law school with at least two years of resident, undergraduate college work. Those applying as accountants must possess a four-year resident college degree with a major in accounting. Linguists must have a four-year resident college degree and fluency in a foreign language. Candidates for consideration under the Modified Program need three years of full-time work experience in addition to a four-year resident college degree, or two years of such work experience if they possess an advanced degree. Many options are available under the Science Program, with qualification possible based on a background in such areas as electrical engineering, metallurgy, physics, chemistry, biological science, pharmacology, toxicology, and mathematics. These are not all inclusive, however, as backgrounds in business or public administration, computer science, management information sciences or systems can also be qualifying, as can expertise as a firearms examiner, explosives examiner, document or fingerprint examiner. As in the other programs, candidates under the Science Program must possess a resident college degree with advanced degrees or professional experience necessary in many instances. College transcripts and detailed resumes showing experience must be submitted by candidates seeking to qualify under the Science Program.

Basis of Rating

All candidates must qualify on batteries of *written and oral examinations* designed to measure emotional stability, resourcefulness, interpersonal and communication skills, and the ability to apply analytical methods to work assignments. Since Agents have to be able to use firearms and defensive tactics to participate in dangerous assignments and raids, each individual must pass a rigid physical examination; be capable of strenuous physical exertion; and have excellent hearing, eyesight, and normal color vision. In addition, before hiring, the FBI conducts an extensive background and character investigation.

SECURITIES INVESTIGATOR

Salary

GS-9 to GS-11 at entrance.

Duties

Securities Investigators work under the supervision of a Regional Administrator. They examine the books, records, and financial statements of national securities exchanges, members of national securities exchanges, brokers and dealers in the over-the-counter market, and investment advisers in order to determine their financial condition and compliance with the acts administered by this Commission, its rules and regulations, and the rules and regulations of securities exchanges and national securities associations. They also conduct investigations involving fraud and other provisions of the acts requiring the examination of books and records of individuals and various business organizations and prepare reports of such examinations in accordance with accepted accounting principles.

Requirements

Except for the substitution of education for general experience, applicants must have had, as a minimum, experience of the length specified in the table below and of the types described in the paragraphs following. The grade level and rating assigned to the applicant will depend primarily on the quality, scope, and responsibility of experience rather than the length.

Grade of Position	Experience Required		
	General	Special	Total
GS-9	3 years	2 years	5 years
GS-11	3 years	3 years	6 years

The general experience must have been progressively responsible accounting or accounting-investigative experience of a scope and quality sufficient to demonstrate conclusively the ability to handle complex technical accounting assignments commensurate with the duties of the position.

In addition to the required general experience, applicants must have acquired responsible accounting, auditing, investigative, or administrative experience in the securities field which experience has provided a broad knowledge of stock exchange procedure and stock brokerage accounting—what is generally known in the trade as "back office" experience.

Basis of Rating

Competitors will not be required to report for a written test but will be rated on a scale of 100, on the extent and quality of their experience and training relevant to the duties of the position. Such ratings will be based upon competitors' statements in their applications and upon any corroborative evidence obtained.

INTERNAL REVENUE AGENT

Salary

GS-5 and GS-7 at entrance.

Duties

Internal Revenue Agents examine and audit the accounting books and records of individuals, partnerships, fiduciaries, and corporations to determine their correct federal tax liabilities.

Requirements

Applicants must have a minimum of four years of college with concentration in accounting, three years of experience comparable to a full four-year professional accounting curriculum, any time-equivalent combination of education and experience, or possession of a Certified Public Accountant certificate.

Basis of Rating

Applicants qualifying on a basis of education will be rated on their academic achievement. Those qualifying on a basis of experience or possession of a CPA certificate will be rated on the quality, diversity, and extent of their experience. Applicants qualifying on a basis of experience will be required to take a written test on accounting principles not required of those qualifying on a basis of education or possession of a CPA certificate.

TREASURY ENFORCEMENT AGENT

Salary

GS-5 and GS-7 at entrance.

Duties

Treasury Enforcement Agents enforce the laws coming under the jurisdiction of the Treasury Department. Positions are located in the enforcement arms of the Treasury: Bureau of Alcohol, Tobacco and Firearms; Bureau of Engraving and Printing; Customs Service; Internal Revenue Service Criminal Investigation Division and Internal Security Division; and Secret Service. The techniques employed range from surveillance and undercover work to presenting evidence to government prosecutors and testifying in court.

Requirements

Experience in dealing with groups and in criminal investigation, four years of college study, membership in the Bar, or possession of a CPA certificate. Only persons over the age of 21 are eligible because of the hazardous nature of these positions.

Basis of Rating

Applicants are rated on the basis of their performance on the Treasury Enforcement Agent examination.

SPECIAL AGENT, INTERNAL REVENUE SERVICE

Salary

GS-5 and GS-7 at entrance.

Duties

Special Agents conduct investigations of alleged criminal violations of federal tax laws, make recommendations with respect to criminal prosecution, prepare technical reports, and assist the United States Attorney in the preparation of cases and during trials.

Requirements

Three years of responsible experience requiring the knowledge and application of commercial accounting and auditing principles and practices sufficient to demonstrate the ability to analyze accounting and audit records and reports or a law degree or four years of college level study that included 12 semester hours in accounting. A written test is required.

Basis of Rating

Applicants are rated on the basis of their performance on the Treasury Enforcement Agent examination.

CORRECTIONAL OFFICER

Salary

GS-6 at entrance.

Duties

The work involves supervising, safeguarding, and training inmates of federal institutions.

Requirements

These applicants must have excellent character backgrounds, be cool in emergencies, and have good morals, patience, and capacity for leadership. Applicants must be physically able to do the work. There are no height or weight limits, but weight must be in proportion to height. Vision may not be less than 20/100 in each eye, corrected to 20/30 with glasses, and hearing in both ears must be normal. Applicants with hernia, organic heart disease, severe varicose veins, serious deformities of extremities (including weak feet), mental or nervous disorder, chronic constitutional disease, marked abnormality of speech, or facial disfigurement will be rejected. At appointment, a correction officer must be under the age of thirty-seven. Applicant must also have had at least three-and-a-half years of progressively responsible experience which required dealing effectively with individuals or groups of persons. Some substitution of higher or specialized education is permitted. U.S. citizenship is required.

Basis of Rating

Evaluation of experience and training.

Opportunities for Advancement

The federal prison system offers a career; persons who start as correctional officers can advance to several kinds of higher positions. Opportunities are available in the institution where the officer happens to be stationed, and throughout the prison system. Supervisory and administrative positions which may be reached by promotion and transfer include work in such fields as custody, education, vocational training, skilled trades, social services, parole, recreation, culinary service, accounting, and farm activities.

GUARD

Duties

Guards patrol buildings or other premises to prevent trespass, fire, theft, damage, or defacement of premises or their contents; prevent unlawful removal of property; protect the occupants of the buildings from outside annoyances and interferences; control traffic; etc.

Requirements

No experience is required for GS-2. One year of active service in the armed forces, Coast Guard, Merchant Marine, or in any position where duties were those described above is required for GS-3. Applicants' vision must be correctible to 20/30; color blindness disqualifies; hearing must be normal. Physical defects which would interfere with the work cause rejection. The minimum age limit for these positions is twenty-one; this age limit, however, does not apply to persons entitled to Veterans' Preference.

Basis of Rating

All competitors will be required to take a written test of reading comprehension and ability to follow oral directions. Competitors for these positions will be rated on the written test on a scale of 100. Competitors must attain a rating of at least 70 on the written test as a whole and will be required to attain a rating of 70 on each of the two parts of the test. Applicants will be notified when and where to report for the written test.

Inspector Positions

Inspection work is related to investigating jobs. Inspectors see that building construction, elevators, fire escapes, plumbing, and other projects comply with regulations. They test weights and measures and act to enforce sanitary, food and drug, and public health laws. Among the various kinds of inspection are electrical, elevator, materials (seeing that supplies such as cement, asphalt, tile, and coal meet specifications of quality and weight), motor vehicle inspection, playground inspection, industrial-safety inspection, waterpipe inspection, lock and vault inspection, boiler inspection, wage-hour-law inspection, mattress inspection, and food-law inspection.

A government inspector may check public works, street lighting and overhead lines, transportation, or public-safety devices.

SAFETY INSPECTOR

Salary

GS-5 at entrance.

Duties

The Safety Inspector enforces the Interstate Commerce Commission's motor carrier safety regulations. Safety inspectors advise bus companies and others in the development of safety activities, accident prevention plans, and driver education; inspect motor vehicles for the condition of equipment; investigate causes of accidents; and work with state agencies.

Requirements

Two years' experience investigating highway accidents, inspecting motor vehicles, conducting hearings on traffic violations, maintaining motor carrier fleets, or important work on highway safety programs. Work as a traffic officer, motor vehicle dispatcher, or insurance claims adjuster does not qualify. The applicant must never have been held criminally responsible for any motor vehicle accident involving loss of life. One year of appropriate education in transportation or mechanical engineering may be substituted for each six months of experience.

Basis of Rating

Applicants for GS-5 positions are rated entirely on the basis of a written test.

PATENT EXAMINER

Salary

GS-5 through GS-13 at entrance.

Duties

The Patent Examiner performs professional scientific and technical work in the examination of applications for United States Patents. He or she evaluates the invention, determines if it will perform as claimed, uncovers any previous teachings or knowledge comparable to the invention claimed in the application, and determines if the application and its claimed invention meet all legal requirements for the granting of patents.

Requirements

All applicants must have completed the requirements for a bachelor's or higher degree in professional engineering or in a scientific option at an accredited college. Experience may be combined with education if the combination is equivalent to the standard four-year college course. Applicants for the higher grades must have had additional experience, or education, or both. Superior college students or those with trainee experience may qualify for higher grades than those to which their experience and education would otherwise entitle them.

Basis of Rating

Competitors will not be required to report for a written test but will be rated on a scale of 100 on the extent and quality of their experience and training relevant to the duties of the position. Such ratings will be based upon the competitors' statements in their applications and upon any additional evidence which may be secured.

Medicine, Dentistry, and Nursing Positions

With the growth of social services in the past fifty years, the government has developed a need for physicians, medical researchers, nurses, and similar workers in more and more fields. Wars have led to the establishment of a permanent corps of medical specialists and their assistants. The growth of psychiatric concepts, the development of occupational therapy, the public demand that veterans who need medical care should have it—all these factors demand a force of practitioners working for the government.

Research activities include the study of bacteriological warfare, the hunt for protection against the effects of radioactivity, the preparation of new vaccines, serums, and other biological products. Medical jobs involve inspection of laboratories and testing of pharmaceuticals, running such public-relations campaigns as the one against syphilis, examining those entering the public service, the medical care of Native Americans on reservations, and straight medical work from the care of colds to the most complex plastic surgery.

Medical and related work in the federal service includes these jobs: Medical Officer, Hospital Administrator, Medical Technician, Dental Officer, Pharmacist, Physical Therapist, Public Health Nurse, Hospital Nurse, Dietitian, First-aid Attendant, Hospital Attendant, Dental Hygienist, Dental Mechanic, Occupational Therapist, Physiotherapist, Psychiatrist, Psychiatric Nurse, Coroner, and Embalmer. To this group might be added the Veterinarian and the Veterinary Inspector.

The department which employs most medical workers in peacetime is the Veterans' Administration. The Army and Navy have medical and dental corps, which, of course, grow enormously during war. Other agencies which need doctors and their aides are the Public Health Service, a department which does notable work in improving public health and guarding against dangerous mass diseases; the Food and Drug Administration; the Children's Bureau of the Department of Health, where extensive research is conducted in maternal and child health and services are provided for handicapped children; the Bureau of Indian Affairs of the Interior Department, where, besides serving in hospitals, doctors make home calls and field trips, conduct school examinations, and administer general public-health measures among the Native Americans. American physicians also accompany our missions in the Foreign Service. Incidentally, the Public Health Service supervises hospitals serving the Coast Guard, Merchant Marine, Army

Engineer Corps, Army Transport Service, and federal employees injured in the line of duty. Many federal agencies employ nurses in the in-house medical facilities which they maintain for their employees. Nurses also serve in U.S. hospitals, and serve as consultants to state health departments on programs to control tuberculosis and venereal disease.

The government maintains an extensive nurse training program, paying student nurses while teaching them.

Now let us have a look at some of the medical positions with their qualifications and requirements.

MEDICAL OFFICER

Medical officers occupy positions in the Public Health Service; in the Food and Drug Administration; in the Children's Bureau; in the Department of Health; in the Office of Indian Affairs, Department of the Interior; in the Veterans' Administration; and in many other federal agencies.

They are on duty in marine hospitals where they care for members of the Merchant Marine and Coast Guard and for civilian employees of the Government who are injured in the line of duty; they are also assigned to duty in marine quarantine stations and airports where they inspect vessels and airplanes entering the ports, harbors, and airfields of the United States and where they examine aliens entering the United States.

Medical officers determine that medicines are labeled according to their composition and content; they conduct extensive research in maternal and child health and in services to handicapped children. They serve in Indian hospitals, make calls to the homes of Native Americans who are ill, make field trips, and administer special health measures among the Native Americans. They serve as district physicians in small government dispensaries. They have the opportunity of working in teaching hospitals in the federal service which are approved by the American Medical Association; here they may obtain a wide variety of medical experience, particularly in the field of tropical diseases.

PROFESSIONAL NURSE

Professional nurses serve in hospitals on Indian reservations. Civilian nurses are employed at times in hospitals of the Department of the Army when there are not sufficient nurses from the Army Nurse Corps to meet hospital needs. The Department of the Navy employs some civilian nurses for duty in Navy hospitals to care for dependents of Regular Navy personnel.

There are two personnel systems through which nurses in the Public Health Service may seek employment—the Commissioned Corps and the Federal Civil Service. The majority of available positions are in the U.S. Public Health Service hospitals located in the major port cities in the United States, the Clinical Center at the National Institutes of Health, and hospitals and clinics of the Indian Health Service. The level of nursing positions ranges from staff nurse through nurse consultant and chief of a division.

Public-health nursing consultants are employed in the Children's Bureau where they work with state agencies in connection with maternal and child-health programs, handicapped children's programs, and programs concerned with the care of children with rheumatic heart disease.

Applicants for all positions of professional nurse must have completed a full three-year course in residence in an approved school of nursing, or a full two-year course plus additional appropriate nursing experience or pertinent education. Applicants must also be currently registered as professional nurses in a State or territory of the United States or the District of Columbia or expect to apply for registration at the first opportunity.

In addition, for positions in grades GS-6 and above, they must have had progressively responsible specialized professional experience appropriate to the position for which they apply. For Nurse Anesthetist positions, additional courses of study in an approved school of anesthesia or certain prescribed experience will be necessary to meet the requirements. For some positions, part of the experience or training must have been gained within the past two to five years, depending on the position for which applying.

The degree of responsibility involved and the scope of the experience required must have been proportionately greater for each successive higher grade.

For Public Health Nurse and Nursing Consultant positions, training must have included or been supplemented by at least 30 semester hours in a program of study in public health nursing.

The entrance salary for a professional nurse in the position of staff nurse is GS-5 to GS-7 and in the position of head nurse, GS-7 to GS-9.

Nurse consultant positions pay GS-11 to GS-13. The education and experience requirements vary with the grade of the position.

The pay of public-health nurse positions is from GS-7 to GS-9 at entrance.

DENTAL ASSISTANT

Salary

GS-4 at entrance.

Duties

Dental Assistants perform duties of either a specialized or a general nature. They receive and prepare patients, assist the dentist in both non-surgical and surgical dentistry, and may perform dental X-ray or prosthetic work. They keep records of appointments, examinations, treatments, and supplies.

Requirements

Applicants must have had two years of dental assistant experience including or supplemented by one year of specialization in restoration, dental X-raying, dental surgery, dental prosthetics, or a combination of these appropriate to the position being filled. Applicants may substitute successful completion of dental assistant courses approved by the American Dental Assistants Association on a month-for-month basis for experience. The successful completion of dental assistant courses in the Armed Forces, in government or private hospitals, or in schools other than those mentioned above will receive credit appropriate to their length and content. Only training clearly dealing with a specialization may be substituted for experience in specialization.

Basis of Rating

No written test is required. Applicants' qualifications will be rated on a scale of 100 and will be judged from a review of the information furnished concerning their education and training and also on corroborative evidence.

DENTAL HYGIENIST

Salary

GS-4 to GS-5 at entrance.

Duties

Dental Hygienists give oral prophylaxis to patients in hospitals and clinics. They conduct programs of oral hygiene education and instruct hospital and clinic personnel in the techniques of the maintenance of oral hygiene.

Requirements

Applicants for all grades must be currently licensed to practice as dental hygienists in the United States. Applicants for GS-4 must have completed successfully a full course of two years in Dental Hygiene accredited by the Council on Dental Education of the American Dental Association. Applicants with one year of experience and one year of education and those with two years of experience will also qualify.

Applicants for GS-5 must have successfully completed a full course of two academic years in Dental Hygiene accredited by the Council on Dental Education of the American Dental Association and have one year of experience; or they may have one year of education and two years of experience; or they may have three years of experience.

Each academic year of education leading toward a bachelor's degree in Dental or Oral Hygiene or in closely related fields will count as six months of experience for those positions involving instruction and demonstration of oral hygiene for groups.

Basis of Rating

No written test is required. Applicants will be rated on a scale of 100 on the extent and quality of their education, experience, and personal qualities required in these positions. Such ratings will be based on information in the applications and upon any corroborative evidence.

OTHER POSITIONS

Other positions in the medical and nursing field include medical technician, laboratory helper, X-ray technician, photofluorographic operator, occupational therapist, orthopedic technician, dental technician, and veterinarian. Entrance salaries for these positions range from GS-3 to GS-14.

Economics and Statistics Positions

The complexities of modern government require the services everywhere of people who "understand figures." Hardly an activity exists in any department which does not demand the work of an accountant, statistician, economist, or mathematician. Every citizen knows of the work done by the people in the Internal Revenue Service. Statisticians in the Census Bureau prepare all kinds of data for businesses and keep facts on the ups and downs of business. Other statisticians work with scientists, collecting and analyzing statistical reports on agriculture, for instance, reports which are frequently the basis of long-range national policy. They work on problems dealing with production, marketing, distribution, taxation, and other economic questions.

Accountants and budget examiners go over the dollars and cents spent by various departments, submit estimates, and sometimes cut spending programs. They make up payrolls, work on retirement mathematics, examine the books of stock exchange firms. They study the backgrounds of bankruptcies, audit the books of public utility companies, check into the financial conditions of banks. In another sphere they may analyze the fiscal policy of the United States and determine methods of adapting that policy to the economic needs of the country. They make up the nation's budget and suggest appropriations for all government activities.

Mathematicians work with scientists in all their activities, from plotting the course of planets to devising formulas in atomic physics. They work with engineers building bridges, solve equations about heat conduction or electrical circuits, make computations to predict weather, and determine the path of missiles and the intensity of earthquakes.

The "figures" people are so important that it is no overstatement to say modern government could not function without them. The Department of Agriculture, the Tennessee Valley Authority, the Department of Labor and its Bureau of Labor Statistics, the National Labor Relations Board, the Census Bureau, the Treasury Department and the Securities and Exchange Commission are only some of the agencies which need workers with mathematics or economics backgrounds.

As the government grows more complex, the need for people who can work with the intangibles of statistics and economics, as well as those who can examine a set of figures in books, will grow. Salaries range from GS-5 to GS-15.

Some typical government positions in these fields are examined below.

ACCOUNTING ASSISTANT

Salary

GS-5 and GS-7 at entrance.

Duties

The duties of this position vary, depending upon the agencies. They are all alike, however, in that they all give an opportunity for a diversity of experience in a program emphasizing the systematic development of full professional skill.

Requirements

For GS-5, applicants must meet one of the following: four years' study in accounting above the high-school level; three years' progressive experience; an equivalent combination of both; a C.P.A. certificate.

For GS-7, applicants must meet the requirements for GS-5 plus completion of one year of graduate study in accounting or one year of experience in professional accounting.

Basis of Rating

Applicants qualifying on a basis of education only or a C.P.A. certificate do not take an examination. Those who offer some qualifications of experience must take an examination.

ACCOUNTANT AND AUDITOR

Salary

GS-9 through GS-15.

Duties

Accountants and Auditors collect and evaluate data, maintain and examine accounting records, plan new accounting systems and revise old ones, prepare accounting statements, examine transactions to determine their accuracy and legality, and analyze financial reports.

Requirements

Applicants must have experience of a length and quality like that shown in the following table:

		Professional		
Grade of Position	General	Type A	Type B	Total
GS-9	3 years	1 year	1 year	5 years
GS-11 through GS-15	3 years	1 year	2 years	6 years

Basis of Rating

Applicants for Grades GS-9, 11, and 12 who have completed four years of college with concentration in accounting or who possess a CPA certificate and applicants eligible for Grade GS-13 and above are the only applicants exempt from the written accounting test. All competitors who meet the experience requirements and pass the written test will be rated on a scale of 100 on the quality, diversity, and extent of their experience. Such ratings will be based on information in the application forms and on additional evidence obtained.

REVENUE OFFICER

Salary

GS-5 and GS-7 at entrance.

Duties

Revenue Officers perform personal contact work involved in the collection of delinquent taxes and the securing of delinquent tax returns. They deal with corporate executives, attorneys, accountants, and individual taxpayers in all walks of life. They investigate and analyze business situations, negotiate agreements to satisfy tax obligations, enforce tax law by seizure and sale, and perform other related work to safeguard the government's interest.

Requirements and Basis of Rating

Preferably, graduates should have 24 semester hours in subjects such as accounting, business administration, business economics, finance, and law.

TAX TECHNICIAN

Salary

GS-5 and GS-7 at entrance.

Duties

Tax Technicians represent the Internal Revenue Service in consultations with taxpayers of all kinds—individual wage earners, small business owners, professionals, corporate executives, and others. They talk with taxpayers in the office and correspond with them to identify and explain tax issues and to determine correct tax liability.

Requirements and Basis of Rating

An examination may be used to fill this position. Preferably, graduates should have 24 semester hours in subjects such as accounting, business administration, business economics, finance, and law.

STATISTICIAN

Salary

GS-9 through GS-15.

Duties

Statisticians do professional work or provide professional consultation requiring the application of statistical theory and techniques in a variety of subject-matter fields including the social, natural, and physical sciences and administration.

Requirements

Applicants must have completed a full four-year course leading to a bachelor's degree in an accredited college with specialization in mathematics and statistics. They must also have had from two to three years of experience in statistics. Substitutions of experience for education may be made.

Basis of Rating

No written test will be given. Applicants will be rated on a scale of 100 based upon statements in applications and any additional information acquired. As vacancies occur, the qualifications of those who meet the basic requirements will be reviewed. Competitors may be asked to supply additional information at such time.

ECONOMIST

Salary

GS-9 and GS-11 through GS-15.

Duties

Economists research economic phenomena and interpret economic data, prepare reports on economic facts and activities, investigate and evaluate reports for their economic implications, write economic reports for official publication, and provide consultant services for government policy makers.

Basis of Rating

Applicants will be rated on a scale of 100 on the amount and quality of their experience, education, and training in relation to the requirements of the position for which they apply.

MANAGEMENT ANALYST

Salary

GS-9 to GS-12 at entrance.

Duties

The management analyst's work includes the evaluating of administrative systems and facilities for the management and control of government operations and developing new or improved procedures, systems, and organization structures.

Requirements

Applicants must have had five or six years of experience (depending on the grade applied for) that has included two or three years in the development, evaluation, or revision of programs, organization, methods, or procedures; specialty systems in such fields as tabulation and machine accounting, forms control, records management; or budgetary preparation and presentation. Graduate study in appropriate subjects may be substituted for this experience.

Basis of Rating

Applicants must pass a written examination.

BUDGET EXAMINER

Salary

GS-9 to GS-12 at entrance.

Duties

Budget examiners survey government programs, review budgets, and present budgets to the proper authorities. They are often responsible for the development and operation of systems for reporting work performed and funds expended.

Requirements

The requirements for this position are the same as for management analyst (see above).

Basis of Rating

Applicants must pass a written examination.

Teaching and Library Positions

Although teaching is primarily a function of state and local governments, the federal government employs teachers and educators for a number of services. With the new emphasis on vocational guidance, the opportunities for qualified teachers in the federal service has increased. Rates of pay compare favorably with those of the larger cities.

Among the agencies which employ teachers and educators are the Bureau of Indian Affairs of the Department of the Interior, the Veterans' Administration, the Department of Agriculture, and the Department of Education. The Indian Affairs Bureau alone employs more than 1200 teachers. In the Veterans' Administration, there is informal class teaching or individual bedside instruction, and teachers assist in arranging correspondence courses. The requirements for the job include college or teacher-training education and some teaching experience. A number of teaching positions are available abroad. The Department of Health uses highly trained education experts to work with colleges, universities, and state educational systems in setting up educational programs. Qualified persons are comparatively well paid.

Among the other teaching jobs in the federal service are educational research; in-service training work in all agencies of the government, training of federal employees for greater efficiency on their jobs; playground and recreation directing.

Almost every federal agency has a librarian who takes care of the agency's reading and reference material. Agencies which usually service the public with such information use many librarians; such agencies include the Departments of Agriculture and Commerce. In Washington librarians assist federal employees in their work by giving them reference material and by doing research for them. Branches of the Veterans' Administration have libraries which offer limited opportunities for trained librarians in the areas where they are located.

The largest number of librarians is employed in the Library of Congress; the jobs there are of great diversity and complexity—locating books and documents, hunting up facts for congressmen, working on major research projects, and writing reports which sometimes influence American policy. Employees of the Library of Congress are not under the civil service; applicants should write directly to the Director of the Library, in Washington, D.C.

Librarians are employed in two categories, subprofessional and professional. At the lowest levels no actual library experience is required. The higher levels require extensive educational qualifications. Salaries have risen in recent years. Positions may be rated as high as GS-15.

Here are some of the teaching and library posts available in the federal service.

BUREAU OF INDIAN AFFAIRS
(Department of the Interior)

The Bureau of Indian Affairs, Department of the Interior, is responsible for the education of Native American children who are not educated by public schools in the states where they live and for a program of adult education which can bridge the gap between life on the reservation and the mainstream of contemporary America. When you work in an Indian school, you act as cross-cultural interpreter as well as a classroom teacher.

BIA operates 254 schools and 18 dormitories for children who attend public schools, serving over 50,000 students. Adult education aids over 31,000 Native Americans in 303 communities. Arizona, New Mexico, Alaska, North Dakota, and South Dakota have the largest concentration of Native American population and schools, although some educators are needed each year in California, Oklahoma, Oregon, Utah, Kansas, Florida, Mississippi, Montana, North Carolina, and Louisiana.

Classroom teachers and guidance counselors are especially needed. Most Bureau schools are located in isolated rural locations more than 30 miles from the nearest urban community. The work involved in combatting physical isolation as well as physical and emotional poverty demands dedication, imagination, and strength, but, as one young teacher put it, "Here I work among a culturally rich but culturally different people. The environment just has to be stimulating, and it is. I work twice as hard as I did in public school teaching, and my rewards are multiplied many, many times."

AGENCY FOR INTERNATIONAL DEVELOPMENT
(Department of State)

AID administers America's foreign aid program in the developing countries of Asia, Africa, and Latin America. Since the progress of a developing country hinges critically on the ability of its people to read and comprehend and to learn the skills by which they can support and govern themselves, education plays an important part in that program.

As an AID educator, you would work with local officials on projects which range from selecting textbooks to setting up educational TV. Your job would be to help plan educational programs that meet needs for particular areas and train the people of each area to run the programs themselves.

AID hires advisors in the fields of elementary education, higher education, human resources development, teacher education, trade-industrial education, and vocational education. Classroom teaching alone does not provide the experience needed, and positions usually require advanced degrees and several years of administrative and program responsibility.

If you meet the rigid professional standards, work with AID offers you the stimulation of working with other American and foreign professionals and the opportunity to make unique, long-range contributions in your field. At a time when unrest is aggravated by the disparity between industrial and third-world nations, your work with AID can help close the gap.

For jobs with AID, write to:

Chief, Talent Search
Office of Personnel and Manpower
Agency for International Development
Washington, D.C. 20523

DEPARTMENT OF DEFENSE
Overseas Dependents Schools

Did you know the ninth largest American school system lies entirely outside the continental United States? Schools in 27 foreign countries are set up by the Department of Defense to provide education for children of overseas military and civilian personnel. More than 167,000 dependents attend 292 such schools around the world.

The largest single group of educators (7,100 of them) work for the government in this system. Jobs in the DOD schools correspond to those in any large American school system, including positions as administrators, counselors, classroom teachers, teachers of the physically and mentally handicapped, teachers of special subjects, and librarians. Two years of teaching experience is required.

Working with the DOD school system offers you the chance to live and travel in a foreign country and pursue your career at the same time. Vacations may be spent touring neighboring countries as well. Many dependent school teachers enroll in foreign institutes, language schools, and universities, or work on advanced degrees through attendance at or correspondence with American universities and foundations overseas. So, in both the teaching and learning sense, the world is your classroom.

For jobs with Department of Defense Overseas Dependents Schools, contact your local United States Employment Service office.

FEDERAL CORRECTIONAL INSTITUTIONS

Far from the hardened master-criminal stereotype, the average inmate in a federal correctional institution is under 30 years old, has an educational level of fifth grade, and is serving time for auto theft. The inmate is, as one prison official put it, a "double dropout," having dropped out of school and out of life outside the institution. Educational programs within the system are aimed at helping him or her make a success of this second chance at useful citizenship.

On the basis of social history, age, nature of offense, and rehabilitative potential 21,000 offenders are assigned to 36 institutions, from pre-release guidance centers to penitentiaries of 2,000 inmates. Academic programs range from remedial reading for functional illiterates to instruction at the high school level. Vocational training is aimed at providing marketable skills, including work as dental technicians, computer training, welding, masonry, small engine repair, and auto repair for the inmate who has loved cars "not wisely, but too well."

The Bureau of Prisons employs people in the fields of remedial reading, library work, academic and vocational subjects, arts and crafts, recreation, guidance, supervisory and administrative work, occupational therapy, and research and development.

Since the educational program in federal prisons is geared to reaching people who haven't succeeded in conventional educational systems, teachers are allowed both freedom to try experimental methods in getting their ideas across and the time to do so.

For the prisoner, a high school diploma or a union card may make the difference between success or failure on reentering society. As the teacher you can help make that difference.

DEPARTMENT OF EDUCATION

Office of Education

The Office of Education links federal education programs with state and local agencies, colleges and universities, international education organizations, and professional associations. Its role has many facets, ranging from school desegregation under the Civil Rights Act to administering funds for library construction; from research in educating handicapped children to compiling statistics; from consulting services to programs of adult and vocational education.

Surprisingly, while OE is involved in so many phases of education, it has virtually no opportunities for classroom teachers as such. The need is for experienced professionals, including college and university presidents and deans, department heads, administrators, research scholars, staff assistants, vocational and technical specialists, counseling and testing experts, and curriculum specialists. If you meet these qualifications, you will find being involved in the broad scale of OE programs interesting and stimulating work.

Note. Each year the Office of Education hires young men and women with bachelor's and master's degrees who are not educators as such. As a recent college graduate, you can put your general education background to work in an administrative capacity in many of the programs at OE.

Public Health Education

The Public Health Educator specializes in getting health facts accepted and used. The work requires a rare blend of specific training and the ingenuity needed to communicate and work with widely varying groups of people. For those few who meet the professional standards, it's a challenging, relatively new field for educators in government.

EDUCATION RESEARCH AND PROGRAM SPECIALIST

Salary

GS-9 to GS-15.

Duties

An appointee may perform any of the following: make appraisals of education practices both here and abroad; plan, conduct and evaluate surveys and research; publish or promote publication of educational articles and bulletins; act as educational consultant to local, state, national or international bodies; plan and administer grants in aid. He or she may be assigned to any of these functions in one or more fields of specialization such as elementary education, vocational, school administration, guidance, or international education.

Requirements

Specialists must have finished a four-year college course including or supplemented by major study in education and have had extensive experience in educational administration, educational research, or other activities in the field of education. The experience must demonstrate ability to plan and supervise, to recommend improvements in curricula, school service, or school finance, and to write or edit manuals. For the jobs at GS-14 and higher, the applicant must have made significant contributions to education and earned outstanding recognition in his or her special field. Credit is given for appropriate part-time and unpaid experience.

Basis of Rating

No written examination is required; candidates are judged on their background and experience. These factors are considered in assigning ratings: knowledge of current developments in the field of specialization; ability to plan and conduct scholarly research, organize an educational program, speak and write effectively, co-operate with colleagues, direct professional employees, and work harmoniously with staff. Evidence of leadership in the specialty is demanded.

LIBRARY ASSISTANT

Salary

GS-3 to GS-5 at entrance.

Duties

Persons appointed to these positions will perform such duties as stack maintenance; book and bindery preparation; circulation work; making additions to serial, shelf-list, and catalog records; arranging inter-library loans; compiling lists of books; answering simple reference questions; checking in and routing periodicals; and other work of a comparable nature. GS-5 involves the supervising of library assistants in lower grades who are engaged in the activities listed above.

Requirements

Depending upon the grade applied for, from one to three years of experience. Two thirds of this experience must have been specialized, including such duties as circulation work, answering simple reference questions, making additions to library records, book and bindery preparation, and stack maintenance. Undergraduate study may be substituted on the basis of one year of education for nine months of experience. Also, each three semester hours of library science is equal to three months of experience.

Basis of Rating

As described below for archives assistant.

LIBRARIAN

Salary

Grades GS-5 through GS-15.

Duties

Librarians perform or direct the performance of work in federal libraries involving acquisitions, cataloging and classification, or reference and bibliography. As many of the libraries are highly specialized, the work often lies in one field. Because many publications are in foreign languages, librarians in many positions must have a knowledge of one or more foreign languages.

At the higher levels, librarians may (1) assume complete charge of a large library containing both general and specific collections; (2) organize and direct the activities of a division in a large library; or (3) serve as consulting specialists to research personnel.

Requirements

Applicants must have successfully completed a four-year course of study in an accredited college including or supplemented by at least 24 semester-hours in library science; or they may have four years of progressive experience equivalent in quality to the course of study described above, six months of which was at a level of difficulty comparable to the next lower grade, or one year of which was comparable in difficulty to the second lowest grade, in the Federal service; or they may combine experience and education to equal four years.

For positions at GS-7 and above, the following experience requirements must be met in addition to those already specified:

Grade of Position	Additional Experience Required
GS-7	1 year
GS-9	2 years

The quality of the experience rather than the length of time employed will be given primary consideration.

Applicants for GS-7 who have completed all the work for a master's degree or one full year of graduate study leading to a higher degree in addition to all work required for a bachelor's degree may qualify in full. Education may be substituted for experience only when it may be substituted in full, i.e., in grades GS-5 and GS-7. Applications will be accepted from students who are otherwise qualified and expect to complete all scholastic requirements within nine months of filing the application.

Basis of Rating

Applicants for GS-5 and GS-7 who qualify on experience alone or on a combination of education and experience and who do not meet the experience requirements for grades GS-9 and above will be required to take a written test. All competitors who meet the experience requirements and who pass the written test when required will be rated on a basis of 100 upon an evaluation of their experience and training in library work. Consideration will be given for specialized experience in the field for which the examination is being given.

ARCHIVES ASSISTANT

Salary

GS-3 to GS-5 at entrance.

Duties

Persons appointed perform work in receiving, sorting, filing, classifying, and indexing noncurrent records and documents; searching for, charging out, and providing information as requested; packing, sorting, and preserving noncurrent records. At GS-5 many of the positions involve supervisory duties.

Requirements

Depending upon the grade applied for, from one to three years of experience in the organization, maintenance, or servicing of the records of a public or private institution; or from 12 to 18 semester hours of college courses in either history, government, political science, sociology, economics, or public administration.

Basis of Rating

A written clerical abilities examination consisting of alphabetizing, arithmetic, and verbal abilities (including word meaning, spelling, and the meaning of written paragraphs) is given. Competitors for grade GS-5 positions will also be required to take a test of supervisory judgment.

Social Work Positions

Twentieth century concepts of government include the notion that the state must exercise some responsibility for the welfare of U.S. citizens. Thus there has grown up, in comparatively recent times, a new grouping of government activities built around certain basic needs of the people—social security, old age and unemployment insurance, and various welfare projects. The federal government interests itself in the blind, the poor, and the handicapped. It takes a hand in the dissemination of nutrition and health education, publishes cookbooks, and advises upon the proper care of babies. It grants aid to states for dealing with people suffering from emotional and psychological problems and to some extent aids these people directly. Much of this work is performed by trained social workers.

Let us look into the duties and the qualifications needed for one of these positions.

SOCIAL WORKER—CORRECTIONS

Salary

GS-7 and GS-9.

Duties

Social Workers work in correctional institutions to develop personal histories of new inmates, prepare progress reports on their adjustment both within the institution and in the outside environment, explain rules, policies, and decisions to prisoners, plan with them regarding parole and release, and advise them about personal and family problems. They make recommendations to the prison administration regarding the prisoners' special needs and requests and are responsible for the detention of prisoners assigned to them. Social Workers at grade GS-7 work as trainees; those at grade GS-9 work with a large degree of independence.

Requirements

Applicants for GS-7 positions must have had five years of experience in social case work, one year of which involved work in a correctional institution or in a crime or delinquency prevention program. A course of study leading to a bachelor's degree from an accredited college may be substituted for four of the five years of experience, but not for the year of correctional work. Completion of all the requirements for a master's degree in social work may be substituted for all five years; one year of graduate work in sociology in an accredited college may be substituted for the one year of correctional experience; and any combination of education and experience which is the equivalent of the three educational options listed above is acceptable. Those applicants who have fulfilled all the requirements for a master's degree in social work are eligible for GS-9. Other applicants must have, in addition to the requirements for GS-7, one additional year of correctional work or one year of graduate study in social work at an accredited college or university. Applications will be accepted from students who expect to fulfill all requirements within six months of filing the application. The quality of an applicant's experience will be evaluated to see if it is comparable with the position for which he or she is applying.

Basis of Rating

No written test is required. Applicants will be rated on a scale of 100 on the extent and quality of their experience. Such ratings will be based upon competitors' statements in their applications and upon any additional information.

Science and Engineering Positions

Scientific research and development are carried out in 25 federal departments and agencies, principally in the laboratories of the Departments of the Army, Navy, and Air Force, the National Aeronautics and Space Administration, the Department of Agriculture, the National Institutes of Health, the National Bureau of Standards, the Department of the Interior, the Federal Aviation Agency, and the Veterans Administration.

Recently, employment conditions for the scientist in the federal service have been radically improved. Now there are more than 71,000 employees in science and 116,000 in engineering, constituting 11½ percent of the white-collar work force.

In August of 1964 the Civil Service Commission, the predecessor to the Office of Personnel Management, issued new salary schedules for scientists and engineers in the federal service, setting pay rates for many professional engineering, scientific, and medical positions even above the newly enacted rates of the general salary schedule. The Office took this action under the authority of the Federal Salary Reform Act of 1962, on the basis of a decision that the higher salaries were necessary to meet non-governmental pay standards in occupations in which there is a shortage of manpower.

The 1962 Salary Act included several special features that help the federal service attract and retain high-quality personnel and stimulate excellent performance. One of these was the special salary-rate authority mentioned above. Pay differentials between grades were increased for the middle and higher grades, and pay steps within the grade were also increased. (The classified salary structure consists of 15 regular grades and three "supergrades." There are several levels or steps within each grade, except for grade 18, the highest.) In addition to the regular periodic within-grade step increase, an additional step increase can be granted for high-quality performance; also, the regular within-grade increase can be withheld if work is not of an acceptable level of competence.

Professional positions in the physical and natural sciences, medicine, and research engineering were removed from the restrictions limiting the number of positions in grades 16, 17, and 18 (the "supergrades"). Federal agencies may now recommend to the Office of Personnel Management, for its approval, inclusion of as many such positions in those grades as duties and responsibilities warrant. This change goes far toward eliminating a potent barrier to the proper matching of pay and responsibility at the highest levels.

A second highly significant legislative step was passage of the Government Employees Training Act of 1958. The Training Act authorizes employee training at full pay within the federal agency or at colleges, universities, professional institutes, industrial laboratories, or research foundations; full or partial payment of tuition and related costs; payment of travel expenses and registration fees for attendance at professional meetings; and cooperation among agencies in opening up training courses across agency lines.

Also, in shortage occupations, officials of federal agencies can now make immediate offers to well qualified candidates on the assumption that their names will be high enough on the appropriate register of eligibles when the grading of the civil service examination they have taken is completed.

Position classification in the federal civil service—the process by which the grade and salary level of a job is determined—is a flexible procedure in scientific fields. Traditionally, "the position, not the person, is classified," but in determining the grade level of research positions the qualifications, professional stature, and scientific contributions of the scientist are primary considerations. Also, the job can be tailored to fit the qualifications of an outstanding scientist.

Within the framework of government-wide personnel laws and policies, agency and laboratory directors can maintain a creative environment by providing privileges and recognition for their scientific personnel. This is done in ways such as the following: by (1) encouraging staff members to attend meetings of professional societies and to publish in professional journals; (2) giving them credit lines on official publications of the laboratory; (3) giving them freedom to teach and serve as consultants on the outside and to write books; (4) maintaining a liberal patent policy; (5) providing reasonable flexibility of working hours; (6) establishing meaningful professional titles; and (7) encouraging co-workers of different grades to consider themselves colleagues, not boss and subordinate.

In the federal service there are some restrictions regarding conflict of interest and disclosure of classified material, but otherwise laboratory directors are given considerable discretion in using the measures listed above to build the type of environment they seek.

The jobs considered below are only a small portion of those that exist. They illustrate requirements, bases of rating, and salary levels for typical federal scientific and engineering positions.

CHEMIST

Salary

GS-5 to GS-15, depending on past experience.

Requirements

For GS-5, a four-year college or university course leading to a bachelor's degree in chemistry or four years of experience in the field of chemical engineering.

Basis of Rating

For Grades GS-5 through GS-12, no written test is required. Applicants' qualifications will be rated on a scale of 100 by subject specialists and will be determined by an evaluation of their experience, education and training.

For Grades GS-13 through GS-15, no written test is required. A preliminary review will be made of the training and experience of each applicant as described in his or her application form. As vacancies occur, the qualifications of the applicants who meet the basic requirements will be evaluated in relation to the specific positions to be filled.

PHYSICIST

Salary

GS-5 to GS-15 at entrance.

Duties

Appointees will perform professional work in one or more of the branches of physical science, conducting or assisting in technical projects and applying scientific knowledge to the solution of scientific problems.

Requirements

For GS-5, a four-year college course leading to a bachelor's degree. This study must include courses in physics totaling at least 24 semester hours.

Requirements for GS-7 through GS-15: In addition to meeting the appropriate requirements shown in the first part of this section for the GS-5 grade of the position for which application is made, applicants must meet the experience requirements listed below:

Grade	Total Professional Experience	Specialized Experience in Physics
GS-7	1 year	1 year
GS-9	2 years	1 year
GS-11, 12, 13, 14, 15	3 years	2 years

Basis of Rating

Applicants' qualifications will be rated on a scale of 100 and will be judged from a review of their experience, education, and training and on corroborative evidence.

ENGINEER

Salary

GS-5 through GS-15 at entrance.

Fields of Engineering

Agricultural, Civil (Bridge, Highway, Sanitary, Surveying-Topographic, and Hydraulic), Electrical, Electronic, Mining, and others.

Requirements

All applicants must have successfully completed a full four-year course in engineering leading to a bachelor's degree. They may also have a combination of engineering education and experience equivalent in quality and quantity to a four-year college course. They must also have passed the Engineer-in-Training Examination, participated in certain specialized courses, or have demonstrable professional stature. Applicants for grades higher than GS-5 must have, in addition, either education or experience of the following amounts and types:

Grade of Position	General	Specialized	Total
GS-7	1 year	none	
GS-9	1 year	1 year	2 years
GS-11 through GS-15	2 years	1 year	3 years

Superior academic achievement, creative research or development contribution, or extensive graduate work may qualify applicants in all grades for higher positions.

Basis of Rating

All applicants except those for GS-13 and GS-15 will be rated on a basis of 100 on experience, education, and training. Ratings will be made for grade levels and for specialties. Applicants for GS-13 and GS-15 will be notified upon review of their applications of the engineering specialties for which they are qualified. As vacancies occur, the qualifications of the applicants who meet the requirements of the specialization will be reviewed. For all grades, applicants' qualifications will be judged from a review of their experience.

ENGINEERING DRAFTSMAN

Salary

GS-2 through GS-7 at entrance.

Duties

Engineering Draftsmen perform drafting work which is directly related to highly technical engineering activities of a professional and scientific nature. Draftsmen use arithmetical calculations and drafting instruments in making working drawings, assemblies, and layouts of various types of equipment. They exercise care in maintaining uniformity in line weights and widths for similar features, details, and symbols.

Requirements

For all grades, applicants must meet the specified experience requirements as modified by the indicated substitutions for education.

Grade	General Experience	Specialized Experience	Total
GS-2	6 months	None	6 months
GS-3	1 year	None	1 year
GS-4	1 year, 6 months	6 months	2 years
GS-5	2 years, 3 months	9 months	3 years
GS-7	3 years	1 year	4 years

General experience must be in performing the work of a cartographic, engineering, or statistical draftsman; experience in skilled and mechanical trades and related scientific and engineering technician occupations in which the interpretation of blue-prints or schematic diagrams was required may be substituted for up to half of the required general experience.

Education at the high-school level and above may be substituted, with special provisions, for both general and specialized experience in specified amounts. Education may not be substituted for the specialized experience required for GS-7.

Basis of Rating

Competitors for GS-2 and GS-3 will be rated on a written test on a scale of 100 and must achieve a rating of at least 70 to be eligible.

Competitors for GS-4, GS-5, and GS-7 will be rated on a scale of 100 on the extent and quality of their experience, education, and training relevant to the position. The rating will be based on the statements in the application, on the sample (consisting of three drawings) of engineering drafting work submitted, and on any additional information.

ENGINEERING AID (HIGHWAY)

Salary

GS-3.

Duties

Engineering Aids will be assigned to sub-professional engineering tasks in the highway construction field. They assist on highway location surveys, highway construction, and minor inspection of highway and/or bridge construction and make minor mathematical calculations. Assignments involve acting as *chair* and/or *rodman,* marking and driving stakes, recording survey notes, reducing simple cross section notes, and plotting cross sections and profiles. Work is performed under supervision of higher-grade employees.

Requirements

Applicants must have had one and one-half years' total experience. The experience must have been in engineering, but experience in mathematics or in the physical sciences may be substituted up to the extent of one year. The successful completion of a full four-year or senior high school curriculum may be substituted for one year of the required experience, and, depending on quality and quantity, education at a higher level that included courses in drafting, mathematics, applied engineering sciences, or engineering may be substituted.

Basis of Rating

Competitors will be rated on a basis of 100 on the extent and quality of their education, experience, and training. Such ratings will be based upon competitors' statements in their applications and upon any additional information and evidence.

GEOLOGIST

Salary

GS-9 to GS-15.

Duties

Persons appointed to these geologist positions will perform professional geological work in one or more of the major occupational fields or specialties within these fields. Typical duties involve geological mapping, making and recording geological field observations and collecting samples for laboratory analysis, identifying and studying samples, compiling and interpreting field, laboratory, and published data, making special studies, and preparing professional scientific and economic reports for publication.

Requirements

Applicants must show successful completion of a four-year course leading to a bachelor's degree with concentration in geology and related sciences or a combination of education and professional experience equivalent in quality and quantity to the four-year course.

Grade	Education Requirement	OR	Experience Requirement		
			General	Specalized	Total
GS-9	2 years graduate study		1 year	1 year	2 years
GS-11	All requirements for Ph.D.		1 year	2 years	3 years
GS-12 to GS-15	No substitution		1 year	2 years	3 years

Superior academic achievement, professional work experience combined with this experience, and creative investigation or research contribution may qualify applicants for higher grades. Students who expect to complete all education requirements within nine months of filing application may apply for positions at GS-9 and GS-11.

Basis of Rating

No written test is required. All ratings will be based on an evaluation of experience, education, and training which may be obtained. Each applicant will be rated in the option for which best qualified.

Applicants for grades GS-9 through GS-13 will be assigned numerical ratings on a basis of 100. Applicants for grades GS-14 and GS-15 will be notified as to whether they meet the basic requirements for these positions. As vacancies occur, the qualifications of candidates who meet the basic requirements will be evaluated in relation to the specific position to be filled, and candidates will be rated accordingly.

METALLURGIST

Salary

GS-5 and GS-7 at entrance.

Requirements

For grade GS-5, a four-year college course including at least 20 semester hours in metallurgy. For GS-7, an additional requirement is one year of professional experience in metallurgy or one year of graduate study in metallurgy.

Basis of Rating

Applicants are assigned numerical ratings on a scale of 100 based on an evaluation of their education and experience.

RESEARCH PSYCHOLOGIST

Salary

GS-9 to GS-15 at entrance.

Types of Work

Experimental and Physiological Psychology; Personnel Measurement and Evaluation; Social Psychology; Engineering Psychology.

Requirements

Depending upon the grade applied for, applicants must have had from two to four years of progressively responsible professional experience which must have included the administration or conduct of significant research or applied studies in the specific field of psychology for which the applicant is being rated. Up to two years of graduate study may be substituted for experience.

Basis of Rating

No written examination is required. Applicants will be rated on an evaluation of their personal and professional qualifications.

Forestry, Agriculture, and Conservation Positions

Two departments of the government—Agriculture and Interior—employ people who know soil, forestry, and water resources. Although the work they do is often difficult and sometimes dangerous, those who hold these positions express a real love for the tasks they perform. The pay is not always high, but it has been increasing. As the nation learns how vital it is to conserve and improve its natural resources, the jobs should grow in importance. Occupational experts believe that jobs in forestry, agriculture, and conservation are "good bets" in coming years.

Among the tasks performed by government workers in agriculture, horticulture, soil science, conservation, and farming are the development, standardization and use of agricultural techniques and products; inspecting and grading samples of farm products; care of trees; experimental landscape gardening; research on soils to see what they can grow; testing fruits, vegetables, trees, shrubs; dairy sanitation and efficiency studies; determining the mineral, water, and agricultural resources of public lands; control and prevention of soil erosion; moisture conservation; research to bring about rapid reforestation; experimental farming; grazing research; the care, breeding, and feeding of farm and dairy animals; research to conserve forests and to use their products; and the economics of all these subjects.

AGRICULTURAL MANAGEMENT

Description of Work

Perform a broad range of functions in carrying out supervised credit and technical assistance programs for people in rural communities. The work involves such activities as crop and livestock production, preparation and marketing of products, and supporting financial, management, rural housing, and community resource development activities.

Course Requirements

Major in farm, livestock, or ranch management, agricultural economics, agricultural education, agronomy, husbandry, agricultural engineering, general agriculture, horticulture, etc. Those qualifying on the basis of combined education and experience must have 30 semester hours in such courses.

AGRONOMY

Description of Work

Perform research, administer or advise on scientific work in the fundamental principles of plant, soil, and related sciences as they apply to crop breeding and production, conservation, propagation and seed production, ground maintenance, and plant adaptation and varietal testing.

Course Requirements

Thirty semester hours, or equivalent, in the basic plant sciences (e.g. botany, plant taxonomy, plant ecology, plant breeding or genetics, microbiology, soil science), with a minimum of 15 semester hours in agronomic subjects such as those dealing with plant breeding, crop production, and soil and crop management.

FORESTRY

Description of Work

Work in the development, production, conservation, utilization, and protection of natural forest resources; management of these resources, including timber, forage, watersheds, wildlife, and land, to meet present and future public needs. Research work involves development of new, improved or more economic scientific instruments and techniques necessary to perform such work.

Course Requirements

Twenty-four semester hours in forestry, sufficiently diversified to fall into at least four of the following areas: (1) silviculture, i.e., such subjects as forest soils, forest ecology, dendrology, silvics, and silviculture; (2) forest management; (3) forest protection; (4) forest economics, i.e., such subjects as forest finance and forest valuation; (5) forest utilization, i.e., such subjects as logging and milling; product preparation and use of wood, etc.; (6) related studies, i.e., such subjects as forest engineering, forest recreation, watershed management, wildlife management. To assure proper diversification of course work, no more than six semester hours credit will be given for courses in any one of the specializations listed. Those qualifying on the basis of combined education and experience must have 30 semester hours in any combination of the biological, physical, or mathematical sciences or engineering, including 24 hours in forestry subjects as described above. For administrative positions, applicants must meet the requirements above or have college education in range conservation, soil science, wildlife, biology, geology, or engineering. The training must have been supplemented by a sufficient amount of professional experience gained in a work situation which required the joint application of professional knowledge of forestry and related fields in solving highly technical and complex problems concerned with the planning, developmental, and administrative phases of multiple-use forest land management.

HUSBANDRY

Description of Work

Develop and improve methods of breeding, feeding, and nutrition of poultry and livestock; improve the management and utilization of poultry and livestock and the quality of meat, poultry, and dairy products.

Course Requirements

Thirty semester hours, or equivalent, in basic biological and agricultural sciences with a minimum of 20 hours in animal sciences. Of these, 10 semester hours must be in the appropriate field of husbandry.

PLANT QUARANTINE AND PEST CONTROL

Description of Work

Apply knowledge of the biological and plant sciences and of the transportation and shipping industries and quarantine techniques to the establishment and enforcement of plant quarantines governing movement of injurious plant pests of economic significance, or to the survey, detection, identification, control, or eradication of plant pests.

Course Requirements

Twenty semester hours, or equivalent, of course work in any combination of one or more of the following: entomology, botany, plant pathology, nematology, horticulture, mycology, invertebrate zoology, or closely related fields. Those qualifying on the basis of combined education and experience must have 30 semester hours in such fields.

RANGE CONSERVATION

Description of Work

Inventory, analyze, improve, protect, utilize, and manage the natural resources of rangelands and related grazing lands; regulate grazing on public rangelands; develop cooperative relationships with range users;

assist landowners to plan and apply range conservation programs; develop technical standards and specifications; conduct research on the principles underlying rangeland management; and develop new and improved instruments and techniques.

Course Requirements

Thirty semester hours, or equivalent, of coursework in any combination of the plant, animal, and soil sciences, and natural resources management.

SOIL CONSERVATION

Description of Work

Advise on, administer, coordinate, perform, or supervise scientific work in a coordinated program of soil, water, and resource conservation which requires the application of a combination of agricultural sciences in order to bring about sound land use and to improve the quality of the environment.

Course Requirements

A major in soil conservation, or closely related agricultural or natural resource sciences, such as agronomy, forestry, wildlife biology, regional planning, agricultural education, or agricultural engineering. The study must have included 30 semester hours, or equivalent in natural resources or agricultural fields including the equivalent of three semester hours in soils.

SOIL SCIENCE

Description of Work

Study and investigate soils from the standpoint of their morphology, genesis, and distribution; their interrelated physical, chemical, and biological properties and processes; their relationships to climatic, physiographic, and vegetative influences; and their adaptation to use and management in agriculture.

WILDLIFE BIOLOGY

Description of Work

Work in the conservation and management of wildlife, or in the determination, establishment, and application of the biological facts, principles, methods, techniques, and procedures necessary for the conservation and management of wildlife.

WILDLIFE REFUGE MANAGEMENT

Description of Work

Develop management and operational plans for bird and game refuges; see that the wildlife is properly protected; and work with individuals, organizations, and the general public on matters pertaining to refuge and related wildlife management programs.

Course Requirements

Nine semester hours, or equivalent, in zoology; six semester hours in such wildlife courses as mammalogy, ornithology, animal ecology, or wildlife management, or equivalent studies in the subject matter field; and nine semester hours in botany.

ZOOLOGY

Description of Work

Administer or perform research in the occurrence, structure, identification, and life histories of parasitic and nonparasitic organisms affecting plants and domestic and wild animals; pathology, epidemiology, immunology, physiology, and host relationships; and biological, physical, and chemical control.

Course Requirements

Thirty semester hours, or equivalent, in biological science, including at least 20 hours in zoology and related animal sciences.

P A R T

TWO

Working for the U.S. Postal Service

CONTENTS

OCCUPATIONS IN THE POSTAL SERVICE

The United States Postal Service is an independent agency of the Federal Government. As such, employees of the Postal Service are federal employees who enjoy the very generous benefits offered by the government. These benefits include an automatic raise at least once a year, regular cost-of-living adjustments, liberal paid vacation and sick leave, life insurance, hospitalization, and the opportunity to join a credit union. At the same time, the operation of the Postal Service is businesslike and independent of politics. A postal worker's job is secure even though presidential administrations may change. An examination system is used to fill vacancies. This system provides opportunities for those who are able and motivated to enter the Postal Service and to move within it.

Most people are familiar with the duties of the city carrier and the post-office window clerk. Yet few are aware of the many different tasks required in processing mail and of the variety of occupations in the Postal Service.

At all hours of the day and night, a steady stream of letters, packages, magazines, and papers moves through the typical large post office. City carriers have collected some of this mail from neighborhood mailboxes; some has been trucked in from surrounding towns or from the airport. When a truck arrives at the post office, mail handlers unload the mail. Postal clerks then sort it according to destination. After being sorted, outgoing mail is loaded into trucks for delivery to the airport or nearby towns. Local mail is left for carriers to deliver the next morning.

To keep buildings and equipment clean and in good working order, the Postal Service employs a variety of service and maintenance workers, including janitors, laborers, truck mechanics, electricians, carpenters, and painters. Some workers specialize in repairing machines that process mail.

Postal inspectors audit the operations of post offices to see that they are run efficiently, that funds are spent properly, and that postal laws and regulations are observed. They also prevent and detect crimes such as theft, forgery, and fraud involving use of the mail.

Postmasters and supervisors are responsible for the day-to-day operation of the post office, for hiring and promoting employees, and for setting up work schedules.

The Postal Service has historically utilized many technological innovations to improve mail distribution and delivery. The first extensive application of technology started in the late 1960s when Multi-Position Letter Machines or MPLSMs began replacing manual mail-sorting equipment. Mechanized MPLSMs represented a significant change in the way mail was processed. In the early 1980s more advanced automated technology, Optical Character Readers and Bar Code Sorters, were introduced and are now essential components in the mail processing environment. These machines are not the ultimate creation. New technologies continue to evolve at an ever-increasing rate. Mail processing by automation is critical to future postal success.

The latest technical advance is the Remote Bar Coding System (RBCS), and the newest job title in the Postal Service is that of Data Conversion Operator.

Almost 85 percent of all postal workers are in jobs directly related to processing and delivering mail. This group includes postal clerks, city carriers, mail handlers, rural carriers, and truck drivers. Postmasters and supervisors make up nearly 10 percent of total employment, and maintenance workers about 4 percent. The remainder includes such workers as postal inspectors, guards, personnel workers, and secretaries.

Training, Other Qualifications, and Advancement

An applicant for a Postal Service job must pass an examination and meet minimum age requirements. Generally, the minimum age is 18 years, but a high school graduate may begin work at 16 years if the job is not hazardous and does not require use of a motor vehicle. Many Postal Service jobs do not require formal education or special training. Applicants for these jobs are hired on the basis of their examination scores.

Some postal jobs do have special education or experience requirements, and some are open only to veterans. Any special requirements will be stated on the announcement of examination.

Male applicants born after December 31, 1959, unless for some reason they are exempt, must be registered with the Selective Service System.

The Immigration Reform and Control Act of 1986 applies to postal workers. All postal workers must be citizens of the United States or must be able to prove identity and right to work in the United States (permanent resident alien status—Green Card).

Applicants should apply at the post office where they wish to work and take the entrance examination for the job they want. Examinations for most jobs include a written test. A physical examination, including drug testing, is required as well. Applicants for jobs that require strength and stamina are sometimes given a special test. For example, mail handlers must be able to lift mail sacks weighing up to 70 pounds. The names of applicants who pass the examinations are placed on a list in the order of their scores. Separate eligibility lists are maintained for each post office. Five extra points are added to the score of an honorably discharged veteran and 10 extra points to the score of a veteran wounded in combat or disabled. Disabled veterans who have a compensable, service-connected disability of 10 percent or more are placed at the top of the eligibility list. When a job opens, the appointing officer chooses one of the top three applicants. Others are left on the list so that they can be considered for future openings.

New employees are trained either on the job by supervisors and other experienced employees or in local training centers. Training ranges from a few days to several months, depending on the job. For example, mail handlers and mechanics' helpers can learn their jobs in a relatively short time. Postal inspectors, on the other hand, need months of training.

Advancement opportunities are available for most postal workers because there is a management commitment to provide career development. Also, employees can get preferred assignments, such as the day shift or a more desirable delivery route, as their seniority increases. When an opening occurs, employees may submit written requests, called "bids," for assignment to the vacancy. The bidder who meets the qualifications and has the most seniority gets the job.

In addition, postal workers can advance to better-paying positions by learning new skills. Training programs are available for low-skilled workers who wish to become technicians or mechanics.

Applicants for supervisory jobs must pass an examination. Additional requirements for promotion may include training or education, a satisfactory work record, and appropriate personal characteristics such as leadership ability. If the leading candidates are equally qualified, length of service is also considered.

Although opportunities for promotion to supervisory positions in smaller post offices are limited, workers may apply for vacancies in a larger post office and thus increase their chances of promotion.

Earnings and Working Conditions

Postal Service employees are paid under several separate pay schedules depending upon the duties of the job and the knowledge, experience, or skill required. For example, there are separate schedules for production workers such as clerks and mail handlers, for rural carriers, for postal managers, and for postal executives. In all pay schedules, except that of executives, employees receive periodic "step" increases up to a specified maximum if their job performance is satisfactory.

The conditions that follow are subject to collective bargaining and may well be different by the time you are employed by the Postal Service.

Full-time employees work an 8-hour day, 5 days a week. Both full-time and part-time employees who work more than 8 hours a day or 40 hours a week receive overtime pay of one-and-a-half times their hourly rate. In addition, pay is higher for those on the night shift.

Postal employees earn 13 days of annual leave (vacation) during each of their first 3 years of service, including prior federal civilian and military service; 20 days each year for 3 to 15 years of service; and 26 days after 15 years. In addition, they earn 13 days of paid sick leave a year regardless of length of service.

Other benefits include retirement and survivorship annuities, free group life insurance, and optional participation in health insurance programs supported in part by the Postal Service.

Most post office buildings are clean and well-lit, but some of the older ones are not. The Postal Service is in the process of replacing and remodeling its outmoded buildings, and conditions are expected to improve.

Most postal workers are members of unions and are covered by a national agreement between the Postal Service and the unions.

EXAMINATION ANNOUNCEMENTS

Postal Clerk

Duties of the Job

People are most familiar with the window clerk who sits behind the counter in post office lobbies selling stamps or accepting parcel post. However, the majority of postal clerks are distribution clerks who sort incoming and outgoing mail in workrooms. Only in a small post office does a clerk do both kinds of work.

When mail arrives at the post office it is dumped on long tables where distribution clerks and mail handlers separate it into groups of letters, parcel post, and magazines and newspapers. Clerks feed letters into stamp-canceling machines and cancel the rest by hand. The mail is then taken to other sections of the post office to be sorted by destination. Clerks first separate the mail into primary destination categories: mail for the local area, for each nearby state, for groups of distant states, and for some of the largest cities. This primary distribution is followed by one or more secondary distributions. For example, local mail is combined with mail coming in from other cities and is sorted according to street and number. In post offices with electronic mail-sorting machines, clerks simply push a button corresponding to the letter's destination, and the letter drops into the proper slot.

The clerks at post office windows provide a variety of services in addition to selling stamps and money orders. They weigh packages to determine postage and check to see if their size, shape, and condition are satisfactory for mailing. Clerks also register and insure mail and answer questions about postage rates, mailing restrictions, and other postal matters. Occasionally they may help a customer file a claim for a damaged package. In large post offices a window clerk may provide only one or two of these services and be called a registry, stamp, or money order clerk.

Working Conditions

Working conditions of clerks differ according to the specific work assignments and the amount and kind of labor-saving machinery in the post offices. In small post offices clerks must carry heavy mail sacks from one part of the building to another and sort the mail by hand. In large post offices, chutes and conveyors move the mail, and much of the sorting is done by machine. In either case, clerks are on their feet most of the time, reaching for sacks of mail, placing packages and bundles into sacks while sorting, and walking around the workroom.

Distribution clerks may become bored with the routine of sorting mail unless they enjoy trying to improve their speed and accuracy. They also may have to work at night, because most large post offices process mail around the clock.

A window clerk, on the other hand, has a greater variety of duties, has frequent contact with the public, generally has a less strenuous job, and never has to work a night shift.

New clerks are trained on the job. Most clerks begin with simple tasks to learn regional groupings of states, cities, and ZIP codes. To help clerks learn these groupings, many post offices offer classroom instruction. A good memory, good coordination, and the ability to read rapidly and accurately are important. These traits are measured by performance on Exam 470.

Distribution clerks work closely with other clerks, frequently under the tension and strain of meeting deadlines. Window clerks must be tactful when dealing with the public, especially when answering questions or receiving complaints.

City Carrier

Duties of the Job

Most city carriers travel planned routes delivering and collecting mail. Carriers start work at the post office early in the morning, where they spend a few hours arranging their mail for delivery, readdressing letters to be forwarded, and taking care of other details.

A carrier typically covers the route on foot, toting a heavy load of mail in a satchel or pushing it in a cart. In outlying suburban areas where houses are far apart, a car or small truck is sometimes needed to deliver mail. Residential carriers cover their routes only once a day, but carriers assigned a business district may make two or more trips. Deliveries are made house to house except in large buildings, such as apartment houses, which have all the mailboxes on the first floor.

Besides making deliveries, carriers collect c.o.d. fees and obtain signed receipts for registered and sometimes for insured mail. If a customer is not home, the carrier leaves a notice that tells where special mail is being held. Carriers also pick up letters to be mailed.

After completing their routes, carriers return to the post office with mail gathered from street collection boxes and homes. They may separate letters and parcels so that stamps can be canceled easily, and they turn in the receipts and money collected during the day.

Many carriers have more specialized duties than those just described. Some deliver only parcel post. Others collect mail from street boxes and office mail chutes.

Working Conditions

Most carriers begin work early in the morning, in some cases as early as 6 A.M. if they have routes in the business district. Carriers spend most of their time outdoors in all kinds of weather, walking from house to house with their heavy mailbags. Even those who drive must walk when making deliveries and must lift heavy sacks of parcel post when loading their vehicles.

The job, however, has its advantages. Carriers who begin work early in the morning are through by early afternoon. They are also free to work at their own pace as long as they cover their routes within a certain period of time. Moreover, full-time postal employees have more job security than workers in most other industries.

Applicants must have a driver's license and pass a road test if the job involves driving. They also must pass a physical examination and may be asked to show that they can lift and handle mail sacks weighing up to 70 pounds. Applicants who have had health conditions that might interfere with work must have a special review to determine their eligibility.

City carrier applicants must take Exam 470.

Distribution Clerk, Machine (Letter Sorting Machine Operator)

Duties of the Job

Distribution clerks work indoors. Often clerks must handle sacks of mail weighing as much as 70 pounds. They sort mail and distribute it by using a complicated scheme that must be memorized. Machine distribution clerks must learn computer codes for the automatic routing of mail. Clerks may be on their feet all day. They also have to stretch, reach, and throw mail. The work of the distribution clerk is more routine than that of other postal clerks; however, the starting salary is higher. Distribution clerks begin at postal pay level six while other clerks and carriers begin at level five. Increasing automation within the postal service has made the job of the distribution clerk quite secure.

Although the amount of mail post offices handle is expected to grow as both the population and the number of businesses grow, modernization of post offices and installation of new equipment will increase the amount of mail each clerk can handle. For example, machines that semiautomatically mark destination codes on envelopes are now being introduced. These codes can be read by computer-controlled letter-sorting machines which automatically drop each letter into the proper slot for its destination. With this system, clerks read addresses only once, at the time they are coded, instead of several times, as they do now. Eventually this equipment will be installed in all large post offices.

Applicants must be physically able to perform the duties described. Any physical condition that causes the applicant to be a hazard to him or herself or to others will be a disqualification for appointment.

The distant vision for clerk positions must test at least 20/30 (Snellen) in one eye (glasses are permitted). Some distribution clerk positions may be filled by the deaf.

A physical examination, drug test, and psychological interview are required before appointment.

Letter sorting machine operator applicants must take Exam 470.

Flat Sorting Machine Operator

Duties of the Job

The work of the Flat Sorting Machine Operator is very similar to that of the Letter Sorting Machine Operator except that the Flat Sorting Machine Operator works with large, bulky packages. Greater physical strength and stamina are required in this position.

The postal pay level at entry is level six, and with ever-increasing automation and mechanization of post offices, job security is virtually assured.

Flat sorting machine operator applicants must take Exam 470.

Mail Handler

Duties of the Job

The mail handler loads, unloads, and moves bulk mail, and he or she performs duties incidental to the movement and processing of mail. Duties may include separation of mail sacks; facing letter mail; canceling stamps on parcel post; operating canceling machines, addressographs, and mimeographs; operating a fork-lift truck; rewrapping parcels; and so forth.

Mail handler applicants must take Exam 470.

Strength and Stamina Test

A physical examination is required before appointment. Persons who have had an arm, leg, or foot amputated should not apply.

When eligibles are within reach of appointment, they are required to pass a test of strength and stamina. In this test they are required to lift, shoulder, and carry two 70-pound sacks 15 feet—one at a time—and load them on a hand truck. They are required to push the truck to an area containing some 40-, 50-, and 60-pound sacks. They are required to load the sacks onto the truck. They next have to unload the truck and return the truck to its original location. Eligibles are notified when and where to report for the test of strength and stamina.

Persons with certain physical conditions are not permitted to take the test of strength and stamina without prior approval of a physician. These physical conditions include hernia or rupture, back trouble, heart trouble, pregnancy, or any other condition that makes it dangerous to the eligible to lift and carry 70-pound weights. Persons with these physical conditions are given special instructions at the time they are notified to report for the strength and stamina test.

An eligible being considered for an appointment who fails to qualify on the strength and stamina test is not tested again in the same group of hires. If the eligible fails the test a second time, his or her eligibility for the position of mail handler is canceled.

Mail Processor

Duties of the Job

A mail processor performs such tasks as:

1. Operating mail-processing equipment, including bar code sorters and optical bar code readers;
2. Acting as minor trouble-shooter for the equipment;
3. Collating and bundling processed mail and transferring it from one work area to another;
4. Processing by hand mail that cannot be handled by the machines;
5. Loading mail into bins and onto trucks;
6. Other related tasks.

Mail processor applicants must take Exam 470.

Physical requirements for mail processors are not as stringent as those for mail handlers because the work is not as strenuous. Since the demands of the work are less, mail processors enter at postal pay level three rather than at the level four of mail handlers.

Mark-Up Clerk, Automated

Duties of the Job

The mark-up clerk, automated, operates an electro-mechanical machine to process mail that is classified as "undeliverable as addressed." In doing this, the mark-up clerk operates the keyboard of a computer terminal to enter and extract data to several databases including change of address, mailer's database, and address-correction file. The mark-up clerk must select the correct program and operating mode for each application, must affix labels to mail either manually or with mechanical devices, and must prepare forms for address-correction services. Other duties may include distribution of processed mark-ups to appropriate separations for further handling, operation of a photocopy machine, and other job-related tasks in support of primary duties.

Qualification Requirements

An applicant for a mark-up clerk position must have had either six months of clerical or office-machine-operating experience or have completed high school or have had a full academic year (36 weeks) of business school. The record of experience and training must show ability to use reference materials and manuals; ability to perform effectively under pressure; ability to operate any office equipment appropriate to the position; ability to work with others; and ability to read, understand, and apply certain regulations and procedures commonly used in processing mail that is undeliverable as addressed.

For appointment, a mark-up clerk must be 18 years old, or 16 years old if a high school graduate. An applicant who will reach his or her eighteenth birthday within two years from the date of the exam may participate. A mark-up clerk must be able to read, without strain, printed material the size of typewritten characters and must have 20/40 (Snellen) vision in one eye. Glasses are permitted. In addition, the applicant must pass a computer-administered alpha-numeric typing test. Candidates with high scores on the competitive exam, Exam 470, and with the requisite experience are called to the alpha-numeric typing test individually as openings occur and hiring is likely. The exam is administered on a personal computer with its numeric keyboard disabled so that the candidate must use only the main keyboard. The Postal Service does not distribute sample questions for this typing test, but the instructions at the test site are very clear and ample time is allowed for preparation. The alpha-numeric typing test is not a competitive test. The candidate needs only to pass to qualify.

Rural Carrier

Duties of the Job

The work of the rural carrier combines the work of the window clerk and the letter carrier but also has special characteristics of its own. The rural carrier's day begins with sorting and loading the mail for delivery on his or her own route. Then comes a day's drive, which may be over unpaved roads and rough terrain. The rural carrier does most deliveries and pickups of outgoing mail from the car. Occasionally, however, bulky packages must be delivered directly to the homeowner's door. Since rural postal patrons may be far from the nearest post office, the rural carrier sells stamps, weighs and charges for packages to be mailed, and performs most other services performed by window clerks in post offices. At the end of the day, the rural carrier returns to the post office with outgoing mail and money collected in various transactions. The rural carrier must be able to account for the stamps, postcards, and other supplies with which he or she left in the morning and must "balance the books" each day.

A rural carrier enjoys a great deal of independence. No supervisor looks over his or her shoulder. On the other hand, there is no supervisor to turn to for advice on how to handle a new situation that may come up.

Since the rural carrier's job requires driving, the minimum age for a rural carrier is 18. The rural carrier must have a valid driver's license, good eyesight, and the ability to hear ordinary conversation (glasses and hearing aid are permitted). In addition, the rural carrier must demonstrate physical stamina and ability to withstand the rigors of the job.

Rural carrier applicants must take Exam 460, which is identical in every way to Exam 470.

Clerk-Typist

Duties of the Job

A clerk-typist types records, letters, memorandums, reports, and other materials from handwritten and other drafts or from a dictating machine; he or she sets up the material typed in accordance with prescribed format and assembles it for initialing, signing, routing, and dispatch. The clerk-typist also cuts mimeograph stencils and masters for duplication by other processes. The miscellaneous office clerical duties of the position include: making up file folders, keeping them in the prescribed order, and filing in them; making and keeping routine office records; composing routine memorandums and letters relating to the business of the office, such as acknowledgments and transmittals; examining incoming and outgoing mail of the office, routing it to the appropriate persons, and controlling the time allowed for preparation of replies to incoming correspondence; receipting and delivering salary checks and filling out various personnel forms; acting as receptionist and furnishing routine information over the telephone; relieving other office personnel in their absence; operating office machines such as the mimeograph, comptometer, and adding machine.

The applicant for a position as clerk-typist must have had one year of office experience or four years of high school business courses or 36 weeks of business or secretarial school. The applicant must also show that he or she has enough of the skills, abilities, and knowledge to read and understand instructions; perform basic arithmetic computations; maintain accurate records; prepare reports and correspondence if required; and operate office machines such as calculators, adding machines, duplicators, and the like. The applicant for a clerk-typist position must pass a test of clerical abilities and a "plain copy" typing test administered on a personal computer, with a speed of 45 wpm and good accuracy.

Clerk-Stenographer

Duties of the Job

The clerk-stenographer performs all of the functions of the clerk-typist. In addition, the clerk-stenographer takes dictation, in shorthand or on a shorthand writing machine, of letters, memorandums, reports, and other materials given by the supervisor of the office and other employees. He or she then transcribes it on the typewriter, or word processor, setting up the material transcribed in accordance with prescribed format and assembling it for required initialing, signing, routing, and dispatch. In consideration of the extra training and skill required in the taking of dictation, the clerk-stenographer is rated at salary level five, rather than at the salary level four of the clerk-typist.

The applicant for the position of clerk-stenographer must meet all the requirements of the applicant for clerk-typist in terms of education or experience and in terms of skills, abilities, and knowledge. In addition to passing the test of clerical ability and the computer-administered plain-copy typing test, the clerk-stenographer applicant must also pass a stenography test.

Data Conversion Operator

Duties of the Job

Data conversion operators use a computer terminal to prepare mail for automated sorting equipment. They read typed or handwritten addresses from a letter image on the terminal screen and then select and type essential information so that an address bar code can be applied to the letter. Depending on the quality of the address information shown on the image, the data conversion operator will be prompted to key the five-number ZIP code or an abbreviated version of the street and city address. Abbreviated addresses must conform to strict encoding rules so that the abbreviation can then be expanded to a full address by the computer so that it can find the correct ZIP + 4 code. Unlike some other types of data entry, this job is not just "key what you see."

Data conversion operators are the vital personnel in the Remote Bar Coding System (RBCS), a system designed to allow letter mail that cannot be read by a machine to be bar coded and processed in the automated mail stream. RBCS technology has created a new operation called a remote encoding center (REC). RBCS has two major elements: an input sub system (ISS) and an output sub system (OSS).

At the processing plant, ISS takes a video picture or image of each letter and then attempts to look up the address to find a ZIP + 4 code. For letters for which the ISS computer cannot find a ZIP + 4 code, corresponding images are transmitted by telephone lines to data conversion operators at the remote encoding center for further processing. At the REC, data conversion operators working at video display terminals are presented with images one at a time. Using specific rules, operators key data for each image so that the computers can find the correct ZIP + 4 code.

At the plant, the output sub system sprays letters with correct ZIP + 4 bar codes and performs initial sorting. Letters are then processed by bar code sorters. These elements are linked together by a communication system consisting of cabling and telephone or microwave telecommunications.

Working Conditions

Remote encoding centers offer a possibility for flexible scheduling. The basic work hours are between 3:00 P.M. and 1:00 A.M. Individual work schedules range between four and eight hours. RECs operate seven days a week. Persons filling data conversion operator positions as temporary or transitional employees will earn one hour of leave for every 20 hours worked but no other benefits. Career employees receive a full benefits package including health and life insurance, sick and annual leave, federal employees retirement system, and eligibility to participate in the thrift savings plan.

Qualification Requirements

All applicants are required to pass the test of clerical abilities with a score of 70 or better. Names are placed on a hiring list in rank order. As an applicant reaches consideration for employment, he or she will be called for a computer-based exam which is a job-simulated data entry performance test. Typing or data-entry experience is a prerequisite for this position.

Applicants must have vision of 20/40 (Snellen) in one eye and the ability to read without strain printed material the size of typewritten characters. Corrective lenses are permitted. The ability to distinguish basic colors and shades is desirable. Applicants under consideration for employment are subject to urinalysis drug screening.

Cleaner, Custodian, Custodial Laborer

Duties of the Job

Workers who serve as cleaners, custodians, or custodial laborers are charged with the maintenance of postal buildings. Their duties include routine and periodic heavy cleaning, routine maintenance such as replacing light bulbs, and responsibility for noticing when specialized maintenance or repair work is called for and for following through to be certain that whatever must be done is done at the proper time.

While the work of custodial laborers, cleaners, and custodians is not generally noticed by the public, their work is vital to the operation of post offices and to the health and safety of postal workers and patrons.

Qualification Requirements

The positions of cleaner, custodian, and custodial laborer are open *only* to veterans of the United States Armed Services. Applications from nonveterans will be rejected. While these positions are at the low end of the postal pay scale, they do afford the veteran an opportunity to earn a steady wage and to enjoy all the fringe benefits and security of all other postal employees. The person who starts his or her career with the Postal Service as a cleaner, custodian, or custodial laborer can advance to positions of greater responsibility within the custodial service or can prepare for examinations for other positions with the Postal Service, either more specialized jobs within building maintenance or completely different jobs such as mail handler, letter clerk, and others. People who already work for the Postal Service in any capacity need not wait for an exam that is open to the public to be announced. After being employed at their present position for a year, they may ask to take an exam at any time. Although this request may or may not be granted, this is one special advantage of postal employees that makes the Veterans-Only feature of this position so valuable. A veteran who wants a postal career can break in at the bottom and rise rapidly.

There are no educational or experience requirements for these positions and no age restrictions. Applicants must, of course, have the physical health and stamina required for the job. They must also qualify on a one-and-a-half-hour examination that tests their ability to follow directions.

Garageman-Driver, Tractor-Trailer Operator, Motor Vehicle Operator

Duties of the Job

What all these jobs have in common is driving various Postal Service vehicles on the highway and within the lots and properties of the Postal Service.

Garagemen are responsible for seeing that each vehicle is in the proper place at the proper time and that each vehicle is roadworthy before it is released. (Though the official job title has historically been "garageman," this position is equally open to qualified women.) Garagemen must keep accurate records of all activity as it affects each vehicle and must follow through on what movement or maintenance is required.

Tractor-trailer operators drive huge mail rigs from city to city along superhighways, delivering large quantities of mail as quickly as possible within the bounds of safety. The work of a Postal Service tractor-trailer operator is really no different from the work of a tractor-trailer operator for private industry.

Motor vehicle operators drive various other Postal Service vehicles as needed, both within and between towns and cities. They pick up and deliver bulk quantities of mail at postal installations, mailing concerns, railroad mail facilities, and airports.

The exam for all these positions is designed to test powers of observation, ability to express oneself, accuracy in record keeping, familiarity with road signs, and ability to follow instructions. The exam is in two parts of 40 questions each. You will have sixty minutes to answer each part. The test requires concentration and careful attention to details. The sample questions that the Postal Service sends to applicants provide a good idea of what to expect from the exam itself.

Since all these positions require a Commercial Driver's License (CDL), people appointed to them must be experienced drivers over the age of 21. In addition, applicants must have good eyesight and hearing and be in excellent health and physical condition. A physical exam, drug testing, and strength and stamina tests are part of the hiring process. Candidates must also take training on the specific type of vehicle they are required to drive.

To qualify for motor vehicle operator, persons must have a Class A or Class B commercial license and at least two years of driving experience, one of which must have been driving a five-ton truck. Applicants for tractor-trailer operator must have a Class A commercial license and at least one year of experience driving a tractor-trailer. All applicants for these positions must have safe driving records.

Postal Police Officer

Duties of the Job

A postal police officer is essentially a security guard at post offices and at other postal installations and facilities. The postal police officer may work inside postal buildings or out of doors at loading docks and in parking lots. A postal police officer may be armed.

Qualification Requirements

An applicant for the position of postal police officer must be at least 20 years of age, and, unless a veteran, cannot be appointed until reaching the age of 21 years. The postal police officer must be physically able to perform the duties of the job, must have weight in proportion to height, must have good color vision and good distant vision (no weaker than 20/40 in one eye and 20/50 in the other eye correctable to 20/20), and must have keen hearing. Emotional and mental stability are essential for the armed officer, and drug testing and a psychological interview are part of the qualification process. The candidate must demonstrate the ability to deal with the public in a courteous and tactful manner; to work in stress situations; to collect, assemble, and act on pertinent facts; to prepare clear and accurate records; to deal effectively with individuals and groups; and to express himself or herself in both oral and written communications. A background investigation will be made on all otherwise qualified candidates. In order to be considered, each applicant must pass a written qualifying exam with a score of 70 or better out of a possible 100. Accepted candidates must complete and pass a rigorous eight week training program at the Federal Law Enforcement Training Center at Glynco, GA, before assignment to duty.

Maintenance Positions

BUILDINGS AND EQUIPMENT

Duties of the Job

Activities of the Postal Service take place in a great number of facilities. These facilities consist not only of post offices but also of warehouses, processing centers, repair shops, garages, and office buildings. These buildings require the same maintenance services as nonpostal buildings that serve the same purposes.

Housed within the postal facilities is a myriad of machinery and equipment. Machines and equipment all require maintenance and service.

Rather than hiring maintenance workers from the private sector, the postal service retains a full staff of maintenance workers to care for its facilities and equipment.

Applicants for positions in the following titles must all qualify on the same exam, Test M/N 931. The maintenance titles are:

- Area Maintenance Specialist
- Area Maintenance Technician
- Building Equipment Mechanic
- Building Maintenance Custodian
- Carpenter
- Machinist
- Maintenance Electrician
- Maintenance Mechanic 4
- Maintenance Mechanic 5
- Mason
- Painter
- Plumber
- Welder

ELECTRONIC EQUIPMENT

Duties of the Job

As the Postal Service moves into the twenty-first century, more and more postal operations are being handled automatically by highly sophisticated electronic equipment. The variety of sorting, stamping, coding, and routing machines is expanding rapidly, and as more post offices join the switch to automation the sheer number of these machines is also growing dramatically. Needless to say, all this electronic equipment requires regular maintenance and repair as needed.

The Postal Service retains its own teams of electronic technicians to care for its electronic equipment. These electronic technicians are hired at two levels, Electronic Technician 9 and Electronic Technician 10. The duties and responsibilities are similar, but there are some differences. The exam is Test M/N 932.

MAINTENANCE MECHANIC AND OVERHAUL SPECIALIST

These last two titles in the maintenance selection system represent specialized, higher-level positions within the building and equipment maintenance areas. In this group are the titles Maintenance Mechanic 7 and Overhaul Specialist 8. Exam M/N 933 covers the KSAs (knowledge, skills, and abilities) necessary for performance of these jobs. As with other maintenance positions, not all KSAs are needed for performance of duties in both job titles; only questions that measure relevant KSAs for the job enter into score calculations.

Qualification Requirements

The examinations in the M/N series test a number of KSAs (knowledge, skills, and abilities) that are required in the various maintenance positions. There is much overlap, but the three exams do not all test precisely the same KSAs. Further, not all positions within a group require all of the KSAs tested by any one exam. Only questions measuring the relevant KSAs are scored for any particular position.

The knowledge, skills, and abilities tested by the three exams in the M/N series (M/N 931, M/N 932, and M/N 933) are:

(1) *Knowledge of basic mechanics* refers to the theory of operation, terminology, usage, and characteristics of basic mechanical principles as they apply to such things as gears, pulleys, cams, pawls, power transmissions, linkages, fasteners, chains, sprockets, and belts; and includes hoisting, rigging, roping, pneumatics, and hydraulic devices.

(2) *Knowledge of basic electricity* refers to the theory, terminology, usage, and characteristics of basic electrical principles such as Ohm's Law, Kirchhoff's Law, and magnetism, as they apply to such things as AC/DC circuitry and hardware, relays, switches, and circuit breakers.

(3) *Knowledge of basic electronics* refers to the theory, terminology, usage, and characteristics of basic electronic principles concerning such things as solid state devices, vacuum tubes, coils, capacitors, resistors, and basic logic circuitry.

(4) *Knowledge of digital electronics* refers to the terminology, characteristics, symbology, and operation of digital components as used in such things as logic gates, registers, adders, counters, memories, encoders, and decoders.

(5) *Knowledge of safety procedures and equipment* refers to the knowledge of industrial hazards (e.g., mechanical, chemical, electrical, electronic) and procedures and techniques established to avoid injuries to self and others such as lock-out devices, protective clothing, and waste disposal techniques.

(6) *Knowledge of basic computer concepts* refers to the terminology, usage, and characteristics of digital memory storage/processing devices such as internal memory, input-output peripherals, and familiarity with programming concepts.

(8) *Knowledge of lubrication materials and procedures* refers to the terminology, characteristics, storage, preparation, disposal, and usage techniques involved with lubrication materials such as oils, greases, and other types of lubricants.

(12) *Knowledge of refrigeration* refers to the theory, terminology, usage, and characteristics of refrigeration principles as they apply to such things as the refrigeration cycle, compressors, condensers, receivers, evaporators, metering devices, and refrigerant oils.

(13) *Knowledge of heating, ventilation, and air-conditioning (HVAC) equipment operation* refers to the knowledge of equipment operation such as safety considerations, start-up, shut-down, and mechanical/electrical operating characteristics of HVAC equipment (e.g., chillers, direct-expansion units, window units, heating equipment). This does not include the knowledge of refrigeration.

(19) *Ability to perform basic mathematical computations* refers to the ability to perform basic calculations such as addition, subtraction, multiplication, and division with whole numbers, fractions, and decimals.

(20) *Ability to perform more complex mathematics* refers to the ability to perform calculations such as basic algebra, geometry, scientific notation, and number conversions, as applied to mechanical, electrical, and electronic applications.

(21) *Ability to apply theoretical knowledge to practical applications* refers to mechanical, electrical, and electronic maintenance applications such as inspection, trouble-shooting equipment repair and modification, preventive maintenance, and installation of electrical equipment.

(22) *Ability to detect patterns* refers to the ability to observe and analyze qualitative factors such as number progressions, spatial relationships, and auditory and visual patterns. This includes combining information and determining how a given set of numbers, objects, or sounds are related to each other.

(23) *Ability to use written reference materials* refers to the ability to locate, read, and comprehend text material such as handbooks, manuals, bulletins, directives, checklists, and route sheets.

(26) *Ability to follow instructions* refers to the ability to comprehend and execute written and oral instructions such as work orders, checklists, route sheets, and verbal directions and instructions.

(31) *Ability to use hand tools* refers to knowledge of, and proficiency with, various hand tools. This ability involves the safe and efficient use and maintenance of such tools as screwdrivers, wrenches, hammers, pliers, chisels, punches, taps, dies, rules, gauges, and alignment tools.

(32) *Ability to use portable power tools* refers to the knowledge of, and proficiency with, various power tools. This ability involves the safe and efficient use and maintenance of power tools such as drills, saws, sanders, and grinders.

(35) *Ability to use technical drawings* refers to the ability to read and comprehend technical materials such as diagrams, schematics, flow charts, and blueprints.

(36) *Ability to use test equipment* refers to the knowledge of, and proficiency with, various types of mechanical, electrical, and electronic test equipment such as VOMS, oscilloscopes, circuit tracers, amprobes, and tachometers.

(37) *Ability to solder* refers to the knowledge of the appropriate soldering techniques, and the ability to apply them safely and effectively.

Supervisory Positions

Supervisory positions are never filled by open competitive examinations. In order to become a supervisor, you must first prove yourself as a worker in the department or function that you would like to supervise. The person who wishes to grow into a supervisory position must first prove his or her reliability, efficiency, and initiative on the job over a period of time. Then that person must take a test of supervisory aptitude to demonstrate promise of success in a supervisory role. The test of supervisory aptitude includes questions on understanding human behavior, judgment in social situations, and judgment in business situations.

Postal Inspector

Near the top of the postal pay schedule is the position of postal inspector. Postal inspectors are law enforcement officers within the Postal Service. They perform varied, highly responsible duties that lead to the detection, prosecution, and conviction of people committing mail fraud and other crimes related to the Postal Service. Their work is exciting, difficult, dangerous, and well paid. No one may become a postal inspector without previous Postal Service experience. All postal inspectors have risen from the ranks of postal employees. In addition, postal inspectors have passed a four-hour examination consisting of 118 questions, mostly reading comprehension and vocabulary, and have undergone and passed a rigorous eleven-week training program.

P A R T

THREE

State and Municipal Employment

CONTENTS

STATE AND MUNICIPAL JOB OPPORTUNITIES

State and local governments provide a very large and expanding source of job opportunities in a wide variety of occupational fields. Over 11.8 million people work for state and local agencies; nearly three-fourths of these work in units of local government, such as counties, municipalities, towns, and school districts.

Educational services account for the majority of jobs in state and local government. About 5.9 million employees work in public schools, colleges, or other educational services.

In addition to the nearly 3 million classroom and college teachers, school systems, colleges, and universities also employ administrative personnel, librarians, guidance counselors, nurses, dietitians, clerks, and maintenance workers. Three-fourths of these work in elementary and secondary schools, which are administered largely by local governments. State employment in education is concentrated chiefly at the college, university, and technical school levels.

The next two largest fields of state and local government employment are health services and highway work. The almost 1.4 million workers employed in health and hospital work include physicians, nurses, medical laboratory technicians, and hospital attendants. More than 600,000 people work in highway activities such as construction and maintenance. Highway workers include civil engineers, surveyors, operators of construction machinery and equipment, truck drivers, concrete finishers, carpenters, and construction laborers.

General governmental control and financial activities account for about 840,000 workers. These include chief executives and their staffs, legislative representatives, and persons employed in the administration of justice, tax enforcement and other financial work, and general administration. These functions require the services of individuals such as lawyers, judges, and other court officials, city managers, property assessors, budget analysts, stenographers, and clerks.

Police and fire protection is another large field of employment. Over 600,000 persons are engaged in police work, including administrative, clerical, and custodial personnel, as well as uniformed and plainclothes police. Local governments employ all of the 300,000 firefighters, many of whom work only part time.

Other state and local government employees work in a wide variety of activities: local utilities (such as water or electricity), transportation, natural resources, public welfare, parks and recreation, sanitation, correction, local libraries, sewage disposal, and housing and urban renewal. These activities require workers in diverse occupations such as economist, electrical engineer, electrician, pipefitter, clerk, forester, and bus driver.

Clerical, administrative, maintenance, and custodial work make up a large portion of employment in most government agencies. Among the workers involved in these activities are clerk-typists, stenographers, secretaries, office managers, fiscal and budget administrators, bookkeepers, accountants, carpenters, painters, plumbers, guards, and janitors.

LOCATING STATE AND MUNICIPAL JOB OPPORTUNITIES ON THE WORLD WIDE WEB

All 50 states and the District of Columbia have state sites on the web. Each state offers information of its own choosing at its site. Many states include descriptions of job openings in state government—detailing what the job entails, qualification requirements, location of openings, salary and benefits, career path, and application procedures. In addition, some state sites will connect you to county or city sites within the state. If you are a savvy computer user, you should be able to directly access existing city home pages as well. The state URLs are:

Alabama: alaweb.asc.edu/
Alaska: www.state.ak.us/
Arizona: www.state.az.us/
Arkansas: www.state.ar.us/
California: www.state.ca.us/
Colorado: www.state.co.us/
Connecticut: www.state.ct.us/
Delaware: www.state.de.us/
District of Columbia: www.dchomepage.net/
Florida: www.state.fl.us/
Georgia: www.state.ga.us/
Hawaii: www.state.hi.us/
Idaho: www.state.id.us/
Illinois: www.state.il.us/
Indiana: www.state.in.us/
Iowa: www.state.ia.us/
Kansas: www.state.ks.us/
Kentucky: www.state.ky.us/
Louisiana: www.state.la.us/
Maine: www.state.me.us/
Maryland: sailor.lib.md.us/mec/
Massachusetts: www.state.ma.us/
Michigan: www.migov.state.mi.us/
Minnesota: www.state.mn.us/
Mississippi: www.state.ms.us/
Missouri: www.state.mo.us/
Montana: www.mt.gov/
Nebraska: www.state.ne.us/
Nevada: www.state.nv.us/
New Hampshire: www.state.nh.us/
New Jersey: www.state.nj.us/
New Mexico: www.state.nm.us/
New York: www.state.ny.us/
North Carolina: www.state.nc.us/
North Dakota: www.state.nd.us/
Ohio: www.state.oh.us/
Oklahoma: www.state.ok.us/
Oregon: www.state.or.us/
Pennsylvania: www.state.pa.us/
Rhode Island: www.state.ri.us/
South Carolina: www.state.sc.us/
South Dakota: www.state.sd.us/
Tennessee: www.state.tn.us/
Texas: www.state.tx.us/
Utah.: www.state.ut.us/
Vermont: www.state.vt.us/
Virginia: www.state.va.us/
Washington: www.wa.gov/
West Virginia: www.state.wv.us/
Wisconsin: www.state.wi.us/
Wyoming: www.state.wy.us/

REPRESENTATIVE CIVIL SERVICE CAREERS

Nearly all states and municipalities use trained business, technical, and professional employees in a variety of fields. College men and women who have prepared for such positions are encouraged to step directly from the classroom into the state and municipal service at the bottom rung of any one of the many career ladders in its numerous departments, institutions, and agencies.

Many state constitutions require that appointments and promotions in the state civil service and all its civil divisions be made according to merit and fitness to be ascertained so far as practicable by examinations. The constitutions further provide that such examinations, so far as practicable, shall be competitive. The entrance positions described in this list are filled competitively by appointment from appropriate civil service eligible lists. Civil service law usually requires that when a vacancy above the entrance level is to be filled, the appointment must be made, if possible, by promotion from among persons holding positions in a lower grade in the department, office, or institution where the vacancy exists. This law increases opportunities for advancement of those employees who come into the service at the lowest rung of the state or municipal career ladder, and emphasizes the importance of the recruitment of well-trained, intelligent personnel in these entrance positions.

The following groups of positions outlined should not be considered all-inclusive. While these specifications may present a true picture today, state and municipal services do not remain static. Fluctuations in the labor market, reorganization within departments, and other factors affect revisions.

Clerical Positions

Clerical support staff are employed throughout state and municipal government and are at the center of communications throughout these organizations. They perform a wide variety of administrative and clerical duties that are necessary to run and maintain the responsibilities of state and local government.

SAMPLE EXAM ANNOUNCEMENTS

State—Municipal
Entry-Level Clerical Positions

Job Descriptions

Messenger. These positions involve sorting and carrying mail, documents, or other materials between offices or buildings. This may involve the operation of a motor vehicle. Lifting and carrying moderately heavy bags or packages is required in the majority of these jobs. A currently valid state driver's license may be required for some jobs.

Clerk I and II. Employees in these positions perform clerical duties such as gathering and providing information, sorting, filing, and checking materials. The complexity of these duties varies from limited (Clerk I) to moderate (Clerk II).

Requirements

Applicants must attain passing scores on a written examination to have their names placed on the eligible lists.

Test Information

Written Test. The test will consist of a 12-minute Name and Number Checking speed test, and a 70-minute Clerical Abilities test. The type and number of questions for each position are as follows:

Subject Areas	Number of Questions
Messenger	
Perceptual speed and accuracy (name and number checking)	70
Coding (sorting mail)	20
Clerk I	
Perceptual speed and accuracy (name and number checking)	70
Coding (sorting mail)	20
Coding (sorting file material)	10
Filing (alphabetizing)	15
Clerk II and Intermittent Clerk II	
Perceptual speed and accuracy (name and number checking)	70
Coding (sorting mail)	20
Coding (sorting file material)	10
Filing (alphabetizing)	15
Information forwarding (taking telephone messages)	15

Test Results. Applicants will receive a Notice of Examination Results in the mail. If they pass the tests, the notice will tell their relative standing on the lists and how long their names will remain on the lists. These lists may be used to fill positions in other comparable job titles.

State Secretary—Typist I

Job Description

Performs secretarial duties which usually involve typing correspondence, reports, and statistical material while acting as a secretary to one or more employees; does related work as required.

Distinguishing Characteristics. Works under direct supervision. Performs repetitive and routine work including frequent operation of a typewriter; performs other secretarial duties such as evaluating correspondence, typing manifests, materials, and processing mail. Exercises some independent judgment and resourcefulness in laying out work procedures. Where work is more repetitive, takes added responsibility for final action; requests detailed instructions when initiating change in procedures or when advice is needed with regard to unusual or difficult matters. Upon assignment, exercises partial supervision over other clerical employees who are performing routine tasks and gives instructions in department procedures and methods.

Examples of Typical Tasks. Performs responsible secretarial duties such as typing forms and correspondence and completing accounting and financial statements, vouchers, departmental reports, permits or other materials from copy, rough draft, dictating equipment, or general instructions. Maintains routine bookkeeping, financial, and cost records where no technical knowledge is required but where frequent procedural problems arise; prepares or checks payrolls, vouchers, requisitions, and purchase orders; maintains personnel, financial and similar records. Gives standard information to other divisions and the public, applying knowledge of departmental rules, regulations, and procedures.

Requirements

1. Completion of high school or its equivalent, including or supplemented by courses in office procedures and typing or the equivalent.
2. One year's experience in an office or secretarial job or in a position at the level of Secretary Typist Trainee or any equivalent combination of education and experience.
3. Considerable knowledge of typewriter operations including its functions. Working knowledge of Business English, spelling, and arithmetic. Working knowledge of office practices and procedures. Skill in typing. Ability to maintain fiscal or departmental records and prepare reports from such records. Ability to make arithmetical computations and tabulations accurately and with reasonable speed. Ability to assign, check, and review the work of other employees. Ability to establish and maintain effective working relationships with the public and other employees.
4. Must be able to pass a typing test at a speed of 40 words per minute.

Test Information

All applicants must take a typing test.

City
Bookkeeper I

Test Information

The examination you are scheduled to take is a written, multiple- choice test of 104 items. The test contains five sections. Each section consists of items which are similar to job duties performed by Bookkeepers. The following are brief descriptions of the five item types contained on the test.

Section I: *Vocabulary*
This section consists of questions regarding the knowledge of bookkeeping terminology and procedures.

Section II: *Filing*
The test taker is required to answer questions regarding filing terminology. Also in this section, the test taker must perform alphabetical filing.

Section III: *Name/Number Comparison*
This section of the test requires the test taker to determine whether two names or two numbers are alike.

Section IV: *Report Writing*
This section requires the test taker to read a paragraph and then determine the best or most effective method of expressing a selected phrase or sentence.

Section V: *Mathematics*
The test taker is required to calculate simple math functions. This section will include addition, subtraction, multiplication, and division.

State
Clerk II

Job Description

Performs varied clerical work involving moderately complex work methods and problems; does related work as required.

Distinguishing Characteristics. Works under the immediate supervision of a superior. Performs repetitive, routine work performing a wide variety of clerical functions which require the application of independent judgment and the interpretation of policies and regulations on the basis of training and knowledge gained through experience on the job. Exercises partial supervision over other employees, assigning, instructing, and supervising a small group of clerical subordinates who perform routine operations.

Examples of Typical Tasks. Assigns, instructs, and supervises a small group of clerical subordinates who perform routine operations. Supervises work production and flow in central files, record management, or similar operating unit of moderate size that maintains more complex indexes and files. Makes final checks for proper coding, classification, and mathematical accuracy in compliance with procedures; posts invoices, vouchers, and other fiscal, statistical, and administrative data; prepares routine correspondence; performs the more complex arithmetical and tabulating assignments.

Requirements

1. Completion of a four-year high school course or its equivalent including supplemental courses in business practices.
2. One year of experience performing similar clerical work in an office; one year of appropriate formal post-high school training may be substituted for the required experience.
3. Some knowledge of modern office practices, procedures, and equipment. Some knowledge of departmental rules, procedures, and functions. Ability to understand and carry out moderately complex oral and written instructions and to make relatively complex arithmetical computations and tabulations accurately and with reasonable speed. Ability to make minor decisions on the basis of precedents and regulations and to apply them to work problems. Ability to train, assign, supervise, and review work of subordinate employees. Ability to prepare clear and concise oral and written reports and to establish and maintain effective working relationships with other employees and the general public.

State—Municipal
Clerical/Secretarial Positions

Job Descriptions

Clerk Typist I and II, Intermittent Clerk Typist II. These positions involve typing and clerical duties such as providing information, composing short letters and memos, sorting, filing, and checking materials. These duties vary in complexity from limited (Clerk Typist I) to moderate (Clerk Typist II).

Clerk Stenographer I and II. These positions involve taking dictation and transcribing the notes. Other duties from limited to moderate complexity include typing, providing information, composing letters and memos, and sorting and filing materials.

Library Assistant. Employees in these positions perform moderately complex clerical work in a library, such as maintaining files and records, sorting and shelving books, and checking materials for accuracy.

Requirements

All applicants must achieve a passing score on a written examination.

Test Information

The clerical examination is made up of three major parts: a written test, a typing test, and a stenography test. The parts of the test that you take will depend upon the position(s) for which you have applied. Applicants for Clerk Typist I and II, Clerk Stenographer I and II, and Intermittent Clerk Typist II, must take a typing test. For these job titles, the written test will be weighted 50 percent and the typing test score will be weighted 50 percent. Applicants for Clerk Stenographer I and II must pass a stenography test. The stenography test will not be weighted as part of the final score. You must pass all parts of the test to be considered for employment. Any part of the tests may be canceled and the weight added to the remaining parts.

Written Test. The written test for these positions contains eight sections. The number of questions an applicant answers will depend upon the position(s) for which he or she has applied. The time allotted for the written test is 1 hour and 42 minutes. The type and number of questions for each position are as follows.

	Number of Questions by Job Title	
Subject Matter Area	Clerk Typist I	Clerk Typist II, Clerk Stenographer I and II, Library Assistant I, Intermittent Clerk Typist II
Name and number checking (perceptual speed and accuracy)	65	65
Sorting file material (coding)	10	10
Alphabetizing (filing)	15	15
Taking telephone messages (following directions)	15	15
Capitalization/punctuation/ grammar (language usage)	15	15
Effective expression	10	10
Spelling	25	25
Arithmetic operations	—	15

Typing Test. The typing performance test will consist of a 4-minute practice exercise followed by the actual test, which will have an eight-minute time limit. A score of 30 words per minute, after deduction for errors, must be achieved in order to pass the typing performance test. Applicants *may* provide their own typewriters for the typing test.

Stenography Test. The stenography test will consist of a three-minute practice exercise followed by the actual test, which will have a three-minute time limit. Dictation will be given at the rate of 80 words per minute. Applicants will have 30 minutes to transcribe their notes into answers on an answer sheet. Applicants for Clerk Stenographer I must not have more than 10% errors on the stenography test. Applicants for Clerk Stenographer II must not have more than 5% errors on the test. Any stenography system including the use of a shorthand machine is acceptable. Applicants who wish to use shorthand machines must provide their own.

City
Clerk Stenographer I

Job Description

The city employs Clerk Stenographers I in all of its operating departments. Under supervision, Clerk Stenographers take dictation, type letters, reports, records, and other documents, and perform related clerical duties.

Employees are eligible for a promotional examination upon completion of two years of office experience which includes a substantial amount of typing or stenography and after at least six months as a regularly appointed employee of the city.

Requirements

1. Ability to take dictation at 80 words per minute (wpm) and type at a minimum of 45 wpm.
2. Graduation from high school or successful completion of high school equivalency or G.E.D. test is desirable.
3. Residence in the city within six months of appointment.

Test Information

The examination will include a written test of clerical skills and performance tests of typing and dictation skills. Only electronic typewriters will be available. Candidates must receive a minimum qualifying rating on each part of the examination. The minimum speeds needed to qualify are ability to take dictation at the rate of 80 wpm and typing speed of 45 wpm.

The tests are weighted as follows: Written Test, 5; Typing Test, 1; and Dictation Test, 1.

This is a continuous examination. All qualified candidates will be notified of the date, time, and place of the examination. Examination sessions will be scheduled as often as necessary to meet the needs of the City Service.

City
Stenographer

Written Test

This is designed to test for knowledge, skills, and/or abilities in such areas as

1. Spelling: These questions are designed to test the candidate's ability to spell words that office employees might encounter in their daily work.
2. Alphabetizing: These questions are designed to test a candidate's ability to file material accurately in alphabetical order.
3. Clerical operations with letters and numbers: These questions are designed to test a candidate's visual perception and basic clerical accuracy in working with alphanumeric characters. The candidate is required to read, compare, check, reorder, and count letters and numbers following specific directions for each question. Knowledge of the alphabet and the ability to count are required.
4. Arithmetic computation: These questions are designed to test a candidate's ability to perform basic computations using addition, subtraction, multiplication, and division. Questions may also involve the use of fractions, decimals, averages, and percents. Word problems are not included in these questions.

A performance test in dictation will be administered on the same day as the written exam. The test involves taking and transcribing dictation of limited difficulty at the rate of 80 wpm.

A performance test in typing will be administered to candidates who pass the written test and the performance test in dictation. A minimum speed of 35 wpm is required.

The Commission reserves the right to retest candidates who fail the typing portion of this examination. This testing would be scheduled at a later date.

Job Description

Performs routine stenographic and clerical work: takes and transcribes dictation; performs related duties as required.

Requirements

Candidates must meet the following requirements on or before the date of the written test: Graduation from high school, including, or supplemented by, courses in stenography and typing. Be sure to indicate when and where you completed the required courses in shorthand and typing.

Satisfactory office experience in clerical work which involved taking and transcribing dictation may be substituted for high school education, including course work, on a year-for-year basis up to a maximum of two years.

Test Information

The examination has three parts: a written test and performance tests in dictation and typing. Candidates must attain a score of 70 percent in each part of the examination. The eligible list will be established on the basis of the average of the scores received on all parts of the examination.

State
Advanced Clerical/Secretarial Positions

Job Description

All positions involve providing training and guidance to new employees and functioning as a lead worker.

Clerks perform advanced clerical duties which involve gathering and providing information, sorting, filing, and checking materials.

Clerk Typists, in addition to performing the duties above, also type documents of various degrees of complexity and compose letters and memoranda.

Clerk Stenographers, in addition to performing all of the duties above, take dictation of a complex nature and transcribe the notes.

Executive Secretaries perform highly responsible secretarial work as staff assistants to Executive Directors. Supervision may be exercised over a small clerical staff.

Requirements

To speed up test scheduling, your qualifications may not be reviewed until after you have taken the test. Please make sure you meet *all* requirements, because if you *do not,* your test results *will not* be counted. If you are not sure if you qualify, contact one of the Commission's offices.

You must be a state resident, of good moral character, and capable of performing the physical activities of the job.

For promotion examinations, you must have regular or probationary civil service status.

Clerk III (State, Local, and Housing Authority). Six months as a Clerk II and high school education; or one year of progressively complex clerical experience and completion of high school; or six months of complex clerical experience and completion of a post-high school business curriculum; or any equivalent experience and/or training which provide the required knowledge and abilities.

Clerk Typist III (State, Local, and Housing Authority). Six months as a Clerk Typist II and educational development to the level of completion of high school; or one year of progressively complex clerical typing experience and completion of high school; or six months of moderately complex clerical typing work and completion of a post-high school business curriculum; or any equivalent experience and/or training which provide the required knowledge, skills, and abilities.

Clerk Stenographer III (State, Local, and Housing Authority). Six months as a Clerk Stenographer II and educational development to the level of completion of high school; or one year of progressively complex clerical stenographic experience and completion of a high school business curriculum; or six months of moderately complex clerical stenographic experience and completion of a post-high school business curriculum; or any equivalent experience and/or training which provide the required knowledge, skills, and abilities.

Executive Secretary (Housing Authority). Five years of progressively responsible experience in secretarial work. Appropriate formal post-high school secretarial training may be substituted for the required experience on a year-for-year basis up to four years; or any equivalent combination of experience and training.

Test Information

Applicants must pass all parts of the test to be considered for employment. Any part of the tests may be canceled by the Commission and the weight added to the remaining parts.

The clerical examination is made up of three major parts: a written test, a typing performance test, and a stenography performance test. *All applicants must take the written test, which is weighted 100%.* All applicants for Clerk Typist III, Clerk Stenographer III, and Executive Secretary must also pass a typing performance test. All applicants for Clerk Stenographer III and Executive Secretary must also pass a stenography performance test. The performance tests will not be weighted as part of your final score but will be scored on a pass/fail basis.

Written Test. The two and one-half hour written test will cover the subject areas noted below.

Subject Areas	Number of Questions
Office procedures and practices	15
Spelling	10
Punctuation and capitalization	10
Grammar	10
Proofreading	35
Arithmetic computations	10
Reports—basis concepts	10
Office management and planning	25
Total	125

Typing Test. The typing performance test will have an eight-minute time limit. A score of 30 words per minute, after deduction for errors, must be achieved in order to pass the typing performance test. Applicants *may* provide their own typewriters.

Stenography Test. The stenography performance test will have a three-minute time limit. Dictation will be given at the rate of 80 wpm. Any stenography system is acceptable. Applicants who wish to use shorthand machines must provide their own.

Computer-Related Positions

Computers are becoming steadily more important in all branches of the civil service and for many functions of state and municipal government, they are now essential. The duties of computer personnel vary with the size of the installation, the type of equipment used, and the policies of the employer. As computer usage grows in government organizations, so will the need for computer professions and related occupations.

SAMPLE EXAM ANNOUNCEMENTS

State—Municipal
Data Entry Machine Operator

Job Description

Data Entry Machine Operators operate a variety of data entry equipment, using an alphanumeric keyboard to enter information from various source documents onto magnetic tape or disks. They may also enter information directly into a computer. They may use video display units to verify information and may be required to operate auxiliary equipment and perform editing and coding incidental to the transcription of data.

Requirements

On or before the date of the written test, you must have either three months of experience operating a data entry machine in a production environment, or three months of training in a simulated production environment in the operation of a data entry machine such as key-to-tape, key-to-disk, or key-to-computer. Part-time and volunteer experience which can be verified will be accepted on a prorated basis.

Test Information

There will be a *performance test* which candidates must pass in order to be considered for appointment. Candidates must be able to perform at a rate of 8,000 key strokes per hour on key-to-disk or direct entry machines to qualify. Work must be 98% accurate. The test will be given on key-to-disk and direct entry equipment *only.*

Note. This position is also filled at the trainee level from the Typist eligible list. If you do not have the training or experience to qualify for this examination, but you can type 35 wpm, you may qualify as a trainee.

State—Municipal
Computer Operator Trainee

Job Description

Computer Operator Trainees are trained to monitor and control the operation of electronic data processing equipment in conformance with programmed instructions. They may also operate peripheral equipment such as disc and tape drives and printers.

Requirements

Qualifying Experience for Taking the Test. On or before the date of the written test, candidates must have had four months of appropriate status in a position allocated to Grade 3 or higher.

For Appointment from the Eligible List. Candidates must have one year of qualifying experience to take the test.

Test Information

There will be a written test which candidates must pass in order to be considered for appointment. The written test will be designed to test for knowledge, skills, and/or abilities in such areas as

1. *Name and Number Checking under Time Limitations:* These questions will be designed to test candidates' ability to distinguish between sets of letters, words, and/or numbers which are almost exactly alike. Material will usually be presented in two or three columns, and candidates are to determine how the first entry compares with the second and possibly the third. Answers are recorded according to a designated code provided in the directions. Speed as well as accuracy will be stressed in these questions.
2. *Following Directions:* These questions will require candidates to follow directions given in coded form. Sufficient reading ability to understand the questions and the ability to work with simple codes are required.
3. *Coding/Decoding Information:* These questions will be designed to test candidates' skill in following and applying written directions in order to keep records, using given sets of coding rules. Two formats are used. The first set of questions will be based on detailed instructions requiring candidates to work from coded information to uncoded information; the second set of questions will be based on detailed instructions that require candidates to work from uncoded information to coded information.

Because this will be a test of skill in following directions carefully and accurately, all information necessary to answer the questions will be presented in the detailed written instructions. Therefore, no prior knowledge of or training in any coding system is required.

State—Municipal Computer Operator

Job Description

This position exists in various state departments and agencies at locations throughout the state.

Computer Operators monitor and control or assist in controlling electronic computers in conformance with written instructions describing each computer application. They also operate magnetic tape and disk drives, printers, and other peripheral devices. In some installations, they may operate the console and may be required to work night, weekend, and/or compressed work shifts. They may confer with Programmers and/or System Analysts on procedural matters and problems.

Requirements

On or before the date of the written test, candidates must meet one of the following requirements:

1. Six months of satisfactory full-time paid experience in the operation of an installed computer. Use or operation of microcomputers, personal computers, or word processing equipment will *not* be considered qualifying experience; or
2. Successful completion of a six-month course in electronic computer operations which included supervised "hands-on" computer operation by the student as a major portion of the course; or
3. An associate degree in EDP.

Appropriate part-time and volunteer experience which can be verified will be accepted on a prorated basis. All degrees and/or credit hours must have been awarded by an accredited college or university.

Test Information

Candidates must pass a *written test* in order to be considered for appointment. The written test will be designed to test for knowledge, skills, and/or abilities in such areas as:

1. *Use, operation, and routine maintenance of computer hardware and peripheral equipment:* These questions will be designed to test for technical knowledge and concepts relevant to data processing and the operation of an electronic computer and associated peripheral equipment. Although the questions asked will not be specific to any vendor or any model of computer, the questions on storage media and peripheral equipment may cover, but not necessarily be confined to, characteristics of magnetic tape and magnetic disk as storage media, basic data communications terms, and the operation of peripheral equipment.

2. *Reading and interpreting instructions relating to data coding and the execution of computer programs:* These questions will be designed to test for skill in following and applying written directions expressed as generalized operator instructions. These instructions will be presented with specific rules for applying them, and the information needed to answer the questions is presented in the test booklet. Therefore, training on any particular computer system is not required.

State—Municipal Computer Specialist (Applied Programming)

Job Description

This class of positions encompasses highly complex technical or supervisory responsibilities involved in the development and maintenance of application programs and systems development projects for use in the operation of a large or medium-size computer installation of varying degrees of difficulty and with varying degrees of latitude for independent initiative and judgment. There are three assignment levels within this class of positions. All personnel perform related work.

1. *Assignment Level I:* Under general supervision, with considerable latitude for the exercise of independent initiative and judgment, investigates complex systems development problems and recommends appropriate solutions; or supervises a number of applications programming units of substantial size or one applications programming unit of substantial size engaged in work of more than ordinary difficulty, complexity, and responsibility in a medium-size electronic computer installation by performing tasks such as are indicated below under Examples of Typical Tasks.
2. *Assignment Level II:* Under general supervision, with wide latitude for the exercise of independent initiative and judgment, supervises a unit engaged in systems development work of great difficulty, complexity, and responsibility in a large multi-programming computer system; or serves as project leader performing complex staff work and the full range of computer systems analysis functions utilizing general knowledge of and involvement with programming languages, operating systems, software and software systems analysis in highly complex systems development projects of a medium-size EDP installation; or supervises the activities of a number of applications programming units of substantial size engaged in work of more than ordinary difficulty, complexity and responsibility in a large electronic computer installation by performing tasks such as are indicated below under Examples of Typical Tasks.

3. *Assignment Level III:* Under direction, with broad scope for the exercise of independent initiative and judgment, supervises the units responsible for systems development and applications programming in an agency, instructing, directing and checking the work of subordinates; or is routinely responsible for the coordination and direction of data processing task forces organized to plan and implement complex integrated software development projects in a very large multi-programming computer system operating in an on-line mode in a communications environment by performing tasks such as are indicated below under Examples of Typical Tasks.

Examples of Typical Tasks. Conducts and supervises the conduct of surveys, definition studies, feasibility studies, and the writing of comprehensive reports. Prepares specifications for complex and detailed systems designs; prepares program specifications. Supervises the scheduling of personnel in applications programming and systems analysis projects. Evaluates the systems and programming work products of subordinates. Coordinates the activities of the applications programming staff or project staff with other units in the applications programming section or with other sections within the information system division.

Requirements

1. A bachelor's degree from an accredited college and four years of satisfactory full-time paid programming or systems analysis experience, at least one year of which shall have been programming experience involving the use of either COBOL, BAL, PL/1, or FORTRAN; or
2. An associate degree from an accredited college or completion of two years of study (60 credits) at an accredited college and six years of satisfactory full-time paid programming or systems analysis experience, at least one year of which shall have been programming experience involving the use of either COBOL, BAL, PL/1, or FORTRAN; or
3. High school graduation or evidence of having passed an examination for a high school equivalency diploma and eight years of satisfactory full-time paid programming or systems analysis experience, at least one year of which shall have been programming experience involving the use of either COBOL, BAL, PL/1, or FORTRAN; or
4. Education and/or experience which is equivalent to (1), (2), or (3). However, all candidates must have the four years of experience described under subdivision 1.

Foreign education will be evaluated by the Department of Personnel to determine comparability to education received in domestic accredited educational institutions to determine the extent to which it will be credited toward meeting the requirements for this examination.

All eligibles must pass a background investigation by the Department of Investigation in order to be eligible for this position.

Test Information

Written, weight 100, 70% required. The test may include questions on techniques of supervision and administration in a computer environment; development, installation, management, operation, and maintenance of computer application programs and systems development projects; and other related areas.

Advancement

Employees in the title of Computer Specialist (Applications Programming) are accorded promotion opportunities, when eligible, to the title of Computer Systems Manager.

State—Municipal
Computer Specialist (Data Base Administration)

Job Description

This class of positions encompasses technical or supervisory responsibilities for the design, implementation, enhancement, and maintenance of Data Base Management Systems performed at varying levels of difficulty and with varying degrees of latitude for independent initiative and judgment. There are three assignment levels within this class of positions. All personnel perform related work.

1. *Assignment Level I:* Under supervision, with considerable latitude for the exercise of independent judgment, is responsible for the maintenance, design, and enhancement of Data Base Management Systems; for assisting other computer personnel with technical advice, as required, including identification, coding, and implementation of complex technical programming projects; performs tasks such as are indicated below under Examples of Typical Tasks.
2. *Assignment Level II:* Under supervision, with considerable latitude for the exercise of independent judgment, performs logical and physical data administration functions working with applications and systems programmers and other technical personnel of the data processing installation; performs tasks such as are indicated below under Examples of Typical Tasks. Supports applications and systems programmers and other technical personnel of the data processing installation in determining data specifications for new information systems or for enhancement of existing systems. Sets standards, ensures that there is no data redundancy, and may lead design reviews to ensure adherence to standards and that the systems design is both complete and feasible. Performs tasks such as are indicated below under Examples of Typical Tasks.
3. *Assignment Level III:* Under general supervision with wide latitude for the exercise of independent initiative and judgment, performs the following: supervises a unit of Data Base Administration Specialists and is fully responsible for execution of projects of the highest complexity in the design, implementation, enhancement, and maintenance of the Data Base Management Systems of the data processing installation. Performs tasks such as are indicated below under Examples of Typical Tasks.

Examples of Typical Tasks. Assists analysts with technical design considerations. Develops approaches for modifying existing systems. Maintains state-of-the-art knowledge in computer systems technology. Is responsible for the maintenance and enhancement of general purpose applications software. Ensures the completeness and accuracy of coded programs, creates program test data and program test plans, and prepares system acceptance test plans and systems test data. Provides on-the-job programming training of subordinate technical personnel to ensure efficient and accurate utilization of state-of-the-art techniques. Ensures that the data center is knowledgeable in the hardware and software requirements, job flow, required inputs, and expected outputs; prepares operational specifications.

Controls and coordinates logical, internal, and external data element definition and data relationships for all applications. Defines physical structures and organizations of data bases/data sets to best meet the logical requirements of the applications, reviewing and modifying as new requirements are specified. Monitors the performance of the data base software and tunes as necessary to optimize performance. For new applications, estimates performance via simulation or benchmark test. Performs approved updates to dictionary system and makes dictionary information available to analysts and programmers. Generates all DBMS control blocks and data structures required by application programs. Defines and implements procedures for backup/recovery/restart for all data. Monitors DBMS output from recovery and backup executions. Determines appropriate reorganization frequency for the data base. Determines device storage space requirements for the data base and data compression strategies. Ensures data security using the features of the DBMS or, if necessary, developing requirement specifications for security routines. Provides training for application programmers, systems programmers, and operations personnel in the use of DBMS and special purpose utility software. Provides application programming DBMS-related diagnostic error detection support. Coordinates implementation of applications changes across multiple divisions of the data processing installation. Develops approaches for addressing security violation detection and tracking and auditing the integrity of the data in the data base. Reviews and approves application systems prior to implementation for adherence to DBA standards in design, systems and programming specifications, systems tests, and final documentation. Develops data definition, documentation, programming, testing, and systems acceptance standards. Provides program specification for internal Data Base Administration programs. Directs the activities of the Data Base Administration librarians. Assists in the selection of appropriate DB access methods.

Requirements

1. A bachelor's degree from an accredited college and four years of satisfactory full-time paid applications or systems programming experience involving the use of either COBOL, BAL, PL/1, or FORTRAN, at least one year of which shall have been in a data base management environment; or
2. An associate degree from an accredited college or completion of two years of study (60 credits) at an accredited college and six years of satisfactory full-time paid applications or systems programming experience involving the use of either COBOL, BAL, PL/1, or FORTRAN, at least one year of which shall have been in a data base management environment; or
3. High school graduation or evidence of having passed an examination for a high school equivalency diploma and eight years of satisfactory full-time paid applications or systems programming experience involving the use of either COBOL, BAL, PL/1, or FORTRAN, at least one year of which shall have been in a data base management environment; or
4. Education and/or experience which is equivalent to (1), (2) or (3). However, all candidates must have the four years of experience described under subdivision 1.

Foreign education will be evaluated by the Department of Personnel to determine comparability to education received in domestic accredited educational institutions to determine the extent to which it will be credited toward meeting the requirements for this examination.

All qualified candidates must pass a background investigation by the Department of Investigation in order to be eligible for this position.

Test Information

Written, weight 100, 70% required. The test may include questions on techniques of supervision and administration in a computer environment; design, implementation, enhancement, and maintenance of Data Base Management Systems, including logical and physical data administration functions; and other related areas.

Advancement

Employees in the title of Computer Specialist (Data Base Administration) are accorded promotion opportunities, when eligible, to the title of Computer Systems Manager.

State—Municipal Computer Programmer

Job Description

Computer Programmers prepare detailed instructions to adapt various operations to data processing, prepare input and output layouts and block diagrams to show the sequence of computations for solution of problems on computers and peripheral equipment, and use programming languages to develop machine instructions for data manipulations.

Requirements

On or before the date of the written test, candidates must meet one of the following requirements:

1. One year of full-time programming experience; or
2. A minimum of 60 college semester credit hours including at least 15 credit hours in EDP courses (an associate degree in EDP will be considered as meeting this requirement).

All degrees and/or credit hours must have been awarded by an accredited college or university. If successful on the written test, you may receive a job commitment prior to completion of the requirements, but you cannot be appointed until you submit proof of your degree and data processing credits to the Department of Civil Service or the appointing authority. Qualifying EDP courses must be listed on your application together with the credits awarded for each. This is not necessary if you have the appropriate associate degree. Your application must show the college(s) attended and the total number of credits awarded. Appropriate part-time and volunteer experience which can be verified will be accepted on a prorated basis.

The list established as the result of this examination may also be used to fill the position of Computer Programmer (Scientific). If you achieve a passing score on the written test and have had 12 semester credit hours in math and/or statistics, including one course in differential or integral calculus, you may be considered for appointment as a Computer Programmer (Scientific).

Test Information

There will be a written test which candidates must pass in order to be considered for appointment. The written test will be designed to test for knowledge, skills, and/or abilities in such areas as indicated below:

1. Programming techniques and concepts, including the use of a pseudolanguage: The questions will be designed to test for basic structures of higher-level computer programming languages and their applications. They may cover, but will not necessarily be confined to, such areas as program documentation, programming terminology, and flowchart interpretation. Use of a pseudolanguage will test for ability to read and interpret programs written in a programming language uniquely constructed for computer programmer examinations and to answer questions based upon these programs. The pseudolanguage will be defined completely in the test booklet in the form of a higher-level programming language. Programs may be supplemented with sample data, formats, or simple decision tables.

2. Systems analysis and symbolic logic: These questions will be designed to test for knowledge of terminology used by systems analysts. They may cover, but will not necessarily be confined to, documentation, feasibility studies, and system implementation and control. The questions on symbolic logic will be designed to test for ability to reason logically. They may cover, but will not necessarily be confined to, truth tables, logical implications (i.e., if A and B, then C), and relations (i.e., greater than, etc.). Knowledge of addition, subtraction, multiplication, and division is necessary, but neither mathematical sophistication nor computational speed is needed.
3. Data processing concepts and terminology: These questions will be designed to test for knowledge of computer characteristics and operations that are relevant for computer programming and analysis. They may cover, but will not necessarily be confined to, basic terminology of data processing, data entry, data access, and data communications; basic characteristics of storage media and data bases; types of data processing (i.e., time-sharing), the functions of operating systems, and hierarchies of computer memory.

Financial, Accounting, Actuarial, and Purchasing Positions

Officials in government must have up-to-date financial information to make important decisions. Accountants and auditors prepare, analyze, and verify financial reports that furnish that kind of information. In addition, government accountants and auditors maintain and examine the records of government agencies and audit private businesses and individuals whose dealings are subject to government regulations.

SAMPLE EXAMINATION ANNOUNCEMENTS

State—Municipal
Assistant Accountant

Job Description

Assistant Accountants, under close supervision, are trained in and perform beginning-level professional accounting for state or city departments or agencies; assist in making field investigations and in auditing of business firms; perform related work.

Examples of Typical Tasks. Under close supervision, are trained in and perform the following tasks: Maintaining general and special books of account according to established account classifications, including cash books, purchase books, financial registers, general ledgers, and general journals; posting entries from books of original entry to general and subsidiary ledgers; making adjusting and closing entries; preparing trial balances, bank reconciliations, operating statements and schedules; maintaining records of contracts, appropriations, allocations, authorizations, and payment; examining invoices, claims, vouchers, and payrolls, and verifying their accuracy by consulting supporting records and data; receiving remittances, making disbursements, and issuing appropriate receipts; setting up and maintaining codes for funds and reserves; allocating costs and charges, classifying receipts and expenditures; auditing books of business enterprises and preparing reports.

Requirements

1. Sixty credits from an accredited college with at least 12 credits in accounting; or
2. High school graduation or equivalent and 12 credits in accounting from an accredited college and three years of full-time paid professional accounting or auditing experience; or
3. A satisfactory equivalent combination of education and experience.

Experience as a cashier, account clerk, payroll clerk, bank teller, bookkeeper, or any other subprofessional capacity will not be credited. However, all candidates must have 12 credits in accounting from an accredited college.

Test Information

Written, weight 100, 70% required. There is also an oral qualifying test (see below). Written test will be of the multiple-choice and essay type and may include questions on accounting and auditing principles and practices; maintenance, examination, and review of financial books, records, and transactions; financial statements, budgets, and supporting documents and schedules; interpretation and understanding of financial written material; human relationships including verbal ability; and related areas.

Oral Test. The ability to speak, understand, and be understood in English is required of all candidates. This ability may be demonstrated by either

1. Attendance at an intermediate school, junior high school, high school, and/or college at the undergraduate level for at least four years of full-time study where standard English, as spoken in the United States, is used as the primary language of instruction (part-time study will be accepted on a pro rata basis); or
2. Passing a qualifying oral test, which will be given to affected candidates prior to appointment.

Eligibles will be required to pass a qualifying medical test prior to appointment.

Advancement

Employees permanently employed in the title of Assistant Accountant who possess a baccalaureate degree, including or supplemented by 18 credits in accounting, including at least one course each in advanced accounting, auditing, cost accounting, and taxation, will receive an appointment to Accountant at the end of one year of satisfactory service. In addition, employees in the title of Assistant Accountant are accorded promotion opportunities, when eligible, to the title of Accountant by passing a promotion examination. However, all employees must have served permanently in the title of Assistant Accountant for a total period of not less than one year immediately preceding the date of promotion or advancement.

State—Municipal Associate Accountant

Job Description

Associate Accountants work under general supervision, with wide latitude for the exercise of independent judgment; perform difficult and responsible work in accounting and auditing, or supervise a clearly differentiated accounting unit or auditing group comprising a substantial accounting staff; perform related work.

Examples of Typical Tasks. Participate in and review the processing of fiscal documents, claims, tax bills, financial statements, and the accounting for the receipt, deposit, and disbursement of large sums of money. Make desk and field audits and confer with taxpayers' representatives to settle disputed tax liability determinations. Prepare complex budgetary estimates and authorizations. Examine, analyze, reconcile, adjust, and prepare reports and correspondence affecting various accounts. Do research. Interpret rules and regulations, methods, and procedures for subordinates. Advise subordinates on procedures to be followed in unusual and exceptional cases. Assign work and evaluate the quantity and quality of work performed by the accounting staff. Review reports and completed assessments submitted by subordinates. Supervise staff in auditing the books and records of landlords, housing companies, or contractors. Confer with subordinates, taxpayers, and taxpayers' representatives to settle disputes and secure consent assessments. Perform financial analyses and make projections; prepare financial forecasts.

Requirements

1. A bachelor's degree from an accredited college including or supplemented by at least 24 credits in accounting, including at least one course each in advanced accounting, auditing, cost accounting, and United States taxation, and two years of full-time paid professional accounting or auditing experience; or
2. High school graduation or equivalent and 24 credits in accounting from an accredited college, including at least one course each in advanced accounting, auditing, cost accounting, and United States taxation, and six years of full-time paid professional accounting or auditing experience; or
3. A valid state C.P.A. license; or
4. A satisfactory equivalent combination of education and experience.

However, all candidates must have at least 18 credits in accounting from an accredited college including at least one course each in advanced accounting, auditing, cost accounting, and United States taxation. One year of full-time paid professional accounting or auditing experience, under a C.P.A. or in a governmental agency, if beyond the two years described in (1) above or the six years described in (2) above, may be substituted for six of the required 24 credits in accounting but not for any of the specifically required courses in advanced accounting, auditing, cost accounting, or United States taxation. Graduate study in accounting in an accredited college may be substituted for experience up to a maximum of one year in (1) above.

Applicants may be summoned for the written test prior to the determination of whether they meet the minimum requirements. To verify course credits you will later be required to have your college send an official transcript.

Foreign education will be evaluated to determine comparability to education received in domestic accredited educational institutions.

Test Information

All candidates must take a written test. The written test will consist of two parts to be given in one session on the same day. You must attain a score of at least 70% on each part of the test. The essay part will be rated only for those candidates who pass the multiple-choice part.

1. *Part I* (weight 65%) of the written test will be of the multiple-choice type and may include questions on accounting and auditing principles and practices; reading and interpretation of relevant rules, laws, and regulations; report writing and editing; financial and management auditing; analysis and critique of accounting systems; supervision, training, and human relations in job situations; planning and organizing work; performing accounting research; standards of employee conduct; and other related areas.
2. *Part II* (weight 35%) of the written test will be of the essay type and may include questions on accounting, auditing, and supervision.

Advancement

Employees in the title of Associate Accountant are accorded promotion opportunities, when eligible, to the title of Administrative Accountant.

State—Municipal Assistant Actuary

Job Description

Assistant Actuary positions exist in the state government with the Insurance Department, the Department of Audit and Control, the State Teachers' Retirement System, the State Insurance Fund, and the Department of Civil Service and involve moderately difficult actuarial work involving the application of actuarial and statistical methods.

In the **Insurance Department,** Assistant Actuaries assist in checking approximate methods submitted by companies in valuing various categories of policies, special benefits, or special liability items. They check reserve formulae, methods, and calculations and assist in the preparation of valuation memoranda for periodic examination of domestic companies. They also assist in the review of casualty insurance company rate filings for compliance with the standards prescribed by the Insurance Law and Department Regulations.

In the **Department of Audit and Control,** Assistant Actuaries work in the State Employees' Retirement System and the State Policemen's and Firemen's Retirement System. They assist higher level actuaries in performing the annual valuation of the System's liabilities, in determining pension contributions, in performing research projects, and in calculating actuarial tables.

In the **State Teachers' Retirement System,** Assistant Actuaries compute reserves for transfers, disability, and deferred allowances. They are responsible for annual computation of cost-of-living factors for supplemental pensions paid to annuitants. They also check computer computations for valuation and service retirement allowances.

In the **State Insurance Fund,** Assistant Actuaries apply actual theory and methods to the review of claims records in death and disability cases for the purpose of establishing proper estimates of eventual incurred losses. They compare loss reserves on death and permanent disability cases and calculate the present value of Workers' Compensation cases and the amount payable to claimants in death and disability cases.

In the **Department of Civil Service,** Assistant Actuaries assist in the compilation of data from various employee benefit programs and perform the calculation of various statistical measures thereof. Under supervision, the Actuary will compute anticipated premium levels, dividends, and actuarial reserves and review such calculations of various companies insuring portions of the program.

Requirements

Candidates are qualified for this examination if, on or before the date of filing application, they have successfully completed Part I (General Mathematics) of the Society of Actuaries' or Casualty Actuarial Society's examination. For information regarding the Societies' examinations, contact the Society of Actuaries, 475 North Martingale Road, Schaumberg, Illinois 60173 or the Casualty Actuarial Society, 1100 North Glebe Road, Suite 600, Arlington, Virginia 22201.

Test Information

There is no written test. The training and experience of applicants who meet the minimum qualifications will be evaluated in relation to the duties and requirements of the position. You must include with your application:

1. A list of probability, statistics, actuarial or computer science, accounting, economics, or law courses successfully completed and the number of semester hours credited for each;
2. A copy of the notification of the Society of Actuaries' or Casualty Actuarial Society's examination score(s) which you received; and
3. A detailed description of your employment experience.

It is essential that you provide complete and accurate information so that your qualifications may be fully evaluated. Final scores will be based upon the rating received on the evaluation of training and experience.

State—Municipal Life Actuaries

Job Description

Senior Actuaries (Life) assist higher level actuaries in checking actuarial reserve formulae and calculations of net premiums and reserves for life insurance, retirement benefits, annuities, disability, and double indemnity life insurance, and life insurance departments of savings banks under the jurisdiction of the Insurance Department. They also prepare statistical tables in the development of trends of reserves and check methods and calculations of approximations employed for special reserve liabilities.

Associate Actuaries (Life) in the Department of Audit and Control are responsible for planning and developing difficult projects and studies. These could include such areas as development of funding procedures to match the expanding benefit structure, continuing analyses of the actuarial gains and/or losses of the systems' operations, and formulating applications of new actuarial concepts to the existing systems. In the Insurance Department, they recommend solutions to difficult actuarial problems connected with valuation of reserves; assist in the preparation of valuation reports covering methods, procedures, and accuracy of reserve valuations submitted by domestic life insurance companies; analyze mortality experience; and examine adequacy of premium rates for life insurance and annuities. They also assist in investigation and studies of problems of reserves, annual statements, policy forms, rates, and other matters.

Principal Actuaries (Life) perform actuarial studies in various phases of life insurance and retirement systems. These studies include the testing of the effectiveness of current department regulations and consideration of the need for modification of such regulations and/or the addition of new regulations. They determine proper reserve bases for life insurance annuities, disability benefits, accidental death benefits, and contingent liabilities of life insurance companies and fraternal societies. They review proposals by domestic life insurance companies to revise their valuation procedures to provide for the application of electronic data processing equipment for upgrading of such equipment at their home offices. They also review policy forms for actuarial compliance with the Insurance Law and regulations concerning credit life insurance, minimum cash values, and guidelines concerning wholesale insurance, and determine the reasonableness of accident and health rates.

Supervising Actuaries (Life) supervise the Actuarial Bureau staff in the annual review of reserve valuation of domestic life companies and the fraternal societies and supervise the adherence to regulations pertaining to life insurance, particularly credit life. They review studies of experience and recommend new regulations and modification of current regulations, supervise the actuarial review of policy forms, and assist in establishing actuarial guidelines. Concerning non-profit hospital and medical corporations, they review and approve premium rates and experience rating formulas. They also recommend approval of employee benefits programs, assist in providing actuarial considerations for policy decisions to be made by the superintendent, and assist in the actuarial review of proposed legislation.

Requirements

Candidates must meet the following requirements:
For Senior Actuary:

1. Successful completion of three of the ten parts of the examination of the Society of Actuaries; and
2. One year of full-time paid experience in professional actuarial work.

For Associate Actuary:

1. Successful completion of four of the ten parts of the examination of the Society of Actuaries; and
2. Two years of full-time paid experience in professional actuarial work.

For Principal Actuary:

1. Successful completion of six of the ten parts of the examination of the Society of Actuaries; and
2. Three years of full-time paid experience in professional actuarial work of which one year shall have been in one or more of the following: directing actuarial computations for regular and special policy forms as to premium rates, reserves, and non-forfeiture values of life insurance policies or annuities; independently investigating and drawing professionally sound conclusions regarding such actuarial problems as approximate reserve methods, valuation procedure, or determination of special reserve items; and drafting, or directing the drafting of, policy forms, riders, and/or endorsements for adoption.

For Supervising Actuary:

1. Successful completion of eight of the ten parts of the examination of the Society of Actuaries; and
2. Four years of full-time paid experience in professional actuarial work of which two years shall have been in one or more of the following: directing and drawing professionally sound conclusions from studies concerning mortality experience and expense analyses; responsibility for determining the specific liability items to be reported in the annual statements of life insurance companies, retirement systems, fraternal societies, etc.; responsibility for correspondence with official governmental regulatory agencies or insurance companies regarding actuarial aspects of life insurance contracts or methods, policy changes, dividends, net costs, procedures, reinstatements, etc.; responsibility for the calculation of reserve liabilities including the determination of insurance in force, valuation standards, methods of valuation; and preparation of written reports including conclusions and recommendations on methods, standards, and results of actuarial investigations.

Test Information

There is no written test. The training and experience of those applicants who meet the minimum qualifications will be evaluated against the general background of the position(s). It is essential, therefore, that you give complete and accurate information on your application.

State
Bank Examiner Trainee, Bank Examiner

Job Description

Bank Examiner Trainees begin a two-year training program which will include field assignments supervised by the Banking Department's examining staff; Department-sponsored training which is conducted in-house or through specialized schools; and training sessions at selected banks. During the in-bank training, trainees have the opportunity to observe and participate in the major operations of commercial banks, savings banks, and foreign branches or agencies. Upon successful completion of the first year of training, trainees advance automatically to the **Bank Examiner Trainee II** level. Although training will follow the same basic format during the second year, the nature of the work while on field assignments will grow in scope as the trainee progresses. Performance as a trainee and in the prescribed training and development programs will be observed and evaluated. An appointee not meeting required standards can be terminated at any time after the initial eight weeks and before the completion of the two-year traineeship. Upon successful completion of the two-year traineeship, individuals are automatically advanced to Bank Examiner without further examination.

Bank Examiners assist in conducting in-depth examinations of banking and other financial service institutions regulated by the State Banking Department. They either perform on-site examinations and reviews of institutions' financial condition, operating procedures, and management controls or, when assigned to one of the Department's specialized office divisions, review and analyze field examination reports and periodic financial reports submitted by various types of institutions. The field examinations and office analyses are conducted to ensure that the operations and policies of state-chartered financial institutions conform with state banking laws and the banking Superintendent's Rules and Regulations.

Requirements

On or before the date of the written test, candidates must have a bachelor's or graduate degree (from an accredited college or university) in one of the following major areas of study: accounting, auditing, banking, business administration, economics, or finance. Course work must have included, or been supplemented by, six credit hours of accounting. You must include with your application a list of all accounting courses successfully completed and the number of credit hours received for each. Failure to include this information can result in your disqualification.

Test Information

There will be a written test which you must pass in order to be considered for appointment. This written test will be designed to test for knowledge, skills, and/or abilities in such areas as:

1. *Understanding and interpreting written material:* These questions will be designed to test how well you comprehend written material. You will be provided with brief reading selections and asked questions relating to the selections. All of the information required to answer the questions will be presented in the selections; you are not required to have any special knowledge relating to the content area covered in the selections.
2. *Elementary accounting:* These questions will be designed to test for familiarity with accounting principles and practices at an elementary level. The questions will attempt to test for recognition of accounting terminology, concepts, and relationships; for ability to record accounting transactions; and for acquaintance with financial statements and books of account.
3. *Preparing written material:* These questions will be designed to test how well you can express yourself in writing. Particular emphasis is placed upon two major aspects of written communication: how to clearly and accurately express given information and how to present written material in the most logical and comprehensive manner.
4. *Understanding and interpreting tabular material:* These questions will be designed to test your ability to understand, analyze, and use the internal logic of data presented in tabular form. You may be asked to complete tables, to draw conclusions from them, to analyze data trends or interrelationships, and to revise or combine data sets. The concepts of rate, ratio, and proportion will be tested. Mathematical operations will be simple, and computational speed and accuracy will not be major factors in the test.

State—Municipal Senior Budget Examiners

Job Description

Senior Budget Examiners are responsible for the central oversight and control of the fiscal operations of state departments, agencies, and public authorities. They review and analyze budget requests relative to expenditure history and projected requirements and recommend program priorities and appropriation levels for the ensuing fiscal year. Senior Budget Examiners develop expenditure projections and monitor agency compliance with revenue limitations. They anticipate changes in operating procedures, develop appropriate program evaluation techniques, survey agency operations, and make recommendations for improvement. They analyze and prepare formal recommendations on program legislation, draft correspondence for the Governor's Office, and participate in the explanation of state programs to public interest groups and other citizens.

Senior Budget Examiners (Employee Relations) review and analyze policies and practices involved in the state's employee relations programs and, as needed, review the employee relations programs of private and other public sector employers. They monitor social and economic developments to anticipate those which would impact on the state's employee relations program and recommend studies, legislative changes, and other appropriate actions accordingly. They represent the Division of the Budget at management negotiating team meetings and negotiation sessions and assist the negotiator in evaluating and responding to employee organization demands. They also provide assistance as required in the preparation and review of material to be submitted at negotiations. They draft employee compensation and benefits legislation and analyze bills passed by the Legislature and drafts of bills proposed by various state departments and agencies for introduction in the Legislature, recommending appropriate action to the Budget Director on the basis of each bill's probable impact on the employee relations programs, its fiscal implications, and its relationship to other programs.

Senior Budget Examiners (Management) analyze programs, policies, organization, and management practices of departments and agencies and make recommendations for their improvement. They collect and analyze data by personal interview and independent research, hold conferences with department personnel, plan and install new or revised systems and procedures, and determine related manpower requirements. Senior Budget Examiners (Management) assist in establishing new programs and agencies and present their findings and conclusions in oral and written reports. They review the effectiveness of new systems, advise other budget staff and departmental administrators on management and systems practices, and prepare memoranda of recommendations on proposed legislation.

Senior Budget Examiners (Public Finance) supervise, plan, and conduct difficult studies, including program analysis, in the fields of public finance, economics, and government and examine intergovernmental fiscal and program relationships, including state and federal aid problems and local fiscal and program needs. They analyze and make recommendations relative to the administrative, economic, social, and fiscal effects of proposed legislation. They also develop official estimates of current and projected expenditures and revenues based on past experience, current developments, and statutory, economic and administrative changes. Senior Budget Examiners (Public Finance) assist in the preparation of the Budget Message and write comprehensive analytical reports.

Requirements

Candidates must meet the following requirements on or before the date of the written tests:

1. Minimum Training: bachelor's degree; and
2. Minimum Experience: three years of full-time paid administrative experience including one year in a position in which the primary (at least 50%) duty involves:

Senior Budget Examiner: the analysis, evaluation and development of recommendations on major budgetary decisions

Examiner (Employee Relations): development and analysis of issues in labor relations

Examiner (Management): the conduct of program, policy, or organizational analysis

Examiner (Public Finance): the evaluation of fiscal needs or intergovernmental relations

Note. A master's degree in public administration, economics, government, business administration, labor relations, or other closely related fields may be substituted for one year of the general experience.

Test Information

There will be a written test that candidates must pass in order to be considered for appointment. The written tests will be designed to test for knowledge, skills, and/or abilities as follows:

For Senior Budget Examiner:

1. The identification and analysis of current governmental problems, situations, and roles, including the ability to recognize the implications of intra- and intergovernmental activities and relationships.
2. Preparation of written material.
3. Principles and practices of governmental budgeting and finance.
4. Application, principles, practices, and guidelines concerning budget formulation and implementation.

For Senior Budget Examiner (Employee Relations): Test factors 1, 2, and 3 as described above and knowledge of employee relations and benefit programs available to and/or in use by public and private employers and recognition of fiscal, social, and policy issues pertaining to such programs.

For Senior Budget Examiner (Management): Test factors 1, 2, and 3 as described above and knowledge of principles, practices, and alternative techniques used in the analysis of programs, policies, and management practices and of development and installation of new programs, organization structures, and management systems.

For Senior Budget Examiner (Public Finance): Test factors 1, 2, and 3 as described above and knowledge of public finance and its applications and indicators as both of these relate to all levels of government and of pertinent policies and issues at the federal, state and/or local level which may impact upon other levels of government.

City
Financial Analyst, Grade 15

Job Description

Under direction, a Financial Analyst reviews and processes financial statements submitted by contractors bidding on city projects; determines the financial capacity of contractors bidding on specific projects; investigates the financial background of contractors to determine their solvency; conducts an annual mass mailing to alert contractors to update their financial records with the city; maintains a confidential file on contractors' financial and performance records; performs related duties as required.

Requirements

A bachelor's degree in finance or a directly related field from an accredited college or university, supplemented by four years of progressively responsible experience in the analysis of financial records, including one year of experience in a supervisory capacity, or an equivalent combination of training and experience is required. College transcripts and resumes must be submitted at the time of application.

Residency. An applicant must be an actual resident of the city. Proof of residency will be required at the time of application.

Test Information

Selection will be based on an evaluation of applicants' training and experience. Successful applicants may be required to appear for and pass additional examinations at the time of certification.

Names of candidates who pass this examination will be placed on an employment list. Passing an examination does not guarantee an offer of employment. It is a statement of eligibility.

Law Enforcement, Firefighting, and Property Protection Positions

LAW ENFORCEMENT OCCUPATIONS

Law enforcement in America is fragmented and specialized; there are some 40,000 separate law enforcement agencies representing municipal, county, state, and federal governments. It is the municipal police officer that is familiar to most people. Highly trained police officers are found in both large and small cities. Of the more than 17,000 cities in the U.S., 55 have populations exceeding a quarter of a million, and these employ about one-third of all police personnel. Of the law enforcement units at state level, two of the best known are the state police and the highway patrol. State police engage in a full range of law enforcement activities, including criminal investigation. Highway patrol units are concerned almost entirely with traffic control and enforcement and have limited general police authority.

SAMPLE EXAM ANNOUNCEMENTS

Municipal Police Officer

Requirements

Age. The examination is open to males and females who are at least 19 years old and not yet 32 years old on or before the final date for the filing of applications for this examination. A birth certificate should be submitted at the examination center on the date of examination. However, if a birth certificate cannot be obtained, the applicant must provide proof of birth date to satisfy this requirement prior to consideration for appointment.

Medical. Applicants selected for appointment will be required to pass a medical examination in accordance with established guidelines. The medical examination could include a psychological evaluation.

Education or Military Experience. Applicants must have graduated from high school, or must possess an equivalency certificate issued by the State Department of Education, or must have served at least three years in the armed forces of the United States, the last discharge or release from which must have been under honorable conditions.

Character. No person who has been convicted of any felony shall be appointed as a police officer. Following a hearing by the Personnel Administrator, a candidate may be disqualified for character clearly unsuited for police services.

Test Information

Written Examination. Applicants must pass a written examination. This examination will consist of multiple-choice questions which test for abilities required for success as a police officer. Questions will test mental abilities such as interpretation of hypothetical rules and regulations, verbal reasoning, number series, table interpretation, and reading comprehension.

Spanish Examination. The examination may also be taken in Spanish. Applicants who take the examination in Spanish will have to pass an additional examination that will test the ability to read and understand the English language.

Special Qualifications. If it is determined that a certain Police Services position in a Police Department requires specific unique skills, competition for that position may be limited to persons who have such skills in the order of their grade on the examination. In the past, such selective certifications have been made for persons who hold certificates as Emergency Medical Technicians and for persons who are able to converse in Spanish or Chinese.

State Trooper

Job Description

The employee is required to work on a rotating shift basis, be available for duty 24 hours a day, work on state and national holidays, work and drive in inclement weather. A state trooper is subject to transfer on a temporary or permanent basis anywhere in the state, must carry firearms and may be required to use them in the line of duty. The employee must maintain the capability to perform strenuous tasks requiring muscular strength and cardiovascular endurance.

First-year employees receive training in the knowledge and skills required to function independently as a law enforcement officer. The employee is initially assigned to residence in the State Police Trooper Training School for approximately 16 weeks where he or she completes a basic police training curriculum of law enforcement course work and physical training. Upon graduation from school, the employee is assigned to a State Police post as a probationary trooper. In the company of an experienced trooper, the employee patrols an area to detect or prevent traffic and criminal law violations, investigates complaints of law violations, and provides a variety of related services to the general public.

After completion of one year of satisfactory service at the entry level classification, the employee will be appointed to the position of State Police Trooper II. Should an employee fail to meet the requirements for the position, that employee will be separated from the job.

Requirements

Citizenship. A citizen of the United States at the time of the written test.

Residence. A resident of the state for at least one year immediately prior to taking the written examination; or for 4 years between the ages of 17 and 35 years. State residents in the armed forces and students attending colleges or universities out of state for the past school year will be considered as meeting this requirement.

Age. At least 21 years of age at the time of the written examination and less than 36 years of age as of the date of hire.

Education. Graduation from high school or General Education Development Test (G.E.D.) results meeting State Department of Education standards. (G.E.D. tests must have been taken at an official G.E.D. center. A standard score of 35 or above on each of the five tests *and* an average of 45 for the five tests must have been attained. G.E.D. results should be submitted at the time of application if they are not already on file with Civil Service.)

Driver's License. Possession of a valid state operator's or chauffeur's license without restrictions applying to time, area, special mechanical control devices or conditions (except corrective lenses).

Vision. At least 20/50 vision in each eye without lenses, corrected to 20/20 with lenses prior to appointment to a Training School. Must have adequate color and depth perception and a visual field of no less than 70 degrees in the horizontal meridian in each eye. Must have normal vertical and lateral muscle balance.

Hearing. Must have normal hearing in both ears. Hearing deficiency, if any, must not exceed 25 decibels (I.S.O.) in either ear in the frequency ranges 500, 1,000, 2,000, 3,000 cycles. Deficiencies in higher frequency ranges (4,000–6,000 cycles) must not exceed an average of 40 decibels.

Convictions of Law Violations or Civil Infractions. May serve as a basis for disqualification. The applicant's total record will be evaluated. The pattern of law violations, the seriousness, the surrounding circumstances, and number and recency will be considered. The convictions noted below will be cause for automatic disqualification:

1. Conviction of a felony.
2. Lost driving privilege through suspension or revocation of license, due to an unsatisfactory driving record as defined by the state driver's license point system.

Exception: Those who maintain a driving record free of license suspension or revocation and moving violation conviction/s or civil infraction determination/s in the two years previous to taking the written examination through appointment to a training school will be accepted.

In the four years previous to taking the written examination through appointment to a training school:

3. Conviction of driving while license was suspended or revoked.
4. Conviction of driving while under the influence of alcohol or drugs. (This includes driving while ability impaired.)
5. Two or more convictions of reckless driving.

In the two years previous to taking the written examination through appointment to a training school:

6. Accumulated eight or more points on the driving record.
7. Conviction or civil infraction determination of three or more moving violations.
8. A record of two or more traffic accidents each resulting in a moving violation conviction or civil infraction determination.

Test Information

Written Examination. A written test containing multiple-choice and true-false questions pertaining to accuracy of observation and memory and ability to read and comprehend reports, manuals, and laws will determine 40 percent of the final score. The written test will be administered by the Department of Civil Service at various examination centers throughout the state.

Background Investigation. Applicants who pass the written test may be scheduled to participate in the remainder of the examination process (oral appraisal) based on departmental work force needs. The candidates will be subjected to a thorough background investigation designed to assist in measuring suitability for police work. The background investigation will include fingerprinting and a vision test. Evidence of unsuitability may serve as a basis for disqualification from the oral appraisal examination process. Applicants who are disqualified will receive notification of the disqualification by mail.

Oral Appraisal Examination. Applicants who pass the background investigation will be scheduled for the oral appraisal examination in which a board of examiners will assess their communication skills and personal fitness. Questions asked by the oral board will pertain to the applicant's background investigation and employment objectives. The oral appraisal examination will determine 60 percent of the final score.

Medical Examination. Applicants who are called to a training school must pass a medical examination. The applicant's physical condition must be adequate for performance of the work as determined by an examining physician. A hearing test, blood test, urinalysis, and blood pressure examination will be included. The applicant must be free from any chronic diseases, organic or functional conditions or physical defects which may tend to impair efficient performance of a trooper's duties. Failure to meet medical standards will result in removal from the Employment List for this job classification. Correction of a medical deficiency may result in a return to the Employment List.

Physical Performance Test. Prior to hire applicants will be called to the Training School for a physical performance test. Failure to meet required standards will result in rejection of the applicant for the Training School. There are six test parts designed to assess strength to push, pull, drag, and lift; cardiorespiratory endurance for strenuous work and running; and abdominal strength and spine flexibility to avoid low back pain, problems of strains, and loss of mobility and agility. The physical performance test consists of the following:

1. *Pushups:* This is a standard pushup where the back and legs are kept straight. The event starts in the up position and the count occurs when the applicant returns to the up position, after having touched an audible beeper on the mat with his/her chest. The applicant is to do as many pushups as possible in sixty seconds.
2. *Grip:* Using a hand grip dynamometer, the applicant squeezes the meter while keeping the arm extended parallel to the leg. Both right and left grips are tested and recorded in kilograms of pressure.
3. *Obstacle Course:* The total distance for this obstacle course is 90 feet and it is run for time. The applicant runs 20 feet, crawls 6 feet through a 2½ foot high simulated tunnel, runs 20 feet, climbs a 6 foot, 6 inch barrier with footholds and handholds. The applicant then runs 20 feet to and around a set of pylons, then back to the barrier which has footholds and handholds on it. After climbing the barrier a second time, the applicant runs 4 feet to the stop position.
4. *165 Pound Drag:* The applicant drags a 165-pound lifeform dummy 30 feet for time. The dummy is gripped in the armpits and dragged backwards.
5. *95 Pound Carry:* The applicant lifts a 95 pound bag which has handholds and runs with it 30 feet and places it on a 32-inch high platform for time.
6. *Half-Mile Shuttle Run:* The applicant runs between two pylons placed 88 feet apart for a total of 15 round trips for time.

Examinees are encouraged to practice ahead of time for the physical performance test. All physical tests, and especially the half-mile run, are aided by conditioning ahead of time. Physical training for law enforcement positions requires that new hires be physically fit when they are hired. This physical performance test screens for minimal levels of physical fitness required for State Police Trooper I. It is very important that applicants adequately prepare themselves to pass the physical performance test. It is recommended that applicants consult a medical doctor before attempting the physical performance skills.

FIREFIGHTING OCCUPATIONS

Nature of the Work

Every year, fires take thousands of lives and destroy property worth billions of dollars. Firefighters help protect the public against this danger.

During duty hours, firefighters must be prepared to respond to a fire and handle any emergency that arises. Because firefighting is dangerous and complicated, it requires organization and teamwork. At every fire, firefighters perform specific duties assigned by an officer such as a lieutenant, captain, or chief. They may connect hose lines to hydrants, operate a pump, or position ladders. Their duties may change several times while the company is in action. They may rescue victims and administer emergency medical aid, ventilate smokefilled areas, operate equipment, and salvage the contents of buildings. Some firefighters operate fire apparatus, ambulances, emergency rescue vehicles, and fireboats.

Most fire departments also are responsible for fire prevention. They provide specially trained personnel to inspect public buildings for conditions that might cause a fire. They may check building plans, the number and working condition of fire escapes and fire doors, the storage of flammable materials, and other possible hazards. In addition, firefighters educate the public about fire prevention and safety measures. They frequently speak on this subject before school assemblies and civic groups, and, in some communities, they inspect private homes for fire hazards.

Between alarms, they have classroom training, clean and maintain equipment, conduct practice drills and fire inspections, and participate in physical fitness activities.

SAMPLE EXAM ANNOUNCEMENTS

Municipal Firefighter

Job Description

Under supervision, assists in the control and extinguishment of fires and in the enforcement of laws, ordinances, rules, and regulations regarding the prevention, control, and extinguishment of fires; performs inspectional, investigational, and regulative duties connected with prevention, control, and extinguishment of fires; performs all additional functions for the rank prescribed by orders, directives, or regulations of the Fire Department and performs special duties or assignments as directed by the Fire Commissioner. Candidates appointed to this position may be required to work rotating tours or shifts including Saturdays, Sundays, and holidays.

Requirements

Education. At the time of appointment, high school graduation or evidence of having passed an examination for the high school equivalency diploma (GED).

License. At the time of appointment, eligibles must possess a valid state motor vehicle driver's license.

Age. Only persons who have passed their 18th birthday but not their 29th birthday on the date of the written test qualify for this examination. However, only persons who have reached their 21st birthday shall be appointed. Applicants must have passed their 18th birthday by the date of the written test. This minimum requirement shall in no case prohibit an applicant who is within six months of this minimum age requirement from taking the written test.

All persons who were engaged in military duty as defined in Section 243 of the Military Law may deduct from their age the length of time which they spent in such military duty, not exceeding a total of four years.

At the time of investigation, applicants will be required to present proof of date of birth by transcript of record of the Bureau of Vital Statistics or other satisfactory evidence.

Character. Proof of good character is an absolute prerequisite to appointment. Persons convicted of a felony are not eligible for positions in the uniformed force of the Fire Department. In addition, the rules of the Department of Personnel provide that no person who has been dishonorably discharged from the Armed Forces shall be certified for appointment as a Firefighter.

Height. Applicants must be not less than 5 feet 4 inches (bare feet) in height. Height will be taken after strenuous physical activity.

Vision. 20/50 each eye separately without glasses; 20/40 both eyes together without glasses.

Test Information

There will be a written test of the multiple-choice type and a physical test. Only candidates who achieve the minimum passing mark of 70% in the written test will be summoned for the physical test. The weight of the written test will be announced by the date of the written test.

Written Test. The written test will be of the multiple-choice type and will be designed to test the candidates' ability to read and understand English and their capacity to learn and perform the work of a Firefighter. It may include questions on understanding job information; applying laws, rules, and regulations to job situations; recognizing appropriate behavior in job situations; understanding mechanical devices; and remembering details of a floor layout.

Physical Test. The physical test will be designed to test the candidates' capacity to perform the physical aspects of the work of a Firefighter.

Advancement. Employees in the title of Firefighter are accorded promotion opportunities, when eligible, to the title of Lieutenant, Fire Department.

State
Assistant Fire Marshal, Fire Marshal in the Department of Public Welfare

Job Description

Assistant Fire Marshals and Fire Marshals are responsible for the implementation, direction, and coordination of the fire safety program at state mental hospitals and state schools for the mentally retarded. Employees inspect institutional buildings and grounds for fire hazards. They test and maintain firefighting and fire prevention equipment to ensure proper operating conditions. Employees are responsible for organizing and training fire brigades which serve as first-level firefighting teams at the institutions. Assistant Fire Marshals and Fire Marshals conduct fire drills and train institutional personnel in emergency evacuation procedures. In the event of a fire, employees are responsible for the proper utilization of personnel and equipment to extinguish or control the fire and to evacuate occupants until outside firefighting companies arrive. Employees are responsible for writing reports of fires and reports of fire prevention inspections. Employees are also responsible for maintaining cooperative working relationships with local fire departments.

The duties of Assistant Fire Marshals and Fire Marshals are similar in nature but different in the degree of responsibility. A Fire Marshal is responsible for the supervision of the Assistant Fire Marshal and has total responsibility for the fire safety program at a state institution. The Assistant Fire Marshal performs work as assigned, but generally will work independently and under minimum supervision. Employees may be required to work rotating shifts depending on the institution at which they are employed.

Requirements

Applicants must be state residents, of good moral character, and physically capable of performing the duties of the position. Residency means a current address in the state and the intention to remain a resident.

Assistant Fire Marshal

1. Two years of experience in firefighting and fire prevention work and such training as may have been gained through graduation from a standard high school or vocational school; or
2. Any equivalent combination of experience and training.

Fire Marshal

1. Four years of experience in firefighting and fire prevention work and such training as may have been gained through graduation from a standard high school or vocational school; or
2. Any equivalent combination of experience and training.

Acceptable training is training in fire prevention or firefighting that can be substituted for the required experience at the rate of 300 clock hours or 18 semester hours for one year's experience to a maximum substitution of one year for the Assistant Fire Marshal and two years for the Fire Marshal position. Training can be administered by colleges, states or other jurisdictions, fire departments, or the military services. To receive credit, these courses must be relevant to civilian firefighting or fire prevention.

Acceptable experience is full-time paid experience as a fire inspector or firefighter with a fire department. Volunteer fire department experience evaluation is dependent on the estimated number of hours per month the applicant served as a firefighter or participated in fire prevention programs. This experience will be converted to full-time equivalency on the basis of a 40-hour week. *However, time spent on a standby basis or in routine maintenance or in organizing social activities will not be credited.* Military and industrial fire prevention or firefighting experience is acceptable as full-time experience if fire prevention and firefighting were major duties. If candidates fully meet the experience requirements, high school graduation will be assumed.

Test Information

There is no written test. The examination will consist of a rating of each candidate's experience and training. Applicants must attain passing scores to have their names placed on eligible lists. All applicants will be notified in writing of their examination results.

Eligible Lists. Names of successful candidates will be placed on employment and promotion lists in order of final earned ratings. Promotion lists are limited to current employees with regular or probationary civil service status. Candidates' eligibility for employment will continue for 24 months. Promotion eligibility will continue for 36 months.

CORRECTION OFFICERS

Correction officers are charged with the safekeeping of persons who have been arrested and are awaiting trial or who have been tried and convicted of a crime and sentenced to serve time in a correctional institution. They maintain order within the institution, enforce rules and regulations, and often supplement the counseling that inmates receive from mental health professionals.

State
Correction Officer Trainee Positions in State Correctional Institutions

Job Description

This is entry-level correctional work of a training nature. Trainees participate in formal courses to develop the skills and techniques for the proper supervision and custody of inmates. Training covers areas such as law, sociology, psychology, counseling, firearms, and crisis prevention and intervention. Work assignments are routinely performed under senior officer supervision and include maintaining security and order, monitoring inmate movement, inspecting grounds and buildings, and searching for contraband.

Starting salary will be based on a normal 40 hour work week. There will be salary increases of approximately 3½% after both six months and nine months of service. After satisfactory completion of the full one-year training period, trainees will be promoted to Correction Officer 1 and receive a salary increase of approximately 7½%. No test is required for this promotion.

Requirements

Candidates who pass the written and oral tests will be considered to have met the education and experience requirement.

Candidates must be state residents. This means a current address in the state and the intention to remain a resident.

Candidates must be at least 21 years old on the date of application.

Test Information

The examination will consist of a written test and an oral test, each counting 50% of the final score.

The tests will be given only at the state correctional institutions. Applicants should be prepared to spend at least one-half of a day at the institution. During this time, they will tour the institution and will be given the written and oral tests. Candidates who pass the written and oral tests and who are under consideration for employment will be scheduled at later dates for an employment interview, physical fitness tests, a medical examination, and psychological tests.

Any part of the examination may be cancelled by the Commission and the weight added to the remaining part(s).

Written Test. The written test will have 75 multiple-choice questions. The score will be the number of right answers. The test will last approximately one and one-half hours.

Description of Questions	Number of Questions
Observation/memory: ability to remember details and visual impressions based on the study of photographs of typical correctional settings	20
Associative memory: ability to remember and associate combinations of written information and pictures	30
Reading comprehension: ability to understand written language and answer questions based on material read	25
Total written questions	75

Oral Test. The oral test will be used to determine job interest, poise and self-confidence, ability to organize and express thoughts, and problem-solving abilities. The test will consist of a series of questions and will last no longer than one-half hour. There will be two or three raters on the oral board.

All candidates will be asked to respond to standard questions, but the raters may ask some follow-up questions. The oral board members may include officers and administrators from correctional facilities as well as civilian personnel specialists.

For further information on testing and other topics, refer to the "General Instructions" section of the "Application for Employment."

Retests. If you do not pass either the written or oral tests or would like to try for a better score, you may be retested on both tests after a **six-month** wait. A new application is required for a retest.

Supplement to Civil Service Application Correction Officer Trainee

Correction Officer Trainees work under unique and demanding conditions. The job duties include the potential danger of physical harm in the form of assaults by inmates or in quelling disturbances among them. Institutions must be staffed 24 hours a day, 7 days a week. Trainees may be assigned to any one of three work shifts. You should be aware of these conditions and be willing to accept them.

Meals and parking are provided to those on duty.

You must complete and **sign** this form and submit it with your application. If you are unwilling to comply with any one of the 8 conditions of employment listed below, you will not be considered for the job of Correction Officer Trainee.

CONDITIONS OF EMPLOYMENT

	Yes	No
1. Are you willing to work at the correctional institution where you are applying to take the examination?	___	___
2. Are you willing to work on any shift and to occasionally work overtime?	___	___
3. Are you willing to work on those weekends and holidays which occur during your normal work schedule?	___	___
4. Are you willing to attend a four-week training program at the Central Training Academy? (You must successfully complete all phases of training, including firearms proficiency, to continue being employed.)	___	___
5. Are you willing and able to report for work under adverse weather conditions? (Days off for adverse weather will not be approved.)	___	___
6. Are you willing to accept the possibility that you may have to use physical force during inmate disturbances?	___	___
7. Are you willing to work "locked inside" an institution unarmed and be exposed to the danger of physical harm?	___	___
8. Are you willing to take physical fitness tests, a medical examination, a urinalysis test to detect drug usage, psychological tests, and to undergo a background investigation?	___	___

ADDITIONAL INFORMATION

List the names of any friends or relatives who are serving sentences in state correctional institutions. Your knowledge of anyone serving a sentence is not a bar to employment, but may affect your assignment within a correctional institution.

	PERSON	INSTITUTION
(1)	________________	________________
(2)	________________	________________
(3)	________________	________________

OATH

I swear (affirm) that all the information I have provided in this supplement is complete and accurate. I understand that the oath on my civil service application applies to all of the information in this supplement.

PLEASE SIGN BELOW.

____
Signature Date

____
(Type or print name)

State—Municipal Correction Officer

Job Description

This is a law enforcement position which requires close contact with inmates. A Correction Officer may be assigned to supervise inmates of either sex. A Correction Officer, under supervision, maintains security within correctional facilities and is responsible for the custody, control, care, job training, and work performance of inmates of detention and correctional facilities, and performs related work. Correction Officers are required to work rotating tours and shifts, including nights and Saturdays, Sundays, and holidays.

Examples of Typical Tasks. Maintains constant watch over and supervises activities of detainees, sentenced inmates, civil prisoners, etc. Enforces maximum security and maintains constant control over Departmental property, keys, gates, etc. Performs tours in cell blocks, dormitories or other housing areas, prison wards or detention areas, or at dining, recreation, exercise, inmate work sites, or other locations. May be assigned to continuous surveillance of prisoners or detainees while they are in transit.

Maintains security of prisoners or detainees hospitalized outside of prison wards or when outside the fixed security areas maintained by the Department. May help locate escaped inmates. Enforces additional emergency security measures in special situations. Enforces maximum security when assigned to tasks of receiving prisoners or detainees, periodically counting them or checking for contraband. Enforces security during movement of vehicles, articles, and visitors into and out of correctional facilities.

Is responsible for adherence to all directives, rules, and regulations of the Department of Correction, all applicable laws, court orders, and administrative requirements. Reports all inmate violations and infractions of standing or special orders, inmate grievances and proper requests, and unusual incidents. Performs duties as assigned in connection with activities for or by prisoners which are intended to improve their adjustment to society.

Requirements

Education. High school graduation or evidence of having passed an examination for the high school equivalency diploma. Foreign education will be evaluated to determine comparability to education received in domestic accredited educational institutions to determine the extent to which it will be credited toward meeting the requirements or for additional credit in this examination.

Age. Candidates must not have reached their 29th birthday by the first date of the filing period. However, they must have reached their 20th birthday by the date of appointment.

Exceptions to age requirements

All persons who were engaged in military duty, as defined in Section 243 of the Military Law, may deduct from their actual age the length of time spent in such military duty provided the total deduction for military duty does not exceed six years, of which not more than four years may be for voluntary service.

Character. Proof of good character is an absolute prerequisite to appointment. The following are among the factors which would ordinarily be cause for disqualification:

1. Conviction of an offense the nature of which indicates lack of good moral character or disposition toward violence or disorder or which is punishable by one or more years imprisonment;
2. Repeated convictions of an offense where such convictions indicate a disrespect for the law;
3. Discharge from employment where such discharge indicates poor behavior or inability to adjust to discipline;
4. Addiction to narcotics or to a controlled substance or excessive use of alcoholic beverages;
5. Dishonorable discharge from the Armed Forces. In accordance with provisions of law, persons convicted of a felony are not eligible for appointment to these positions.

Eligibles must also meet, at the time of appointment, the standards for obtaining firearms permits.

Investigation. At the time of investigation and at the time of appointment, candidates must present originals or certified copies of all required documents, including but not limited to proof of date and place of birth by transcript of record of the Bureau of Vital Statistics or other satisfactory evidence, naturalization papers if necessary, proof of any military service, and proof of meeting educational requirements. Any willful misstatement or failure to present any required documents will be cause for disqualification. Investigation must be completed prior to appointment.

Probationary Period. The probationary period is one year. As part of the probationary period, probationers will be required to successfully complete a prescribed training course. Unsatisfactory probationers will be terminated.

Test Information

Education and experience weigh 100%, a minimum score of 75% is required. There is a written test; a minimum score of 70% is required. There are also qualifying physical and medical exams.

Education and Experience. Education and experience will be calculated on the basis of candidates' responses. This rating will be verified on the basis of information contained in the Experience Paper. Therefore, the Experience Paper must be filled out completely and in detail including exact dates, number of hours per week worked, and salary earned. Candidates are advised to list *all* education and experience for which credit may be given as described below, since they will not be permitted to add any education or experience once they have filed their applications. Education or experience will not be found acceptable unless satisfactory and verifiable. Education and experience listed on the Experience Paper will receive credit only if described clearly and in detail.

The maximum score is 100. Applicants who meet the minimum educational requirement will receive a score of 75. Additional credit will be given to candidates who have additional education and/or experience as explained in the following paragraphs.

Experience Credit. Up to eight years of paid work experience including military service but not including self-employment may be given experience credit. Additional credit may also be given for up to four of the eight years of experience if such experience falls within the specialized experience described below. However, each year of specialized experience may be credited under only one category of specialized experience.

Full-time experience means 30 hours or more per week on a regular basis. Part-time experience is less than 30 hours per week but must be at least 15 hours per week to receive credit.

General Experience. At least 6 months with each employer. General Experience credit will be granted as follows: one point for 6–17 months; two points for 18–29 months; three points for 30–41 months; four points for 42–53 months; five points for 54–65 months; six points for 66–77 months; seven points for 78–89 months; eight points for 90 months and above.

Specialized Experience. At least 12 months with each employer. Specialized Experience credit will be granted as listed below.

For experience as a correction officer, military policeman assigned to a disciplinary facility or equivalent correctional experience: three points for 12–21 months; six points for 22–23 months; nine points for 34–45 months; 12 points for 46 months and above.

For experience as a police officer, military policeman, parole officer, probation officer, court officer, or equivalent law enforcement experience; two points for 12–21 months; four points for 22–33 months; six points for 34–45 months; eight points for 46 months and above.

For experience as a supervisor or for each year of active duty in military service culminating in honorable discharge or separation provided at least one year was served: one point for 12–21 months; two points for 22–33 months; three points for 34–45 months; four points for 46 months and above.

Part-Time Experience. 15 to 29 hours per week. Candidates must have a total of at least 12 months of part-time experience to receive any credit. To earn this credit, candidates must have worked at least six months for each employer. Credit will be granted as follows: one point for 12–34 months; two points for 35–57 months; three points for 58–82 months; four points for 83 months and above.

Education Credit. One point will be given for 15 to 36 semester-hours of education at an accredited college. An additional one point will be given for 37 to 72 semester-hours of education at an accredited college. An additional one point will be given for 73 or more semester-hours of education at an accredited college. An additional one point will be given for completion of at least three courses in criminal justice, law enforcement, or correctional administration, or completion of a certificate program in any of these areas at an accredited college. An additional one point will be given for possession of an associate, baccalaureate, or any other degree from an accredited college.

Rating of Education and Experience. In addition to the Experience Paper, candidates must fill out and submit an Answer Sheet in accordance with the Instruction Sheet. The Answer Sheet submitted by the candidate will be the basis for calculating a rating and for ranking on the eligible list, subject to changes after investigation of information contained in the Experience Paper. Candidates will not be allowed to make any changes on their Experience Papers or Answer Sheets once they have filed for this examination. Candidates who fail to submit an Answer Sheet or who fail to fill in their identifying information and responses to the questions listed in the Instruction Sheet will be marked Not Qualified in the Education and Experience Test.

Qualifying Written Test. The qualifying written test will be of the multiple-choice type and will be designed to measure the ability to learn to perform the duties of the position as described above. It may include questions on understanding written instructions, human relations and communication, filling out forms and maintaining records, basic arithmetic, report writing including English usage, and related areas.

Qualifying Physical and Medical Examination. Eligibles will be rejected for any medical and/or psychiatric condition which impairs their ability to perform the duties of the class of positions for which they are being examined. Medical reexamination of probationary and permanent employees in these titles may be required.

Advancement

Employees in the title of Correction Officer are accorded promotion opportunities to the title of Captain.

State—Municipal Juvenile Counselor

Job Description

Under direct supervision, is responsible for the custody, supervision, direct care, and counseling of juveniles in the custody of the Department of Juvenile Justice; performs related work.

Examples of Typical Tasks. During an assigned tour of duty, supervises juveniles in dormitories, corridors, dining rooms, recreation rooms, and related facilities where their attendance is required to ensure maintenance of their safety and order; assists in the maintenance of the security of premises and conducts searches to ensure the custody and safety of juveniles; implements constructive programs designed to establish a harmonious environment; identifies and reports any unusual occurrences that may affect the general social atmosphere of the juvenile care facility; confers regularly with appropriate staff members regarding special problems of individual juveniles; guides and directs group and play activities; counsels and helps juveniles, individually or in groups, to assist them in adjustment and the development of socially desirable habits and behavior patterns; supervises and accompanies juveniles during their transit to and presence at locations where their attendance is required; drives vehicles for the transportation of juveniles in care; regularly takes attendance of juveniles; prepares records and reports as required; performs related work.

Requirements

1. High school graduation or its equivalent plus four years of satisfactory full-time paid experience in group, community, or institutional work involving juveniles (ages 10–18); or
2. An associate degree from an accredited college or completion of 60 credits of study at an accredited college, plus two years of experience as described above under (1); or
3. A combination of education and/or experience which is equivalent to (1) or (2). However, all candidates must possess a high school diploma or its equivalent, and must have at least one year of experience as described under (1) above.

Foreign education will be evaluated by the Department of Personnel to determine comparability to education received in domestic accredited educational institutions to determine the extent to which it will be credited toward meeting the requirements for this examination.

License. At the time of appointment as a Juvenile Counselor, possession of a valid motor vehicle driver's license is required.

Test Information

There is a written qualifying test. A minimum score of 70% is required. Education, training and experience, weigh 100%, 70% required. The written test will be of the multiple-choice type and may include questions on juvenile care practices; understanding and interpreting the criminal justice system as it relates to juveniles; understanding and preparing written reports, including completing standardized forms and performing simple arithmetic calculations; and other related areas. Only those candidates who qualify on the multiple-choice test will have their education, training, and experience rated.

The education, training, and experience rating will be based on statements on the Experience Paper, which must be filled out completely and in detail, including dates and number of hours per week worked and salary earned. Candidates are advised to list all education, training, and experience for which credit may be given as described below. Once they have filed their application, candidates will not be permitted to add additional education, training, and experience beyond that needed to meet the minimum requirements.

Education, training, and experience will not be found acceptable unless it is verifiable. Education, training, and experience listed on the Experience Paper will receive credit only to the extent that they are described clearly and in detail.

You will receive a score of 70% for meeting the minimum requirements.

After the minimum requirements are met, credit will be given for a maximum of an additional six years of full-time paid experience with delinquent, violent, or emotionally disturbed juveniles (ages 10–18) on the following basis:

1. Three points per year will be given for each additional year of full-time paid experience as a case worker with juveniles in an institutional setting or long-term facilities such as detention centers, shelters, residential treatment centers, rehabilitation centers for delinquents, or child care institutions for juveniles.
2. Four points per year will be given for each additional year of full-time paid experience with juveniles as a group leader or recreation worker.
3. Five points per year will be given for each additional year of full-time paid experience as a child care worker, counselor, or houseparent with juveniles in an institutional setting or long-term facilities such as detention centers, shelters, residential treatment centers, rehabilitation centers for delinquents, or child care institutions for juveniles.

Experience as a guidance counselor in a school setting, or as a teacher, will not be accepted for the purpose of obtaining additional credit on the test for education, training, and experience. Acceptable part-time paid experience will be prorated.

The maximum allowable rating for this examination is 100.

Investigative, Social Welfare, and Legal Positions

INVESTIGATIVE OCCUPATIONS

The range of activities performed by modern state and municipal authorities means that they have a great need for information. Hence the need for investigators. Investigators have a wide variety of functions: to examine claims for benefits or compensation to ensure that they are valid and conform with the relevant regulations; to gather evidence of fraud and other wrongdoing to be used in various legal actions; to discover violations of rules and regulations.

SAMPLE EXAMINATION ANNOUNCEMENTS

State
Compensation Claims Investigator I, II

Job Description

Compensation Claims Investigators investigate Workers' Compensation and Disability Benefits claims. They obtain necessary information and documents from employers, claimants, witnesses, co-workers, government officials, medical personnel, other insurance carriers, and any other concerned parties. They may be required to conduct on-site personal interviews, at any location, in order to obtain the necessary information regarding a claim. They may also work in the office to aid the Claims Unit in the preparation of cases and to prepare reports and provide information to employers, claimants, and others regarding the Worker's Compensation Law and other related matters. Field work and/or office duties, as necessary, are required of Compensation Claims Investigators I; extensive field work and more complex assignments are required of Compensation Claims Investigators II.

Requirements

On or before the date of the written tests, candidates must have had satisfactory experience in a field investigative position requiring the submission of detailed narrative reports as follows:

1. For Compensation Claims Investigator I, two years.
2. For Compensation Claims Investigator II, three years.

Qualifying experience includes experience in positions such as police detective, detective-investigator, insurance investigator, private investigator, Federal, state, or military investigator or similar positions which involve trial preparation.

Nonqualifying experience includes tax collection, auditing, credit checking, inspection, compliance monitoring, research, and patrol, guard, or watch duty.

Study at an accredited college or university may be substituted for the above experience on the basis of one year of study (30 credits) being considered the equivalent of one year of experience. Substitution of college study will be accepted for up to two years of the required work experience. Appropriate part-time and volunteer experience, which can be verified, will be accepted on a prorated basis.

At the time of appointment, successful candidates may be required to possess a valid license to operate a motor vehicle or otherwise demonstrate their capacity to meet the transportation needs of the job. Field work travel expenses will be reimbursed on a fixed schedule.

Test Information

There will be a written test which candidates must pass in order to be considered for appointment. The written test will be designed to test for knowledge, skills, and/or abilities in such areas as

1. Reasoning clearly and selecting the proper course of action in conducting investigations.
2. Investigative techniques.
3. Evaluating information and evidence.
4. Understanding and interpreting written material.
5. Preparing written material.

State—Municipal Investigator

Job Description

Under supervision, makes investigation designed to prevent or detect violations of laws relating to tax liabilities and delinquencies or violations of miscellaneous rules and regulations of various state or local agencies; makes investigations designed to determine qualifications for civil service employment; performs related work.

Examples of Typical Tasks. Investigates both clients and personnel of the Department of Social Services to obtain information about possible violations of Social Service Law; interviews applicants in their homes or in the office to determine eligibility for public assistance. Obtains information regarding liability of delinquent taxpayers. Investigates corporations and organizations soliciting funds from the public. Makes searches in depositories of public and private records to determine financial standing of tax debtors. Apprehends violators of laws governing solicitation of funds from the public, causes arrests, signs complaints, makes physical inspections and diagrams at scenes of accident. Locates and interviews prospective witnesses in actions in which the state or city or its agencies are defendants, conducts examinations under oath, and serves legal process. Investigates complaints about state or city prison inmates. Acts as internal security investigator for various city agencies. May issue summonses and seize evidence; may be required to carry firearms.

Assembles and verifies data pertinent to settlement or adjudication of tort claims. Verifies information concerning education, experience, and other personal qualifications bearing upon character and fitness of applicants for employment in the civil service. Examines and analyzes records and documents. Reports on results of personal interviews or interrogation of witnesses. Testifies at hearings and in court proceedings.

Requirements

1. High school graduation or evidence of having passed an examination for the high school equivalency diploma (GED) and four years of full-time paid experience as an investigator, at least two years of which must have been as an investigator in the field; or
2. An associate degree from an accredited college or completion of two years of study (60 credits) at an accredited college and two years of experience as an investigator; or
3. A bachelor's degree from an accredited college: or
4. A combination of education and/or experience which is equivalent to (1), (2), or (3) above. All candidates who qualify under (4) must have at least one year of full-time paid experience as an investigator in the field.

For appointment to the Special Investigations Unit of the Department of Finance, an individual must be eligible for certification as a Peace Officer under the State Criminal Procedures Law.

Foreign education will be evaluated by the Department of Personnel to determine comparability to education received in domestic accredited educational institutions to determine the extent to which it will be credited toward meeting the requirements for this examination.

Test Information

The rating on this examination will be based solely on education and experience. *There will be no other competitive test.* Education and Experience weigh 100%, a minimum of 70% is required.

Education and Experience. Education and experience will be calculated on the basis of candidates' responses on the Answer Sheet. This rating will be verified on the basis of information contained in the

Experience Paper. Therefore, the Experience Paper must be filled out completely and in detail including exact dates, number of hours per week worked, and salary earned. Candidates are advised to list *all* education and experience for which credit may be given as described below since they will not be permitted to add any education or experience once they have filed their applications. Education or experience will not be found acceptable unless satisfactory and verifiable. Education and experience listed on the Experience Paper will receive credit only if described clearly and in detail. You will receive a score of 70% for meeting the minimum requirements. After the minimum requirements have been set, additional credit will be granted for education and/or experience on the following basis:

1. Five points will be granted for each year of full-time paid experience as a claim examiner, claim adjuster, or insurance investigator investigating claims for personal, casualty, or property loss or damage; a police officer or state trooper engaged in investigation activities; a licensed private investigator; an investigator or claim examiner for the state or the federal government; an agent for the Federal Bureau of Alcohol, Tobacco and Firearms or similar federal law enforcement body; an investigator for the Criminal Investigation Division in the United States Armed Forces; or experience in the title of Investigator, Confidential Investigator, or Claim Examiner for an agency or department of the City government.

   Full-time experience means 30 hours or more per week on a regular basis. Part-time experience is less than 30 hours per week but must be at least 15 hours per week to receive credit.
2. One point will be granted for each three-credit course in criminal justice, criminalistics, or paralegal studies from an accredited college.

The maximum rating that can be granted on this education and experience test is 100.

Advancement

Employees in the title of Investigator are accorded promotion opportunities, when eligible, to the title of Senior Investigator.

State
Unemployment Insurance Investigator Trainee
Unemployment Insurance Investigator

Job Description

Unemployment Insurance Investigators investigate cases of alleged fraud or collusion by claimants or employers, cases of employee misconduct, complex cases involving self-employing entities and corporations to determine employee status and claimant eligibility, and cases where complex issues and facts require lengthy exploration to establish proper findings. They conduct formal examinations involving sworn testimony of employers, claimants, and witnesses. They locate, collect, collate, and analyze evidence for comprehensive written reports covering facts upon which to make and issue determinations on behalf of the Commissioner of Labor. They need to be free to travel and provide a satisfactory means of transportation whenever necessary.

Unemployment Insurance Investigator Trainees receive on-the-job training while performing duties similar to those described for Unemployment Insurance Investigator. Upon satisfactory completion of a one-year traineeship they will be advanced to the position of Unemployment Insurance Investigator without further examination.

Requirements

On or before the date of the written tests, candidates must meet the following requirements:

1. For Unemployment Investigator Trainee: a bachelor's degree from an accredited college or university.
2. For Unemployment Investigator:
   a. *Specialized experience:* one year of experience in a field investigative position requiring the submission of detailed narrative reports.
   b. *General experience:* four years of business experience or experience in a public contact position. College credits can be substituted for up to four years of this general experience only, at the rate that 15 semester credit hours equals six months of experience. However, you still must indicate one year of specialized experience.

Field investigation is gathering and securing information and evidence from a variety of sources, away from your official work station, through independent, nonstructured activities, including the preparation and submission of detailed narrative reports, in support of legal activities which could lead to prosecution. Experience in positions such as Police Detective, Insurance Investigator, Private Investigator, Federal Investigator, an investigative position in the Armed Forces, or in field investigation positions involving trial preparation are examples of what might be considered as meeting the experience requirement.

Experience in auditing, inspection, research or in positions in tax collecting, credit checking, police patrolling, guarding or watching, would not be considered as meeting the experience requirement.

Appropriate part-time and volunteer experience, which can be verified, will be accepted on a pro-rated basis.

Applicants for both examinations who expect to meet the educational requirement by __ 19__ will be admitted to the written test. If they pass the written test, they will not be considered for appointment until such time as they submit proof of successful completion of the educational requirement to the State Department of Civil Service.

As these positions require substantial travel, especially in carrying out field investigations, successful candidates must either possess a currently valid license to operate a motor vehicle and have access to a motor vehicle on a daily basis or otherwise demonstrate their capacity to meet the transportation needs of the job in carrying out their responsibilities in any location where these positions exist in order to be considered for appointment. Field work travel expenses will be reimbursed on a fixed schedule.

Test Information

Unemployment Investigator Trainee: There will be a written test which candidates must pass in order to be considered for appointment.

Unemployment Investigator: There will be a written test and an oral test. Candidates must pass both in order to be considered for appointment. Only those candidates who pass the written test will be notified to appear for the oral test. The Department of Civil Service reserves the right to call to the oral test only a sufficient number of candidates necessary to fill existing and anticipated positions. Only passing scores on the written test will be considered in computing final scores.

Scope of Written Tests. The written tests will be designed to test for knowledge, skills, and/or abilities in such areas as:

1. Reasoning clearly in selecting the proper course of action in investigating techniques
2. Interviewing and investigative techniques
3. Evaluating information and evidence
4. Understanding and interpreting written material
5. Preparing written material

Candidates for Unemployment Insurance Investigator Trainee will be tested on factors 1, 3, 4, and 5. Candidates for Unemployment Investigator will be tested on factors 2, 3, 4, and 5.

State
Employment Interviewer Supervisor
Employer Relations Representative

Job Description

Employment Interviewer Supervisor performs supervisory or advanced employment service work in interviewing and referring job applicants. Employees in this class supervise a small group of employment interviewers and clerical personnel engaged in interviewing and referral activities in a local employment office; or, in the absence of supervisory responsibilities, independently perform all interviewing, referral, and related functions in a claims office, itinerant office, or within the community.

Occasional travel may be necessary. Offers of Employment will be made only if candidates are willing to travel and are willing to drive a government vehicle or arrange or provide their own transportation. Travel expenses will be reimbursed at specified rates.

Employer Relations Representatives perform promotional and technical work in developing and maintaining employer relations to promote the services of the Department of Labor and Industry's Office of Employment Security. Employees in this class are responsible for promoting the use of placement and technical services offered to employers by the Office of Employment Security. They are responsible for providing advice and assistance with respect to the selection and placement of workers and for explaining the technical personnel services offered the employer through employment services.

Employees will be required to travel. Offers of employment will be made only if candidates are willing to drive a government vehicle or arrange or provide their own transportation. Travel expenses will be reimbursed at specified rates.

Requirements

To speed up test scheduling, your qualifications may not be reviewed until after you have taken the test. Please make sure you meet *all* requirements, because if you *do not,* your test results *will not* be counted. If you are not sure if you qualify, contact one of the Commission offices.

Candidates must be state residents, of good moral character, and capable of performing the physical activities of the job.

Employment Interviewer Supervisor

1. One year as an Employment Interviewer; or
2. Five years of responsible public contact work or demonstrated community leadership which involved obtaining, providing, and evaluating information concerning employment or employability; or
3. Any equivalent combination of experience and training.

Employer Relations Representative

1. One year as an Employment Interviewer; or
2. Five years of employment service work or public contact work related to employment service activities; or
3. Any equivalent combination of experience and training.

Substitution of Training for Experience: College-level training with major coursework in job-related areas such as counseling, sociology, business administration, etc., may be substituted for the required experience on the basis of *one* year of training for *one* year of experience to a maximum of *four* years. Non-job-related college level training may be substituted for the required experience to a maximum of two years.

Test Information

The examination will consist of a written test. Applicants must pass the test to be considered for employment. This will be a three-hour multiple-choice test covering the subject areas noted below.

Subject Areas	Number of Questions by Job Title	
	EIS	ERR
Interpretation of written material (reading comprehension)	15	15
Labor economics: industry and employment	20	20
Office of Employment security services and programs	15	15
Principles, practices, and techniques of employment interviewing, referral, and placement	25	25
Principles, practices, and techniques of employment services promotion and public relations	20	45
Principles, practices, and techniques of supervision	25	—
Total	120	120

SOCIAL WELFARE OCCUPATIONS

Those involved in the social welfare field are community troubleshooters. Through direct counseling, referral to other services, or policymaking and advocacy, they help individuals, families, and groups cope with their problems. Those in the area of planning and policy help people understand how social systems operate and propose ways of bringing about needed change in institutions such as health services, housing, or education. Among the major helping professions, social work is distinguished by a tradition of concern for the poor and the disadvantaged.

State—Municipal Social Worker

Job Description

Under supervision, is responsible for the provision of psychosocial services to children, adults, families, and/or groups in a public agency or setting, such as a municipal hospital, prison health service, or social services center; performs related tasks.

Examples of Typical Tasks. Conducts or participates in the intake process to obtain information relevant to formulating a psychosocial evaluation and social work treatment plan; interviews patients/clients, relatives, agency staff, or members of the community regarding patients'/clients' ability to function in the community; implements treatment plan by providing individual and group counseling and/or concrete services; plans for discharge and/or aftercare; makes referrals to agencies or community resources, or provides direct services; confers and consults with professional and technical personnel in implementing a multidisciplinary approach to patient/client care; attends meetings, staff conferences, social work staff meetings and rounds; orients and educates members of other professional disciplines in social work concepts and functions; participates in work of selected staff committees; serves as liaison with community agencies; may supervise fieldwork placement of graduate and undergraduate social work students; may supervise volunteers and other auxiliary personnel; initiates and/or participates in special studies and research projects; maintains appropriate case records and statistical reports and prepares other reports as required; may practice within one or more social work specialities, i.e., casework, group work, or community organization; determines the desirability of the placement of children; provides adoption services; assists unmarried pregnant women by arranging for maternity shelter care and by planning for suitable care of the child; interviews children and parents to discuss behavior problems and to determine appropriate services indicated; prepares children and parents to accept services; analyzes neighborhood or area problems and needs; evaluates alternate care arrangements for the elderly; provides social work services in a prison setting.

Requirements

Education. A master's degree in social work from an accredited school of social work. Foreign education will be evaluated by the Department of Personnel to determine comparability to education received in domestic accredited educational institutions.

Certificate Requirements. All candidates will be required to have a valid certificate of Certified Social Worker (CSW) issued by the State Department of Education within one year of the date of appointment. This certificate must be presented to the appointing officer at the time of appointment or, if it is obtained after appointment, at the time it is received. Employees who fail to obtain their certificate within one year after their appointment will automatically have their probationary period extended for no more than six months.

Test Information

Education and experience, weight 100, 70% required. There will be no competitive test other than an evaluation of education and experience.

Your education and experience rating will be based on your statements on the Experience Paper which must be filled out completely and in detail, including dates and number of hours worked per week. List all education and experience for which credit may be given as described below, since you will not be able to add information after filing has closed. Education or experience will not be found acceptable unless it is verifiable. Education and experience listed on the Experience Paper will receive credit only to the extent that they are described clearly and in detail.

You will receive a score of 70 for meeting the minimum requirements.

After the minimum requirements are met, you may receive credit for a maximum of an additional 9 years of experience, accrued within the last 10 years, on the basis of the categories described below. Each year of experience may be credited under only one category.

1. One point will be granted for each year of full-time paid social work experience, prior to receiving the master's degree in social work, in a recognized child welfare, adult or family services agency, or in a hospital, mental health, or prison setting.
2. Three points will be granted for each year of full-time paid social work experience, subsequent to receiving the master's degree in social work, in a recognized child welfare, adult or family services agency, or in a hospital, mental health, or prison setting.

Additionally, three points will be credited for possession, at the time of filing the application, of a valid certificate of Certified Social Worker (CSW) issued by the State Department of Education.

The maximum rating that can be granted on the education and experience test is 100.

Advancement

Employees in the title of Social Worker are accorded promotion opportunities, when eligible, to the title of Supervisor I (Social Work).

State
Social Work Assistants II, II (Spanish-speaking), III, III (Spanish-speaking) and Psychiatric Social Work Assistants, II, II (Spanish-speaking), III, III (Spanish-speaking)

Job Description

Social Work Assistants II and III and Social Work Assistants II and III (Spanish-Speaking) are employed in the residential facilities and community programs of the State Office of Mental Retardation and Developmental Disabilities. Psychiatric Social Work Assistants II and III and Psychiatric Social Work Assistants II and III (Spanish-speaking) are employed in the residential facilities and community programs of the State Office of Mental Health and in the treatment centers of the State Division of Alcoholism and Alcohol Abuse. Positions exist in various locations throughout the state.

Social Work Assistants II or **Psychiatric Social Work Assistants II** function as members of an interdisciplinary treatment team and assist professional level social work staff in providing a full range of social work services to clients.

Social Work Assistants III or **Psychiatric Social Work Assistants III** have duties similar to those of an Assistant II, but are required to handle more complex issues and to exercise more independent judgment in performing those duties.

If appointed to a Spanish-speaking position, performs duties similar to those described above but works primarily with Spanish-speaking clients.

Requirements

On or before the date of the written tests, all candidates must have a bachelor's degree in social work, social service, human services, or community mental health. Only degrees with majors specifically entitled "Social Work, Social Service, Human Services, or Community Mental Health" will be considered qualifying. In addition, candidates for Social Work Assistant III and Psychiatric Social Work Assistant III must have had one year of post-bachelor's social work or social service experience.

If candidates have a master's degree in social work, they will be conditionally admitted into both the Assistant II and Assistant III examinations. However, if they achieve passing scores on the written test, they will not be considered for appointment until such time as they submit proof of their degree to the Department of Civil Service.

If candidates expect to receive an appropriate bachelor's degree, they will be admitted conditionally into the Assistant II examinations. However, if they achieve passing scores on the written test, they will not be considered for appointment until such time as they submit proof of their degree to the Department of Civil Service.

Substitution

1. Thirty credits in a graduate program in one of the four fields listed above may be substituted for the bachelor's degree.
2. An appropriate bachelor's degree plus thirty graduate credits in social work can be substituted for the one year of required experience for Social Work Assistant III and Psychiatric Social Work Assistant III.

Note

1. Education must have been received from a regionally accredited college or university.
2. Appropriate part-time and volunteer experience, which can be verified, will be accepted on a prorated basis.

3. Candidates interested in the Spanish-speaking position must be able to understand Spanish as spoken in the areas assigned and to speak it fluently. Fluency must be demonstrated at the time of the appointment interview.

Test Information

Selection. There will be a written test which candidates must pass in order to be considered for appointment. The written tests will be designed to measure knowledge and skills in such areas as:

1. **Interviewing.** These questions will test for a knowledge of the principles and practices employed in obtaining information from individuals and making certain judgments based on that information as an integral part of carrying out the programs or services of a public agency. Questions generally require candidates to apply the principles, practices, and techniques of effective interviewing to hypothetical interviewing situations. Some questions will present an interviewing situation in which some problem has arisen. The candidate's task is to choose which of the four alternative courses of action shown should most appropriately be taken under the given circumstances.
2. **Development and Maintenance of Client Records.** These questions may include, but will not necessarily be limited to, combining or extracting information, recognizing concise summaries, recognizing objective versus subjective narratives, distinguishing central from peripheral information, and classifying information into appropriate categories.
3. **Characteristics, Behavior, and Problems of the Disabled and Nondisabled.** These questions may include, but will not necessarily be limited to, causes and prognosis for various disabilities; physical, psychological, intellectual, and social characteristics of the disabled; normal and abnormal human behavior; body language and nonverbal communication; and value conflicts and personal bias.
4. **Principles and Practices of Social Casework.** These questions may include, but will not necessarily be limited to, social work standards and points of view; purposes and functions of an interdisciplinary treatment team; client and family rights; confidentiality; developing, implementing, and evaluating client treatment plans; conflict resolution, supportive counseling approaches; behavior modification principles and techniques; programs of client assistance; and situations requiring supervisory consultation.

State—Municipal
Promotion to Supervisor I (Social Work)

Job Description

Under supervision, supervises a unit or group of social work, auxiliary and other personnel engaged in providing social work services in a municipal hospital; performs related work.

Examples of Typical Tasks. Screens cases, makes work assignments, reads and reviews workers case records and reports, and evaluates work performance; gives guidance to subordinate staff in social work techniques, methods, and practices; conducts individual and group staff conferences; trains staff in relevant policies and procedures; works cooperatively with physicians, nurses, and other professional personnel; participates in conferences with higher level supervisory personnel and with representatives of federal, state, city, and voluntary social work agencies, organizations and groups; cooperates with community service agencies to utilize available resources; handles a caseload, including more difficult cases; prepares and supervises the preparation of case records and required reports.

Requirements

Eligibility. Open to each employee of the Health and Hospitals Corporation who, on the day of the written test, is permanently employed in the title of Social Worker and is not otherwise ineligible. However, certification from the promotion list shall be limited to those employees who have served permanently in the eligible title for a period of not less than one year prior to the date of promotion.

Certification Requirement. All candidates will be required to have a valid and current certificate of Certified Social Worker (CSW) within one year of the date of appointment. This certificate must be presented to the appointing officer at the time of appointment or, if it is obtained after appointment, at the time it is received. Candidates who fail to obtain their certificate by the end of six months will automatically have their probationary period extended for up to six months.

Test Information

Written, weight 85; seniority, weight 15. A score of at least 70% on the written test is required. The written test is multiple-choice and may include questions on principles and techniques of supervision; interpersonal relations, including developing constructive working relationships with staff, patients/clients, public and private agency representatives and hospital personnel of other disciplines; knowledge and interpretation of agency rules, regulations, and procedures relative to social service, health and mental health standards, as mandated by regulatory agencies; generic social work principles, practices, and techniques including knowledge of social systems and support services; principles and techniques of teaching, training, and staff development; and other related areas.

Selective Certification. The eligible list resulting from this examination may be selectively certified to fill vacancies which require a working knowledge of both English and another language.

State—Municipal

Caseworker

Job Description

Under supervision, with considerable latitude for independent action, individually or as a team member, identifies, develops, and implements social service plans for disadvantaged clients, including recipients of public assistance and child welfare services, and adults/children receiving institutional care; may also determine eligibility for these services; may perform investigative activities; performs related work.

Examples of Typical Tasks. Provides comprehensive health-related and social services to disadvantaged clients such as aged, disabled, or handicapped adults, multi-problem families, and the unemployed or underemployed. Reads and analyzes case records for information on background, agency contacts, and other matters bearing on eligibility or need for services. Confers with supervisor on an individual basis to evaluate progress of cases. Helps the client to identify the need for services and develops service plan with client; provides supportive counseling or undertakes activity to facilitate the securing of these services. Makes referrals to and confers with representatives of other agencies in such areas as education, rehabilitation, housing, employment, and health-related services; follows up to determine whether services were provided and utilized. Maintains case folders and administrative forms and controls to report activity and to provide information for evaluative studies of effectiveness of such activity. May function as a member of a team, as well as on an individual basis; may confer regularly with the total team to evaluate progress, share information, and plan future activity in identifying and implementing services. Interviews applicants, at their homes or in the office, and determines eligibility for institutional or hospital care, foster home care, or day care placement of children. Investigates and verifies information obtained on family composition, income, financial and other resources, past employment, legally and socially responsible relatives, status of children. Makes collateral visits to employers, relatives, friends, hospitals, schools, other public and private agencies, and community resources as may be required. Makes social studies of clients, indicating interpersonal relationships of members of the family, problem areas, strengths, and weaknesses of members. May investigate cases of child abuse and neglect and locate absent parents.

Requirements

A bachelor's degree from an accredited college is required.

Foreign education will be evaluated by the Department of Personnel to determine comparability to education received in domestic accredited educational institutions to determine the extent to which it will be credited toward meeting the requirements for this examination.

Test Information

Written, weight 100, 70% required. The written test will be of the multiple-choice type and may include questions on interviewing methods; interpersonal relations, including counseling and developing rapport with disadvantaged clients, and working effectively with others; interpretation of rules, regulations, and procedures, and Social Service laws and guidelines; methods of investigating child abuse, and locating absent parents; forms completion and record keeping; basic arithmetic; and other related areas.

Selective Certification. The eligible list resulting from this examination may be selectively certified to fill vacancies in the title of Caseworker which require a working knowledge of both English and another language.

Advancement

Employees in the title of Caseworker are accorded promotion opportunities, when eligible, to the title of Supervisor I (Welfare).

State
Casework Supervisors I, II, and III

Job Description

Employees in these job titles perform direct, supervisory, or administrative social casework services in the field of human services.

A **Casework Supervisor I** directs and trains caseworkers and casework trainees. Work includes providing direct casework services for clients and may include administering a small autonomous social services program, a specialized program, or a definitive major program area.

A **Supervisor II** directs a group of caseworkers who are engaged in providing a wide variety of social services.

A **Casework Supervisor III** supervises a group of casework supervisors. In the smaller counties the work is on county-wide basis and includes responsibility for development and maintenance of the county's social services program under the direction of the county administrator.

Requirements

To speed up test scheduling, your qualifications may not be reviewed until after you have taken the test. Please make sure you meet *all* requirements, because if you *do not,* your test results *will not* be counted. If you are not sure if you qualify, contact one of the Commission's offices listed at the end of this announcement.

Candidates must be willing to travel. Travel expenses will be paid.

Candidates must be state residents, of good moral character, and capable of performing the physical activities of the job.

Test Information

The two-hour written test will cover the subject areas noted below.

Subject Areas	Number of Questions		
	CWS 1	CWS 2	CWS 3
Basic principles of supervision	20	20	20
Social casework principles and techniques	20	20	20
Human behavior	20	20	20
Social service program interpretation and community organization	—	20	20
Community social service program planning and development	—	—	20
Total	60	80	100

Written tests will be scheduled as soon as possible after applications are received. This requires an appointment which can be obtained by submitting your application directly to the office where you wish to be tested. Note that not all locations are used all the time.

After you take the test, retests will not be allowed.

Minimum Requirements

Casework Supervisor I. Two years of experience in public or private social work *and* a bachelor's degree.

Casework Supervisor II. Three years of experience in public or private social work, including one year in a public welfare program *and* a bachelor's degree.

Casework Supervisor III. Four years of experience in public or private social work, including two years in a public welfare program one of which must have been in a supervisory capacity, *and* a bachelor's degree.

All Job Titles. Any equivalent combination of the above experience and training will be acceptable.

State
Parole Officer, Parole Officer (Spanish-speaking)

Job Description

Parole Officers are employed by the State Division of Parole and are assigned to State Correctional Facilities and in the field offices of the Division. Parole Officers assigned to an area field office provide supervision and guidance to an assigned case load of releasees from state and local correctional facilities and help releasees comply with the terms and conditions of their release. In a correctional facility, you would assess needs, prepare evaluations, and provide guidance to an assigned case load of inmates and help prepare them for release to the community. In some cases, you would supervise juvenile offenders and work releasees. You might be assigned to any of these assignments at any time. You would have both social work and law enforcement functions, requiring firearms training and a knowledge of arrest procedures. You would work with community-based organizations to deliver needed services to an offender population under court-imposed sentences.

Probation. Appointees will be required to serve a 26- to 52-week probationary period during which performance will be periodically reviewed and carefully evaluated. Those who do not perform satisfactorily during the probationary period may be terminated at any time after eight weeks of probationary service.

Requirements

Minimum Qualifications. On or before the date of the written test, candidates must have a bachelor's degree. You must also have had three years of experience as a social caseworker or group-worker in a recognized social services, correctional, criminal justice, community, or human welfare agency. A law degree or a master's degree in social work, probation and parole, sociology, criminal justice, psychology, or in a related social service or criminal justice field may be substituted for up to one year of the required experience. Appropriate part-time and volunteer experience, which can be verified, will be accepted on a prorated basis.

Education must have been received at an accredited college or university. To qualify for this examination, casework experience must have focused primarily on the establishment of an on-going, one-to-one relationship between the caseworker and client, with the development of treatment plans and implementation of appropriate treatment services. Group-worker experience must have focused primarily on responsibility for conducting group sessions designed to provide the participants with therapeutic services for significant social problems such as alcohol and drug abuse, mental and emotional problems, family disturbance, and delinquency. An important criterion used in determining acceptable group work experience is the applicant's formalized training in group dynamics or social work as opposed to participation in informal group sessions.

Types of experience that would not be considered qualifying are group work oriented toward behavior modification in such areas as self-improvement or the use of tobacco; teaching; para-professional aide; job placement; house parenting; camp counseling; and nonsocial work therapy, i.e., speech and hearing, recreation, occupational or physical therapy.

Additional Requirements. Successful candidates must also satisfy the following requirements at the time of appointment:

Character. Candidates must be qualified to serve as a public officer of the state. This requires U.S. citizenship and state residence. Conviction of a felony will bar appointment. Conviction of a misdemeanor or other violations of the law may bar appointment. Because of the nature of the position, successful candidates will undergo an investigative screening which may include a thorough character investigation.

Physical/Medical. Candidates must meet the physical/medical standards for Parole Officer, which include a vision requirement. Physical examinations will be administered prior to appointment.

License. Appointees may be required to travel in order to perform field work duties of the position. Therefore, at the time of appointment, candidates will be required to possess a valid license to operate a motor vehicle or demonstrate ability to travel by alternate means in their assigned area. Authorized travel will be reimbursed according to a fixed schedule.

These are peace officer positions under state law. All appointees will be required to participate in, and satisfactorily complete, all requirements of a training program. Training will include classroom instruction in such areas as basic law, social work practice and case management, firearms training, and arrest procedures. Successful completion of the training program is mandatory for continued employment.

Successful candidates who are considered for appointment as Parole Officer (Spanish-speaking) will be required, at the time of the interview, to demonstrate proficiency in speaking Spanish as spoken in the areas assigned. Candidates who cannot demonstrate proficiency in Spanish will still be considered for appointment as Parole Officer.

Test Information

There will be **a written test** which you must pass in order to be considered for appointment. The written test will be designed to test for knowledge, skills, and/or abilities in such areas as:

1. Preparing written material;
2. Interviewing;
3. Principles and practices of casework and counseling in a correctional/parole rehabilitation setting;
4. Knowledge and understanding of social issues related to minorities, the poor, and ethnic groups and cultures.

Successful candidates will be notified, in score order, to appear for the physical examination and investigative screening prior to appointment.

State
Parole Investigators and Parole Agents

Job Description

Parole Investigator. This is technical investigative work in the state parole and probation system. Employees conduct investigations and evaluate offenders' backgrounds prior to their parole, sentence, or pardon. Investigators write reports and make recommendations based on the data obtained. Work involves performing some beginning level parole agent duties as part of the formal on-the-job training program to develop technical competence and understanding of the occupational area. Work is performed under the supervision of a parole supervisor.

Parole Agent. Employees provide counseling and related services to probationers and parolees to aid them in their adjustment to community life. Agents maintain contacts with families, friends, social service agencies, employers, and clergy to assist offenders in their adjustment. Employees develop rehabilitation plans, supervise probationers and parolees, and investigate their activities to determine if they are violating regulations. Agents determine if rehabilitation plans are satisfactory and prepare follow-up reports. There may be an element of physical danger involved in working with probation and parole violators. Although this work is regulated by law and detailed procedures, employees are required to make decisions directly affecting the public safety and personal liberties of individuals.

The Parole Agent I is the beginning level of the series and receives formal and on-the-job training. Supervision is received from a parole supervisor.

Requirements

Parole Investigator

1. Three years of experience in criminal justice, human services, or related fields including one year of investigative work which involved detailed and legally valid fact-finding and reporting assignments; *or*
2. Any equivalent combination of experience and training.

Parole Agent

1. A bachelor's degree; *or*
2. Any equivalent combination of experience and training.

Applicants must be state residents, of good moral character, and capable of performing the physical activities of the job.

Applicants must have a valid state driver's license.

Evaluation Policy

Parole Investigator. Acceptable experience in investigative work would include the following job titles: police officer, detective, drug investigator, enforcement officer, corrections counselor, insurance adjuster or investigator, field auditor, etc.

Acceptable human services experience must be providing direct services to disadvantaged clients. Examples of human service agencies: welfare agencies, employment service agencies, human relations agencies, Peace Corps, etc.

Background Investigation. Prior to appointment, a complete background investigation will be conducted by the State Police in conjunction with the Board of Probation and Parole. Section 10 of the Civil Service Commission Application for Employment/Promotion *must* be thoroughly and accurately completed in order to facilitate the investigation.

Medical Examination. Prior to appointment, a complete medical examination will be conducted by a physician appointed by the Board of Probation and Parole.

Both the Background Investigation and the Medical Examination must be successfully completed to the satisfaction of the Board of Probation and Parole and the Civil Service Commission before any appointments will be made.

Test Information

This will be a three-hour multiple-choice test covering the subject areas noted below.

Subject Matter Area	Number of Questions by Job Title	
	Parole Investigator	Parole Agent I
General criminology	15	15
Behavior, motivation, adjustment	25	25
Investigation	30	30
Community resources	15	15
Correspondence—reports	15	15
Social casework	—	20
Total	100	120

State
Social Services Disability Analyst Trainee I, II

Job Description

These positions exist with the Office of Disability Determinations of the State Department of Social Service. The traineeships for which these examinations are being announced lead to appointment at the journey level as Social Services Disability Analyst I.

Social Services Disability Analyst Trainees I serve a two-year traineeship which includes extensive classroom and on-the-job training in all aspects of processing claims for disability benefits under Titles II and XVI of the Social Security Act. After satisfactory completion of the first year of the traineeship, candidates are advanced to Trainee II without further examination.

Social Services Disability Analyst Trainees II serve a one-year traineeship, during which they receive classroom training in processing initial disability claims and also undergo extensive training in evaluating continuing claims for disability benefits. After satisfactory completion of this year of traineeship, candidates would be advanced to Social Services Disability Analyst I without further examination.

Candidates who achieve a passing score on the written test who are interested in appointment to the Spanish-speaking positions must demonstrate their ability to speak Spanish, as spoken in the areas assigned, at the time of the employment interview.

Requirements

On or before the date of the written tests, candidates must meet the following requirements: for Trainee I, a bachelor's degree; for Trainee II:

1. A license to practice as a registered professional nurse (RN) or as a Physician's Assistant, in any state or territory of the United States *and* one year of full-time experience as an RN or as a Physician's Assistant; or
2. A bachelor's degree in the natural sciences field with at least 24 credit hours in one or a combination of the following: biology, biochemistry, human anatomy, or human physiology; or
3. A bachelor's degree in psychology with 24 credit hours in psychology; or
4. A master's degree in vocational rehabilitation; or
5. One year of experience adjudicating disability claims under Titles II and XVI of the Social Security Act; or
6. Four years of full-time experience in evaluating claims for medical benefits during which you were primarily responsible for making determinations as to the appropriateness and compatibility of medical evidence to treatment prescribed. **Important!** Experience in routine processing and/or adjusting of claims, or clerical experience involving forms completion, transmittal, or review is *not* acceptable.

Substitution. Successful completion of college course work may be substituted for the experience required on the basis that 60 credit hours equals one year of experience.

Appropriate part-time and volunteer experience, which can be verified, will be accepted on a prorated basis.

Education must have been received at a regionally accredited college or university.

Test Information

Trainee I. There will be a **written test** which candidates must pass in order to be considered for appointment.

Trainee II. There will be a **written test** and an **oral test.** Candidates must pass both in order to be considered for appointment.

Only those candidates who achieve a passing score on the written tests will be notified to appear for the oral tests. Passing scores on the written tests will be considered when computing final scores.

Scope of Written Tests. The **written test** will be designed to test for knowledge, skills, and/or abilities in such areas as

1. Preparing written material.
2. Understanding and interpreting written material.
3. Interviewing.
4. Analyzing medical case information (in order to answer questions in this category, it is not necessary for candidates to have prior medical knowledge).
5. Understanding medical terminology.

State—Municipal Rehabilitation Counselor

Job Description

In the Health and Hospitals Corporation, under supervision, assists in the vocational rehabilitation of clients with disabilities or impairments; performs related work.

Examples of Typical Tasks. Interviews, orients, and gives individual and/or group counseling to patients in terms of their educational and occupational background, socio-economic status, medical prognosis, and test results; selects, administers, scores, and interprets vocational aptitude and other standardized tests; prepares reports of test findings used for vocational and educational training of patients; reviews case records for information relating to occupational adjustment; secures cooperation of public and private organizations and employers in the vocational training or placement of patients; participates in conferences and consultations on programs to assist patients in solving problems resulting from hospitalization, disability, or maladjustment; helps coordinate vocational programs in a hospital with medical, educational, recreational, and other nonmedical services made available by community agencies; refers patients to other services in the hospital; observes the progress of patients in vocational training programs, prepares case summaries and progress reports; keeps records; assists in maintenance of an occupational information library; assists in in-service training programs; applies pertinent federal, state, and local legislation.

Requirements

1. A master's degree from an accredited college in rehabilitation counseling or vocational rehabilitation counseling issued after completion of a two-year course of study which includes a supervised internship; or
2. A master's degree or 30 graduate credits from an accredited college in rehabilitation counseling or vocational rehabilitation counseling in a course of study which does not include a supervised internship, plus one year of full-time experience in rehabilitation counseling or vocational rehabilitation counseling; or
3. A bachelor's degree from an accredited college plus four years of full-time experience in rehabilitation counseling or vocational rehabilitation counseling; or
4. A combination of education and experience which is equivalent to 1, 2, or 3 above. However, except for those candidates who qualify under (1) above, all candidates must possess at least one year of full-time rehabilitation counseling or vocational rehabilitation counseling experience dealing with the mentally or physically disabled, handicapped, or aged. All candidates must possess a bachelor's degree.

Foreign education will be evaluated by the Department of Personnel to determine comparability to education received in domestic accredited educational institutions to determine the extent to which it will be credited toward meeting the requirements for this examination.

Test Information

Education, training, and experience weight 100, 70% required. There will be no competitive test other than an evaluation of education, training, and experience. The education, training, and experience rating will be based on your statements on the Experience Paper which must be filled out completely and in detail, including dates and numbers of hours per week worked and salary earned. List *all* education, training, and experience for which credit may be given as described below. Once you have filed your application, any additional education, training, or experience you add will not be evaluated beyond that needed to meet the minimum requirements.

Education, training, or experience listed on the Experience Paper will not be found acceptable unless it is verifiable, and will receive credit only to the extent that it is described clearly and in detail. You will receive a score of 70% for meeting the minimum requirements. After the minimum requirements are met, you may receive credit for a maximum of an additional ten years of experience on the following basis:

1. Credit at the rate of *one* point per year will be granted for each year of full-time paid experience in vocational guidance, occupational therapy, or psychological counseling, or other related therapeutic or counseling experience.
2. Credit at the rate of *two* points per year will be granted for each year of full-time paid experience in rehabilitation counseling or vocational rehabilitation counseling.
3. Credit at the rate of *three* points per year will be granted for each year of full-time paid experience supervising staff performing rehabilitation, counseling, or vocational rehabilitation counseling duties.

In addition to the above, *three* points will be granted for certification as a Certified Rehabilitation Counselor (CRC) granted by the Commission on Rehabilitation Counseling Certification (CRCC).

Acceptable part-time experience will be credited on a prorated basis.

The maximum rating that can be granted on this education, training, and experience test is 100 points.

Advancement

Employees in the title of Rehabilitation Counselor are accorded promotion opportunities, when eligible, to the title of Senior Rehabilitation Counselor.

Municipal Eligibility Specialist

Job Description

This position encompasses the performance of tasks under supervision with some latitude for independent action or decision. This work is performed under well-defined procedures of the Department of Social Services in Income Maintenance, Food Stamps, and Medical Assistance; determining and verifying initial and continuing eligibility for Public Assistance, Medicaid, and Food Stamps through the use of agency procedures, automated systems, and/or based on face-to-face client interviews; all personnel perform related work. There are three assignment levels in this class of positions; the following are examples of typical tasks for each level:

Assignment Level I. Determines initial eligibility, or verifies continuing eligibility and reapplications for Medicaid, Food Stamps, and/or Public Assistance via use of agency procedures and automated systems with incidental or no face-to-face client contact. Receives and reviews all required documents from clients/applicants to determine eligibility for Public Assistance, Medicaid and/or Food Stamps. Computes and determines the amount of financial assistance for Public Assistance, Food Stamps, and/or Medicaid for eligible participants. Forwards case records and other documentation for supervisory review and approval. Authorizes statistical and financial changes in assistance and/or budgets resulting from information received from active clients and prepares all required forms to effect processing. Maintains records to provide a continuing history of pertinent action in each case. Assumes responsibility for substantiating the reason for evaluation in all eligibility decisions. Prepares reports on activities and makes other reports as required.

Assignment Level II. Performs duties as described in Level I in direct client contact. Conducts face-to-face interviews with clients/applicants to determine initial eligibility, or to verify continuing eligibility and reapplications for Medicaid, Public Assistance, and/or Food Stamps. Makes referrals during interview for other services; prepares necessary memoranda for referral.

Assignment Level III. Performs duties as described in Levels I and II within a caseload concept Income Maintenance Center. Maintains a caseload of clients as assigned by the group supervisor. Determines appropriate employability status of members of households of clients/applicants, refers to employment programs, takes required case actions based upon employability coding. Makes appropriate entries in public assistance case records; provides assistance and instructs applicants; computes budget amounts of public assistance grants; prepares and verifies documentation from clients; takes required actions to provide assistance grants. Contacts landlords/agents and/or other agencies/officials to obtain or maintain suitable housing for clients/applicants; processes all housing actions such as rent increases, change of address, rent advances, and relocation.

Requirements

1. An associate degree from an accredited college or completion of two years of study (60 credits) at an accredited college; or
2. A high school diploma, or evidence of having passed an examination for the high school equivalency diploma, and two years of full-time paid experience in the following areas: interviewing for the determination of eligibility for public assistance, unemployment, health, or other insurance benefits; bookkeeping; preparation of statistical reports; validation of vouchers, warrants, invoices; or
3. Education and/or experience equivalent to (1) or (2) above, but all candidates must have a high school diploma or its equivalent.

Foreign education will be evaluated by the Department of Personnel to determine comparability to education received in domestic accredited educational institutions.

Test Information

Your score will be determined by a written test: a multiple-choice test, weight 100. A score of at least 70% is needed in this test in order to pass.

The written multiple-choice test may include questions on reading comprehension; basic arithmetic reasoning and computation; office procedures including knowledge of filing systems and techniques; English usage, including punctuation, spelling, and grammar; obtaining relevant information from documents, printouts, files, etc.; good writing skills, including report writing; human relations problems, both on the telephone and face-to-face, including interviewing; and related areas.

Selective Certification. The eligible list resulting from this examination may be selectively certified to fill vacancies in the title of Eligibility Specialist which require a working knowledge of both English and another language.

Advancement

Employees in the title of Eligibility Specialist are accorded promotion opportunities, when eligible, to the title of Principal Administrative Associate.

State—Municipal
Housing and Community Development Assistant

Job Description

Housing and Community Development Assistants engage in the review and processing of applications and related documents submitted by sponsors, builders, community organizations, and local officials in connection with programs for the development of new housing, rehabilitation of existing housing, and the revitalization of communities. This includes determining the need for program and/or technical reviews of particular applications; attending project review meetings; reviewing and analyzing recommendations of technical personnel; and preparing summary analyses of applications. They also visit project sites and prepare field reports verifying progress made in achieving objectives.

Requirements

On or before the date of the written test, candidates must have had three years of experience in urban planning, community development, community organization, real estate development or financing, or in the management or administration of publicly assisted multidwelling housing projects.

College study may be substituted for up to one year of experience at the rate of 30 credit hours equaling three months of experience. Graduate study in urban planning, urban studies, suburban studies, public administration, public management, law, political science or government; or in Puerto Rican studies. Afro-American studies, or social sciences, with a concentration in urban or rural studies, may be substituted for up to one year of experience at the rate of 30 credit hours equaling one year of experience. Education must have been received at an accredited college or university. Appropriate part-time and volunteer experience, which can be verified, will be accepted on a prorated basis.

License. Because these positions require substantial travel, successful candidates must either possess a valid license to operate a motor vehicle or otherwise demonstrate their ability to meet the transportation needs of the job in carrying out their responsibilities in any location to which travel is required, including some locations not accessible by public transportation. Field work travel expenses will be reimbursed on a fixed schedule.

Test Information. There will be a *written test* which candidates must pass in order to be considered for appointment. The test will be designed to test for knowledge, skills, and/or abilities in such areas as:

1. Understanding, interpreting, and applying housing and community development laws, rules, and regulations: These questions will test for the candidates' ability to read, understand, and apply provisions of a variety of state and federal laws, rules, and regulations. The candidates will be provided with a brief reading selection based on or extracted from a passage of legal text followed by a paragraph describing a hypothetical situation. The candidate must read the selection and the paragraph and then answer one or more questions based on the selection's application to the paragraph. All factual information needed to answer the questions is provided in the readings. That the content of the readings may not pertain directly to the duties of each position being tested is immaterial. The questions seek only to determine the candidates' ability to read and comprehend written material of a particular style and difficulty.
2. Real property and community development terminology, documents, and forms: These questions will test for the candidates' knowledge of terminology, documents, and forms commonly used or encountered in the conduct of work in the real property and/or community development fields.
3. Preparing written material: These questions will be designed to test how well the candidates can express themselves in writing. Particular emphasis is placed on two major elements of written communications: clarity and organization.

State
Medicaid Review Analyst II (SUR) III

Job Description

Medicaid Review Analysts II (Surveillance and Utilization Review) work as part of a team which applies medical expertise and knowledge to the development, review, and evaluation of recipient utilization records to monitor the necessity, appropriateness, and quality of care provided to individuals enrolled in the Medicaid program. You would be required to review computer reports, case files, and other information sources and prepare detailed summaries of findings.

Medicaid Review Analysts III (Surveillance and Utilization Review) supervise a team of Medicaid Review Analysts II (Surveillance and Utilization Review) in the performance of their duties in the review and reporting of findings or recipient utilization of Medicaid.

Requirements

On or before the date of filing application, candidates for both examinations must have a current state license to practice as a professional registered nurse or a current state registration as a physician's assistant. A current state license to practice as a pharmacist will also be accepted as qualifying for Medicaid Review Analyst II (SUR). Candidates must also meet one of the following requirements:

Examination	Education		"A" Experience*		"B" Experience*
Medicaid Review Analyst II	1. Either *a.* a bachelor's degree; or *b.* an associate's degree (or 60 credit hours) in health sciences or a related field; or	and	2 years	and	1 year
	2. No coursework	but	3 years	and	1 year
Medicaid Review Analysts III	1. Either *a.* a bachelor's degree; or *b.* an associate's degree (or 60 credit hours) in health sciences or a related field; or	and	3 years	and	2 years†
	2. No coursework	but	4 years	and	2 years†

* **"A" Experience:** Administrative/clinical experience in a health care program which, for purposes of these examinations, is defined as any public or private program which is responsible for the funding, delivery, monitoring, or evaluation of health care services. **"B" Experience:** Experience in a two-function program involving periodic monitoring of postpayment Medicaid program claim information to identify billing or medical utilization aberrancies by examining and comparing specific health care provider and recipient utilization practices with standard medical practices. The two functions are defined, for purpose of this examination, as: **Surveillance:** directed to the administrative aspects of the program in that it detects improper or illegal utilization by providers and recipients; **Utilization Review:** concerned with the quality and level of medical care delivered to medical clients.

† One year of this experience must have been in a supervisory capacity.

Test Information

There is no written exam. There will be an evaluation of training and experience which candidates must pass in order to be considered for appointment. The training and experience of those candidates who meet the minimum qualifications will be evaluated against the general background of the position(s). It will, therefore, be necessary for candidates to include all pertinent education and experience in detail so that this information may be fully evaluated. Vagueness and omissions will *not* be interpreted in the candidate's favor. Qualified candidates will then be sent a questionnaire in which they will be asked specific information concerning their training and experience. The evaluation will be based on the information solicited by this questionnaire.

LEGAL POSITIONS

The legal activities of many of the state departments require the services of attorneys of various grades. A great deal of important state legal work is handled by lawyers in the office of the Attorney-General. In addition to these are many legal positions, some under specialized titles, which are filled from open-competitive civil service lists. The state offers opportunity for legally trained employees to rise to highly responsible, well-paid positions.

State—Municipal Legal Assistant I, II

Job Description

Legal Assistants I, under the direction of staff attorneys, are responsible for compiling and organizing documentation, preparing and assisting in the preparation of legal documents and forms, logging information, and preparing correspondence and subpoenas. They respond to inquiries and complaints; track cases; ensure that deadlines are met; and maintain various calendars. They also conduct research into legal matters, analyzing materials and presenting both verbal and written comments of their findings. They prepare and maintain files, record and monitor the status of legislation, and gather materials and summaries of legislation pertinent to the agency.

Legal Assistants II are distinguished from the Legal Assistants I by their increased responsibility, their greater freedom of judgment, and their degree of expertise in interpreting the overall mission of the Bureau and Agency.

Requirements

On or before the date of the written tests, candidates must meet the following requirements:

Legal Assistant I:

1. An associate's degree in paralegal studies; or
2. Satisfactory completion of general practice legal specialty training (normally comprised of 150 classroom hours or more) resulting in a certificate from an accredited institution or one cited by the American Bar Association as following acceptable practices.

Legal Assistant II:

1. A bachelor's degree in paralegal studies; or
2. a. An associate's degree in paralegal studies *and* one year of full-time experience as a paralegal assistant (see definition below); or
   b. Satisfactory completion of general practice legal specialty training (normally comprised of 150 classroom hours or more) resulting in a certificate from an accredited institution or one cited by the American Bar Association as following acceptable practices *and* one year of full-time experience as a paralegal assistant (see definition below).

Definition

A paralegal assistant applies knowledge of the law and legal procedures in rendering direct assistance to lawyers, clients, and courts; prepares and interprets legal documents; researches, compiles, and uses information from a law library; and analyzes and handles procedural problems that involve independent decisions.

Substitution

Candidates for Legal Assistant II may substitute a bachelor's degree for the one year of required experience.

1. General clerical or secretarial duties performed in a law office will NOT be deemed as experience as a paralegal assistant.
2. Appropriate and verifiable part-time and volunteer experience will be accepted on a prorated basis.
3. Education must have been received at an accredited college or university.

Important! All candidates must provide a copy of the transcript issued following completion of the required course work in paralegal studies. This transcript must accompany the application form.

Test Information

There will be a written test which candidates must pass in order to be considered for appointment. The written test will be designed to test for knowledge, skills, and/or abilities in such areas as:

1. Record keeping and preparing written material in a legal context including legal documents and forms.
2. Understanding and interpreting legal material including legal terminology.
3. Conducting research into legal matters.

State—Municipal Attorney

Job Description

Under direction, with latitude for the exercise of independent judgment and unreviewed action and decision, performs legal work involving issues of fact and questions of law; performs related work.

Examples of Typical Tasks. Performs legal work in preparation for and trial and argument of cases before courts or quasi-judicial bodies; appears in all courts and argues motions, writs, and other proceedings; prepares briefs, motions, legal opinions, affidavits, memoranda, and other legal papers; determines the advisability of presenting witnesses, admissibility of types of evidence, and matters of legal strategy; assists, guides, and supervises subordinates in pretrial preparation and legal research and reviews work for completeness, compliance with policy and professional standards; confers with subject matter specialists, technical experts, and counsel for litigants; recommends settlements and adjustments; conducts legal investigations, holds informal hearings, and interrogates prospective witnesses; determines those legal questions requiring higher legal opinion and refers them with appropriate memoranda to proper authority; may advise on legal aspects of enforcement and administration of acts, rules, laws, and regulations; may conduct legal investigations and may hold informal hearings regarding compliance with pertinent laws, rules and regulations; may study and report on existing law and may recommend statutory revisions; may interpret laws and regulations and may advise executive and administrative personnel on legal matters.

Requirements

1. A license to practice law in the state
2. One year of satisfactory full-time, paid legal experience acquired within the last three years, subsequent to admission to any state bar.

Test Information

Education and experience, weight 100, 70% required. There will be no competitive test other than an evaluation of education and experience. Education and experience rating will be based on candidate's statement on the Experience Paper, which must be filled out completely and in detail, including dates and number of hours per week worked and percentage of time worked in areas described below.

Candidates are warned to list all education and experience for which credit may be given as described below. Once they have filed their application, candidates will not be permitted to add additional education and experience for purposes of having such education and experience evaluated beyond the minimum requirements. Only training and experience which is verifiable and explained in sufficient detail will be considered. You will receive a score of 70% for meeting the minimum requirements.

After the minimum requirements have been met, credit will be given for a maximum of an additional five years of satisfactory full-time paid legal experience acquired within the last six years, subsequent to admission to any state bar:

1. Four points will be granted for each year of additional legal experience within the last four years.
2. Three points will be granted for each year of additional legal experience up to a maximum of two years.

To receive credit beyond the minimum requirements all legal experience must have been in one or more of the following areas, and must constitute at least 50 percent of the candidate's work year. The areas are practice before courts, including appellate units, and/or Administrative Tribunals; enforcement, defense, and settlement of claims; practice relating to enforcement of civil rights or criminal law; negotiation, drafting, and preparation of written interpretation of contracts, agreements, or leases relating to commercial, or real estate transactions or labor-management or intergovernmental relations. Candidates must indicate on the Experience Paper amount of time spent in each legal area for which they are requesting additional credit.

Note. Two hundred workdays, five hours a day, constitute one full year; but no more than the maximum points indicated in 1 or 2 above will be granted per calendar year.

3. Three points per degree granted for each advanced legal degree beyond the JD or LLB up to a maximum of two degrees.
4. Two points will be granted for each postgraduate publication on legal matters, such as legal texts, articles, reports in recognized professional publications, maximum of three publications. (Copy to be submitted on request at time of investigation.)
5. Membership on the editorial board of a law school's law review, membership on an editorial board of a satisfactory legal publication other than the school's law review, and/or membership on the school's Moot Court Board. Two points per membership (maximum of four points.)

The maximum rating that can be granted on this Training and Experience test is 100%.

Advancement

Employees in the title of Attorney are presently accorded promotion opportunities, when eligible, to the title of Associate Attorney.

Health-Related Positions

With the continuing growth of social services, state and local governments continue to need physicians, medical researchers, nurses, and similar workers in more and more fields. The growth of psychiatric concepts, the development of occupational therapy, the public demand that veterans who need medical care should have it, and the increasing demands that an aging population will place on society in general and the health-care industry in particular—all these factors demand a force of health-care practitioners working for the government at the state and local levels as well as at the federal level.

SAMPLE EXAMINATION ANNOUNCEMENTS

State
Nurses I, II, IV, V, VI and Nurse Supervisor

Job Description

Nurse I. These perform staff nursing in acute, long-term, or comparable-level patient care.

Nurse II. These function as head nurses in acute or long-term care or as staff nurses with specialized responsibilities.

Nurse Supervisor. These function as shift supervisors or supervisors of nursing care areas with responsibilities comparable to shift supervisors.

Nurse IV. These direct, or assist in directing, nursing services in a small hospital or supervise a substantial portion of all nursing services at a large hospital.

Nurse V. These direct, or assist in directing, nursing services in a hospital or supervise where responsibilities are complex or extensive.

Nurse VI. These direct nursing services at a large general hospital.

Requirements

Nurse I. Possession of a current license to practice as a registered nurse.

Nurse II. Two years of professional nursing experience.

Nurse Supervisor. Four years of professional nursing experience including two years at the advanced professional nursing level.

Nurse IV. Three years of professional nursing experience including one year in a supervisory or administrative capacity and graduation from an accredited school of nursing or graduation from college with a bachelor's degree in nursing or nursing education.

Nurse V. Four years of professional nursing experience including two years in a supervisory or administrative capacity and graduation from an accredited school of nursing with a bachelor's degree in nursing or nursing education.

Nurse VI. Five years of professional nursing experience including three years in a supervisory or administrative capacity and graduation from an accredited school of nursing with a bachelor's degree in nursing or nursing education.

For All Job Titles Except Nurse I. Any equivalent combination of experience and training.

Necessary Special Requirement For All Job Titles. Possession of a current license to practice as a registered nurse as issued by the State Board of Nurse Examiners or eligibility for such licensure. Nurses licensed in other states must apply for and receive state endorsement within one year of the date they begin employment. Nurses licensed in countries other than the United States must pass the licensure examination before accepting nursing employment with the state. Licensure status must be reported in item number 9 on your application.

Test Information

No written test is required. The test will consist of a rating of experience and training. Applicants will receive a score based on what they report on their application and application supplement. It is important to provide complete and accurate information. Failure to do so may delay the processing of the application or result in a lower-than-deserved score. Call any of the Commission's offices if there are any problems or questions.

If, after taking the test, applicants obtain additional qualifications and want to take the test again, they may be retested after six months. A new application is required for a retest.

Test Results. Employment and promotion lists will be established. You will be notified in writing of your test results.

State—Municipal Public Health Nurse

Job Description

Under supervision, performs public health nursing functions in a generalized public health nursing program which includes clinics, schools, and home nursing; performs related tasks.

Examples of Typical Tasks. Administers routine screening tests; interprets, evaluates, and reports the results; counsels patients or family on results of diagnostic tests, treatment procedures, and medication prescribed; administers oral and topical medications, therapeutic injections, and immunization, being alert and watching for adverse side effects or reactions; maintains medical charts and records on patients; teaches patients and family about nutrition, hygiene, prevention, rehabilitation, and community resources available; maintains community resource file, makes referrals to other agencies, acts as patient advocate and follows up; controls, keeps an inventory, and orders supplies; ensures proper labeling, security, and storage of medications and specimens; supervises and/or coordinates delivery of services with other health care personnel; assigns work, supervises activities and evaluates performance of subordinates; sets up, coordinates, and implements delivery of required health care practices in the public and parochial school systems; answers requests for interpretation and explanation of Department of Health policies and regulations and general information on public health matters; makes home visits to follow up on patients, school students, and their families; gathers information on sudden infant deaths (SIDS), window fall accidents, lead poisoning, and unregistered home births; observes and reports environmental and/or sociological health hazards; and writes narrative reports on activities.

Special Working Conditions. In the event of emergencies, appointees may be subject to call on a 24-hour-a-day, seven-day-a-week basis. Appointees in the Department of Health may be assigned to clinics and health stations for which evening and/or weekend hours are scheduled.

Requirements

1. A bachelor of science degree in nursing, or nursing education from a college accredited for public health nursing preparation by the National League for Nursing; and
2. A current license issued by the State Department of Education to practice as a Registered Professional Nurse.

Test Information

Education, training, and experience, weight 100; 70% required. There will be no other competitive test.

The education, training, and experience rating will be based on candidates' statements on the Experience Paper, *which must be filled out completely and in detail, including dates and number of hours per week worked and salary earned.* Candidates are advised to list all education, training, and experience as described below. Once the application has been filed, candidates will not be permitted to add additional education, training, and experience beyond that needed to meet the minimum requirements. Education, training, and experience listed on the Experience Paper will not be found acceptable unless they are verifiable and will receive credit only to the extent that they are described clearly and in detail.

A score of 70% will be given for meeting the minimum requirements. After the minimum requirements are met, additional credit will be given on the following basis.

1. *Experience.* Credit will be given for up to eight years of experience, accrued within the last ten years, if such experience falls within the categories described below. Each year of experience will be credited under only one category. Full-time experience means 30 hours or more per week on a regular basis. Part-time experience is less than 30 hours per week, but must be at least ten hours per week to receive credit.
   a. One point will be given for each year of full-time paid experience as a Public Health Assistant performing work in the nonprofessional phases of the delivery of public health services in a school, clinic, or health station.
   b. Two points will be given for each year of full-time paid experience as a Registered Professional Nurse.
   c. Three points will be given for each year of full-time paid experience as a Pediatric Nurse Associate or Nurse Practitioner (with a Certificate of completion of a 12-month course of classroom and clinical training in pediatric and nursing practice which meets the joint guidelines of the American Academy of Pediatrics); or as a Junior Public Health Nurse or Public Health Nurse in a school, clinic, or public health station.
   d. Four points will be given for each year of full-time paid experience as a nurse-in-charge at a Public Health Clinic.
2. *Education and Training.* Four points will be given for either (a) a master's degree in public health nursing education; (b) a master's degree in public health administration; or (c) a master's degree in public health.

The maximum rating that can be granted on this education, training, and experience test is 100%.

Advancement

Employees in the title of Public Health Nurse are accorded promotion opportunities, when eligible, to the title of Supervising Public Health Nurse.

State—Municipal Physician's Assistant

Job Description

Under the direct supervision and control of a licensed physician, and within the scope and practice of that physician, assists in providing such medical service as is assigned to him or her by the supervising physician and is appropriate to the Physician's Assistant's education, training, and experience in the delivery of health care to patients in ambulatory and in-patient medical institutions, including health centers, child health stations, correctional institutions, and hospitals; or, under the supervision of a licensed physician, performs medical services, within the scope and practice of such supervising physician, in a department clinic, at an inpatient medical facility, or while making home visits as part of a department medical program; performs related work.

Examples of Typical Tasks. Obtains detailed case histories of patients on admission, and compiles and records detailed narrative case summaries; obtains medical histories, makes detailed narrative summaries and compiles medical records with respect to employees of a department; as directed, may perform physical examinations and record and present resulting data to the supervising physician, makes home visits to department personnel to perform medical examinations, and such diagnostic evaluations as may be required as part of a medical leave program; performs such administrative tasks and makes such medical decisions as may be required to effectuate a medical leave program such as making reports, scheduling home visits where deemed appropriate, conducting reviews of employees' medical records and histories, and issuing resumption to work orders; as directed, may perform such routine procedures as injections, immunizations, and the suturing and care of wounds; assists supervising physician in the delivery of service to patients requiring continuing care, including the review and monitoring of treatment and therapy plans; performs evaluative and treatment procedures necessary to provide appropriate response to life-threatening emergency situations; may perform or assist in the performance of routine laboratory or related procedures; may be required to operate a motor vehicle in connection with the performance of duties related to a department medical leave program.

Special Working Conditions. Appointees to the Department of Correction may be required to work rotating shifts around the clock, including Saturdays, Sundays, and holidays, depending upon the needs of the service.

Requirements

A current State Registration as a Physician's Assistant. This minimum requirement must be met on the date the application is filed.

License. At the time of appointment to Department of Sanitation or Department of Correction, candidates must possess a valid motor vehicle driver's license.

Test Information

Education and experience, weight 100, 70% required. Your education and experience rating will be based on your statements on the Experience Paper and on the Special Insert which must be filled out completely and in detail, including dates and number of hours worked per week. List *all* education and experience for which credit may be given as described below. Education and experience listed on the Experience Paper and on the Special Insert will not be found acceptable unless it is verifiable and will receive credit only to the extent that they are described clearly and in detail. You will receive a score of 70% for meeting the minimum requirement.

After the minimum requirement is met, you may receive credit for a maximum of an additional five years of full-time paid experience on the following basis:

1. Experience
   a. One point will be given for each year of active duty in the United States Military Services performing Medical Corpsman duties in the M.O.S. of Medical Corpsman in the Army or equivalent M.O.S. in other United States Military Services.
   b. Three points will be given for each year of full-time paid experience, after acquisition of the State Registration as a Physician's Assistant, performing the duties of a Physician's Assistant in an office of a licensed physician engaged in private practice.
   c. Six points will be given for each year of full-time paid experience, after acquisition of the State Registration as a Physician's Assistant, performing the duties of a Physician's Assistant in a hospital, clinic, or facility rendering medical care.

Acceptable part-time paid experience will be prorated. The maximum rating that can be given on this education and experience test is 100%.

2. Education: One point will be given for possession of a bachelor's degree from an accredited college or university.

Foreign education will be evaluated by the Department of Personnel to determine comparability to education received in domestic accredited educational institutions.

State—Municipal Public Health Assistant

Job Description

Under direct supervision, the public health assistant assists medical staff in a public health clinic by performing nonprofessional duties; performs related work.

Examples of Typical Tasks. Performs vision, hearing, and simple urinanalysis tests; weighs and measures patients; takes pulse, respiration rates, and temperatures; collects specimens; prepares patients for examination and helps professional staff perform examination; operates related equipment; may administer simple first aid; interviews clients to obtain identifying and routine medical information; explains clinic procedures; answers routine questions and makes appropriate referrals; makes and receives related telephone calls; comforts children; reports relevant observations and information to the professional staff; accompanies nurses on home visits; prepares, maintains, and files medical folders, charts, and forms; reviews for completeness and enters data onto appropriate documents; labels specimens; arranges appointments; sends and receives medical records and notices; collects and records statistical data; maintains logs and schedules; requests, arranges, and maintains equipment and supplies; does light housekeeping and cleaning of instruments and equipment.

Requirements

1. High school graduation or its equivalent; or
2. Successful completion of the 11th grade of high school and one year of full-time paid experience performing health-related or clerical duties; or
3. Experience and/or education which is equivalent to (1) or (2).

However, all candidates must have successfully completed the 11th grade of high school.

Test Information

Written, weight 100, 70% required. The written test will be of the multiple-choice type and may include questions on reading and understanding instructional material, medical charts, and statistical forms; completing forms; filing and organizing simple data; spelling, simple arithmetic, and measurements; working cooperatively with staff and interacting with patients; and related information.

State—Municipal Public Health Sanitarian

Job Description

Under supervision, makes inspections to assure compliance with pertinent laws, rules, and regulations governing the areas of food, drugs, and general environmental sanitation; performs related work.

Examples of Typical Tasks. May make periodic inspections of food processing plants, slaughterhouses, warehouses, wholesale and retail food and drug establishments, and pasteurizing plants to ensure a pure food and drug supply and to enforce pertinent laws, rules, and regulations; inspects business establishments, stores, schools, institutions, day camps, nurseries, recreational and other areas for occupational hazards, defective plumbing, inadequate water supply, overflowing cesspools, condition of sewers, condition of gas heating equipment, animals not properly controlled or housed, insect or rodent infestation or noxious odors; instructs operators in establishments under permit or jurisdiction of the Department of Health in principles of sanitation, vermin control, and other areas of environmental health; investigates complaints regarding nuisances, unsanitary conditions, quality and purity of foods, improper food handling and personal habits of handlers, and inadequate or unsuitable water supply; condemns adulterated, contaminated, or decomposed foods; seals unsanitary equipment against further use; makes necessary arrests of health code violators; investigates applications for permits to operate beauty parlors, barber shops, pet shops, and stables for compliance with laws, rules, and regulations; inspects premises of purveyors of inhalation therapy; investigates outbreaks of food poisoning, diarrhea, dysentery, or other communicable diseases in hospitals or institutions; collects samples of beach or drinking water for bacteriological and chemical examination; tests milk to determine if substandard or low in total solids; evaluates performance of fumigators and exterminators, and examines equipment; selects and processes samples of food for chemical analysis; assists in the conduct of special studies and surveys; represents the Department of Health with the media and at public meetings and performs other public relations tasks; supervises and instructs staff members.

Requirements

1. A bachelor's degree from an accredited college, with at least 30 credits in the physical and biological sciences; or
2. An associate degree from an accredited college, with 12 credits in the physical and biological sciences and five years of experience as a public health technician assisting sanitarians and engineers in carrying out the various elements of prevention and control programs affecting the public's health; or
3. A combination of education and experience which is equivalent to (1) or (2).

The Experience Paper listing all completed courses in the physical and biological sciences must be filled out and filed with the application.

Foreign education will be evaluated by the Department of Personnel to determine comparability to education received in domestic accredited educational institutions to determine the extent to which it will be credited toward meeting the requirements for this examination.

Test Information

Tests. Written, weight 100, 70% required. The written test will be of the multiple-choice type and may include questions on biological, chemical, and physical factors affecting health and physical well-being; selection and performance of appropriate field tests, including sample collection and data recording; job-related situations, including dealing with the public diplomatically; reading comprehension, arithmetic, and report writing appropriate to the duties of the position; and other related areas.

Advancement

Employees in the title of Public Health Sanitarian are accorded promotion opportunities, when eligible, to the title of Senior Public Health Sanitarian.

State
Pharmacist, Chief Pharmacist

Requirements

Necessary Special Requirement (Both Levels). Possession of a license to practice pharmacy as issued by the State Board of Pharmacy.

Pharmacist

No experience required.

Chief Pharmacist

Two years of experience as a pharmacist in a hospital pharmacy.

Applicants must be state residents, of good moral character, and capable of performing the physical activities of the job.

Job Description

Pharmacist. This is professional pharmaceutical work of a staff nature in a state facility. Employees dispense physicians' prescriptions including ointments, powders, solutions, medicines, and drugs. The work may include directing pharmacy assistants and/or custodial and nontechnical personnel. Supervision is received from a Chief Pharmacist.

Chief Pharmacist. This is professional pharmaceutical work directing all pharmaceutical services in a state facility. Employees develop and/or implement all policies, procedures, and controls for the dispensing of pharmaceuticals and certain pharmaceutical supplies. The work involves the supervision of pharmacists, pharmacy assistants, clerical staff, and custodial personnel. Supervision is received from a medical or administrative superior.

Test Information

Both Levels. Applicants will be evaluated for possession of a license to practice pharmacy as issued by the State Board of Pharmacy.

Chief Pharmacist. Applicants will be evaluated for possession of the required experience.

Applicants who fail to qualify may reapply after six months (during the life of this announcement) upon attaining the specified qualifications. A new application will be required.

If these tests do not produce enough candidates for a particular geographic area, a testing program will be announced locally. That announcement will tell when and how to apply.

Advancement

Most Pharmacists and Chief Pharmacists are employed by the Department of Public Welfare in state mental hospitals, state centers for the mentally retarded, restoration centers, and the Bureau of Utilization Review.

A small number are also employed by the Department of Labor and Industry and the Department of Military Affairs.

State
Dietitian I, II; Therapeutic Dietitian in State Hospitals and Centers

Job Description

Dietitians I plan and supervise food production and perform at least two administrative functions (such as directing, coordinating, inspecting, and evaluating food production in accordance with standards) in a general hospital food service operation or other functions of comparable scope and complexity.

Dietitians II direct the operation of a state general hospital food service department or other food service department of comparable scope and complexity or may assist a food service manager who has comparable administrative and supervisory responsibility. As a director, the employee carries total responsibility for the department including planning and modifying standard and therapeutic menus; preparing orders for food and supplies; reviewing and maintaining cost records; determining staffing needs; interviewing and hiring or recommending applicants for employment, directing, coordinating, and inspecting all food preparation, service, and sanitation.

Therapeutic Dietitians plan and supervise an institutional diet program which requires planning nutritional diets through special diet menu modifications and medical staff consultations and maintain special diet records.

Requirements

Dietitian I. Experience in planning, organizing, and supervising an institutional food preparation and service operation that involved the application of the principles and practices of dietetics.

Dietitian II. Experience in the administrative aspects of dietetics and food management in an institutional food service operation.

Therapeutic Dietitian. Experience in the development and administration of a therapeutic diet program which included therapeutic and special menu planning.

All Job Titles. Any combination of experience and/or training which provided the applicant with the appropriate required knowledge, skills, and abilities is acceptable. (See "Equivalency")

Evaluation Policy

General. As used in the Requirements section, "institutional food service preparation and service operation" means an organization which provides for the planning, preparation, and service of three meals a day for a core of regular clients such as in a hospital, nursing home, residential school, etc.

Dietitian 1. Creditable experience must include **planning, organizing, and supervising. Equivalency:** Any background deemed acceptable by the ADA (American Dietetic Association) for its internship program.

Dietitian 2. Creditable experience must include administrative aspects of dietetics and food management (menu planning, purchasing, personnel, finance, and therapeutics). Any job experience of a nature similar to Dietitian 1. **Equivalency:** Successful completion of an ADA internship; or similar experience coupled with a background deemed acceptable by the ADA to enter its internship program. Any Registered Dietitian is assumed to have satisfied this option.

Therapeutic Dietitian. Creditable experience must include the development and administration of a therapeutic diet program (in or for an institution). **Equivalency:** Any background deemed acceptable by the ADA for its internship program by way of the administrative dietetics option.

Note. Candidates will be expected to provide documentation to satisfy evaluative conditions. (Include copy of ADA Form: "Preliminary Evaluation of University Transcripts for Dietetic Internship"; or other evidence that you satisfy these requirements.)

General Requirements. Applicants must be state residents of good moral character and capable of performing the physical activities of the job. They must be free of communicable diseases or any other physical conditions that may hinder their work or endanger the health and well-being of others. Health examinations may be required as a condition of employment. Dietitians may have to have a physical examination annually during their employment.

Test Information

The test will consist of a rating of experience and training. You must pass the test to have your name placed on the eligible lists.

You will receive a score based on the experience and training reported on the Application and Work Background Questionnaire which must be submitted with the Application. It is therefore important to provide complete and accurate information. Failure to do so may delay the processing of the application or result in a lower than deserved score. Call any of the Commission offices if there are any problems or questions.

Applicants who do not pass the rating of experience and training test or who would like to try for a better score may be retested after six (6) months during the life of this announcement. A new application and Work Background Questionnaire No. 050-9-1 are required for a retest.

If these tests do not produce enough candidates for a particular geographic area, a testing program will be announced locally. That announcement will tell when and how to apply.

State—Municipal
Physical Therapist, Senior Physical Therapist

Job Description

These positions exist in the state government in the residential facilities and community programs of the State Offices of Mental Health and Mental Retardation and Developmental Disabilities; in the rehabilitation centers of the Department of Health; and in the facilities of the Department of Correctional Services.

Physical Therapists perform the duties of a first level professional clinician, under the supervision of a Senior Physical Therapist. They might supervise Physical Therapy Assistants.

Senior Physical Therapists function as advanced clinicians and may supervise Physical Therapists and Physical Therapy Assistants.

Requirements

On or before the date of filing application, applicants must have a limited permit or a license and current registration to practice physical therapy in the state in order to be considered for either examination.

In addition, applicants for Senior Physical Therapist must have had one year of professional physical therapy experience. If, after appointment an employee's permit expires and he or she does not obtain a license or does not maintain the license and registration, the appointment will be revoked.

Appropriate part-time and volunteer experience, which can be verified, will be accepted on a prorated basis.

How to Apply for the Positions. To apply for these positions, contact the Personnel Office of the agencies where you are interested in working. You may apply to more than one personnel office. You can be appointed only at agencies where you have submitted an application.

Test Information

There is no written test. If applicants meet the minimum qualifications, their education and experience will be evaluated against the general background of the position(s), and a rating will be assigned by the Personnel Office of each facility to which they apply. Names will be placed on an eligible list for each facility in final score order. As score and rank will be based solely on the rating received in the evaluation of education and experience, it is essential to include all pertinent details in the application. Vagueness and omissions will not be resolved in the applicant's favor.

Municipal Occupational Therapist

Job Description

Upon the referral of a licensed physician, assists in the physical and psychosocial rehabilitation of patients through occupational therapy in hospitals, clinics, and patients' homes; performs related work.

Examples of Typical Tasks. Evaluates, treats, and advises patients who are limited by physical and/or psychosocial dysfunction, developmental or learning disability, or the aging process; provides evaluation and remediation services for limitations in activities of daily living skills, range of motion, muscle strength, voluntary movement, cognitive-perceptual motor skills, and sensory integration; uses specifically designed crafts, instructional programs, games, exercises, and handling techniques to improve functional performance; designs, fabricates, applies, and instructs in the use of selected orthotic and prosthetic devices and adaptive equipment; sets up programs for guidance of families and patients in the home/community; may instruct students and personnel of other disciplines in theory and practice of occupational therapy; participates in in-service educational activities; may supervise support personnel and students; maintains equipment, cares for and requisitions supplies; keeps records, interprets results of treatment, and makes reports.

Requirements

1. A valid state license to practice occupational therapy; or
2. A valid one-year limited permit to practice occupational therapy pending receipt of a license.

License. All candidates will be required to possess a valid Occupational Therapist license or a valid one-year limited permit to practice occupational therapy, pending receipt of a license. The license or limited permit, issued by the State Department of Education, must be presented to the appointing officer at the time of appointment. Candidates who possess a limited permit and fail to obtain their license within one year after the date of appointment will be terminated.

Test Information

Education and experience, weight 100, 70% required. The education and experience rating will be based on the statements on the Experience Paper, which must be filled out completely and in detail, including dates and number of hours per week worked. List *all* education and experience for which credit may be given as described below. Once the application has been filed, no additional education or experience will be evaluated beyond that needed to meet the minimum requirements. Education or experience will not be found acceptable unless it is verifiable. Education and experience listed on the Experience Paper will receive credit only to the extent that they are described clearly and in detail. Applicants receive a score of 70% for meeting the minimum requirements. After the minimum requirements are met, applicants may receive credit for a maximum of an additional five years of experience, accrued within the last ten years, on the following basis:

1. Credit at the rate of *three* points per year will be granted for each year of full-time paid experience performing the duties of a Certified Occupational Therapist Assistant.
2. Credit at the rate of *four* points per year will be granted for each year of full-time paid experience performing the duties of an Occupational Therapist in a school or community setting.
3. Credit at the rate of *five* points per year will be granted for each year of full-time paid experience performing the duties of an Occupational Therapist in a hospital setting.
4. Credit at the rate of *six* points per year will be granted for each year of full-time paid experience performing the duties of an Occupational Therapist and supervising paraprofessionals, occupational therapy students, and/or occupational therapists.

In addition to the above, *two-tenths* point will be granted for each graduate credit towards an advanced master's degree in occupational therapy for graduates of an occupational therapy bachelor's program.

Acceptable part-time experience will be credited on a prorated basis.

The maximum rating that can be granted on this education and experience test is 100.

Advancement

Employees in the title of Occupational Therapist are accorded promotion opportunities, when eligible, to the title of Senior Occupational Therapist.

State—Municipal Occupational Therapy Assistant I, II

Job Description

These positions exist in the residential facilities and community programs of the Offices of Mental Health and Mental Retardation and Developmental Disabilities; in the rehabilitation centers of the Department of Health; in the alcoholism treatment centers of the Division of Alcoholism and Alcohol Abuse; and in the facilities of the Department of Correctional Services.

Occupational Therapy Assistants I or **Occupational Therapy Assistants II** function under the supervision of a licensed Occupational Therapist or Senior Occupational Therapist. Both positions are paraprofessional.

Requirements

On or before the date of filing application, applicants must be certified and currently registered to practice as an Occupational Therapy Assistant in the state.

In addition, if applying for Occupational Therapy Assistant II, applicants must have had two years of post-certification occupational therapy experience. If, after appointment, an employee loses certification, or if he or she does not maintain registration, appointment will be revoked.

Appropriate part-time and volunteer experience, which can be verified, will be accepted on a pro-rated basis.

How to Apply for the Positions. To apply for these positions, applicants contact the personnel office of the agency where they are interested in working. You may apply to more than one personnel office. Be sure to apply to each agency at which you are interested in working. You can be appointed only at agencies where you have submitted an application.

Test Information

There is no written test. If applicants meet the Minimum Qualifications, their education and experience will be evaluated against the general background of the position(s), and a rating assigned by the Personnel Office of each facility to which they apply. Names will be placed on an eligible list for each facility in final score order.

As score and rank will be based solely on the rating received in the evaluation of education and experience, it is essential to include all pertinent details in the application. Vagueness and omissions will not be resolved in the applicant's favor.

State
Occupational Therapist, Senior Occupational Therapist

Job Description

These positions exist in the residential facilities and community programs of the Offices of Mental Health and Mental Retardation and Developmental Disabilities; in the rehabilitation centers of the Department of Health; in the alcoholism treatment centers of the Division of Alcoholism and Alcohol Abuse; and in the facilities of the Department of Correctional Services.

Occupational Therapists perform the duties of a first level professional clinician under the supervision of a Senior Occupational Therapist. They might supervise Occupational Therapy Assistants.

Senior Occupational Therapists function as advanced clinicians and may supervise Occupational Therapists and Occupational Therapy Assistants.

Requirements

On or before the date of filing application, you must have a limited permit or a license and current registration to practice occupational therapy in the state in order to be considered for either examination.

In addition, applicants for Senior Occupational Therapist must have had one year of professional occupational therapy experience. If, after appointment, an employee's permit expires and he or she does not obtain a license or does not maintain the license and registration, the appointment will be revoked.

How to Apply for the Positions. Applicants for these positions must contact the personnel office of the agency where they are interested in working. They may apply to more than one personnel office. They should apply to each agency at which they are interested in working, since they can be appointed only at agencies where they have submitted an application.

Test Information

There is no written test. If applicants meet the minimum qualifications, their education and experience will be evaluated against the general background of the position(s), and a rating will be assigned by the Personnel Office of each facility to which they apply. Names will be placed on an eligible list for each facility in final score order.

As score and rank will be based solely on the rating received in the evaluation of education and experience, it is essential to include all pertinent details in the application. Vagueness and omissions will not be resolved in the applicant's favor.

State—Municipal Physical Therapy Assistant I, II

Job Description

Physical Therapy Assistants I or **Physical Therapy Assistants II** function under the supervision of a licensed Physical Therapist or Senior Physical Therapist. Both positions are paraprofessional.

Requirements

On or before the date of filing application, candidates must be certified and currently registered to practice as a Physical Therapy Assistant in the state.

Applicants for Physical Therapy Assistant II must have had two years of post-certification physical therapy experience. If, after appointment, an employee loses his or her certification or does not maintain registration, the appointment will be revoked.

Appropriate part-time and volunteer experience, which can be verified, will be accepted on a prorated basis.

How to Apply for the Positions. To apply for these positions, you must contact the personnel office of the agency where you are interested in working. You may apply to more than one personnel office. Be sure to apply to each agency at which you are interested in working. You can be appointed only at agencies where you have submitted an application.

Test Information

There is no written test. If applicants meet the minimum qualifications, their education and experience will be evaluated against the general background of the position(s), and a rating will be assigned by the Personnel Office of each facility to which they applied. Names will be placed on an eligible list for each facility in final score order.

As score and rank will be based solely on the rating received in the evaluation of education and experience, it is essential to include all pertinent details in the application. Vagueness and omissions will not be resolved in the applicant's favor.

State
Podiatrist in the Department of Public Welfare

Job Description

This is responsible professional work involving the examination, diagnosis, and treatment of foot ailments such as corns, bunions, calluses, ingrown and deformed toenails, warts, blisters, sprains, arch defects and athlete's foot of patients and residents living in state facilities for the mentally disabled. Employee's responsibility does not extend to those foot ailments which would require the services of an orthopedic surgeon; work requires the exercise of independent judgment based on training and experience in this field. Work is performed in accordance with professional standards and is subject to review by physicians.

Podiatrist positions exist in state mental hospitals, state centers for the mentally retarded, and at restoration centers in the Department of Public Welfare.

Requirements

Graduation from an approved school of podiatry. Applicant must be of good moral character and capable of performing the physical activities of the job.

Necessary Special Requirement. Possession of a state license to practice podiatry as issued by the State Board of Podiatry Examiners.

Test Information

No written test is required. Applicants will be evaluated for possession of a current certification as a Podiatrist as issued by the State Board of Podiatry Examiners. Applicants must show on their Civil Service Application for Employment/Promotion in Section 9 their registration number, when and where acquired, and expiration date of current certification. Failure to include this information may result in delay in processing the application or in disqualification.

Applicants who fail to qualify may reapply upon acquiring the qualifications specified. A new application will be required.

Rating of Experience and Training: This is a test and applicants will receive a score based on the experience and training reported on the Civil Service Application for Employment/Promotion. It is therefore important to provide complete and accurate information. Failure to do so may delay the processing of the application or result in disqualification. Call any of the Commission offices if there are any problems or questions.

If these tests do not produce enough candidates for a particular geographic area, a testing program will be announced locally. That announcement will tell when and how to apply.

State—Municipal
Dental Hygienist

Job Description

Under supervision, performs prophylactic work and provides dental hygiene education in a district dental clinic, or classroom, or dental clinic in a public or parochial school. Dental hygienists also perform related work.

Requirement

A valid state Dental Hygienist's license.

Test Information

Training and experience, weight 100, 70% required. There will be no competitive test other than an evaluation of training and experience. The training and experience rating will be based on the applicant's statement on the Experience Paper, which must be filled out completely and in detail, including dates and number of hours worked per week. List all training and experience for which credit may be given as described below.

Training and experience will not be found acceptable unless it is verifiable. Training and experience listed on the Experience Paper will receive credit only to the extent that they are described clearly and in detail. Once the application has been filed, no additional education or experience can be added.

Applicants receive a score of 70% for meeting the minimum requirements. After the minimum requirements are met, credit will be given for a maximum of six years of experience based on the following:

1. One point per year will be given for each year of full-time experience as a dental assistant.
2. Three points per year will be given for each year of full-time experience as a licensed dental hygienist working in a private dentist's office.
3. Five points per year will be given for each year of full-time experience working as a licensed dental hygienist for a hospital, clinic, school, or neighborhood family care center.

In addition, 0.5 point will be given for possession of either a bachelor's or master's degree in a health-related field from a recognized accredited college or university.

Acceptable part-time paid experience will be prorated.

The maximum rating that can be granted on this training and experience test is 100.

State—Municipal Laboratory Technician

Job Description

The position of laboratory technician exists in a number of departments and agencies at various locations throughout the state.

Laboratory Technicians perform a variety of technical laboratory procedures in food, diagnostic, research, and other laboratories. Depending upon the specific assignment, duties might include performing such functions as water and/or environmental chemistries; virological determinations; radiation counts; microscopic examinations; standard bacteriological examinations; testing foods by common methods for adulteration and contamination; preparing media, cultures, reagents, stains, and solutions; and keeping records and carrying out other duties normally encountered in laboratory operation. Appointees in the Department of Correctional Services will be required to demonstrate practical proficiency in obtaining blood by venipuncture.

Requirements

Candidates must meet one of the following requirements on or before the date of the written test:

1. An associate's degree in science technology; or
2. Two years of satisfactory experience in a laboratory, performing technical laboratory tests and procedures; or
3. Satisfactory completion of 18 college or university semester credit hours in biology and/or chemistry (If you qualify under this option, you must include with your application a list of the courses and credits you have successfully completed. A transcript is not necessary.); or
4. A satisfactory equivalent combination of experience and training noted in (2) and (3) above.

Appropriate part-time and volunteer experience, which can be verified, will be accepted on a prorated basis. Education must have been received at an accredited college or university.

Test Information

There will be a written test which you must pass in order to be considered for appointment. The written test will be designed to test for knowledge, skills, and/or abilities in such areas as:

1. *Basic principles of biology, chemistry, and general science.* These questions may include:
   a. Elementary relationships of pressure, volume, and temperature
   b. Chemical elements
   c. Microscopic organisms
   d. Various systems of the body
   e. Scientific and metric terminology.
2. *Basic laboratory equipment and glassware.* These questions will require the candidate to correctly identify common laboratory glassware and equipment.
3. *Laboratory principles and practices.* These questions may include topics such as the following:
   a. Care and handling of toxic and/or dangerous materials
   b. Simple first aid techniques
   c. Proper safety techniques
   d. Metric system
   e. Care and safe use of laboratory glassware and equipment
   f. Common laboratory procedures such as the correct way to prepare solutions
   g. Methods necessary to correct unsafe working conditions
4. *Laboratory calculations.* These questions will require the candidate to perform basic arithmetic functions incidental to solving a particular scientific problem.

State X-ray Technologist I

Job Description

This is technical work in the operation of x-ray, film processing, and related equipment. Close technical supervision is received from a physician or an X-ray Technologist II, Supervisory. Most positions are in state general hospitals. The remainder are in state mental hospitals and mental retardation centers.

Requirements

No experience required. An applicant must be a state resident, of good moral character, and capable of performing the physical activities of the job.

Necessary Special Requirements. Possession of a current certificate as a Registered Radiologic Technologist as issued by The American Registry of Radiologic Technologists or eligibility for such certification.

You must show in Section 9 of your Application for Employment/Promotion the number of your current certificate as a Registered Radiologic Technologist, as issued by the American Registry of Radiologic Technologists (ARRT). If you do not yet have certification, you must submit proof of acceptance to participate in the ARRT Examination for Certification and write "Eligible" in Section 9 of your Application for Employment/Promotion.

Test Information

The test is a rating of experience and training. Scores are based on the qualifications reported on the completed Application for Employment/Promotion. It is therefore important to provide complete and accurate information. Failure to do so may delay the processing of the application or result in a lower-than-deserved score. Call any of the offices if there are any problems or questions. If an applicant has obtained additional qualifications, he or she may reapply after six months (during the life of this announcement). A new application is required for a retest.

If these tests do not produce enough candidates for a particular geographic area, a testing program will be announced locally. That announcement will tell when and how to apply.

State
Public Health Educator, I, II in the Department of Health

Job Description

A **Public Health Educator I** plans and implements a segment of public health educational programs for an assigned geographical area. An employee evaluates needs, determines the best methods to address those needs, and provides technical assistance to health organizations, community groups, and individuals. Work is performed under the direction of an administrative supervisor.

A **Public Health Educator II** independently plans, organizes, and promotes a public health education program which has statewide impact. An employee may supervise a technical staff of Public Health Educators I. Work is reviewed by an administrative superior for compliance with departmental policies and procedures.

Requirements

Please make sure you meet *all* requirements. If you are not sure if you qualify, contact one of the Commission offices.

Applicants will be required to travel. Offers of employment will be made only if applicants are willing to drive a government vehicle or arrange to provide their own transportation. Travel expenses will be reimbursed at specified rates.

Applicants must be state residents of good moral character and capable of performing the physical activities of the job.

Public Health Educator I

1. Such training as may have been gained through graduation from a four-year college or university with major coursework* in natural sciences, social sciences, or education; and a master's degree in public health education**; or
2. Two years as a Health Educator.

Public Health Educator II

1. Two years of experience in the field of public health education including one year with a voluntary or official public health agency; and such training as may have been gained through graduation from a four-year college or university, with major coursework* in the natural sciences, social sciences, or education; and a master's degree in public health education**; or
2. Two years as a Public Health Educator I.

*All bachelor's degrees are acceptable.

**A master's degree in public health is also acceptable.

Test Information

The test will consist of a rating of your experience and training. Applicants receive a score based on the experience and training they report on the Application for Employment/Promotion. It is therefore important to provide complete and accurate information. Failure to do so may delay the processing of the application or result in a lower-than-deserved score. Call any of the Commission offices if there are any problems or questions.

Retests will not be allowed because of the short duration of the testing program.

If these tests do not produce enough names for a localized geographic area, another test may be announced for that area *only*. That announcement will tell when and how to apply.

Test results. You will receive a Notice of Examination Results in the mail which will give your test scores, and if you pass the tests, your relative standing on the lists and how long your name will remain on the lists.

These lists may be used to fill positions in other comparable job titles.

Drafting and Engineering Positions

SAMPLE EXAM ANNOUNCEMENTS

State
Assistant Draftsman

Job Description

Assistant Draftsman assists in the preparation of drawings and working plans including tracings from sketches or notes and makes computations for engineering, architectural, and/or mechanical projects in a drafting room; does related work as required. The incumbent of a position in this class works in the main office under immediate supervision at all times. The duties involve the application of trained draftsmanship to work at the subprofessional level. This work is fairly routine and is assigned and reviewed upon completion by a Draftsman or by the professional employee in charge. The incumbent ordinarily exercises no supervision over others and is responsible only for the neatness, clarity, and accuracy of his or her own work.

Examples of Work

Engineering. Traces drawings for stream bridges, highway-parkway grade separations, and for elimination of highway railroad crossings at grade; traces key sheets and standards; reduces field notes; draws and traces land appropriation maps; revises titles and dimensions on plans; plots cross sections; computes areas by use of planimeters; estimates quantities; maintains files of plans, drawings, and blueprints.

Architectural. Prepares and traces drawings of architectural projects; draws and traces maps and grading plans; prepares and letters schedules from working drawings; revises titles and dimensions on plans; maintains files of plans, drawings, and blueprints.

Mechanical. Draws and traces heating, refrigerating, sanitary, and electrical and ventilating plans; prepares and letters schedules; revises titles and dimensions on plans; plots cross sections; maintains files of plans, drawings, and blueprints.

Requirements

1. Graduation from a standard senior high school and two years of satisfactory drafting experience, of which one year shall have been in the field of specialization indicated in the title; or
2. A satisfactory equivalent combination of education and experience, substituting a year of approved training in an engineering college for each year of required work experience.

Desirable Qualifications. Familiarity with the fundamentals of applied mathematics including trigonometry, surveying, and elementary engineering calculations; familiarity with architectural design and drafting; skill in the use of drawing instruments; ability to make ordinary calculations with accuracy; willingness to learn; ability to follow directions.

Advancement

These positions are found in several state departments, particularly the Department of Public Works. Senior Draftsman positions are filled by open-competitive examination when there is an insufficient number of Assistant Draftsmen in the department who are eligible for promotion. For employees with professional training, promotion lines extend into the professional engineering and architectural service.

ENGINEERS

Engineers design machines, processes, systems, and structures. They apply scientific and mathematical theories and principles to solve practical technical problems. In state and local government, most work in one of the more than 25 specialties recognized by professional societies. Electrical, mechanical, civil, industrial, chemical, and aerospace engineering are the largest. Although many engineers work in design and development, others work in testing, production, operations, and maintenance.

State
Civil Engineer Trainee

Job Description

This is entrance level training work to develop practical proficiency in the use of civil engineering knowledge, skills, and abilities as these are applicable to the mission of the hiring agency.

The employee participates in a variety of beginning level engineering duties associated with the location, design, and construction of roads, bridges, buildings, dams, water supply or waste collection systems, treatment plants, flood control, or other civil engineering projects; transportation planning; and highway traffic control. Work requires occasional travel to project sites.

In the Department of Transportation, employees participate in a fifteen-month training program. In the Department of Environmental Resources, the normal training period is twelve months. Persons hired in these jobs normally advance into Civil Engineer II or Civil Structural Engineer I positions after completion of training, with a corresponding increase in salary.

Requirements

A bachelor's degree in civil engineering or closely related field which includes or is supplemented by major coursework in civil engineering; or four years of civil engineering experience and an

Engineer-in-Training certificate issued by or acceptable to the State Registration Board for Professional Engineers. Appropriate education may be substituted for the required experience on a year-for-year basis.

Evaluation Policy. The phrase "or closely related field" is interpreted to mean a bachelor's degree in civil engineering technology or a bachelor's degree in an engineering major which included or was supplemented by at least 24 credits in civil engineering coursework. Seniors who are within six months of graduation may apply.

Other Requirements, Conditions of Employment. Applicants must also meet the following requirements and conditions of employment. If they cannot, they should not apply for this job.

1. Be in a state of health and physical condition sufficient to permit walking up to one mile on rough and slippery terrain; climbing scaffolding; being able to stoop, bend, and reach; working in close proximity to moving vehicles, noise, and vibrations; and being exposed to extremes of weather and unusual environmental conditions.
2. Have the ability to communicate orally in English sufficient to be understood without difficulty and with no more than occasional repetition.
3. Occasional travel may be necessary. Offers of employment will be made only if applicants are willing to travel and are willing to drive a government vehicle or arrange to provide their own transportation. Travel expenses will be reimbursed at specific rates.

Applicants must be state residents of good moral character and capable of performing the physical activities of the job.

Test Information

No written test is required. The test will consist of a rating of experience and/or training.

Rating of Experience and Training. Applicants will receive a score based on the experience and training reported on the Application for Employment/Promotion and Application Supplement. It is important to submit complete and accurate information on completed college coursework in civil engineering (including coursework they expect to successfully complete if they are students within six months of graduation). Failure to do so may delay the processing of application or result in a lower-than-deserved score. Call any of the Commission offices if you have any problems or questions. Retests will not be allowed because of the short duration of the testing program. If this test does not produce enough names for a localized geographic area, a testing program will be announced locally. That announcement will tell when and how to apply.

Test Results. Applicants will receive a Notice of Examination Results in the mail. If they pass the test, the notice will tell their relative standing on the list and how long their names will remain on the list. The eligible list will be established using a group-scoring method. This means that there are a fixed number of scores (Final Earned Ratings). Everyone with the same score will be considered equal when employment interviews are scheduled. This list may be used to fill positions in other comparable job titles.

State Electrical and Mechanical Engineers

Job Description

Employees in these positions perform professional engineering work, within their specialties, in the design, construction, and inspection of a variety of electrical and mechanical systems and equipment for state buildings and facilities, such as office buildings, colleges, hospitals, water and sewage treatment plants, steam generating plants, parks and recreation areas, highway interchanges, and rest areas. The work performed must conform to accepted engineering standards, agency rules and regulations, and safety laws and codes.

Engineer I-level work normally includes engineering assignments involving component parts of a system when the controlling parameters for such systems have been developed. The work does not normally involve coordinating their specialties with other architectural or engineering disciplines.

Engineers II perform more advanced work with responsibility for complete engineering projects. They work with considerable independence in developing the technical details of the projects. Their work requires coordinating their specialties with other architectural and engineering disciplines and contact with other public agencies, consultants, or contractors to obtain compliance with state standards and needs.

Consultants perform highly advanced engineering work. They are involved in developing solutions to design and construction problems which require advanced and innovative application of engineering principles. They are normally recognized agency experts with responsibility for advising management on the advantages, disadvantages, and effects of utilizing technology and/or changing existing engineering and materials standards. Work is normally self-generated and in response to unusual construction, design, or administrative problems and is performed with considerable independence in approach and scheduling.

Electrical Engineers and Consultants work on such projects, or parts of projects, as complete electrical distribution systems, and substations; conversion of a facility to a total electrical utility base; tunnel and highway interchange lighting and signaling; electrical servicing of highways; parking lot illumination; security and intrusion alarm systems; fire detection and suppression systems; temperature and motor controls; intercommunications systems; and elevators.

Mechanical Engineers and Consultants work on such projects as mechanical systems for internal water supply and other plumbing systems; heating including steam generation, air conditioning, ventilation, and refrigeration for buildings and water and sewage treatment plants; components of recreational facilities such as pumps and filtration for swimming pools and plumbing for camping sites; locks and gates for dams or similar projects; fire suppression and detection; and air pollution control systems.

Employees in these jobs may occasionally travel. For positions where travel is required, offers of employment will be made only to applicants who are willing to travel. If transportation by government vehicle or public transportation is not available or feasible, employees may be required to arrange their own transportation. Travel expenses of employees will be reimbursed at specified rates.

In addition, employees in these jobs are occasionally required to work an unusual schedule or work overtime to meet emergency situations or project deadlines. In such cases, employees are paid overtime or given compensatory time off, as appropriate, in accordance with state Personnel Rules and/or the union contract.

These positions are in the Department of General Services, the primary employing agency; the Departments of Public Welfare, Education, Transportation, and Community Affairs; the State Public Utility Commission; and the State Fish Commission. There are thirteen (13) filled Electrical Engineer positions and twelve (12) filled Mechanical Engineer positions.

Requirements

Necessary Special Requirement. Certain positions in these job titles will require licensure as a professional engineer by the state or a reciprocal jurisdiction. These are positions where there can be no exemption from such licensure, as defined under Section 5, Exemption from Licensure, of the Professional Engineers Registration Law (as amended).

Electrical Engineer I

1. One year as an Electrical Engineer Trainee in state employment; or
2. One year of experience in designing, constructing, or reviewing components of electrical engineering projects which required the application of problem-solving techniques including loading and capacity calculations and the preparation of drawings; and a bachelor's degree in electrical engineering or closely related field.

Electrical Engineer II

1. One year as an Electrical Engineer I in state employment; or
2. Two years of experience in designing, constructing, or reviewing components of electrical engineering projects which required the application of problem-solving techniques including electrical loading and capacity calculations and the preparation of drawings and specifications for the solutions; and a bachelor's degree in electrical engineering or closely related field.

Electrical Engineering Consultant

1. One year as an Electrical Engineer II in state employment; or
2. One year of experience in designing, reviewing, or constructing engineering systems for commercial, educational, or governmental facilities which required the application of problem-solving techniques including electrical loading or power capacity calculations and the preparation of drawings and specifications for the solutions; and a bachelor's degree in electrical engineering or closely related field.

Mechanical Engineer I

1. One year as a Mechanical Engineer Trainee in state employment; or
2. One year of experience in designing, constructing, or reviewing components of mechanical engineering projects which required the application of problem-solving techniques including loading and capacity calculations and the preparation of drawings; and a bachelor's degree in mechanical engineering or closely related field.

Mechanical Engineer II

1. One year as a Mechanical Engineer I in state employment; or
2. Two years of experience in designing, constructing, or reviewing components of mechanical engineering projects which required the application of problem-solving techniques and the preparation of drawings; and a bachelor's degree in mechanical engineering or closely related field.

Mechanical Engineering Consultant

1. One year as a Mechanical Engineer II in state employment; or
2. One year of experience in designing, reviewing, or constructing engineering systems for commercial, educational, or governmental facilities which required the application of problem-solving techniques including loading or capacity calculations and the preparation of drawings and specifications for the solutions; and a bachelor's degree in mechanical engineering or closely related field.

Note. Any equivalent combination of experience and training can be substituted for the above experience and training.

Evaluation Policy

Clarification of the Necessary Special Requirement (NSR). This NSR means some selected positions in these job titles will require licensure as a professional engineer (PE). When a vacancy is to be filled in a position which requires licensure, only candidates who possess a PE license, as defined above, will be considered for employment to the position. After you are on the eligible list for these jobs, you should immediately advise the Civil Service Commission of any changes concerning your PE license.

Acceptable Experience and Training. The phrase "any equivalent combination of experience and training" means that generally:

1. Applicants who do not have an engineering degree in the appropriate discipline can substitute any combination of appropriate engineering experience and education which totals four years and possession of an Engineer-in-Training (EIT) certificate or PE license for the required degree.
2. Applicants can substitute graduate training in the appropriate engineering discipline or a closely related field for the required experience at the rate of 30 semester hours (or equivalent) of coursework for each year of experience. Students in the final term of qualifying training may apply.
3. A bachelor's degree in a closely related electrical engineering field includes a bachelor of engineering or engineering technology degree in such fields as electrical power, electrical science engineering, electrical design, and electrical science and systems.
4. A bachelor's degree in a closely related mechanical engineering field includes a bachelor of engineering or engineering technology degree in such fields as mechanical analysis and design, mechanical design, mechanical engineering and analysis.

Applicants for the Electrical/Mechanical Engineering Consultant job titles must have experience involving a total electrical/mechanical system.

Qualifying experience or training must have included engineering assignments which required the application of engineering problem-solving techniques involving loading and capacity calculations and the preparation of drawings appropriate to the jobs applied for. Acceptable experience will normally commence after receipt of a bachelor's degree in the appropriate discipline. In the absence of such degree, the appropriate engineering experience will not normally commence until after award of an EIT certificate.

Applicants must be of good moral character and be capable of performing the physical activities of the job. State residency is not required for any of these job titles.

Test Information

The tests will consist of a rating of your experience and training. Applicants will receive a score based on the experience and training reported on the Application for Employment and Application Supplement for Electrical Engineers or Application Supplement for Mechanical Engineers. It is therefore important to provide complete and accurate information. Failure to do so may delay the processing of the application or result in a lower than deserved score. Call any of the Commission offices if there are any problems or questions.

Applicants who do not pass the tests or who would like to try for a better score may be retested after six months during the life of this announcement. A new application and application supplement are required for a retest.

If these tests do not produce enough candidates for a particular geographic area, a testing program will be announced locally. That announcement will tell when and how to apply.

State—Municipal Stationary Engineer

Job Description

Stationary Engineers, on an assigned shift, under the general direction of a Senior Stationary Engineer, are responsible for the operation and maintenance of a heating plant. They supervise Assistant Stationary Engineers and Power Plant Helpers; operate various types of heating equipment; and make emergency and running repairs. In addition, they may make mechanical, electrical, and emergency repairs on water, sewage, and gas lines; on elevators; and on electrical, refrigeration and air conditioning systems. Stationary Engineers may supervise, assist in, or perform, the installation of electrical and mechanical equipment, including commercial-type kitchen equipment.

Requirements

Candidates must meet the following requirements:

1. Two years of satisfactory experience in the operation and maintenance of steam and/or high temperature hot water (HTHW) pressure boilers or auxiliary lines conveying steam or HTHW and equipment rated at 15 psi or more; or
2. Graduation from an accredited technical institute or junior college with an associate degree in engineering technology and six months of experience in the operation and maintenance of HTHW or high pressure boilers and/or auxiliary HTHW or steam lines and equipment rated at 15 psi or more; or
3. Satisfactory completion of an appropriate technical institute course in the mechanical-electrical trades and six months experience in the operation and maintenance of HTHW or high pressure boilers and/or auxiliary HTHW or steam lines and equipment rated at 15 psi or more.

Substitution

1. Experience in the operation of large central air conditioning equipment (50 tons and above) or journey-level experience in such trades as electrician, plumber/steamfitter, refrigeration/air conditioning mechanic (50 tons and above) may be substituted for required experience with HTHW or high pressure boilers or auxiliary HTHW or steam lines and equipment on the basis of two months of such substitute experience for one month of HTHW or steam experience. Such substitution may be made for up to one year of HTHW or steam experience under (1) above; for up to six months HTHW or steam experience under (2) above; or for up to three months of HTHW or steam experience under (3) above. Experience in the operation and maintenance of domestic oil, coal, or gas burning equipment will not be considered satisfactory experience. Candidates must state on their applications the type, use, pressure (in psi), and capacity of the boilers and lines of equipment they operated or maintained.
2. Part-time experience which can be verified will be accepted on a prorated basis.

Test Information

There will be a written test which candidates must pass in order to be considered for appointment. The written test will be designed to test for knowledge, skills, and/or abilities in such areas as

1. Operation, maintenance, and repair of steam and high temperature hot water generating and distribution systems, electrical equipment, prime movers, and related mechanical and electrical power plant equipment.

2. Heating, ventilating, air conditioning, refrigeration, plumbing, water supply, and sanitary systems, including related electrical and mechanical trades and machine shop practices.
3. Energy management, conservation, and safety practices.
4. Supervision.

State
Assistant Sanitary Engineer, Senior Sanitary Engineer

Job Description

These positions exist in the state government with the Department of Environmental Conservation and the Department of Health at various locations throughout the state.

Assistant and Senior Sanitary Engineers in the Department of Environmental Conservation are assigned to either the central office or to a field office in a major segment of an environmental quality program such as wastewater treatment and disposal, water pollution control, solid waste management, air pollution control, hazardous and toxic material control, radiological pollution control, or noise control. In the Department of Health, either in the central office or in a field office, these engineers perform sanitary engineering work in such areas as water supply, quality, and use; toxic substances; indoor air quality; hospital, institutional, temporary residence, camp and recreational resort sanitation; food sanitation, rural water supply and sewage disposal; and review of related engineering plans.

In both departments, Sanitary Engineers work with representatives of all levels of government as well as with citizen groups and other professionals. Additional duties may involve instructional activities with employees of municipal operating agencies and developing systems for training plant personnel.

Requirements

Candidates for the following positions must meet these requirements on or before the date they file their application:

Assistant Sanitary Engineer

1. Possession of an acceptable bachelor's or higher-level degree in engineering. (An acceptable degree is one granted in an engineering curriculum which is accredited by the Accreditation Board for Engineering and Technology as a first or second professional degree in engineering or a degree registered by the State Education Department for professional licensing in engineering. ABET-accredited curricula leading to degrees in engineering technology are not acceptable.); and
2. The equivalent of one year of full-time experience in sanitary, environmental, or public health engineering.

Senior Sanitary Engineer

1. The equivalent of two years of full-time experience in sanitary, environmental, or public health engineering; and
2. Possession of a state professional engineer's license and current registration; or
3. Licensure and current registration as a professional engineer in a state or territory of the United States which has commensurate licensing procedures to those used in the state by means of a 16-hour written examination. Candidates appointed to this title must secure a state professional engineer's license within 12 months of appointment in order to continue employment.

Substitutions

1. For Assistant Sanitary Engineer, satisfaction of the license requirement for Senior Sanitary Engineer may be substituted for the degree requirement in (1) of the minimum qualifications.
2. For both examinations, a master's degree in one of the following engineering disciplines (sanitary, environmental, public health, radiological pollution, air pollution control, solid waste, or another closely related engineering discipline) can be substituted for one year of required experience; a doctoral degree in one of the above engineering disciplines may be substituted for two years of required experience.
3. Appropriate part-time and volunteer experience, which can be verified, will be accepted on a pro-rated basis.

Test Information

There is no written test. The training and experience of candidates meeting the minimum qualifications will be evaluated against the duties of the position(s). This evaluation will concentrate on the appropriateness, breadth, and recency of relevant education and experience. It is, therefore, essential that candidates describe their training and experience as completely as possible on their applications; ambiguity, vagueness, or omissions will not be decided in their favor.

Custodial and Service Positions

The following are some examples of the wide range of custodial and service occupations available in state and local government. Many require no formal education, qualification, or experience.

SAMPLE EXAM ANNOUNCEMENTS

State—Municipal
Custodial Assistant

Job Description

Under close supervision, performs work of ordinary difficulty in cleaning public buildings and their immediate grounds; performs related light labor duties; performs related work.

Examples of Typical Tasks. Sweeps, damp mops, and wet mops office floors, toilets, corridors, lobbies, and other assigned floor areas. Cleans wash basins and other toilet room facilities. Washes walls by hand with a brush or by using an electric machine. Scrubs floors with an electric machine; waxes and polishes floors. Hand-scrubs stairs and stair landings. Empties wastebaskets and disposes of refuse. Vacuums rugs and carpets. Dusts and removes and cleans venetian blinds. Performs shoulder high and high dusting of walls. Polishes furniture and metal work. Cleans mirrors and glass in bookcases and doors. Washes electric light fixtures. Replenishes bathroom supplies in toilets. Sweeps sidewalks and removes snow from sidewalks; washes sidewalks and lower portions of buildings with brush and hose. May attend a low pressure heating plant. Occasionally may operate an elevator. Replaces bulbs and fuses. May move furniture or act as watchman or messenger.

Requirements

There are no formal education or experience requirements for this position.

Test Information

Written, weight 100, 70% required. The written test will be of the multiple-choice type and may include questions on knowledge of basic cleaning procedures for buildings; proper operation of cleaning machines; safety as related to custodial work; the ability to understand instructions; and other related areas.

Advancement

Employees in the title of Custodial Assistant are accorded promotion opportunities, when eligible, to the titles of Senior Custodial Assistant, Custodial Foreman, and Junior Building Custodian.

State—Municipal Exterminator

Job Description

Under general supervision, performs work in the prevention, control, and elimination of insects, vermin, and other pests from buildings and surrounding areas; performs related work.

Examples of Typical Tasks. Inspects areas of infestation; selects and uses the most effective insecticides, rodenticides, baits, traps, etc., for exterminating pests as required; prepares poisonous insecticides, rodenticides, etc., used in exterminating; may prepare reports as required, including records of equipment usage, work schedules, and exterminating operations performed.

Requirements

1. One year of satisfactory, full-time paid experience in the preparation, testing, or application of pesticides; or
2. Successful completion of a pesticide application course acceptable to the Department of Environmental Conservation for meeting the requirements for a Commercial Pesticide Applicator Certificate in Structural and Rodent Control.

Candidates who claim to meet the minimum requirements as described in (2) above (successful completion of a pesticide application course) *must* list the name of the course and the full name of the institution where the course was taken.

All candidates will be required to possess a valid Commercial Pesticide Applicator Certificate in Structural and Rodent Control issued by the Department of Environmental Conservation within 18 months of the date of appointment.

Test Information

There will be no competitive test other than an evaluation of your training and/or experience.

Training and Experience test, weight 100. A score of at least 70% is needed in order to pass. The training and experience rating will be based on candidates' statements on the Experience Paper which must be filled out completely and in detail, including dates and number of hours worked per week. List and describe all vocational courses and experience for which credit may be given as described below. Training or experience will not be found acceptable unless it is verifiable. Training and experience listed on the Experience Paper will receive credit only to the extent that they are described clearly and in detail. A score of 70% will be given for meeting the minimum requirements.

After the minimum requirements are met, credit may be given for a maximum of an additional five years of experience on the following basis:

1. Up to two points, depending on quality, will be given for each year of fulltime, paid experience in the preparation and testing of pesticides.
2. Up to four points, depending on quality, will be given for each year of fulltime, paid experience in the application of pesticides.
3. Four points will be given for the successful completion of a pesticide application course acceptable to the Department of Environmental Conservation for meeting the requirements for a Commercial Pesticide Applicator Certificate in Structural and Rodent Control.
4. Six points will be given for the possession of a valid Commercial Pesticide Applicator Certificate in Structural and Rodent Control issued by the Department of Environmental Conservation.

Physical Test. Candidates will be required to satisfactorily complete the following physical test:

1. Stair climb: Eligibles will be required to walk/run up 81 steps (approximately ten short flights of stairs) and return to the starting point within three minutes.
2. Agility: Eligibles will be required to rise from a supine position, scale a vault box three feet high, sprint three yards to a maze of obstacles and dodge through a tunnel approximately four yards in length, and sprint back approximately ten yards to the finish line within 35 seconds.
3. Wall climb: Eligibles will be required to climb three steps to a foothold 44 inches high. The eligible must then step or climb over a 26 inch wall to a platform. The eligible must then descend to the ground by stepping or climbing back over the wall and climbing to the ground within two minutes.

Medical evidence to allow participation in the physical test may be required and the Department of Personnel reserves the right to exclude from the physical test eligibles who, upon examination of such evidence, are apparently medically unfit. Eligibles will take the physical test at their own risk of injury, although every effort will be made to safeguard them.

Advancement

Employees in the title of Exterminator are accorded promotion opportunities, when eligible, to the title of Foreman (Exterminators).

State
Laundry Washman and Supervisor

Job Description

Laundry Washmen perform semi-skilled manual work in the operation of heavy duty washing machines in a state laundry facility. They operate washing machines, extractors, conditioning tumblers, and dryers; use proper amounts of laundry chemicals; load machines; and keep the equipment and surrounding area clean.

Laundry Supervisors supervise the operation of a state laundry facility. They plan, direct, and coordinate laundry operations, requisition materials and supplies, arrange for repairs to equipment or machinery, and train others in work methods, safety hazards, and rules and regulations.

These jobs are in state hospitals and centers operated by the Department of Public Welfare throughout the state. The Department currently has 36 filled Laundry Washman jobs and 24 filled Laundry Supervisor jobs. A few job openings are expected during the coming year. In the past two years, there have been three appointments to Laundry Washman and seven to Laundry Supervisor. Contact the personnel office at the place where you want to work for more information on possible job openings.

Requirements

Laundry Washman

1. One year as a Laundry Worker; or
2. One year of experience as a laundry worker or washman in a commercial or industrial laundry and completion of the eighth grade.

Laundry Supervisor

1. One year as a Laundry Washman; or
2. Three years of experience in the input, process, and output phases of a commercial or industrial laundry and high school graduation.

Equivalent combinations of experience and training are acceptable for both job titles. If you have enough experience to qualify, you don't need to have completed the schooling specified above.

Please make sure you meet *all* requirements. If you are not sure if you qualify, contact one of the Commission's offices listed at the end of this announcement.

For both positions, applicants must be a state resident and of good moral character. They must be willing to work under hot, humid, and noisy conditions, be exposed to unpleasant odors and soiled laundry, and be physically capable of lifting up to 35 pounds, bending, stooping, and standing for long periods. They may be required to pass a physical examination, including a test for color blindness, given by the hiring agency prior to appointment.

Test Information

No written test is required. The test is a rating of experience and training. Applicants will receive a score based on their Application and Application Supplement. It is important to provide complete and accurate information. Failure to do so may delay the processing of the application or result in a lower-than-deserved score. Call any of the Commission's offices if there are any problems or questions.

Retests will not be allowed.

If these tests do not produce enough names for a localized area, another test may be announced for that area *only.*

Test Results. Employment and Promotion lists will be established. Applicants will be notified in writing of their test results.

State—Municipal Laundry Manager I, II

Job Description

These positions exist in certain facilities of the Office of Mental Health; the Office of Mental Retardation and Developmental Disabilities; and the Office of General Services, Executive Department.

Laundry Managers I direct the operations of a large single-facility laundry or of a consolidated laundry (a laundry serving more than one facility). Working under the general direction of an institution administrator, they have responsibility for all matters concerning the laundry operation, including record-keeping, reporting and written communications; employee selection, orientation, training, evaluation, and discipline; laundry department production planning, scheduling, and implementation; overall supervision and evaluation of laundry operations; and policy, procedures, and systems development within the laundry department. They are responsible for the efficient and effective functioning of the laundry in providing all serviced facilities and units with clean, sanitary linen and clothing in a timely manner.

Laundry Managers II have duties substantially the same as the duties of the Laundry Manager I except that they are responsible for a larger or more extensive laundry operation.

Requirements

On or before the date of the written tests, candidates must meet the following requirements:

Laundry Manager I. Four years of experience in a large commercial or institutional laundry, including at least two years as the supervisor of employees, inmates, working patients, or working clients.

Laundry Manager II. Five years of experience in a large commercial or institutional laundry, including at least three years as the supervisor of employees, inmates, working patients, or working clients.

Test Information

There will be a written test which candidates must pass in order to be considered for appointment. The written test will be designed to test for knowledge, skills, and/or abilities in such areas as:

1. Operation of power laundries, including materials, supplies, proper processing of various materials, and the operation and preventive maintenance of powered laundry equipment.
2. Work scheduling.
3. Preparation of written material.
4. Administrative supervision.

Municipal Sanitation Worker

Job Description

Under direct supervision, performs the work and operates the equipment involved in street cleaning, waste collection, snow removal and waste disposal; performs related work. Appointees will be required to serve a probationary period. As part of the probationary period, probationers will be required to complete a training course. Eligibles appointed to this position may be required to work rotating shifts including nights, Saturdays, Sundays, and holidays.

Requirements

There are no formal education or experience requirements for this position.

Minimum Age. Eligibles must have reached the age of twenty and a half by the date of appointment.

Investigation. At the time of investigation and at the time of appointment, candidates must present originals or certified copies of all required documents and proof, including but not limited to proof of date of birth by transcript of record of the Bureau of Vital Statistics or other satisfactory evidence and proof of any military service. Any willful misstatement or failure to present any required documents will be cause for disqualification.

License. At the time of appointment, eligibles must have a valid motor vehicle driver license. Serious moving violations, driver license suspension, accident record or other indication of poor driving ability may disqualify. Appointees will be required to obtain a class B commercial driver license after training.

Test Information

Your score will be determined by a competitive physical test weight 100. A score of at least 70% in the competitive physical test is needed in order to pass. In addition, there will be a qualifying written test designed to measure ability to understand written material in the following areas: filling out load tickets; reading and following administrative procedures and/or orders; reading, verifying, and/or signing vehicle accident statements; writing a statement on injury reports; reading and complying with safety rules and procedures; reading and following route sheets; reading equipment and vehicle operation manuals; filling out forms relating to snow activities; and related areas.

Qualifying Physical and Medical. Periodic reexaminations of employees in this title may be required to ensure they are in good health.

Physical Test. Medical evidence to allow participation in the physical test may be required, and the Department of Personnel reserves the right to exclude from the physical test eligibles who are apparently medically unfit.

State—Municipal
Associate Park Service Worker

Job Description

Under supervision, operates and maintains various types of motorized equipment; performs groundskeeping or gardening work in any park area required including all work in connection with the planting, maintenance, and removal of trees and large shrubs; inspects and performs general maintenance and repair work to buildings, monuments, and similar works of art, equipment, and facilities; and/or serves as an operator in a chlorination, coagulation, and/or filtration plant; performs related work.

Examples of Typical Tasks. Performs all aspects of gardening work including grading, cultivating, fertilizing, seeding, laying sod, mowing, and trimming hedges; sweeping and raking litter and emptying receptacles; planting, cultivating, and caring for trees, flowers, plants, shrubs, and other flora; and operates and cares for hand and power gardening tools and equipment. Operates cars, trucks, and other motorized equipment incidental to the performance of duties and/or operates heavy-duty motorized equipment on a full-time basis; checks vehicles to ensure they are in proper operating condition; changes tires and performs routine servicing. Cleans dirt accumulation and debris from monuments. Assists in or performs general repair work. Assists in climbing and pruning work; and may operate manual power driven equipment in the performance of these duties. Operates and maintains a chlorination, coagulation, and/or filtration plant consisting of chlorine and/or coagulation machine and auxiliary equipment used in purification and chemical treatment of water. Operates a low-pressure heating system; cleans and lubricates the boiler parts. Performs any necessary record-keeping and report writing activities related to the above functions of the Department of Parks and Recreation.

Requirements

1. High school graduation or evidence of having passed an examination for a high school equivalency diploma and six months of full-time paid experience in gardening, grounds maintenance, or in the building construction or maintenance trades; or
2. Two years of full-time paid experience in gardening, grounds maintenance, or in the building construction or maintenance trades; or

3. One year of full-time paid experience as a climber or pruner or tree worker performing climber and tree pruning duties; or
4. A satisfactory equivalent combination of (1) and/or (2) and/or (3) above.

License. At the time of appointment, eligibles must possess a valid commercial driver's license for the operation of trucks and tractors in excess of 18,000 pounds, maximum gross weight (MGW). If the license was issued in a state which did not require a road test with a vehicle in excess of 18,000 pounds MGW, the eligible will be required to demonstrate ability to operate such vehicles to the satisfaction of the appointing officer.

Test Information

Written, weight 100, 70% required. The written test will be of the multiple-choice type and may include questions in the following areas: rudimentary gardening techniques; park area and park building maintenance; cleaning of park, playground, and comfort stations; maintenance of tennis courts, beaches, ball fields, golf courses, and other recreation areas; defensive driving and minor automotive servicing techniques; rudimentary painting and repair techniques including the maintenance of tools; reading and understanding simple instructional materials; the writing of short, simple reports of accidents; arithmetic (addition and subtraction); basic first aid techniques; chlorination and filtration plant operation and low-pressure heating plant operation; and supervision of employees.

Qualifying Physical Tests. Medical evidence to allow participation in the physical test may be required, and the Department of Personnel reserves the right to exclude from the physical test eligibles who, upon examination of such evidence, are apparently medically unfit. Eligibles will take the physical test at their own risk of injury, although every effort will be made to safeguard them. Eligibles will be required to satisfactorily complete the following physical test consisting of two subtests:

1. *Strength subtest.* Eligibles must lift a bag weighing approximately 50 pounds from the floor, place it on a table approximately four feet in height, and then return the bag to the floor under control. The eligible will be required to perform this operation for a total of eight times within three minutes.
2. *Agility subtest.* Eligibles must first climb three steps to a foothold 44 inches high, then step or climb over a 26 inch wall to a platform. The eligible must then descend to the ground by stepping or climbing back over the wall and climbing down to the ground. Eligibles will be required to complete this subtest within three minutes. Eligibles will be given two attempts to complete each subtest.

Qualifying Medical. An eligible will be rejected for any medical condition which impairs his or her ability to perform the duties of Associate Park Service Worker. Periodic reexamination will be required.

Advancement

Associate Park Service Workers are afforded the promotion opportunity, when eligible, to the title of Park Supervisor.

State—Municipal
Consumer Services Specialist Trainee

Job Description

Consumer Services Specialist Trainees perform a variety of activities and tasks in connection with the investigations and resolution of consumer complaints against the investor-owned electric, steam, gas, telecommunications, and water utilities. These complaints include inadequate or substandard service, interruptions in service, disconnection of service, meter problems, billing problems, rate problems, deposit arrangements, deferred payment agreements, transferred balances, utility company policy, or other disputes requiring investigations and formal reply by the Department. They also discuss energy conservation matters with consumers and provide information on utility regulation.

Consumer Services Specialists Trainees also identify trends or problems in complaint handling which are investigated by staff in the Division of Consumer Services Policy and Compliance Section. Upon satisfactory completion of a one-year traineeship, they advance to the position of Consumer Services Specialist 1 without further examination.

Requirements

On or before the date of the written test, candidates must meet the following requirements:

1. A minimum of two years of experience in any one or any combination of the following:
   a. Construction, inspection, repair, or testing of electric or gas meters
   b. Testing gas for heat content and purity
   c. Telephone plant construction, maintenance, or operation
   d. Telephone commercial or traffic operations
   e. Drafting or analyzing utility billing statements
   f. Satisfactory equivalent combination of such experience; or
2. Graduation from a two-year technical institute or college with an associate degree in electronics, electrical technology, instrument technology, engineering technology, computer technology, or applied science; or
3. Completion of two years of a four-year engineering or engineering technology course; or
4. A satisfactory equivalent combination of the above training experience.

Test Information

There will be a *written test* and an *oral test.* Candidates must pass both in order to be considered for appointment. Only candidates who pass the written test will be notified to appear for the oral test. The Department of Civil Service reserves the right to call to the oral test only that number of successful written test candidates necessary to fill existing and anticipated positions. Only passing scores on the written test will be used in computing final scores.

Scope of Written Test. The written test will be designed to test for knowledge, skills, and/or abilities in such areas as

1. Understanding and interpreting tabular material
2. Understanding and interpreting written material
3. Reading of meters, scales, and gauges
4. Evaluating conclusions in the light of known facts
5. Basic interviewing.

Scope of Oral Test. The oral test will be designed to evaluate, against the background of the position, the ability to:

1. Identify and deal effectively with consumer problems
2. Communicate orally
3. Establish satisfactory relationships with others in a complaint-oriented situation.

Mechanical Positions

The following is a selection of the wide variety of mechanical positions available at the state and local levels. Most mechanics acquire their skills on the job following the instructions of experienced workers, reading repair manuals, and solving problems on their own. Increasingly, formal mechanic training acquired in high school, vocational or technical school, community or junior college, or in the Armed Forces is an asset to persons entering mechanic and repairer careers.

SAMPLE EXAM ANNOUNCEMENTS

State—Municipal
Auto Machinist

Job Description

Under supervision, an auto machinist rebuilds, repairs, maintains, and machines parts for automotive, construction, and special equipment powered by internal combustion engines; performs related work.

Examples of Typical Tasks. Repairs and rebuilds internal combustion engines, transmissions, rear ends, and general appurtenances thereto. Operates powered automotive repair equipment such as lathes, drill presses, crankshaft grinders, cylinder borers, valve grinders, etc. Reclaims salvageable automotive equipment. Works to drawings and figures dimensions. Works with and operates shop testing equipment, devices, and measuring instruments. May transmit orders to other journeymen as directed. May supervise machinist helpers, senior automotive servicemen, automotive servicemen, and other personnel as directed. Trains assigned machinist helpers, senior automotive servicemen, automotive servicemen, or other related personnel in the performance of various maintenance and/or repair tasks. May prepare reports and orders and maintain records and inventories of supplies and materials. May operate motor vehicles or equipment in the performance of assigned duties.

Requirements

1. Five years of full-time paid experience acquired within the last fifteen years as a machinist in the repair and maintenance of internal combustion automotive engines and component parts; or
2. Not less than two-and-one half years of experience as described in (1) above plus sufficient full-time paid experience as a helper or apprentice, or training of a relevant nature acquired in an approved trade or vocational high school, to make up the equivalent of five years of acceptable experience. Six months of acceptable experience will be credited for each year of helper or apprentice experience or approved trade or vocational high school.

License. At the time of appointment, candidates must have a state motor vehicle driver's license.

Test Information

The score will be determined by two practical tests: Part I and Part II. The weight of each is 50% and a score of at least 70% in each Part is needed in order to pass. In Part I, you may be required to demonstrate knowledge of principles of operation and construction of internal combustion engines and automotive components, basic mathematics, machine shop instruments, and metals. In Part II, you may be required to demonstrate knowledge and skill in the operation of machine tools, machine shop practices and equipment, and reading of plans and specifications.

Advancement

Employees in the title of Auto Machinist are accorded promotion opportunities, when eligible, to the title of either Foreman of Mechanics (Motor Vehicles) or Foreman Auto Machinist.

State—Municipal Blacksmith

Job Description

Under direction, does general blacksmith work in forging and shaping metal in building, maintaining, and repairing of equipment and appurtenances; performs related work.

Examples of Typical Tasks. Forges and shapes, manually or by power hammer, angle iron, bridle irons, tools, automobile parts and other similar pieces of equipment. Forge welds iron components, repairs metal parts of trucks, automobiles, carts, enclosures, sweepers, and other equipment. Is responsible for and directs the work of Blacksmith's Helpers. Keeps records and makes reports.

Requirements

1. Five years of full-time paid experience as a Blacksmith acquired within the last fifteen years; or
2. Not less than two and one-half years of such experience acquired within the last ten years plus sufficient full-time paid experience as a blacksmith's helper or apprentice or training of a relevant nature acquired in an approved trade or vocational high school to make up the equivalent of five years of acceptable experience. Six months of acceptable experience will be credited for each year of blacksmith's helper or apprentice experience or approved trade or vocational high school; or
3. Education and/or experience which is equivalent to (1) or (2).

Test Information

The score will be determined by a practical-oral test, weight 100. A score of at least 70% is needed in order to pass. In the practical-oral test, candidates will be required to demonstrate knowledge of working heats in the fabrication of tools and parts; shaping of metal using hand forge, gas furnace, steam hammer and related machines and hand tools; forge welding; tool hardening and tempering; properties of various metals (primarily hot-rolled structural steel) in fabrication and application; basic arithmetic and measurement; sketch reading; safety; identification of tools and equipment; and other related areas.

Advancement

Employees in the title of Blacksmith are accorded promotion opportunities, when eligible, to the title of Foreman Blacksmith.

State—Municipal Bus Maintainer

Job Description

Maintain, inspect, test, alter, and repair the electrical, mechanical, hydraulic, pneumatic, and air conditioning equipment of buses, trucks, and other automotive vehicles.

Examples of Typical Tasks. Inspect, test, alter, and repair diesel and gasoline engines, clutches, transmissions, axles, generators, compressors, air conditioning systems, brake assemblies, and electrical accessories. Diagnose troubles and irregularities and make the necessary repairs and adjustments. Align wheels and repair steering equipment. Reline and adjust brakes and clutches. Operate power machine tools and portable power tools and use hand tools as required to rebuild and repair automotive components. If assigned, perform inspection work on new equipment and material at manufacturing plants. Record data and keep records.

Requirements

Candidates must meet one of the following requirements:

1. Four years of full-time paid experience at the mechanic (journeyman) level repairing passenger automobiles, trucks, buses, or aircraft, including engines, transmissions, brakes, electrical systems, and automotive air conditioning; or
2. Three years of full-time paid experience at the mechanic (journeyman) level as described above, plus graduation from a recognized trade high school, vocational high school, or community college with a major sequence of courses of study in auto mechanics or a closely related field.

On the Experience Paper applicants must indicate which of the two alternative requirements described above they are presenting for qualification.

The following types of experience are *not* acceptable: auto body and fender mechanic; auto or truck assembly line mechanic; dealership "make-ready" mechanic; gas station attendant; specialty replacement shop mechanic; salvage and junkyard mechanic.

License. At the time of appointment, eligibles must possess a valid state driver's license. Eligibles must also possess, at the time of the appointment interview, either a commercial driver's license or a valid learner's permit for a commercial driver's license. Eligibles will be appointed subject to the receipt of a commercial driver's license at the end of a special training course. Serious moving violations, license suspensions, or accident record may disqualify.

Test Information

This examination will consist of four parts: a competitive education and experience test; a qualifying written test; a qualifying medical test; and a qualifying physical test. Information on each of the four parts is given below. Candidates must pass all parts to be eligible for employment.

Competitive Education and Experience Test. Weight 100, 70% required. There will be no competitive test other than an evaluation of education and experience. After the minimum requirements have been met, additional credit will be given, as stated in the rating key below, for a maximum of ten additional years of full-time paid experience at the mechanic (journeyman) level, as described in the minimum requirements, or as a supervisor of such mechanics. Education and experience rating will be based on candidate's statements on the Experience Paper, which must be filled out completely and in detail, including names and addresses of employers, dates, salary, and number of hours per week worked for all claimed relevant experience; and including full details of all claimed relevant education. Candidates must list all education and experience for which credit may be given as described below. Once a candidate has filed an application, the candidate will not be permitted to add additional education and experience for purposes of having such education and experience evaluated beyond the minimum requirements.

Education and experience will not be found acceptable unless they are verifiable. Education and experience listed on the Experience Paper will receive credit only to the extent that they are described clearly and in detail.

Rating Key. A rating of 70% will be granted for meeting the minimum requirements as stated above. After the minimum requirements have been met, experience for a maximum of 10 additional years will be credited as follows:

1. Two points per year for each additional year of full-time paid experience at the mechanic (journeyman) level as described in minimum requirements above.
2. Three points per year for each additional year of full-time paid experience as a supervisor of those performing the duties described in minimum requirements above.

In addition, candidates who have full-time paid experience at the mechanic (journeyman) level repairing diesel engines on buses, trucks, or other automotive equipment, will receive an additional two points per year for each year of such experience. For mechanic or supervisory experience, credit will be given to the nearest full quarter of a year.

The maximum rating in this Education and Experience test is 100%.

Qualifying Written Test. Minimum of 70% required. Prior to appointment, eligibles will be required to pass a multiple-choice qualifying test. This test may include questions on safe, proper, and efficient work practices related to maintenance operations in a bus repair shop; proper selection and safe use of hand tools, power tools, and machinery, as required for the performance of work related to bus maintenance and repair; technical knowledge and ability to perform maintenance, repair, and trouble-shooting of engines, transmissions, chassis, running gear, air conditioning, and electrical and mechanical accessories as used in buses, trucks, and other vehicles; reading and interpreting specifications and drawings and performing related mathematical calculations; record keeping; and other related areas.

Candidates who fail the qualifying written test will not be permitted to file again for this examination until at least six months after the date on which they take and fail such qualifying written test.

Qualifying Medical Test. Eligibles will be required to pass a qualifying medical test. Rejection will be based on determination by the examining physician that a condition will interfere with the eligible's ability to engage in the activities performed in this class of positions.

Qualifying Physical Test. Medical evidence to allow participation in the qualifying physical test may be required, and the Department of Personnel reserves the right to exclude from the physical test eligibles who, upon examination of such evidence, are apparently medically unfit. Eligibles will take the physical test at their own risk of injury, although every effort will be made to safeguard them.

The qualifying physical test will consist of two subtests. In one subtest, eligibles will be required to squat without falling and without using any support to keep from falling and to rise to an erect position without falling and without using any support to keep from falling. In the second subtest, eligibles will be required to lift a 50-pound barbell off the floor, raise it to a stop position at shoulder level by bending the arms, press it over the head to a vertical, fully-extended arm position, return it to a stop position at shoulder level by bending the arms, and put the barbell back on the floor. All lifting of the 50-pound barbell must be done under full control and solely by the eligible's sheer muscular effort.

Municipal Transit Authority Car Maintainer—Group B

Job Description

Maintains, installs, tests, alters, and repairs multiple-unit cars, particularly machine shop work, including the operation of lathes, milling machines, boring mills, shapers, and drill presses. Performs such other duties as the city Transit Authority is authorized by law to prescribe in its regulations.

Examples of Typical Tasks. Sets up and operates various types of machines, matching parts according to blueprint specifications. Grinds tool bits, cuts and/or shapes jigs. Reconditions parts for compressors and connecting rods, cleans up bearing surfaces on axles, rebuilds radius bars, rethreads turnion bolts, resurfaces commutators, routs down truck bushings, reseats valves and drills out welds on brake straps. Rebores armature bearings and cylinders on D-3F compressor, replaces worn bushings on door engines, mounts gear housing on axles, measures axle diameters and bores the center of wheels for proper fit onto axles. Works with various measurement tools. Keeps records.

Requirements

Candidates must meet one of the following requirements:

1. Completion of a four-year, full-time paid apprenticeship in the machinist trade conducted or sponsored by a recognized trade union or a recognized industry association or group; or
2. Four years of full-time paid experience at the mechanic (journeyman) level as an all around machinist in a machine shop on machine and bench work, including experience on the lathe, milling, grinding, and shaper machines, boring mill, and drill press; or a satisfactory equivalent; or
3. Three years of full-time paid experience at the mechanic (journeyman) level as described in (2) above, plus graduation from a recognized trade high school, or vocational high school, or community college with a major sequence of courses in machine shop practice; or
4. Three years of full-time paid experience at the mechanic (journeyman) level as described in (2) above, plus at least two years of full-time paid experience as a machinist's helper; or
5. Three years of full-time paid experience at the mechanic (journeyman) level as described in (2) above, plus a combination of relevant education in the machinist trade and full-time paid experience as a machinist's helper, instead of the fourth year of mechanic (journeyman) experience, as follows:
   a. Six months of credit for each year of such helper experience;
   b. Three months of credit for each year of such education at the high school level;
   c. Six months of credit for each year of such education at the community college level.

On the Experience Paper, applicants must indicate which of the five alternative requirements described above they are presenting for qualification.

License. None for Car Maintainer-Group B. (An eligible considered for placement as a Turnstile Maintainer in the Maintenance of Way Department must possess, at the time of appointment, a valid motor vehicle driver's license. Serious moving violations, license suspension, or accident record may disqualify.)

Test Information

Competitive Education and Experience Test. Weight 100, 70% required. There will be no competitive test other than an evaluation of education and experience.

After the minimum requirements have been met, additional credit will be given, as stated in the rating key below, for a maximum of ten additional years of full-time paid experience at the mechanic (journeyman) level, as described in paragraph (2) of the minimum requirements, or as a supervisor of such mechanics. The Education and Experience rating will be based on candidate's statements on the Experience Paper, which must be filled out completely and in detail, including names and addresses of employers, dates, salary, and number of hours per week worked for all claimed relevant experience; and including full details of all claimed relevant education. Candidates must list all education and experience for which credit may be given as described below.

Once a candidate has filed an application, the candidate will not be permitted to add additional education and experience for purposes of having such education and experience evaluated beyond the minimum requirements.

Education and experience will not be found acceptable unless they are verifiable. Education and experience listed on the Experience Paper will receive credit only to the extent that they are described clearly and in detail.

Rating Key. A rating of 70% will be granted for meeting the minimum requirements as stated above.

After the minimum requirements have been met, experience for a maximum of ten additional years will be credited as follows:

1. Two points per year for each additional year of full-time paid experience at the mechanic (journeyman) level as described in paragraph (2) of the minimum requirements above.
2. Three points per year for each additional year of full-time paid experience as a supervisor of those performing the duties described in paragraph (2) of the minimum requirements above.

For mechanic or supervisory experience, credit will be given only for full quarters of a year that have been completed.

The maximum rating in this Education and Experience test is 100%.

Qualifying Physical Test. Eligibles will be required to pass a qualifying physical test prior to appointment. Medical evidence to allow participation in the physical test may be required, and the Department of Personnel reserves the right to exclude from the physical test eligibles who, upon examination of such evidence, are apparently medically unfit. Eligibles will take the physical test at their own risk of injury, although every effort will be made to safeguard them.

Eligibles will be required to satisfactorily complete a physical test consisting of one subtest: Using both arms, eligibles will be required to lift a 50-pound barbell from the floor to shoulder level and from a stop position at shoulder level, lift the barbell to a full-arm vertical position above the head. Under their own power and in full control eligibles must then return the 50-pound barbell to the floor.

Municipal Transit Authority Mechanical Maintainer

Job Description

To maintain, install, inspect, test, alter, and repair elevators, escalators, electrically operated drawbridges, and all allied electrical and mechanical equipment. Perform such other duties as the City Transit Authority is authorized by law to prescribe in its regulations.

Examples of Typical Tasks. Maintain, install, and repair elevator, escalator, and drawbridge electrical and mechanical equipment and components, including generators, motors, electrical control equipment, cars, treads, chains, cables, doors, and door control equipment. If assigned, perform inspection work on new equipment and material at manufacturing plants. Drive trucks and vans; load and unload tools, equipment, and material. Keep records. Make reports.

Requirements

Candidates must meet *one* of the following requirements:

1. Completion of a four-year, full-time paid apprenticeship in the construction, repair, and maintenance of elevators or escalators conducted or sponsored by a recognized trade union or a recognized industry association group; or
2. Four years of full-time paid experience at the mechanic level in the construction, repair, and maintenance of elevators or escalators; or
3. Three years of such experience as described in (2) above, plus one of the following:
   a. Two years of full-time paid experience at the helper level in constructing, maintaining, installing, inspecting, testing, altering, or repairing elevators and associated equipment; or

b. Graduation from a recognized trade high school, vocational high school, or community college with a major sequence of courses of study in electronics; or
c. Three years of full-time paid experience as an electronic technician repairing and maintaining complex electronic equipment.

License. At the time of appointment, eligibles must possess a valid motor vehicle driver's license. Serious moving violations, license suspension, or accident record may disqualify.

Test Information

Education and experience, weight 100, 70% required. There will be no competitive test other than an evaluation of education and experience.

After the minimum requirements have been met, additional credit will be given, as stated in the rating key below, for a maximum of 10 additional years of full-time paid experience at the mechanic level, as described in the minimum requirements, or as a supervisor of such mechanics. Education and experience rating will be based on candidate's statements on the Experience Paper, which must be filled out completely and in detail, including names and addresses of employers, dates, salary, and number of hours per week worked for all claimed relevant experience; and including full details of all claimed relevant education. Candidates must list *all* education and experience for which credit may be given as described below. Once a candidate has filed an application, the candidate will not be permitted to add additional education and experience for purposes of having such education and experience evaluated beyond the minimum requirements.

Education and experience will not be found acceptable unless they are verifiable. Education and experience listed on the Experience Paper will receive credit only to the extent that they are described clearly and in detail.

Rating Key. A rating of 70% will be granted for meeting the minimum requirements as stated above. After the minimum requirements have been met, experience for a maximum of ten additional years will be credited as follows: Two points per year for each additional year of full-time paid experience at the mechanic level as described in (2) of the minimum requirements above.

For mechanic level or supervisory experience, credit will be given to the nearest full quarter of a year. The maximum rating in this Education and Experience test is 100.

Qualifying Physical Test. Eligibles will be required to pass a qualifying physical test prior to appointment. Medical evidence to allow participation in the physical test may be required, and the Department of Personnel reserves the right to exclude from the physical test eligibles who, upon examination of such evidence, are apparently medically unfit. Eligibles will take the physical test at their own risk of injury, although every effort will be made to safeguard them. Eligibles will be required to satisfactorily complete a physical test consisting of the following three subtests:

1. In one subtest, eligibles will be required to squat without falling and without using any support to keep from falling and to rise to an erect position without falling and without using any support to keep from falling.
2. In another subtest, eligibles will be required to lift a 75-pound barbell from floor to waist level, using both hands, carry it in that position for a distance of 50 feet, and return it to the floor under control. All lifting and lowering of the barbell must be done under full control and solely by the eligible's sheer muscular effort.
3. In another subtest, eligibles will be required to climb approximately six and one-half feet up a ladder-type trestle, mount a platform affixed thereto, walk approximately nine feet to another ladder-type trestle, turn around, and climb down, all within 30 seconds.

Advancement

Mechanical Maintainers are accorded promotion opportunities, when eligible, to Foreman (Elevators and Escalators).

State—Municipal
Promotion to Supervisor of Mechanics (Motor Vehicles)

Job Description

Under general supervision, supervises, directs, and is responsible for the work of assigned personnel in connection with the repair, overhaul, and maintenance of motor vehicles; performs related work.

Examples of Typical Tasks. Supervises and directs the work of assigned personnel in repairing, overhauling, dismantling, assembling, and troubleshooting of all automotive equipment such as passenger cars, trucks, flushers, tractors, wreckers, drag lines, cranes, shovels, and various types of snow removal equipment. Makes recommendations and suggestions regarding the purchasing of production machinery. Makes decisions relative to methods of doing work. Keeps records and makes reports.

Requirements

Eligibility. Open to each employee of the Department of Sanitation and Department of Environmental Protection who on the day of the written test:

1. Is permanently employed in the title of Auto Machinist, Auto Mechanic, Auto Mechanic (Diesel), Electrician (Automobile), or Machinist; and
2. Is not otherwise ineligible.

Test Information

The score will be determined by two tests: seniority, weight 15, and a written test, weight 85. The written test will consist of two parts, to be given in one session on the same day.

Part I (weight 90) will be of the multiple-choice type and may include questions on supervision of staff, assigning work, taking disciplinary action, motivating and training staff, practicing human relations skills, understanding and interpreting directives and technical material; standards of employee conduct; providing technical information and expertise on automotive vehicle repairs, production methods, and safe and proper work procedures; estimating time, materials, and costs; reading plans and blueprints; performing job-related arithmetic calculations; and other related areas. A grade of 70% or better is required for Part I. Candidates who do not receive a grade of 70% or better on this part will not have their papers rated for the other part.

Part II (weight 10) will be of the essay type and may include questions on preparing reports, filling out and reviewing forms, ordering materials and keeping records; and other related areas. A grade of 70% or better is required for this essay part.

State—Municipal
Radio Repair Mechanic

Job Description

Under supervision, installs, repairs, aligns, or tunes the following radio, radar, microwave, multiplex, television, and electronic apparatus and appurtenances of the city's communication systems: land, mobile, and marine radio receivers and transmitters, including UHF and VHF equipment; radio power systems; radio antenna systems; miniature radio receivers and transmitters; audio amplifiers and public address systems; television cameras, receivers, and antennas; radar systems; electronic test equipment; multiplex equipment; magnetic tape recorders; various other electronic devices; performs related work.

Examples of Typical Tasks. Locates and isolates defects in electronic equipment. Repairs or replaces defective parts. Adjusts, aligns, or tunes electronic equipment. Installs electronic units and associated electrical elements, including the mounting of radios in automobiles. Keeps records and makes reports.

Requirements

1. Five years' full-time paid experience acquired within the last ten years as a radio repair mechanic; or
2. Not less than three years of such experience plus sufficient training of a relevant nature acquired in an approved trade or vocational high school to make up the equivalent of five years of acceptable experience. Six months of acceptable experience will be credited for each year of approved trade or vocational school.

License. At the time of appointment, candidates must possess a valid motor vehicle driver's license and a Federal Communication Commission (FCC) Commercial Radiotelephone Second Class Operator's license, with a radar endorsement.

Test Information

Written, weight 100, 70% required. The written test will be in two parts: Part I is multiple-choice, and Part II is short essay (the weight of each part is 50).

Part I will be of the multiple-choice type and may include questions on knowledge of electronic and electrical principles; principles of operation of test equipment; operation of radio communication systems and audio frequency intercommunication systems; safety procedures for electronic and electrical equipment; Federal Communication Commission (FCC) rules, regulations, and operating procedures; and other related areas.

Part II will be of the short essay type and may include questions on the ability to troubleshoot, locate, and diagnose malfunctions; knowledge of proper installation and testing of electronic and electrical equipment; report preparation and other related areas.

Candidates must pass Part I (multiple-choice) with a rating of at least 70% in order for Part II (short essay) to be rated.

State—Municipal Machinist's Helper

Job Description

Under direct supervision, assists machinists in the performance of general machine shop work; performs related work.

Examples of Typical Tasks. Assists in the operation of machine shop equipment, such as engine lathes, shapers, milling machines, drill presses, grinders, etc. Uses hand tools in the performance of machine shop work. Is familiar with and uses precision instruments essential to machine shop work.

Requirements

1. Three years of full-time paid mechanical experience as a Machinist's Helper acquired within the last 10 years; or

2. Not less than one and one-half years of such experience acquired within the last seven years plus sufficient training of a relevant nature acquired in an approved trade, vocational, or technical high school to make up the equivalent of three years of acceptable experience. Six months of acceptable experience will be credited for each year of approved trade, vocational, or technical school; or
3. Education and/or experience which is equivalent to (1) or (2) above.

Test Information

The test score will be determined by a written multiple-choice test, weight 100. A score of at least 70% is needed in order to pass. The written multiple-choice test may include questions on knowledge of machine shop operations and practices, tools, materials and machinery, precision measuring instruments, reading comprehension, shop mathematics, safety, and other related areas.

Advancement

Employees in the title of Machinist's Helper are accorded promotion opportunities, when eligible, to the title of Machinist.

State—Municipal Machinist

Job Description

Under supervision, does bench, general shop, and outside machinist's work; performs related work.

Examples of Typical Tasks. Sets up and operates machine shop equipment such as engine lathes, shapers, milling machines, drill presses, grinders, etc. Is familiar with and uses tools and instruments required for all phases of machinist's work. When assigned, does outside machinist's work in the inspection, overhaul, and repair of all types of main and auxiliary stationary power plant, marine propulsion, water and disposal works equipment. May transmit orders to other journeymen as directed. May supervise machinist's helpers, senior automotive servicemen, automotive service men, and other personnel as directed. Trains assigned machinist's helpers, senior automotive servicemen and automotive servicemen or other related personnel in the performance of various maintenance and/or repair tasks. May prepare reports and orders; maintains records and inventories of supplies and materials. May operate motor vehicles or equipment in the performance of assigned duties.

Requirements

1. Five years of full-time paid experience acquired within the last 15 years as a machinist; or
2. Not less than two-and-one-half years of such experience acquired within the last ten years plus sufficient full-time paid experience as a helper or an apprentice or training of a relevant nature acquired in an approved trade or vocational high school to make up the equivalent of five years of acceptable experience. Six months of acceptable experience will be credited for each year of helper or apprentice experience or approved trade or vocational high school.

At the time of appointment to the Department of Sanitation or the Department of Environmental Protection, candidates must have a valid motor vehicle driver's license.

Test Information

The score will be determined by two tests: a written multiple-choice test, weight 50; and a practical test, weight 50. A score of at least 70% is needed in each test in order to pass. The written multiple-choice test may include questions on operation and maintenance of all machine shop equipment; hand tools and machine shop practices; machinery components; measuring devices and instruments; metals and heat treatment; reading comprehension and plan reading; related machine shop mathematics; safety; supervision and reports; and other related areas. In the practical test, the candidate may be required to demonstrate knowledge and skill in the production of a work sample.

Advancement

Employees in the title of Machinist are accorded promotion opportunities, when eligible, to the titles of Foreman Machinist or Foreman of Mechanics (Motor Vehicles).

P A R T

FOUR

Examination Preparation

CONTENTS

PREPARING YOURSELF FOR THE CIVIL SERVICE EXAMINATION

About twelve million people are employed by our state and local departments and agencies. The employment opportunities cover practically every skill and profession in our complex modern social order. Every year thousands of new jobs are created and tens of thousands of replacements are needed on existing jobs.

Most federal, state, and municipal units have recruitment procedures for filling civil service positions. They have developed a number of methods to make job opportunities known. Places where such information may be obtained include:

1. The offices of the State Employment Services. There are almost two thousand throughout the country. These offices are administered by the state in which they are located, with the financial assistance of the federal government. You will find the address of the one nearest you in your telephone book.
2. Your state Civil Service Commission. Address your inquiry to the capital city of your state.
3. Your city Civil Service Commission—if you live in a large city. It is sometimes called by another name, such as the Department of Personnel, but you will be able to identify it in your telephone directory under the listing of city departments.
4. Your municipal building and your local library.
5. Complete listings are carried by such newspapers as *The Chief-Leader* (published in New York City), as well as by other city- and state-wide publications devoted to civil service employees. Many local newspapers run a section on regional civil service news.
6. State and local agencies looking for competent employees will contact schools, professional societies, veterans organizations, unions, and trade associations.
7. School Boards and Boards of Education, which employ the greatest proportion of all state and local personnel, should be asked directly for information about job openings.

The Format of the Job Announcement

When a position is open and a civil service examination is to be given for it, a job announcement is drawn up. This generally contains just about everything an applicant has to know about the job.

The announcement begins with the job title and salary. A typical announcement then describes the work, the location of the position, the education and experience requirements, the kind of examination to be given, and the system of rating. It may also have something to say about veteran preference and the age limit. It tells which application form is to be filled out, where to get the form, and where and when to file it.

Study the job announcement carefully. It will answer many of your questions and help you decide whether you like the position and are qualified for it. The precise duties are described in detail, usually under the heading **Description of Work.** Make sure that these duties come within the range of your experience and ability.

There is no point in applying for a position and taking the examination if you do not want to work where the job is. The job may be in your community or hundreds of miles away at the other end of the state. If you are not willing to work where the job is, study other announcements that will give you an opportunity to work in a place of your choice. A civil service job close to your home has as an additional advantage because of the fact that local residents usually receive preference in appointments.

Most job announcements give a **deadline** for filing an application. Others bear the words, *No Closing Date* at the top of the first page; this means that applications will be accepted until the needs of the agency are met. In some cases a public notice is issued when a certain number of applications have been received. No application mailed past the deadline date will be considered.

Every announcement has a detailed section on **education and experience requirements** for the particular job and for the optional fields. Make sure that in both education and experience you meet the minimum qualifications. If you do not meet the given standards for one job, there may be others open where you stand a better chance of making the grade.

If the job announcement does not mention **veteran preference,** it would be wise to inquire if there is such a provision in your state or municipality. There may be none or it may be limited to disabled veterans. In some jurisdictions surviving spouses of deceased veterans are given preference. All such information can be obtained through the agency that issues the job announcement.

Applicants may be denied examinations and eligible candidates may be denied appointments for any of the following reasons:

1. Intentional false statements.
2. Deception or fraud in examination or appointment.
3. Use of intoxicating beverages to the extent that ability to perform the duties of the position is impaired.
4. Criminal, infamous, dishonest, immoral, or notoriously disgraceful conduct.

The announcement describes the **kind of test** given for the particular position. Please pay special attention to this section. It tells what areas are to be covered in the written test and lists the specific subjects on which questions will be asked. Sometimes sample questions are given.

Usually the announcement states whether the examination is to be **assembled** or **unassembled.** In an assembled examination applicants assemble in the same place at the same time to take a written or performance test. The unassembled examination is one where an applicant does not take a test; instead, he or she is rated on education and experience and whatever records of past achievement are required.

In the competitive examination all applicants for a position compete with each other; the better the mark, the better the chance of being appointed. Also, competitive examinations are given to determine desirability for promotion among employees.

Civil service written tests are rated on a scale of 100, with 70 as the usual passing mark.

Filling Out the Application Form

Having studied the job announcement and having decided that you want the position and are qualified for it, your next step is to get an application form. The job announcement tells you where to send for it.

On the whole, civil service application forms differ little from state to state and locality to locality. The questions, which have been worked out after years of experimentation, are simple and direct, designed to elicit maximum information about you.

Many prospective civil service employees have failed to get a job because of slipshod, erroneous, incomplete, misleading, or untruthful answers. Give the application serious attention, for it is the first important step toward getting the job you want.

Here, along with some helpful comments, are the questions usually asked on the average application form, although not necessarily in this order.

Name of examination or kind of position applied for. This information appears in large type on the first page of the job announcement.

Announcement number or examination number. You will find this at the top of the front of the announcement. It is important that this number appear on all application materials you submit.

Optional job (if mentioned in the announcement). If you wish to apply for an option, simply copy the title from the announcement. If you are not interested in an option, write *None.*

Primary place of employment applied for. The location of the position was probably contained in the announcement. You must consider whether you want to work there. The announcement may list more than one location where the job is open. If you would accept employment in any of the places, list them all; otherwise list the specific place or places where you would be willing to work.

Name and address. Give in full, including your zip plus four. It makes you appear efficient.

Home and office phones. If none, write *None.*

Legal or voting residence. The state in which you vote is the one you list here.

Citizenship and Social Security Number. You MUST give these to be considered.

Date of birth. Give the exact day, month, and year.

Lowest grade or pay you will accept. Although the salary is clearly stated in the job announcement, there may be a quicker opening in the same occupation but carrying less responsibility and thus a lower basic entrance salary. You will not be considered for a job paying less than the amount you give in answer to this question.

Will you accept temporary employment if offered you for (a) one month or less, (b) one to four months, (c) four to twelve months? Temporary positions come up frequently and it is important to know whether you are available.

Will you accept less than full-time employment? Part-time work comes up now and then. Consider whether you want to accept such a position while waiting for a full-time appointment.

Were you in active military service in the Armed Forces of the United States? Veterans' preference, if given, is usually limited to active service during specific wartime or special operations periods, but do ask. Rules and procedures vary.

Do you claim disabled veterans credit? If you do, you have to show proof of a war-incurred disability compensable by at least 10%. This is done through certification by the Veterans Administration.

Special qualifications and skills. Even though not directly related to the position for which you are applying, information about licenses and certificates obtained for teacher, pilot, registered nurse, and so on, is requested. List your experience in the use of machines and equipment and whatever other skills you have acquired. Also list published writings, public speaking experience, membership in professional societies, honors, and fellowships received.

Education. List your entire educational history, including all diplomas, degrees, special courses taken in any accredited or Armed Forces school. Also give your credits toward a college or a graduate degree.

References. The names of people who can give information about you, with their occupations and business and home addresses, are often requested.

Work history. Considerable space is allotted on the form for the applicant to tell about all past employment. Examiners check all such answers closely. Do not embroider or falsify your record. If you were ever fired, say so. It is better for you to state this openly than for the examiners to find out the truth from your former employer.

Getting Ready for the Examination

When you have filled out the application as completely as possible, sign it and send it to the address given on the form. If your examination includes a written test, you must wait until it is scheduled. Shortly before it is to be held, you will be notified where and when to report.

Sometimes the date of the written test appears on the job announcement. Sometimes it does not and you must simply wait until you receive notification of the time and place.

The period between the filing of the application and the taking of the test can be of immense value to you. If you use it wisely, it will help you score high.

MULTIPLE-CHOICE TESTS

All multiple-choice tests consist of a question booklet or booklets and a separate answer sheet. The question booklets begin with general instructions for taking the test. It is at the beginning of the question booklet that you will learn the rules and regulations governing your exam, number of questions, timing, signals, etc. If there are specific directions for different types of questions in the exam, you will find these in the question booklet before each new type of question.

You may usually write in the question booklet—put a question mark next to the number of a question at which you took a guess, calculate the answers to math questions, cross out eliminated answer choices, underline key words, or even just plain doodle in the margins. The one thing you must not do with a question booklet is use it as an answer sheet. If you are not permitted to write in the test booklet, you will be issued scratch paper for figuring and for writing notes to yourself about guesses and when time will run out on each part of the exam. The scratch paper will be collected but it will NOT be scored.

The separate answer sheet that accompanies the test booklet is the only record of answers that is scored. You must mark every answer that you choose in the correct place on the answer sheet. Mark your answer choice by blackening its circle darkly and completely. A correct answer response looks like this: ●. Here are some examples of incorrectly marked responses: ✓●✗●. The scoring machine might not notice these marks. If your answer is not registered by the scoring machine, you cannot get any credit for it. You must mark only one answer for each question. If there is more than one answer for any question, even if one of the answers is correct, the machine will give no credit for that question. You may change your mind and change your answer. However, when you change an answer, you must be careful to fully and cleanly erase the first answer. And mark your new choice with extra care. You do not want the scoring machine to misread your choice. Never cross out an answer in favor of a new choice. You must erase. Ⓐ✗Ⓒ● will not work. The machine will read both old and new answers and will give you no credit.

Another very important aspect of working with the separate answer sheet is to mark every question in the right place. The scoring machine does not read question number and answer choice. The machine scans the page for a pattern of blackened spaces. If you have marked an answer in the wrong place you will have it scored as wrong (unless, of course, the same letter was the correct answer for the space in which you made your mark). If you notice that you have slipped out of line, you must erase all answers from the point of the error and redo all those questions. Most Civil Service tests are not heavily speeded (though some parts of some exams are), but you do not have the luxury of time to waste erasing and reanswering large blocks of questions. Furthermore, an error of this type will fluster you and lead to errors of judgment in choosing answers to other questions. Therefore, do not skip any questions. Do not jump around looking for easy questions to answer first. Do not omit a question even if you have no idea whatsoever of the correct answer. If you are forced to guess so as to answer every question in order, then do so. If you guess, mark the question in the question booklet with a question mark or write its number on your scratch paper. If you have time after you have completed all the questions, go back and give the marked questions more thought. If you answer every question in order, there should be no chance to slip. Even so, it is a good idea to check question number and answer space number as you mark each answer.

The questions on multiple-choice exams consist of the question itself and four or five answer choices. The answer choices are lettered A through D or E. On the answer sheet next to each number are lettered circles. Each question has one BEST answer. You must read the question carefully, think, choose the best answer and blacken the circle that contains the letter of that answer. This method of answering is much easier than filling in a blank or circling a portion of a sentence or paragraph. Provided that you mark your answers neatly, there is no room for scoring error in marking a multiple-choice answer sheet. You can be sure of accuracy and objectivity.

The scoring of most of these exams is simple too. You get one credit for each correct answer. You get no credit for a wrong answer. You get no credit for a question that you did not answer at all. Most important: You do not lose any credit for a wrong answer. A wrong answer is simply not a right answer. You get no credit, but the wrong answer itself does not work against you. What this means is that a guess cannot hurt. The best guess is the educated guess. Sometime you may read a question and not be sure of the right answer. Try to eliminate those answers that are obviously wrong. If you have any idea at all of the answer, you may be able to rule out one or two of the choices. If you can narrow the field and guess from among fewer choices, you can raise your odds of guessing right. If you have no idea at all and must guess from among all four, you have a 1 in 4 chance of guessing right. If you eliminate one choice, your odds are 1 in 3. If you can eliminate two of the four, then your odds become 1 in 2; that's 50-50. You could pick up a number of points by intelligent guessing. And always mark the guesses in the question booklet so that you can try again.

Since a blank space can do you no good, and a wrong answer can do you no harm, it makes sense to answer every question. This means that you must keep track of time. Wear a watch. If you have worked slowly and methodically and find that time is about to run out, pick a letter and mark all the remaining questions with the same response. By the law of averages, you should get some right and should pick up some credit.

A few exams or portions of exams do not follow this scoring rule. These tend to be exam portions which are measuring the applicant's accuracy under time pressure. A part of the Federal Clerical Exam and parts of some postal exams penalize wrong answers. In some cases, the number of wrong answers is subtracted from the number of right answers. More often, a portion (one-fourth, for instance) of the wrong answers are subtracted from the number of correct answers. Whenever there is a penalty for wrong answers, you should not rush to answer remaining questions as time is about to run out. Rather, work as quickly and accurately as you can right up to the end signal; then stop. The printed instructions at the beginning of the exam should tell you if there is a penalty for inaccuracy or for guessing. But it never hurts to ask; you are entitled to have this information.

Not many exams consist of exactly 100 questions. Some contain only 80, others 140 or more. All scores are finally reported on the basis of 100. What this means is that while you get one credit for each correct answer, that answer may not be adding exactly one point to your score. The examiners create a conversion formula that they apply equally to all papers in the same exam. This formula converts raw scores (number right) to the score that is reported. When an announcement specifies "70 percent required" it refers to the score which is reported after the conversion (and before the addition of veteran's credit).

Aside, of course, from actually knowing the answer, the single factor that most influences your choosing the right answer is careful reading. Misreading of directions causes the greatest damage. If the directions ask you to choose the word that means the *opposite* of the underlined word, and you choose the word that means the *same* as the underlined word, you will mark wrong answers for a whole series of questions and do poorly on the exam. If the directions tell you to "Mark (D) if all the names being compared are *alike,*" and you mark (D) when all the names are *different,* you will sabotage your score.

Careful reading must extend beyond reading of directions to reading of each individual question. Qualifying words like: *most, least, only, best, probably, definitely, not, all, every,* and *except* make a big difference in determining the correct answer to a specific question. You want to earn the highest possible score on your exam. A wrong answer caused by careless reading would be a shame.

Actually, reading enters into all multiple-choice questions in one way or another. Directions are always written and must be read. Furthermore, a large proportion of questions are either reading comprehension/interpretation questions or are questions that are based upon material that the test-taker must read. Since reading is so key to success with multiple-choice questions, we are devoting a large part of this chapter to reading and reading-based questions. Once you have mastered the techniques of dealing with reading-based questions, you will be well-equipped to tackle all aspects of your civil service exam. By concentrating so heavily on reading, however, we do not mean to imply that reading questions are more important than arithmetic questions or mechanical ability questions or whatever else you may find on your exam. Usually questions are of equal weight. Each correct answer gives you one credit, unless the exam specifies otherwise. But reading does underlie much of the exam, so read on.

Reading-Based Questions

Some exams include classic reading comprehension questions that present a passage and then ask questions on the details of the passage and, perhaps, on its meaning. Other exams require candidates to indicate proper behavior based on their reading of printed procedures and regulations. Still another type of reading-based question requires candidates to reason and choose next steps on the basis of information presented in a reading passage. There are, of course, nearly as many variations of the reading-based question as there are testmakers. In fact, reading skill enters into form-completion questions, arithmetic problems based on fact situations, and judgment questions as well.

Before you begin to devote attention to strategies for dealing with reading-based questions, give some thought to your reading habits and skills. Of course, you already know how to read. But how well do you read? Do you concentrate? Do you get the point on your first reading? Do you notice details?

Between now and the test day, you must work to improve your reading concentration and comprehension. Your daily newspaper provides excellent material to improve your reading. Make a point of reading all the way through any article that you begin. Do not be satisfied with the first paragraph or two. Read with a pencil in hand. Underscore details and ideas that seem to be crucial to the meaning of the article. Notice points of view, arguments, and supporting information. When you have finished the article, summarize it for yourself. Do you know the purpose of the article? The main idea presented? The attitude of the writer? The points over which there is controversy? Did you find certain information lacking? As you answer these questions, skim back over your underlinings. Did you focus on important words and ideas? Did you read with comprehension? As you repeat this process day after day, you will find that your reading will become more efficient. You will read with greater understanding, and will get more from your newspaper.

One aspect of your daily reading that deserves special attention is vocabulary building. The effective reader has a rich, extensive vocabulary. As you read, make a list of unfamiliar words. Include in your list words that you understand within the context of the article, but that you cannot really define. In addition, mark words that you do not understand at all. When you put aside your newspaper, go to the dictionary and look up *every* new and unfamiliar word. Write the word and its definition in a special notebook. Writing the words and their definitions helps seal them in your memory far better than just reading them, and the notebook serves as a handy reference for your own use. A sensitivity to the meanings of words and an understanding of more words will make reading easier and more enjoyable even if none of the words you learn in this way crops up on your exam. In fact, the habit of vocabulary building is a good lifetime habit to develop.

Success with reading-based questions depends on more than reading comprehension. You must also know how to draw the answers from the reading selection and be able to distinguish the *best* answer from a number of answers that all seem to be good ones, or from a number of answers that all seem to be wrong.

Strange as it may seem, it's a good idea to approach reading comprehension questions by reading the questions—not the answer choices, just the questions themselves—before you read the selection. The questions will alert you to look for certain details, ideas, and points of view. Use your pencil. Underscore key words in the questions. These will help direct your attention as you read.

Next skim the selection very rapidly to get an idea of its subject matter and its organization. If key words or ideas pop out at you, underline them, but do not consciously search out details in the preliminary skimming.

Now read the selection carefully with comprehension as your main goal. Underscore the important words as you have been doing in your newspaper reading.

Finally, return to the questions. Read each question carefully. Be sure you know what it asks. Misreading of questions is a major cause of error on reading comprehension tests. Read *all* the answer choices. Eliminate the obviously incorrect answers. You may be left with only one possible answer. If you find yourself with more than one possible answer, reread the question. Pay attention to catch words that might destroy the validity of a seemingly acceptable answer. These include expressions like: *under all circumstances, at all times, never, always, under no condition, absolutely, entirely,* and *except when.* Then skim the passage once more, focusing on the underlined segments. By now you should be able to conclude which answer is *best.*

Reading-based questions may take a number of different forms. In general, some of the most common forms are as follows.

1. **Question of fact or detail.** You may have to mentally rephrase or rearrange, but you should find the answer stated in the body of the selection.
2. **Best title or main idea.** The answer may be obvious, but the incorrect choices to the "main idea" question are often half-truths that are easily confused with the main idea. They may misstate the idea, omit part of the idea, or even offer a supporting idea quoted directly from the text. The correct answer is the one that covers the largest part of the selection.
3. **Interpretation.** This type of question asks you what the selection means, not just what is says. On police exams, questions based upon definitions of crimes, for example, fall into this category. On firefighter exams, questions based upon categories of building styles might fall into the realm of interpretation.
4. **Inference.** This the the most difficult type of reading comprehension question. It asks you to go beyond what the selection says, and to predict what might happen next. You might have to choose the best course of action to take, based upon given procedures and a fact situation, or you may have to judge the actions of others. Your answer must be based upon the information in the selection and your own common sense, but not upon any other information you may have about the subject. A variation of the inference question might be stated as, "The author would expect that. . . ." To answer this question, you must understand the author's point of view, then make an inference from that viewpoint based upon the information in the selection.
5. **Vocabulary.** Some civil service reading sections, directly or indirectly, ask the meanings of certain words as used in the selection.

Let's now work together on some typical reading comprehension selections and questions.

SELECTION FOR QUESTIONS 1 TO 4

The recipient gains an impression of a typewritten letter before beginning to read the message. Factors that give a good first impression include margins and spacing that are visually pleasing, formal parts of the letter that are correctly placed according to the style of the letter, copy that is free of obvious erasures and overstrikes, and transcript that is even and clear. The problem for the typist is how to produce that first, positive impression of her work.

There are several general rules that a typist can follow when she wishes to prepare a properly spaced letter on a sheet of letterhead. The width of a letter should ordinarily not be less than four inches, nor more than six inches. The side margins should also have a proportionate relation to the bottom margin, as well as the space between the letterhead and the body of the letter. Usually the most appealing arrangement is when the side margins are even, and the bottom margin is slightly wider than the side margins. In some offices, however, a standard line length is used for all business letters, and the secretary then varies the spacing between the date line and the inside address according to the length of the letter.

1. The best title for the preceding paragraph is (A) (B) (C) (D)
   (A) Writing Office Letters
   (B) Making Good First Impressions
   (C) Judging Well-Typed Letters
   (D) Good Placing and Spacing for Office Letters

2. According to the preceding paragraphs, which of the following might be considered the way that people quickly judge the quality of work that has been typed? (A) (B) (C) (D)
   (A) by measuring the margins to see if they are correct
   (B) by looking at the spacing and cleanliness of the typescript
   (C) by scanning the body of the letter for meaning
   (D) by reading the date line and address for errors

3. According to the preceding paragraphs, what would be definitely undesirable as the average line length of a typed letter? (A) (B) (C) (D)
   (A) 4 inches
   (B) 5 inches
   (C) 6 inches
   (D) 7 inches

4. According to the preceding paragraphs, when the line length is kept standard, the secretary (A) (B) (C) (D)
   (A) does not have to vary the spacing at all because this also is standard.
   (B) adjusts the spacing between the date line and inside address for different lengths of letters.
   (C) uses the longest line as a guideline for spacing between the date line and inside address.
   (D) varies the number of spaces between the lines.

Begin by skimming the questions and underscoring key words. Your underscored questions should look more or less like this:

1. The <u>best title</u> for the preceding paragraphs is . . .
2. According to the preceding paragraphs, which of the following might be considered the way that people <u>quickly judge the quality</u> of work that has been typed?
3. According to the preceding paragraphs, what would be definitely <u>undesirable</u> as the <u>average line length</u> of a typed letter?
4. According to the preceding paragraphs, <u>when the line length is kept standard,</u> the secretary . . .

Now skim the selection. This quick reading should give you an idea of the structure of the selection and of its overall meaning.

Next read the selection carefully and underscore words that seem important or that you think hold keys to the question answers. Your underscored selection should look something like this:

> The recipient gains an impression of a typewritten letter before he begins to read the message. Factors that give a good first impression include margins and spacing that are visually pleasing, formal parts of the letter that are correctly placed according to the style of letter, copy that is free of obvious erasures and overstrikes, and transcript that is even and clear. The problem for the typist is how to produce that first, positive impression of her work.
>
> There are several general rules that a typist can follow when she wishes to prepare a properly spaced letter on a sheet of letterhead. The width of a letter should ordinarily not be less than four inches, nor more than six inches. The side margins should also have a proportionate relation to the bottom margin, as well as the space between the letterhead and the body of the letter. Usually the most appealing arrangement is when the side margins are even, and the bottom margin is slightly wider than the side margins. In some offices, however, a standard line length is used for all business letters, and the secretary then varies the spacing between the date line and the inside address according to the length of the letter.

Finally, read the questions and answer choices, and try to choose the correct answer for each question. The correct answers are: 1. **(D)**, 2. **(B)**, 3. **(D)**, 4. **(B)**. Did you get them all right? Whether you made any errors or not, read these explanations.

1. **(D)** The best title for any selection is the one that takes in all of the ideas presented without being too broad or too narrow. Choice (D) provides the most inclusive title for this passage. A look at the other choices shows you why. Choice (A) can be eliminated because the passage discusses typing a letter, not writing one. Although the first paragraph states that a letter should make a good first impression, the passage is clearly devoted to the letter, not the first impression, so choice (B) can be eliminated. Choice (C) puts the emphasis on the wrong aspect of the typewritten letter. The passage concerns how to type a properly spaced letter, not how to judge one.

2. **(B)** Both spacing and cleanliness are mentioned in paragraph 1 as ways to judge the quality of a typed letter. The first paragraph states that the margins should be "visually pleasing" in relation to the body of the letter, but that does not imply margins of a particular measure, so choice (A) is incorrect. Meaning is not discussed in the passage, only the look of the finished letter, so choice (C) is incorrect. The passage makes no mention of errors, only the avoidance of erasures and overstrikes, so choice (D) is incorrect.

3. **(D)** This answer comes from the information provided in paragraph 2, that the width of a letter "should not be less than four inches nor more than six inches." According to this rule, seven inches is an undesirable line length.

4. **(B)** The answer to this question is stated in the last sentence of the reading passage. When a standard line length is used, the secretary "varies the spacing between the date line and the inside address according to the length of the letter." The passage offers no support for any other choice.

Let us try another together.

SELECTION FOR QUESTIONS 5 TO 9

Cotton fabrics treated with XYZ Process have features that make them far superior to any previously known flame-retardant-treated cotton fabrics. XYZ Process treated fabrics endure repeated laundering and dry cleaning; are glow resistant as well as flame resistant; when exposed to flames or intense heat form tough, pliable, and protective chars; are inert physiologically to persons handling or exposed to the fabric; are only slightly heavier than untreated fabrics; and are susceptible to further wet and dry finishing treatments. In addition, the treated fabrics exhibit little or no adverse change in feel, texture, and appearance, and are shrink-, rot-, and mildew-resistant. The treatment reduces strength only slightly. Finished fabrics have "easy care" properties in that they are wrinkle resistant and dry rapidly.

5. It is most accurate to state that the author in the preceding selection presents

(A) facts but reaches no conclusion concerning the value of the process.
(B) a conclusion concerning the value of the process and facts to support that conclusion.
(C) a conclusion concerning the value of the process unsupported by facts.
(D) neither facts nor conclusions, but merely describes the process.

5. Ⓐ Ⓑ Ⓒ Ⓓ

6. Of the following articles, for which is the XYZ Process most suitable?

(A) nylon stockings
(B) woolen shirt
(C) silk tie
(D) cotton bedsheet

6. Ⓐ Ⓑ Ⓒ Ⓓ

7. Of the following aspects of the XYZ Process, which is *not* discussed in the preceding selection?

(A) costs
(B) washability
(C) wearability
(D) the human body

7. Ⓐ Ⓑ Ⓒ Ⓓ

8. The main reason for treating a fabric with XYZ Process is to

(A) prepare the fabric for other wet and dry finishing treatment.
(B) render it shrink-, rot-, and mildew-resistant.
(C) increase its weight and strength.
(D) reduce the chance that it will catch fire.

8. Ⓐ Ⓑ Ⓒ Ⓓ

9. Which of the following would be considered a minor drawback of the XYZ process?

(A) it forms chars when exposed to flame
(B) it makes fabrics mildew-resistant
(C) it adds to the weight of fabrics
(D) it is compatible with other finishing treatments

9. Ⓐ Ⓑ Ⓒ Ⓓ

Skim the questions and underscore the words which you consider to be key. The questions should look something like this:

5. It is the most accurate to state that the author, in the preceding selection, presents
6. Of the following articles, for which is the XYZ Process most suitable?
7. Of the following aspects of the XYZ Process, which is *not* discussed in the preceding selection?
8. The main reason for treating a fabric with the XYZ Process is to
9. Which of the following would be considered a minor drawback of the XYZ Process?

Skim the reading selection. Get an idea of the subject matter of the selection and of how it is organized.

Now read the selection carefully and underscore the words that you think are especially important. This fact-filled selection might be underlined like this:

> Cotton fabrics treated with XYZ Process have features that make them far superior to any previously known flame-retardant-treated cotton fabrics. XYZ Process treated fabrics endure repeated laundering and dry cleaning; are glow resistant as well as flame resistant; when exposed to flames or intense heat form tough, pliable, and protective chars; are inert physiologically to persons handling or exposed to the fabric; are only slightly heavier than untreated fabrics; and are susceptible to further wet and dry finishing treatments. In addition, the treated fabrics exhibit little or no adverse change in feel, texture, and appearance, and are shrink-, rot-, and mildew-resistant. The treatment reduces strength only slightly. Finished fabrics have "easy care" properties in that they are wrinkle resistant and dry rapidly.

Now read each question and all its answer choices, and try to choose the correct answer for each question.

The correct answers are: 5. **(B)**, 6. **(D)**, 7. **(A)**, 8. **(D)**, 9. **(C)**. How did you do on these? Read the explanations.

5. **(B)** This is a combination main idea and interpretation question. If you cannot answer this question readily, reread the selection. The author clearly thinks that the XYZ Process is terrific and says so in the first sentence. The rest of the selection presents a wealth of facts to support the initial claim.

6. **(D)** At first glance you might think that this is an inference question requiring you to make a judgment based upon the few drawbacks of the process. Closer reading, however, shows you that there is no contest for correct answer here. This is a simple question of fact. The XYZ Process is a treatment for cotton fabrics.

7. **(A)** Your underlinings should help you with this question of fact. Cost is not mentioned; all other aspects of the XYZ Process are. If you are having trouble finding mention of the effect of the XYZ Process on the human body, add to your vocabulary list "inert" and "physiologically."

8. **(D)** This is a main idea question. You must distinguish between the main idea and the supporting and incidental facts.

9. **(C)** Obviously a drawback is a negative feature. The selection mentions only two negative features. The treatment reduces strength slightly, and it makes fabrics slightly heavier than untreated fabrics. Only one of these negative features is offered among the answer choices.

You should be getting better at reading and at answering questions. Try this next selection on your own. Read and underline the questions. Skim the selection. Read and underline the selection. Read questions and answer choices and mark your answers. Then check your answers against the answers and explanations that follow the selection.

SELECTION FOR QUESTIONS 10 TO 12

Language performs an essentially social function: It helps us get along together, communicate, and achieve a great measure of concerted action. Words are signs that have significance by convention, and those people who do not adopt the conventions simply fail to communicate. They do not "get along," and a social force arises that encourages them to achieve the correct associations. By "correct" we mean as used by other members of the social group. Some of the vital points about language are brought home to an English visitor to America, and vice versa, because our vocabularies are nearly the same—but not quite.

10. As defined in the preceding selection, usage of a word is "correct" when it is **10.** Ⓐ Ⓑ Ⓒ Ⓓ

(A) defined in standard dictionaries.
(B) used by the majority of persons throughout the world who speak the same language.
(C) used by a majority of educated persons who speak the same language.
(D) used by other persons with whom we are associating.

11. In the preceding selection, the author is concerned primarily with the **11.** Ⓐ Ⓑ Ⓒ Ⓓ

(A) meaning of words.
(B) pronunciation of words.
(C) structure of sentences.
(D) origin and development of language.

12. According to the preceding selection, the main language problem of an English visitor to America stems from the fact that an English person **12.** Ⓐ Ⓑ Ⓒ Ⓓ

(A) uses some words that have different meanings for Americans.
(B) has different social values than the Americans.
(C) has had more exposure to non-English speaking persons than Americans have had.
(D) pronounces words differently than Americans do.

The correct answers are: 10. **(D)**, 11. **(A)**, 12. **(A)**.

10. **(D)** The answer to this question is stated in the next-to-last sentence of the selection.

11. **(A)** This main idea question is an easy one to answer. You should have readily eliminated all of the wrong choices.

12. **(A)** This is a question of fact. The phrasing of the question is quite different from the phrasing of the last sentence, but the meaning is the same. You may have found this reading selection more difficult to absorb than some of the others, but you should have had no difficulty answering this question by eliminating the wrong answers.

Now try this reading selection and its questions. Explanations follow the correct answers. Follow the procedure you have learned, and be sure to read the explanations even if you have a perfect score.

SELECTION FOR QUESTIONS 13 TO 18

Since almost every office has some contact with data-processed records, a Senior Stenographer should have some understanding of the basic operations of data processing. Data processing systems now handle about one third of all office paper work. On punched cards, magnetic tape, or on other mediums, data are recorded before being fed into the computer for processing. A machine such as the key punch is used to convert the data written on the source document into the coded symbols on punched cards or tapes. After data has been converted, it must be verified to guarantee absolute accuracy of conversion. In this manner data becomes a permanent record that can be read by electronic computers that compare, store, compute, and otherwise process data at high speeds.

One key person in a computer installation is a programmer, the man or woman who puts business and scientific problems into special symbolic languages that can be read by the computer. Jobs done by the computer range all the way from payroll operations to chemical process control, but most computer applications are directed toward management data. About half of the programmers employed by business come to their positions with college degrees; the remaining half are promoted to their positions without regard to education, from within the organization on the basis of demonstrated ability.

13. Of the following, the best title for the preceding selection is — 13. Ⓐ Ⓑ Ⓒ Ⓓ
(A) The Stenographer as Data Processor
(B) The Relation of Key Punching to Stenography
(C) Understanding Data Processing
(D) Permanent Office Records

14. According to the preceding selection, a Senior Stenographer should understand the basic operations of data processing because — 14. Ⓐ Ⓑ Ⓒ Ⓓ
(A) almost every office today has contact with data processed records by computer.
(B) any office worker may be asked to verify the accuracy of data.
(C) most offices are involved in the production of permanent records.
(D) data may be converted into computer language by typing on a key punch.

15. According to the preceding selection, the data that the computer understands is most often expressed — 15. Ⓐ Ⓑ Ⓒ Ⓓ
(A) as a scientific programming language.
(B) as records or symbols punched on tape, cards, or other mediums.
(C) as records on cards.
(D) as records on tape.

16. According to the preceding selection, computers are used most often to handle — 16. Ⓐ Ⓑ Ⓒ Ⓓ
(A) management data.
(B) problems of higher education.
(C) the control of chemical processes.
(D) payroll operations.

17. Computer programming is taught in many colleges and business schools. The preceding selection implies that programmers in industry

(A) must have professional training.
(B) need professional training to advance.
(C) must have at least a college education to do adequate programming tasks.
(D) do not need college education to do programming work.

17. Ⓐ Ⓑ Ⓒ Ⓓ

18. According to the preceding selection, data to be processed by computer should be

(A) recent.
(B) complete.
(C) basic.
(D) verified.

18. Ⓐ Ⓑ Ⓒ Ⓓ

The correct answers are 13. **(C)**, 14. **(A)**, 15. **(B)**, 16. **(A)**, 17. **(D)**, 18. **(D)**.

13. **(C)** Choosing the best title for this selection is not easy. Although the Senior Stenographer is mentioned in the first sentence, the selection is really not concerned with stenographers or with their relationship to key punching. Eliminate choices (A) and (B). Permanent office records are mentioned in the selection, but only along with other equally important uses for data processing. Eliminate choice (D). When in doubt, the most general title is usually correct.

14. **(A)** This is a question of fact. Any one of the answer choices could be correct, but the answer is given almost verbatim in the first sentence. Take advantage of answers that are handed to you.

15. **(B)** This is a question of fact, but it is a tricky one. The program language is a symbolic language, not a scientific one. Reread carefully and eliminate choice (A). (B) includes more of the information in the selection than either (C) or (D) and so is the best answer.

16. **(A)** This is a question of fact. The answer is stated in the next to the last sentence.

17. **(D)** Remember that you are answering the questions on the basis of the information given in the selection. In spite of any information you may have to the contrary, the last sentence of the selection states that half the programmers employed in business achieved their positions by moving up from the ranks without regard to education.

18. **(D)** Judicious underlining proves very helpful to you in finding the correct answer to this question buried in the middle of the selection. Since any one of the answers might be correct, the way to deal with this question is to skim the underlined words in the selection, eliminate those that are not mentioned, and choose the appropriate answer.

In the past few years, the federal government has introduced a new style of reading comprehension question into many of its exams. The reading selection itself is very short, and it is followed by only one question. At first glance, the task is deceptively simple. However, the paragraph is often dense with information and difficult to absorb. The question may be phrased in a circular, oblique, or negative fashion. Total concentration is needed for answering this type of reading question. On the plus side, this style of reading question is always scored on a "rights only" basis; so read carefully, think, eliminate obviously wrong answers, and guess if necessary.

SELECTION FOR QUESTION 19

The modern conception of the economic role of the public sector (government), as distinct from the private sector, is that every level of government is a link in the economic process. Government's contribution to political and economic welfare must, however, be evaluated not merely in terms of its technical efficiency, but also in the light of its acceptability to a particular society at a particular state of political and economic development. Even in a dictatorship this principle is formally observed, although the authorities usually destroy the substance by presuming to interpret to the public its collective desires.

19. The paragraph best supports the statement that

19. Ⓐ Ⓑ Ⓒ Ⓓ Ⓔ

(A) it is not true that some levels of government are not links in the economic process
(B) all dictatorships observe the same economic principles as other governments
(C) all links in the economic process are levels of government
(D) the contributions of some levels of government do not need to be evaluated for technical efficiency and acceptability to society
(E) no links in the economic process are institutions other than levels of government

19. The correct answer is **(A)**. This answer can be inferred from the first sentence of the paragraph, which states that *every level of government is a link in the economic process*. It can be deduced that its contradictory statement, *some levels of government are not links in the economic process*, cannot be true.

Response B is not supported by the paragraph because it goes beyond the information given. The third sentence of the paragraph states that a dictatorship observes (at least formally) *one* of the same principles as other governments. It cannot be concluded from this that dictatorships observe more than this one principle in common with other governments.

Responses C and E represent incorrect interpretations of the information given in the first sentence, which states that *every level of government is a link in the economic process*. It cannot be inferred from this statement that *all links in the economic process are levels of government*, only that some are. We know that the category "all levels of government" is contained in the category "links in the economic process," but we do not know if other links in the economic process exist that are not levels of government. In regard to response E, it cannot be inferred that *no links in the economic process are institutions other than levels of government*, because that would be the same as saying that all links in the economic process are levels of government.

Response D is not supported by the passage because the second sentence implies that the contributions of *all* levels of government must be evaluated for technical efficiency and acceptability to society. There is nothing to suggest that the contributions of some levels of society do *not* need to be evaluated.

Note that in this question the correct answer follows basically from one sentence in the paragraph—the first sentence. The rest of the paragraph presents additional information about the public sector and its effects on society, which is relevant to the discussion but not necessary to make the inference. Part of your task in the Reading section is to understand what you read and then to discern what conclusions follow logically from statements in the paragraph. Consequently, in this test, you will find some questions necessitate the use of all or most of the statements presented in the paragraph, while others, such as this one, require only one statement to infer the correct answer.

SELECTION FOR QUESTION 20

All property is classified as either personal property or real property, but not both. In general, if something is classified as personal property, it is transient and transportable in nature, while real property is not. Things such as leaseholds, animals, money, and intangible and other moveable goods are examples of personal property. Permanent buildings and land, on the other hand, are fixed in nature and are not transportable.

20. The paragraph best supports the statement that

(A) if something is classified as personal property, it is not transient and transportable in nature
(B) some forms of property are considered to be both personal property and real property
(C) permanent buildings and land are real property
(D) permanent buildings and land are personal property
(E) tangible goods are considered to be real property

20. Ⓐ Ⓑ ● Ⓓ Ⓔ

20. The correct answer is **(C)**. The answer can be inferred from information contained in the first, second, and fourth sentences. The first sentence is a disjunction; that is, it presents two mutually exclusive alternatives—*all property is classified as either personal property or real property, but not both.* The second sentence states that *if something is classified as personal property, it is transient and transportable in nature.* The fourth sentence states that *permanent buildings and land. . . . are fixed in nature and are not transportable.* It can be concluded that, since permanent buildings and land are not transient and transportable in nature, they are not personal property. In view of the disjunction in the first sentence, it can be seen that they must be real property.

Response A is incorrect because it contradicts the information presented in the second sentence.

Response B is incorrect because it contradicts the first sentence, which states that *all property is classified as either personal property or real property, but not both.*

Response D contradicts the information presented in the second and fourth sentences. The second sentence states that *if something is classified as personal property, it is transient and transportable in nature.* The fourth sentence indicates that permanent buildings and land do not have these qualities. Therefore, it can be concluded that they are not personal property.

Response E seems to be derived from the third sentence, which says that intangible goods are examples of personal property. However, it cannot be concluded from this statement that tangible goods are real property. In fact, the third sentence gives examples of tangible goods that are personal property.

SELECTION FOR QUESTION 21

Personnel administration begins with the process of defining the quantities of people needed to do the job. Thereafter, people must be recruited, selected, trained, directed, rewarded, transferred, promoted, and perhaps released or retired. However, it is not true that all organizations are structured so that workers can be dealt with as individuals. In some organizations, employees are represented by unions, and managers bargain directly only with these associations.

21. The paragraph best supports the statement that **21.** Ⓐ Ⓑ Ⓒ Ⓓ Ⓔ

(A) no organizations are structured so that workers cannot be dealt with as individuals

(B) some working environments other than organizations are structured so that workers can be dealt with as individuals

(C) all organizations are structured so that employees are represented by unions

(D) no organizations are structured so that managers bargain with unions

(E) some organizations are not structured so that workers can be dealt with as individuals

21. The correct answer is **(E)**. This conclusion can be derived from information contained in the third sentence of the paragraph, which states that *it is not true that all organizations are structured so that workers can be dealt with as individuals.* From this statement, it can be inferred that *some organizations are not structured so that workers can be dealt with as individuals.*

Response A is incorrect because it contradicts the information in the third and fourth sentences of the paragraph. With its double negation, response A is in effect saying that all organizations are structured so that workers can be dealt with as individuals. This flatly contradicts the third sentence and also contradicts the fourth sentence, which says that *in some organizations, employees are represented by unions, and managers bargain with these associations.*

Response B is not supported by the paragraph because the paragraph gives no information about working environments other than organizations.

Response C is not supported by the paragraph because the paragraph says only that employees are represented by unions in *some* organizations. One cannot generalize from this to say that employees are represented by unions in *all* organizations.

Response D is incorrect because it contradicts the fourth sentence, which says that managers bargain with unions in some organizations.

Note that in this question the correct answer follows basically from one sentence in the paragraph—the third sentence. The rest of the paragraph presents additional information about personnel administration that is relevant to the discussion, but not necessary to make the inference. Part of your task in the Reading section is to *understand* what you read, and then to *discern* what conclusions follow logically from statements in the paragraph. Consequently, in this test, you will find some questions necessitate the use of all or most of the statements presented in the paragraph, while others, such as this one, require only one statement to infer the correct answer.

SELECTION FOR QUESTION 22

Many kinds of computer programming languages have been developed over the years. Initially, programmers had to write instructions in machine language. If a computer programming language is a machine language, then it is a code which can be read directly by a computer. Most high-level computer programming languages, such as Fortran and Cobol, use strings of common English phrases which communicate with the computer only after being converted or translated into a machine code.

22. The paragraph best supports the statement that

22. Ⓐ Ⓑ Ⓒ Ⓓ Ⓔ

(A) all high-level computer programming languages use strings of common English phrases which are converted to a machine code

(B) if a computer programming language is a machine language, then it is not a code which can be read directly by a computer

(C) if a computer programming language is a code which can be read directly by a computer, then it is not a machine language

(D) if a computer programming language is not a code which can read directly by a computer, then it is not a machine language

(E) if a computer programming language is not a machine language, then it is a code which can be read directly by a computer

22. The correct answer is **(D)**. The answer can be derived from the information presented in the third sentence. That sentence states that *if a computer programming language is a machine language, then it is a code which can be read directly by a computer.* From this statement it can be seen that all machine languages are codes which can be read directly by a computer and that if a computer programming language is not such a code, then it is not a machine language.

Response A goes beyond the information presented in the paragraph, which states only that *most* high level computer programming languages use strings of common English phrases.

Response B represents a complete contradiction of the third sentence of the paragraph.

Response C contradicts the paragraph. We know from the paragraph that at least some coded languages which can be read directly by a computer are machine languages.

Response E is incorrect because the paragraph does not say whether or not computer languages that are *not* machine languages are codes which can be read directly by a computer.

Many exams contain reading passages that relate to legal definitions or laws or to standard designations or to specified rules of procedure. You are not expected to have any knowledge of these definitions or rules. All the information you need to answer the questions will be given to you. On the contrary, if you happen to know that a definition is wrong or that a procedure is not according to current practice, you must still answer on the basis of the information on the page. When reading these passages, you must pay special attention to details relating to exceptions, special preconditions, combinations of activities, choices of actions, and prescribed time sequences. Sometimes the printed procedure specifies that certain actions are to be taken only when there is a combination of factors such as that water pressure has dropped *and* staircase collapse is imminent or, perhaps, that a person has actually broken a window *and* has a gun. At other times, the procedures give choices of action under certain circumstances. You must read carefully to determine if the passage requires a combination of factors or gives a choice, then make the appropriate judgment. When a time sequence is specified, be certain to follow that sequence in the prescribed order.

The remaining reading selections require the special attention to sequence, combinations, and choices that we have just described.

SELECTION FOR QUESTIONS 23 TO 26

Label

BREGSON'S CLEAR GLUE HIGHLY FLAMMABLE	PRECAUTIONS
A clear quick-drying glue	Use with adequate ventilation
For temporary bonding, apply glue to one surface and join immediately	Close container after use
	Keep out of reach of children
For permanent bonding, apply glue to both surfaces, press together after it dries	
	Avoid prolonged breathing of vapors and repeated contact with skin
Use for bonding plastic to plastic, plastic to wood, and wood to wood only	
Will not bond at temperatures below 60°	

23. Assume that you, as a member of a repair crew, have been asked to repair a wood banister in the hallway of a house. Since the heat has been turned off, the hallway is very cold except for the location where you have to make the repair. Another repair crew worker is working at that same location using a blow torch to solder a pipe in the wall. The temperature at that location is about 67°. According to the instructions on the above label, the use of this glue to make the necessary repair is

23. Ⓐ Ⓑ Ⓒ Ⓓ

(A) advisable because the glue will bond wood to wood
(B) advisable because the heat from the soldering will cause the glue to dry quickly
(C) inadvisable because the work area temperature is too low
(D) inadvisable because the glue is highly flammable

24. According to the instructions on the label, this glue should *not* be used for which of the following applications

24. Ⓐ Ⓑ Ⓒ Ⓓ

(A) affixing a pine table leg to a walnut table
(B) repairing leaks around pipe joints
(C) bonding a plastic knob to a cedar drawer
(D) attaching a lucite knob to a lucite drawer

25. According to the instructions on the label, using this glue to bond ceramic tile to a plaster wall by coating both surfaces with glue, letting the glue dry, and then pressing the tile to the plaster wall is

(A) advisable because the glue is quick drying and clear
(B) advisable because the glue should be permanently affixed to the one surface of the tile only
(C) inadvisable because the glue is not suitable for bonding ceramic tile to plaster walls
(D) inadvisable because the bonding should be a temporary one

25. Ⓐ Ⓑ ● Ⓓ

26. The precaution described in the label, to "use with adequate ventilation" means that

(A) the area you are working in should be very cold
(B) there should be sufficient fresh air where you are using the glue
(C) you should wear gloves to avoid contact with the glue
(D) you must apply a lot of glue to make a permanent bond

26. Ⓐ ● Ⓒ Ⓓ

The correct answers are 23. **(D)**, 24. **(B)**, 25. **(C)**, 26. **(B)**.

23. **(D)** In all caps, the label clearly states: BREGSON'S CLEAR GLUE, HIGHLY FLAMMABLE. Since another repair crew worker is working at the same location using a blow torch, it would be most foolhardy to use the glue at this location at this time.

24. **(B)** The glue is for bonding one surface to another, not for repairing leaks. Further, the use of the glue is specific to wood and plastics.

25. **(C)** The glue is suited for bonding plastic to plastic, plastic to wood, and wood to wood only. It will not bond ceramic tile to plaster.

26. **(B)** This is really a vocabulary question. "Sufficient ventilation" means "adequate fresh air."

SELECTION FOR QUESTIONS 27 TO 30

All automotive accidents, no matter how slight, are to be reported to the Safety Division by the employee involved on Accident Report Form S-23 in duplicate. When the accident is of such a nature that it requires the filling out of the State Motor Vehicle Report Form MV-104, this form is also prepared by the employee in duplicate, and sent to the Safety Division for comparison with the Form S-23. The Safety Division forwards both copies of Form MV-104 to the Corporation Counsel, who sends one copy to the State Bureau of Motor Vehicles. When the information on the Form S-23 indicates that the employee may be at fault, an investigation is made by the Safety Division. If this investigation shows that the employee was at fault, the employee's dispatcher is asked to file a complaint on Form D-11. The foreman of mechanics prepares a damage report on Form D-8 and an estimate of the cost of repairs on Form D-9. The dispatcher's complaint, the damage report, the repair estimate and the employee's previous accident record are sent to the Safety Division where they are studied together with the accident report. The Safety Division then recommends whether or not disciplinary action should be taken against the employee.

27. According to the preceding paragraph, the Safety Division should be notified whenever an automotive accident has occurred by means of
    (A) Form S-23
    (B) Forms S-23 and MV-104
    (C) Forms S-23, MV-104, D-8, D-9, and D-11
    (D) Forms S-23, MV-104, D-8, D-9, D-11, and employee's accident record

27. Ⓐ Ⓑ Ⓒ Ⓓ

28. According to the preceding paragraph, the forwarding of the Form MV-104 to the State Bureau of Motor Vehicles is done by the
    (A) Corporation Counsel
    (B) dispatcher
    (C) employee involved in the accident
    (D) Safety Division

28. Ⓐ Ⓑ Ⓒ Ⓓ

29. According to the preceding paragraph, the Safety Division investigates an automotive accident if the
    (A) accident is serious enough to be reported to the State Bureau of Motor Vehicles
    (B) dispatcher files a complaint
    (C) employee appears to have been at fault
    (D) employee's previous accident record is poor

29. Ⓐ Ⓑ Ⓒ Ⓓ

30. Of the forms mentioned in the preceding paragraph, the dispatcher is responsible for preparing the
    (A) accident report form
    (B) complaint form
    (C) damage report
    (D) estimate of cost of repairs

30. Ⓐ Ⓑ Ⓒ Ⓓ

The correct answers are: 27. **(A)**, 28. **(A)**, 29. **(C)**, 30. **(B)**.

27. **(A)** The first sentence makes it clear that regardless of whatever other forms might need to be filed, all automobile accidents should be reported to the Safety Division on Form S-23.

28. **(A)** Follow the steps carefully. The employee fills out Form MV-104 in duplicate and sends both copies to the Safety Division. The Safety Division, in turn, sends both copies to the Corporation Counsel who then sends one copy on to the State Bureau of Motor Vehicles.

29. **(C)** The Safety Division investigates if the information on the Form S-23 indicates that the employee may have been at fault.

30. **(B)** If the employee was indeed at fault, the dispatcher files a complaint on Form D-11.

SELECTION FOR QUESTION 31

When a person commits a traffic infraction, a Police Officer should:

1. Inform the violator of the offense committed.
2. Request the violator to show his or her driver's license, vehicle registration, and insurance identification card. Failure to produce this required material may result in additional tickets. (Taxis, buses, and other rented vehicles do not require insurance identification cards.)
3. Enter only one infraction on each ticket.
4. Use a separate ticket for each additional infraction.

31. Police Officer Herrmann has been assigned to curb traffic violations at the intersection of Main Street and Central Avenue. Officer Herrmann observes a taxi cab going through a red light at this intersection and signals the driver to pull over. The officer informs the cab driver of his violation and asks for the required material. The driver surrenders his license and registration to the officer. Police Officer Herrmann should

31. Ⓐ Ⓑ Ⓒ Ⓓ

(A) issue the cab driver a ticket for the red light violation and issue him a separate ticket for not surrendering his insurance card
(B) issue the cab driver one ticket including both the red light violation and the absence of the insurance card
(C) issue the cab driver a ticket only for the red light violation
(D) issue the cab driver a ticket only for not having an insurance card

The correct answer is **(C)**.

31. **(C)** The taxi driver violated the law by going through a red light. Officer Herrmann correctly informed the driver of this infraction and must issue a ticket. If the violator had been driving a private automobile. Officer Herrmann would have had to issue a separate ticket for his not producing an insurance card (see rules 3 and 4). However, in this case, the exception applies. The exception is that taxis, along with buses and rented vehicles, do not need to have insurance identification cards. You have to read carefully to determine exactly which rule applies in this case.

SELECTION FOR QUESTIONS 32 TO 33

Police Officers while on patrol may observe a recently vacated building that can create a safety hazard. In such situations, Police Officers should follow these procedures, in the order given:

1. Walk through the vacated building to determine if a safety hazard exists.
2. If a safety hazard exists, notify the supervisor on patrol.
3. Write an entry in the Activity Log.

4. Report the facts concerning the safety hazard in the vacant building to the Telephone Switchboard Operator.
5. Place barriers in front of the vacated building if directed by the Patrol Supervisor.

32. Police Officer Wolff notes that a building on his patrol route has recently been vacated. What action should Officer Wolff take next?

(A) Report the safety hazard in the vacant building to the Telephone Switchboard Operator.
(B) Radio the supervisor on patrol.
(C) Make an entry in his Activity Log.
(D) Determine if there is a safety hazard.

32. Ⓐ Ⓑ Ⓒ Ⓓ

33. Police Officer Furumoto has noticed a safety hazard in a vacant building. He first notified the supervisor on patrol and then made an entry in the Activity Log. He is about to place barriers in front of the building to safeguard the public. Officer Furumoto is acting

(A) correctly. Public safety is the police officer's first duty.
(B) incorrectly. The Patrol Supervisor did not direct him to place barriers.
(C) incorrectly. He must first report the safety hazard to the Telephone Switchboard Operator.
(D) incorrectly. He should radio for additional police officers to assist him in protecting the public from this hazard.

33. Ⓐ Ⓑ Ⓒ Ⓓ

The correct answers are: 32. **(D)**, 33. **(C)**.

32. **(D)** The introductory sentence says that a recently vacated building can create a safety hazard, not that it necessarily does so. Officer Wolff must enter the building and look around to determine whether or not there is indeed a safety hazard. Only if he decides that there is a hazard, should he proceed with notification and other actions.

33. **(C)** The procedure lists steps to be taken in the order given. While Officer Furumoto is justly concerned with public safety, the hazard in the vacant building hardly constitutes a pressing emergency. Having made the entry in the Log, his next act must be to notify the Telephone Switchboard Operator. Then he must await instructions from the Patrol Supervisor. The Supervisor may feel that the hazard does not warrant barricades.

SELECTION FOR QUESTIONS 34 TO 35

Police Officer DiSisto has observed that there is a pattern to criminal activity in her sector. She has noticed that burglaries tend to occur on High Street while auto thefts occur on York Street. Most rapes take place on Chapel Street and most assaults on Whitney. The rapes occur between 10 P.M. and 4 A.M., auto thefts between midnight and 6 A.M., burglaries between 10 A.M and 4 P.M., and assaults between 6 P.M, and 10 P.M. Auto thefts seem most common on Monday, Tuesday, and Thursday. Assaults occur most often on Friday, Saturday, and Sunday. Most rapes happen over the weekend and most burglaries on Monday, Wednesday, and Saturday.

34. Police Officer DiSisto would most likely to be able to reduce the incidence of rape by concentrating her patrol on **34.** Ⓐ Ⓑ Ⓒ Ⓓ

(A) York Street between midnight and 8 A.M.
(B) Chapel Street between 7 P.M. and 3 A.M.
(C) High Street between 2 A.M. and 10 P.M.
(D) Chapel Street between 4 P.M. and midnight

35. Auto theft is a special problem in the precinct, and Police Officer DiSisto's supervisor has requested that she make a special effort to eliminate auto theft on her patrol. Officer DiSisto should request assignment to patrol on **35.** Ⓐ Ⓑ Ⓒ Ⓓ

(A) Sunday through Thursday from 10 P.M. to 6 A.M.
(B) Friday through Wednesday from 3 A.M. to 4 P.M.
(C) Monday through Friday from 8 A.M. to 4 P.M.
(D) Wednesday through Sunday from 2 P.M. to 10 P.M.

The correct answers are: 34. **(B)**, 35. **(A)**.

34. **(B)** You must read for details and then use these details to reason. This type of question highlights the value of reading the questions before you read the paragraph. Question 30 deals with rape; question 31 with auto theft. In your initial reading of the paragraph, you will underscore details concerning rape and auto theft, ignoring information relating to burglary and assault. With your information thus narrowed, note that the rape area is Chapel Street. Eliminate choices (A) and (C). The rapes occur in the six-hour span from 10 P.M. to 4 A.M. Choice (B) covers five hours of this six-hour span while (D) covers only the two hours from 10 P.M. to midnight.

35. **(A)** Approach this question in the same way. Auto theft appears to be a mid-week event. Only choices (A) and (C) include the three target days of Monday, Tuesday, and Thursday. Auto thefts occur under cover of darkness making (C) a poor choice.

SELECTION FOR QUESTION 36

Harrassment occurs when a person annoys or alarms another person, but does not intend or cause physical injury.
Menacing occurs when a person threatens to cause serious physical injury to another person, but does not cause a serious physical injury.
Assault occurs when a person causes physical injury to another person.

36. On a foggy Friday night after a work, a group of men met at Jolly-O Tavern for a few beers. The conversation centered on the merits of the two local hockey teams, and Warren Wu stoutly defended his favorite team against that of Tomas Ramos. Ramos could stand just so much taunting. As he became more angry, Ramos told Wu that he had better "shut up" before he, Tomas Ramos, knocked Wu's block off. Wu continued to praise his team, whereupon **36.** Ⓐ Ⓑ Ⓒ Ⓓ

Ramos gave him such a punch to the jaw that Wu's lip was split and a tooth was knocked out. Based on the definitions above, Ramos should be charged with

(A) harassment, menacing, and assault
(B) menacing and assault
(C) assault
(D) no crime

The correct answer is **(C)**.

36. **(C)** The fact of assault seems clear. Ramos caused physical injury to Wu. According to the definitions, assault is the only charge. Harassment requires that no injury be intended, but Ramos stated intent to harm Wu. Menacing requires that no injury be caused. These definitions are mutually exclusive. Only one can apply. Definitions of other crimes may allow for one definition to be included within another. Careful reading is the number one requirement.

Judgment Questions

The need for reading skill is universal. The need for good judgment is not far behind. Even the entry-level employee who works under close supervision has occasions when he or she must rely on his or her own good judgment in dealing with an emergency situation or in choosing priorities when there is no supervisor to consult. Handling of many routine tasks also may depend on the good judgment of the worker. Almost all multiple-choice civil service exams include some questions designed to measure judgment either directly or indirectly. For test-taking purposes, we define judgment as a process of combining knowledge and understanding with common sense. Some examples:

37. Decisions about handcuffing or restraining inmates are often up to the Correction Officers involved. An officer is legally responsible for exercising good judgment and for taking necessary precautions to prevent harm both to the inmate involved and to others. In which one of the following situations is handcuffing or other physical restraint most likely to be needed?

37. Ⓐ Ⓑ Ⓒ Ⓓ

(A) An inmate seems to have lost control of his senses and is banging his fists repeatedly against the bars of his cell.
(B) During the past two weeks, an inmate has deliberately tried to start three fights with other inmates.
(C) An inmate claims to be sick and refuses to leave his cell for a scheduled meal.
(D) During the night an inmate begins to shout and sing, disturbing the sleep of other inmates.

The correct answer is **(A)**.

37. **(A)** The inmate who repeatedly bangs his fists against the bars of his cell is in immediate danger of causing himself bodily harm. This inmate *must* be restrained. The other inmates require attention, and their situations must be dealt with, but they do not require physical restraint.

38. While you are working on a routine assignment, a coworker asks you to help her for a few minutes so that she can complete an assignment that has top priority and must be completed immediately. Of the following, the *best* action for you to take should be to

38. Ⓐ Ⓑ ● Ⓓ

(A) tell her to find somebody who doesn't look busy and ask that person for help
(B) tell her you will help her as soon as you complete your own work
(C) help her to complete her assignment and then go back to your work
(D) tell her that your work is as important to you as her work is to her and continue to work on your own assignment

The correct answer is **(C)**.

38. **(C)** There are a number of points to take into consideration: Your own task is described as routine, the coworker's assignment is described as one which has top priority; and the coworker has asked for only a few minutes of your time. If you were involved in "rush" work yourself, you might refuse to help until you had finished your own task, but under these circumstances, help get the priority work done. A side benefit to be considered here is to maintain a good relationship with the coworker so that you, too, may request assistance at some time when your job demands it.

39. A police officer stationed along the route of a parade has been ordered not to allow cars to cross the route while the parade is in progress. An ambulance driver on an emergency run attempts to drive an ambulance across the route while the parade is passing. Under these circumstances, the officer should

39. Ⓐ ● Ⓒ Ⓓ

(A) ask the driver to wait while the officer calls headquarters and obtains a decision
(B) stop the parade long enough to permit the ambulance to cross the street
(C) direct the ambulance driver to the shortest detour available, which will add at least ten minutes to the run
(D) hold up the ambulance in accordance with the order

The correct answer is **(B)**.

39. **(B)** Without any knowledge of police rules, common sense dictates that saving of lives is the number one priority. An ambulance on an emergency run is on a mission to save a life. Lifesaving takes precedence over the desire for an uninterrupted parade despite the officer's prior orders.

40. An office worker frequently complains to the building custodian that her office is poorly illuminated. The best action for the building custodian to follow is to

40. Ⓐ Ⓑ Ⓒ ●

(A) ignore the complaints as those of an habitual crank
(B) inform the worker that illumination is a fixed item built into the building originally and evidently is the result of faulty planning by the architect
(C) request a licensed electrician to install additional ceiling lights
(D) investigate for faulty illumination features in the room, such as dirty lamp globes, and incorrect lamp wattages

The correct answer is **(D)**.

40. **(D)** The repeated complaints may be quite legitimate if the lighting problem has not been corrected. Do not dismiss the officer worker as a "crank." The custodian should check out the fixtures personally before calling in an electrician. Costs can be held down by having house staff perform those tasks for which they are qualified.

41. Suppose that one of your neighbors walks into the police precinct where you are an Administrative Aide and asks you to make 100 photocopies of a flyer he intends to distribute in the neighborhood. Of the following, what action should you take in this situation?

(A) Pretend that you do not know the person and order him to leave the building.
(B) Call a police officer and report the person for attempting to make illegal use of police equipment.
(C) Tell the person that you will make the copies when you are off duty.
(D) Explain that you cannot use police equipment for nonpolice work.

41. Ⓐ Ⓑ Ⓒ Ⓓ

The correct answer is **(D)**.

41. **(D)** Where calm, reasoned explanation is offered as an answer choice, it is nearly always the correct answer. There is no need to be impolite or hostile toward the neighbor. He may not even realize that he is asking you to do something that is not permitted. He will respect you for obeying the rules.

42. A police officer, walking a beat at 3 A.M., notices heavy smoke coming out of a top floor window of a large apartment house. Out of the following, the action the officer should take *first* is to:

(A) make certain that there really is a fire
(B) enter the building and warn all the occupants of the apartment house
(C) attempt to extinguish the fire before it gets out of control
(D) call the fire department

42. Ⓐ Ⓑ Ⓒ Ⓓ

The correct answer is **(D)**.

42. **(D)** A police officer is a police officer and not a firefighter. Eliminate choices (A) and (C) at once. It is the job of the firefighters to ascertain whether or not there really is a fire and to put it out. Since the building is a large one and fires spread rapidly, the practical move is to call the fire department immediately rather than trying to run through the building alone trying to rouse all occupants. Firefighters' will have greater manpower to do this efficiently and are trained in nighttime rousing procedures.

43. An elevator inspector on routine inspection for the Building Department notices a number of dangerous situations in the basement of the building she is in. Of the following conditions that she notices, which is the most dangerous and should be reported immediately?

(A) Gas is leaking from a broken pipe.
(B) The sewer pipe is broken.
(C) Water is seeping into the basement.
(D) The basement is unlighted.

43. Ⓐ Ⓑ Ⓒ Ⓓ

The correct answer is **(A)**.

43. **(A)** Leaking gas can be ignited, causing a fire. If a large amount of gas collects in the basement and is ignited, an explosion and fire are likely. This is the greatest hazard. The broken sewer pipe and the water seepage can create health hazards and should be reported and repaired, but these corrections do not represent the same emergency situations as the gas leak. An unlit basement is also a safety hazard, but even less of an emergency.

44. There are times when an employee of one City department should notify and seek assistance from employees of another department. A parking enforcement agent is checking meters on a busy one-way street. Of the following situations which he notices, which should he report immediately?

44. Ⓐ Ⓑ Ⓒ Ⓓ

(A) A rat runs out of a building and into the storm sewer across the street.
(B) A wire is dangling over the sidewalk giving off sparks.
(C) A car is parked directly in front of a hydrant.
(D) Two men are sitting on the front steps of a building sharing a marijuana joint.

The correct answer is **(B)**.

44. **(B)** The most urgent hazard is that caused by the sparking wire. A quick call to the Police Department will get the area sealed off and a repair crew to attend to the wire. The Health Department could be notified of rodents in the building, but pest infestation is a chronic problem rather than an emergency. The parking enforcement agent can ticket the illegally parked car. The two men sharing one joint pose no danger.

Communication Skills

No one works entirely alone. Every person must at times communicate information to some other person. The communication may be in the form of written memos or reports or may be oral. No matter the form of the communication, it must be clear and must be readily understood. It must convey all necessary information in usable form. Most city civil service exams include some measure of ability to organize and communicate information. Where the communication is very likely to be written, this measure may be by the way of questions on grammar and English usage. These questions do not ask rules of grammar; rather they offer a choice of sentences and ask which one contains an error, or which is the best and most correct sentence of the group. Where the communication is more likely to be telephoned in to a central post, the measure of ability to communicate may offer a set of facts and ask how you would best organize those facts into a clear and accurate report. Some examples:

*Select the sentence that is **best** with regard to grammar and proper usage.*

45.

45. Ⓐ Ⓑ Ⓒ Ⓓ

(A) There are several ways to organize a good report.
(B) Several ways exist in organizing a good report.
(C) To organize a good report, several ways exist.
(D) In the organization of a good report, there must be several ways.

The correct answer is **(A)**.

45. **(A)** While all four choices get the message across, the first is most straightforward.

46. **46.** Ⓐ Ⓑ Ⓒ Ⓓ

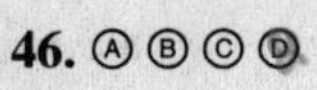

(A) The personnel office has charge of employment, dismissals, and employee's welfare.

(B) Employment, together with dismissals and employees' welfare, are handled by the personnel office.

(C) The personnel office takes charge of employment, dismissals, and etc.

(D) The personnel office is responsible for the employment, dismissal, and welfare of employees.

The correct answer is **(D)**.

46. **(D)** This statement is clear and correct. Choice (A) is incorrect in that the personnel department is in charge of the welfare of more than one employee; the word would have to be "employees'." In choice (B), the subject of the sentence is "employment," which is singular. The verb would have to be "is." "Together with dismissals and employees' welfare" is a parenthetical expression giving additional information, but is not part of the subject. The Latin abbreviation, "etc." means "and so forth." The word "and" before "etc." is superfluous and is incorrect.

Select the sentence that is ***incorrect.***

47. **47.** Ⓐ Ⓑ Ⓒ Ⓓ

(A) In the case of members who are absent, a special letter will be sent.

(B) The visitors were all ready to see it.

(C) I like Leaf's poem "To a Mountain Daisy."

(D) John told William that he was sure he had seen it.

The correct answer is **(D)**.

47. **(D)** This sentence is incorrect because it is unclear. Who is the second *he*? Was John sure that William had seen it or that he had seen it himself? If you were puzzled by choice (C), it is indeed correct. A period *always* goes inside the quotation marks, even if it seems logical to place it outside in a case like this. There are no exceptions to the rule governing placement of period or comma inside quotation marks.

48. **48.** Ⓐ Ⓑ Ⓒ Ⓓ

(A) Being tired, I stretched out on a grassy knoll.

(B) While we were rowing on the lake, a sudden squall almost capsized the boat.

(C) Entering the room, a strange mark on the floor attracted my attention.

(D) Mounting the curb, the empty car crossed the sidewalk and came to rest against a building.

The correct answer is **(C)**.

48. **(C)** The way this sentence currently reads, the strange mark entered the room and attracted my attention. Obviously, this is ridiculous. For clarity and correctness, the sentence should be rewritten: "As I entered the room, a strange mark on the floor attracted my attention." The subject of the sentence is "I." In all three other sentences, the subject is clear.

Below are the details of an incident. Following the details of the incident are four statements. Which one of the statements expresses the information most clearly and accurately?

49. Police Officer Franks arrives at the scene of a frame, two-family house in Brooklyn and observes flames leaping from the door onto the porch. A woman on the sidewalk gives him a description of a man she saw running from the house just before she noticed the fire. The information is:

49. Ⓐ Ⓑ Ⓒ Ⓓ

Place of Occurrence:	1520 Clarendon Road, Brooklyn.
Time of Occurrence:	6:32 A.M.
Type of Building:	Two-family frame dwelling
Event:	Fire, suspected arson
Suspect:	Male, white, approx 6-foot wearing blue jeans
Witness:	Mary Smith of 1523 Clarendon Road, Brooklyn

Officer Franks is about to radio an alert for the suspect. Which of the following expresses the information *most clearly* and *accurately?*

(A) At 6:32 A.M. Mary Smith of 1523 Clarendon Road, Brooklyn, saw a white male wearing approximately 6-foot blue jeans running from the building across the street.

(B) A white male wearing blue jeans ran from the house at 1520 Clarendon Road at 6:32 A.M. Mary Smith saw him.

(C) At 6:32 A.M. a 6-foot white male wearing blue jeans ran from a burning two-family frame structure at 1520 Clarendon Road, Brooklyn. He was observed by a neighbor, Mary Smith.

(D) A two-family frame house is on fire at 1520 Clarendon Road in Brooklyn. A white male in blue jeans probably did it. Mary Smith saw him run.

The correct answer is **(C)**.

49. **(C)** This statement tells what happened, where, and when. It gives a brief description of the suspect and identifies the witness. Choices (A) and (B) neglect to mention the fire; (D) omits the height of the suspect, an important fact, and does not identify the relationship of the witness for later questioning, if necessary.

50. A woman runs to the token clerk at the platform of the subway station to report that her purse was just snatched. She gives the following information to the token clerk:

50. Ⓐ Ⓑ Ⓒ Ⓓ

Time of Occurrence:	1:22 A.M.
Place of Occurrence:	uptown-bound platform, 59th Street Station, 7th Avenue line
Victim:	Juana Martinez
Crime:	purse snatching
Description of Suspect:	unknown, fled down steps to lower platform.

The token clerk is about to call for assistance from the transit police. Which of the following expresses the information *most clearly* and *accurately?*

(A) Juana Martinez had her purse snatched on the subway platform at 59th Street Station. She didn't see him.

(B) A purse was just snatched by a man who ran down the steps. This is the 7th Avenue token booth at 59th Street Station. Her name is Juana Martinez.

(C) It is 1:22 A.M. The person who snatched Juana Martinez' purse is downstairs at 59th Street Station.
(D) This is the 59th Street Station, uptown-bound 7th Avenue token booth. A Juana Martinez reports that her purse was just snatched by a man who fled down the steps to a lower platform.

The correct answer is **(D)**.

50. **(D)** This statement gives the precise location, the event, and a direction in which the suspect might be traced. Since the statement says that the event just occurred, the time is irrelevant. The recipient of the message knows to move quickly. Choice (A) does not give enough details to be of use; (B) makes a disjointed statement; (C) makes a flat statement that is not necessarily true. The purse snatcher may have exited by another route.

Other Test Topics

The purpose of Civil Service exams is to identify those candidates who have the aptitude and ability to learn the job easily and to do it well. The subjects tested on the exam are closely related to the duties of the position. Reading, judgment, and self-expression are common to most jobs. Other subjects are more specific: arithmetic for cashiers, clerical workers, and many positions in the manual trades; observation and memory for police officers, firefighters, correction officers, court officers, and the like; coding, alphabetizing, name and number checking for office workers of all sorts; typing for typists, stenography for stenographers; tool recognition for firefighters, custodians, mechanical workers in many trades, etc. The remainder of this chapter will introduce you to just a few of these.

VOCABULARY

51. FRAUDULENT means most nearly

(A) suspicious
(B) unproven
(C) deceptive
(D) unfair
(E) despicable

51. Ⓐ Ⓑ Ⓒ Ⓓ Ⓔ

The correct answer is **(C)**.

51. **(C)** The word *fraudulent* means "characterized by deceit or trickery, especially deliberate misrepresentation." Therefore, response C, *deceptive,* is the best synonym. Responses A, D, and E could be viewed as slightly related to the meaning of *fraudulent.* Response A, *suspicious,* "sensing that something is wrong without definite proof," could describe a person's reaction to a *fraudulent* situation. Response D, *unfair,* and response E, *despicable,* could both be used to describe a *fraudulent* act. However, the basic meanings of these three words are completely different from the meaning of *fraudulent.* Response B, *unproven,* is clearly unrelated to the meaning of *fraudulent.*

52. ALTRUISTIC means most nearly 52. Ⓐ Ⓑ Ⓒ Ⓓ Ⓔ

(A) unselfish
(B) extended
(C) unimaginative
(D) organized
(E) appealing

The correct answer is **(A)**.

52. **(A)** To be *altruistic* means "to be concerned for or devoted to the welfare of others." Therefore, response A, *unselfish,* is an excellent synonym. Response B could be viewed as slightly related, since *altruistic* people often extend themselves to help others. However, the basic meaning of *extended,* "stretched out," is completely different from the meaning of *altruistic.* Responses C and D are clearly unrelated to the meaning of *altruistic.* A vague connection exists between *altruistic* and response E, *appealing. Altruistic* people often make appeals on behalf of those less fortunate than themselves. Simultaneously, the generosity of *altruistic* people often makes them very *appealing* to other people. Although this vague connection exists between *altruistic* and *appealing,* they do not share a similar meaning.

ARITHMETIC

53. Ⓐ Ⓑ Ⓒ Ⓓ

53. What is the net amount of a bill of $428 after a discount of 6% has been allowed?

(A) $401.10
(B) $402.32
(C) $401.23
(D) $402.23

The correct answer is **(B)**.

53. **(B)** 6% of $428 = $428 × .06 = $25.68

$428 – 6% = $428 – $25.68 = $402.32

54. Ⓐ Ⓑ Ⓒ Ⓓ

54. If a piece of wood measuring 4 feet 2 inches is divided into three equal parts, each part is

(A) 1 foot $4^2/_3$ inches
(B) 1 foot $2^1/_3$ inches
(C) 1 foot 4 inches
(D) 1 foot $^7/_{18}$ inch

The correct answer is **(A)**.

54. **(A)** 4 feet 2 inches = 50 inches (4 × 12 + 2)

50 inches ÷ 3 = 16 $^2/_3$ inches = 1 foot 4 $^2/_3$ inches each

55. A federal agency had a personal computer repaired at a cost of \$49.20. This amount included a charge of \$22 per hour for labor and a charge for a new switch which cost \$18 before a 10 percent government discount was applied. How long did the repair job take? **55.** Ⓐ Ⓑ Ⓒ Ⓓ

(A) 1 hour, 6 minutes
(B) 1 hour, 11 minutes
(C) 1 hours, 22 minutes
(D) 1 hour, 30 minutes

The correct answer is **(D)**.

55. **(D)** $49.20 - (18 - (18 \times .10)) \div 22 = X$

$$X = \frac{33}{22} = 1.5 \text{ hours or 1 hour, 30 minutes}$$

The cost of the switch after the government discount of 10 percent is applied is 18 – (18 × .10) or \$16.20. This amount, when subtracted from the total charge of \$49.20, leaves \$33, which represents the charge for labor. A charge of \$33 at the rate of \$22 per hour represents 1.5 hours, or 1 hour and 30 minutes, of work.

TABULAR COMPLETION

FINANCE COMPANIES—ASSETS AND LIABILITIES: 1970 to 1980
(in millions of dollars)*

ITEM	1970	1975	1980
Total Receivables	(I)	85,994	183,341
Consumer Receivables	31,773	40,814	77,460
Retail passenger car paper and others	11,577	13,399	31,950
Retail consumer goods and loans	20,196	27,415	(IV)
Business Receivables	22,999	39,286	86,067
Wholesale paper and others	14,084	22,012	48,059
Lease paper and others	8,915	17,274	38,008
Other Receivables	2,341	5,894	19,814
Total Liabilities	60,577	(III)	175,025
Loans and Notes Payable to Banks	7,551	8,617	15,458
Short-term	(II)	7,900	7,885
Long-term	969	717	7,573
Commercial Paper	22,073	25,905	52,328
Other Debt	30,953	54,194	(V)

*Hypothetical data.

56. What is the value of I in milions dollars ? 56. Ⓐ Ⓑ Ⓒ Ⓓ Ⓔ

(A) 54,772
(B) 57,113
(C) 63,546
(D) 68,856
(E) none of these

57. What is the value of II in millions of dollars? 57. Ⓐ Ⓑ Ⓒ Ⓓ Ⓔ

(A) 6,582
(B) 14,522
(C) 53,026
(D) 58,236
(E) none of these

58. What is the value of III in millions of dollars? 58. Ⓐ Ⓑ Ⓒ Ⓓ Ⓔ

(A) 62,811
(B) 88,716
(C) 94,610
(D) 97,333
(E) none of these

59. What is the value of IV in millions of dollars? 59. Ⓐ Ⓑ Ⓒ Ⓓ Ⓔ

(A) 45,610
(B) 47,610
(C) 47,611
(D) 54,117
(E) none of these

60. What is the value of V in millions of dollars? 60. Ⓐ Ⓑ Ⓒ Ⓓ Ⓔ

(A) 67,786
(B) 85,147
(C) 107,239
(D) 107,259
(E) none of these

The correct answers are 56. **(B)**, 57. **(A)**, 58. **(B)**, 59. **(E)**, 60. **(C)**.

56. **(B)** Add the values for *Consumer Receivables, Business Receivables,* and *Other Receivables.*

31,773 + 22,999 + 2,341 = 57,113

57. **(A)** Subtract the value for *Long-term* from the value for *Loans and Notes Payable to Banks.*

7,551 – 969 = 6,582

58. **(B)** Add the value of 1975 *Loans and Notes Payable to Banks, Commercial Paper,* and *Other Debt.*

8,617 + 25,905 + 54,194 = 88,716

59. **(E)** Subtract the value of 1980 *Retail passenger car paper and others* from 1980 *Consumer Receivables.*

77,460 – 31,950 = 45,510

60. **(C)** Subtract the sum of the values of *Loans and Notes Payable to Banks* and *Commercial Paper* from 1980 *Total Liabilities.*

175,025 – (15,458 + 52,328) = 107,239

OBSERVATION AND MEMORY

***Directions:** You will have three minutes to study the following picture, to note details about people, time and place, and activities. Then you will have to answer five questions about the picture without looking back at the picture.*

*Picture for questions 61 to 65—***At The Bank**

*Answer questions 61 to 65 on the basis of the picture, "***At The Bank.***" Cover the picture with your hand or a piece of paper. Do not look at the picture again.*

61. The teller is — **61.** Ⓐ Ⓑ Ⓒ Ⓓ Ⓔ

(A) wearing a striped tie
(B) wearing glasses
(C) making change
(D) left-handed

62. The man wearing a hat is also — **62.** Ⓐ Ⓑ Ⓒ Ⓓ Ⓔ

(A) handing money to the teller
(B) wearing a bow tie
(C) talking to another man in the line
(D) smoking a pipe

63. The teller's name is
(A) R. Smith
(B) T. Jones
(C) T. Smith
(D) R. Jones

63. Ⓐ Ⓑ Ⓒ Ⓓ

64. The woman in the striped dress is
(A) carrying a handbag
(B) wearing a pendant
(C) holding gloves
(D) third in line

64. Ⓐ Ⓑ Ⓒ Ⓓ

65. The time of day is
(A) early morning
(B) lunchtime
(C) mid-afternoon
(D) later afternoon

65. Ⓐ Ⓑ Ⓒ Ⓓ

The correct answers are: 61. **(B)**, 62. **(D)**, 63. **(D)**, 64. **(B)**, 65. **(B)**

MECHANICAL APTITUDE, ELECTRONICS INFORMATION, TOOL RECOGNITION, AUTOMOTIVE KNOWLEDGE

66. The saw shown to the right is used mainly to cut
(A) plywood
(B) odd-shaped holes in wood
(C) along the grain of the wood
(D) across the grain of the wood

66. Ⓐ Ⓑ Ⓒ Ⓓ

The correct answer is **(B)**.

66. **(B)** The compass saw is used to cut odd-shaped holes in wood.

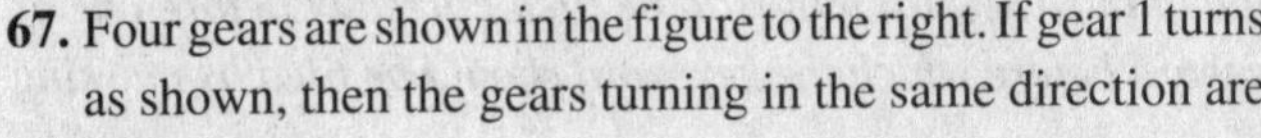

67. Four gears are shown in the figure to the right. If gear 1 turns as shown, then the gears turning in the same direction are
(A) 2 and 3
(B) 2 and 4
(C) 3 and 4
(D) 2, 3, and 4

67. Ⓐ Ⓑ Ⓒ Ⓓ

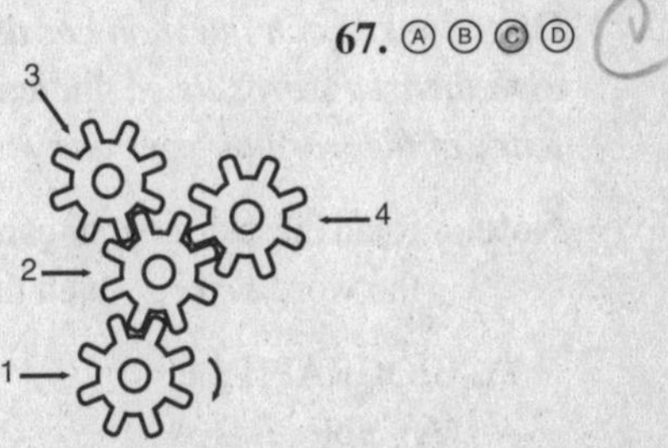

The correct answer is **(C)**.

67. **(C)** Gear 1 turns clockwise; gear 2 turns counterclockwise; gears 3 and 4 turn clockwise.

68. After brakes have been severely overheated, what should be checked for? **68.** Ⓐ Ⓑ Ⓒ Ⓓ

(A) water condensation in brake fluid
(B) glazed brake shoes
(C) wheels out of alignment
(D) crystallized wheel bearings

The correct answer is **(B)**.

68. **(B)** Overheating the brake shoe will cause the brake material to glaze and become slippery. Slippery brakes are dangerous because they take longer to stop a car.

69. The tool shown to the right is used for **69.** 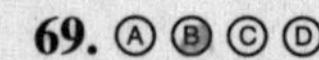

(A) pressure lubricating
(B) welding steel plate
(C) drilling small holes in tight places
(D) holding small parts for heat treating

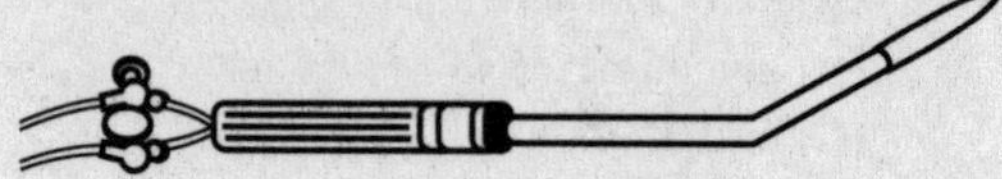

The correct answer is **(B)**.

69. **(B)** The tool is a welding torch used in making metal joint. Welding is generally done with material made of steel.

70. When working on live 600-volt equipment where rubber gloves might be damaged, an electrician should **70.** Ⓐ Ⓑ Ⓒ Ⓓ

(A) work without gloves
(B) carry a spare pair of rubber gloves
(C) reinforce the fingers of the rubber gloves with rubber tape
(D) wear leather gloves over the rubber gloves

The correct answer is **(D)**.

70. **(D)** Leather gloves offer the best protection over the rubber gloves. The leather can withstand severe conditions before it will tear. The rubber acts as insulation.

ALPHABETIZING, FILING, CLERICAL NAME AND NUMBER CHECKING, CODING

Directions: *Each question consist of a capitalized word that is to be filed correctly before one of the alphabetized words listed. Indicate the word before which the key word should be filed by marking the letter of the word on your answer sheet.*

Note: Read these directions carefully. The correct answer is the letter of the word *before* which the key word should be filed.

71. BIOGRAPHY **71.** Ⓐ Ⓑ Ⓒ Ⓓ

(A) bible
(B) bibliography
(C) bilge
(D) biology

The correct answer is **(D)**.

71. **(D)** Biography should be filed before *biology.*

Directions: *In Column I you will find four names to be filed. The names are lettered w, x, y, and z. In Column II are four possible orders for alphabetizing those names. You are to choose which arrangement constitutes the correct filing order according to the rules for alphabetical filing and mark the letter that precedes the correct order.*

72.	**Column I**	**Column II**	**72.** Ⓐ Ⓑ Ⓒ Ⓓ
	(w) Rivera, Ilena	(A) w, x, z, y	
	(x) Riviera, Ilene	(B) z, w, y, x	
	(y) Rivere, I.	(C) w, y, z, x	
	(z) Riviera Ice-Cream Co.	(D) x, z, w, y	

The correct answer is **(C)**.

72. **(C)** The correct order in which to file these names is:
(w) Rivera, Ilena
(y) Rivere, I.
(z) Riviera Ice-Cream Co.
(x) Riviera, Ilene

Directions: *Each question consists of letters or numbers in Columns I and II. For each question, compare each line of Column I with its corresponding line in Column II and decide how many lines in Column II are exactly the same as their counterparts in Column I. Mark your answers as follows:*

Mark (A) if only *ONE* line in Column II is exactly the same as its corresponding line in Column I
Mark (B) if *TWO* lines in column II are exactly the same as their corresponding lines in Column I
Mark (C) if *THREE* lines in Column II are exactly the same as their corresponding lines in Column I
Mark (D) if all *FOUR* lines in Column II are exactly the same as their corresponding lines in Column I

73.	**Column I**	**Column II**	**73.** Ⓐ Ⓑ Ⓒ Ⓓ
	awg3	awg3	
	tyE3	ty3E	
	abhn	abnh	
	24po	24op	

The correct answer is **(A)**.

73. **(A)** Only on the top line are the letter combinations in columns I and II identical. If you got this wrong, look again.

Directions: *Each question consists of a set of names and addresses. In each question the name and address in Column II should be exactly like the name and address in Column I. But there are some mistakes.*

Mark (A) if there is a mistake *only* in the *NAME*
Mark (B) if there is a mistake *only* in the *ADDRESS*
Mark (C) if there are mistakes in *both NAME and ADDRESS*
Mark (D) if there are *NO MISTAKES*

74.	Column I	Column II	74. Ⓐ Ⓑ Ⓒ Ⓓ
	Mr. Brett H. Meyers	Mr. Brett H. Meyers	
	72 Nannyhagen Road	72 Nannyhagen Road	
	Haverford, PA 19042	Haverford, PA 19402	

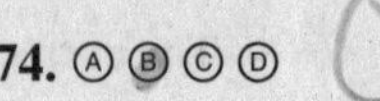

The correct answer is **(B)**.

74. **(B)** The name is identical in both columns, as are street address, city, and state. However, there is a number reversal in the zip code. The total addresses are therefore not identical and the answer must be (B).

The most common variety of coding question found on City Civil Service tests consists of a coding table (which need not be memorized) and a series of questions that requires you to demonstrate your understanding of the use of the code and your ability to follow directions in answering the questions. From one exam to another, the chief variations in coding questions tend to be in the number of digits and letters in each question line and in the directions. Indeed, in New York City, on the same day, two exams were given for two different clerical positions. Both exams contained coding questions, but the directions for answering the questions were different on the two exams. One asked that questions be answered on the basis of correctly coded lines; the other on the basis of how many lines contained coding errors. On one exam the questions and directions looked like this:

Directions: *Each letter should be matched with its number in accordance with the following table:*

Letter	P	S	B	O	Q	K	A	M	E	Y
Number	0	1	2	3	4	5	6	7	8	9

For each question, compare each line of letters and numbers carefully to see if each letter is matched correctly to its corresponding number. Mark your answer according to the number of lines in which all of the letters and numbers are matched correctly.

Mark (A) if NONE of the lines is matched correctly
Mark (B) if only ONE of the lines is matched correctly
Mark (C) if TWO of the lines are matched correctly
Mark (D) if all THREE lines are matched correctly

75.	SEOB	1732	75. Ⓐ Ⓑ Ⓒ Ⓓ
	YMQA	9756	
	BEPM	2806	

The correct answer is **(A)**.

75. **(A)** In the first line, E is incorrectly matched with 7. In the second line, Q is incorrectly matched with 5. In the third line, M is incorrectly matched with 6. Since all of the letters and numbers are matched correctly in none of the lines, the answer is (A).

On the other exam, the directions looked like this:

Directions: *The numbers on each line of each question should correspond with the code letters on the same line in accordance with the table below:*

Code Letter	M	Q	O	H	B	C	I	N	Y	V
Number	0	1	2	3	4	5	6	7	8	9

In some of the lines below, an error exists in the coding. Compare the numbers and letters in each question very carefully. Mark your answers according to the number of lines in which you find an error or errors.

Mark (A) if only ONE line contains an error or errors
Mark (B) if TWO lines contain errors
Mark (C) if all THREE lines contain errors
Mark (D) if NONE of the lines contains an error

76. BCMHIOB 4503624
VYBQNCO 8941752
MHBCNIV 0345869

76. Ⓐ ● Ⓒ Ⓓ

The correct answer is **(B)**.

76. **(B)** Line 1 contains no errors. It is correctly coded. On the second line, *V* is incorrectly coded as *8*, and *Y* is incorrectly coded as *9*. On the third line, *N* is incorrectly coded as *8*. There are three errors, but the three errors occur on only two lines, so the correct answer is (B).

To sum up, the keys to success with multiple-choice questions are care with the use of answer sheets, budgeting of time, and accurate reading of directions and questions.

Study and practice for the specific exam that you must take can, of course, give you a further advantage over the competition. ARCO has prepared a series of test-prep books that give you instruction and advice for handling the various types of questions and that give you extensive practice answering those questions. Most books also contain actual previous exams or exams that we have created to closely resemble the real thing. Taking the real or model exams gives you a chance to learn to pace yourself to finish an exam and to leave time to check it over.

SAMPLE U.S. POSTAL SERVICE EXAMINATION—EXAMS 470 AND 460

Postal Clerk
City Carrier
Distribution Clerk, Machine
Flat Sorting Machine Operator
Mail Handler
Mail Processor
Mark-up Clerk, Automated
Rural Carrier

TEAR HERE

Part A—Address Checking

1 Ⓐ Ⓓ	20 Ⓐ Ⓓ	39 Ⓐ Ⓓ	58 Ⓐ Ⓓ	77 Ⓐ Ⓓ
2 Ⓐ Ⓓ	21 Ⓐ Ⓓ	40 Ⓐ Ⓓ	59 Ⓐ Ⓓ	78 Ⓐ Ⓓ
3 Ⓐ Ⓓ	22 Ⓐ Ⓓ	41 Ⓐ Ⓓ	60 Ⓐ Ⓓ	79 Ⓐ Ⓓ
4 Ⓐ Ⓓ	23 Ⓐ Ⓓ	42 Ⓐ Ⓓ	61 Ⓐ Ⓓ	80 Ⓐ Ⓓ
5 Ⓐ Ⓓ	24 Ⓐ Ⓓ	43 Ⓐ Ⓓ	62 Ⓐ Ⓓ	81 Ⓐ Ⓓ
6 Ⓐ Ⓓ	25 Ⓐ Ⓓ	44 Ⓐ Ⓓ	63 Ⓐ Ⓓ	82 Ⓐ Ⓓ
7 Ⓐ Ⓓ	26 Ⓐ Ⓓ	45 Ⓐ Ⓓ	64 Ⓐ Ⓓ	83 Ⓐ Ⓓ
8 Ⓐ Ⓓ	27 Ⓐ Ⓓ	46 Ⓐ Ⓓ	65 Ⓐ Ⓓ	84 Ⓐ Ⓓ
9 Ⓐ Ⓓ	28 Ⓐ Ⓓ	47 Ⓐ Ⓓ	66 Ⓐ Ⓓ	85 Ⓐ Ⓓ
10 Ⓐ Ⓓ	29 Ⓐ Ⓓ	48 Ⓐ Ⓓ	67 Ⓐ Ⓓ	86 Ⓐ Ⓓ
11 Ⓐ Ⓓ	30 Ⓐ Ⓓ	49 Ⓐ Ⓓ	68 Ⓐ Ⓓ	87 Ⓐ Ⓓ
12 Ⓐ Ⓓ	31 Ⓐ Ⓓ	50 Ⓐ Ⓓ	69 Ⓐ Ⓓ	88 Ⓐ Ⓓ
13 Ⓐ Ⓓ	32 Ⓐ Ⓓ	51 Ⓐ Ⓓ	70 Ⓐ Ⓓ	89 Ⓐ Ⓓ
14 Ⓐ Ⓓ	33 Ⓐ Ⓓ	52 Ⓐ Ⓓ	71 Ⓐ Ⓓ	90 Ⓐ Ⓓ
15 Ⓐ Ⓓ	34 Ⓐ Ⓓ	53 Ⓐ Ⓓ	72 Ⓐ Ⓓ	91 Ⓐ Ⓓ
16 Ⓐ Ⓓ	35 Ⓐ Ⓓ	54 Ⓐ Ⓓ	73 Ⓐ Ⓓ	92 Ⓐ Ⓓ
17 Ⓐ Ⓓ	36 Ⓐ Ⓓ	55 Ⓐ Ⓓ	74 Ⓐ Ⓓ	93 Ⓐ Ⓓ
18 Ⓐ Ⓓ	37 Ⓐ Ⓓ	56 Ⓐ Ⓓ	75 Ⓐ Ⓓ	94 Ⓐ Ⓓ
19 Ⓐ Ⓓ	38 Ⓐ Ⓓ	57 Ⓐ Ⓓ	76 Ⓐ Ⓓ	95 Ⓐ Ⓓ

Part B—Memory for Addresses

1 Ⓐ Ⓑ Ⓒ Ⓓ Ⓔ	23 Ⓐ Ⓑ Ⓒ Ⓓ Ⓔ	45 Ⓐ Ⓑ Ⓒ Ⓓ Ⓔ	67 Ⓐ Ⓑ Ⓒ Ⓓ Ⓔ
2 Ⓐ Ⓑ Ⓒ Ⓓ Ⓔ	24 Ⓐ Ⓑ Ⓒ Ⓓ Ⓔ	46 Ⓐ Ⓑ Ⓒ Ⓓ Ⓔ	68 Ⓐ Ⓑ Ⓒ Ⓓ Ⓔ
3 Ⓐ Ⓑ Ⓒ Ⓓ Ⓔ	25 Ⓐ Ⓑ Ⓒ Ⓓ Ⓔ	47 Ⓐ Ⓑ Ⓒ Ⓓ Ⓔ	69 Ⓐ Ⓑ Ⓒ Ⓓ Ⓔ
4 Ⓐ Ⓑ Ⓒ Ⓓ Ⓔ	26 Ⓐ Ⓑ Ⓒ Ⓓ Ⓔ	48 Ⓐ Ⓑ Ⓒ Ⓓ Ⓔ	70 Ⓐ Ⓑ Ⓒ Ⓓ Ⓔ
5 Ⓐ Ⓑ Ⓒ Ⓓ Ⓔ	27 Ⓐ Ⓑ Ⓒ Ⓓ Ⓔ	49 Ⓐ Ⓑ Ⓒ Ⓓ Ⓔ	71 Ⓐ Ⓑ Ⓒ Ⓓ Ⓔ
6 Ⓐ Ⓑ Ⓒ Ⓓ Ⓔ	28 Ⓐ Ⓑ Ⓒ Ⓓ Ⓔ	50 Ⓐ Ⓑ Ⓒ Ⓓ Ⓔ	72 Ⓐ Ⓑ Ⓒ Ⓓ Ⓔ
7 Ⓐ Ⓑ Ⓒ Ⓓ Ⓔ	29 Ⓐ Ⓑ Ⓒ Ⓓ Ⓔ	51 Ⓐ Ⓑ Ⓒ Ⓓ Ⓔ	73 Ⓐ Ⓑ Ⓒ Ⓓ Ⓔ
8 Ⓐ Ⓑ Ⓒ Ⓓ Ⓔ	30 Ⓐ Ⓑ Ⓒ Ⓓ Ⓔ	52 Ⓐ Ⓑ Ⓒ Ⓓ Ⓔ	74 Ⓐ Ⓑ Ⓒ Ⓓ Ⓔ
9 Ⓐ Ⓑ Ⓒ Ⓓ Ⓔ	31 Ⓐ Ⓑ Ⓒ Ⓓ Ⓔ	53 Ⓐ Ⓑ Ⓒ Ⓓ Ⓔ	75 Ⓐ Ⓑ Ⓒ Ⓓ Ⓔ
10 Ⓐ Ⓑ Ⓒ Ⓓ Ⓔ	32 Ⓐ Ⓑ Ⓒ Ⓓ Ⓔ	54 Ⓐ Ⓑ Ⓒ Ⓓ Ⓔ	76 Ⓐ Ⓑ Ⓒ Ⓓ Ⓔ
11 Ⓐ Ⓑ Ⓒ Ⓓ Ⓔ	33 Ⓐ Ⓑ Ⓒ Ⓓ Ⓔ	55 Ⓐ Ⓑ Ⓒ Ⓓ Ⓔ	77 Ⓐ Ⓑ Ⓒ Ⓓ Ⓔ
12 Ⓐ Ⓑ Ⓒ Ⓓ Ⓔ	34 Ⓐ Ⓑ Ⓒ Ⓓ Ⓔ	56 Ⓐ Ⓑ Ⓒ Ⓓ Ⓔ	78 Ⓐ Ⓑ Ⓒ Ⓓ Ⓔ
13 Ⓐ Ⓑ Ⓒ Ⓓ Ⓔ	35 Ⓐ Ⓑ Ⓒ Ⓓ Ⓔ	57 Ⓐ Ⓑ Ⓒ Ⓓ Ⓔ	79 Ⓐ Ⓑ Ⓒ Ⓓ Ⓔ
14 Ⓐ Ⓑ Ⓒ Ⓓ Ⓔ	36 Ⓐ Ⓑ Ⓒ Ⓓ Ⓔ	58 Ⓐ Ⓑ Ⓒ Ⓓ Ⓔ	80 Ⓐ Ⓑ Ⓒ Ⓓ Ⓔ
15 Ⓐ Ⓑ Ⓒ Ⓓ Ⓔ	37 Ⓐ Ⓑ Ⓒ Ⓓ Ⓔ	59 Ⓐ Ⓑ Ⓒ Ⓓ Ⓔ	81 Ⓐ Ⓑ Ⓒ Ⓓ Ⓔ
16 Ⓐ Ⓑ Ⓒ Ⓓ Ⓔ	38 Ⓐ Ⓑ Ⓒ Ⓓ Ⓔ	60 Ⓐ Ⓑ Ⓒ Ⓓ Ⓔ	82 Ⓐ Ⓑ Ⓒ Ⓓ Ⓔ
17 Ⓐ Ⓑ Ⓒ Ⓓ Ⓔ	39 Ⓐ Ⓑ Ⓒ Ⓓ Ⓔ	61 Ⓐ Ⓑ Ⓒ Ⓓ Ⓔ	83 Ⓐ Ⓑ Ⓒ Ⓓ Ⓔ
18 Ⓐ Ⓑ Ⓒ Ⓓ Ⓔ	40 Ⓐ Ⓑ Ⓒ Ⓓ Ⓔ	62 Ⓐ Ⓑ Ⓒ Ⓓ Ⓔ	84 Ⓐ Ⓑ Ⓒ Ⓓ Ⓔ
19 Ⓐ Ⓑ Ⓒ Ⓓ Ⓔ	41 Ⓐ Ⓑ Ⓒ Ⓓ Ⓔ	63 Ⓐ Ⓑ Ⓒ Ⓓ Ⓔ	85 Ⓐ Ⓑ Ⓒ Ⓓ Ⓔ
20 Ⓐ Ⓑ Ⓒ Ⓓ Ⓔ	42 Ⓐ Ⓑ Ⓒ Ⓓ Ⓔ	64 Ⓐ Ⓑ Ⓒ Ⓓ Ⓔ	86 Ⓐ Ⓑ Ⓒ Ⓓ Ⓔ
21 Ⓐ Ⓑ Ⓒ Ⓓ Ⓔ	43 Ⓐ Ⓑ Ⓒ Ⓓ Ⓔ	65 Ⓐ Ⓑ Ⓒ Ⓓ Ⓔ	87 Ⓐ Ⓑ Ⓒ Ⓓ Ⓔ
22 Ⓐ Ⓑ Ⓒ Ⓓ Ⓔ	44 Ⓐ Ⓑ Ⓒ Ⓓ Ⓔ	66 Ⓐ Ⓑ Ⓒ Ⓓ Ⓔ	88 Ⓐ Ⓑ Ⓒ Ⓓ Ⓔ

Part C—Number Series

1 Ⓐ Ⓑ Ⓒ Ⓓ Ⓔ	7 Ⓐ Ⓑ Ⓒ Ⓓ Ⓔ	13 Ⓐ Ⓑ Ⓒ Ⓓ Ⓔ	19 Ⓐ Ⓑ Ⓒ Ⓓ Ⓔ
2 Ⓐ Ⓑ Ⓒ Ⓓ Ⓔ	8 Ⓐ Ⓑ Ⓒ Ⓓ Ⓔ	14 Ⓐ Ⓑ Ⓒ Ⓓ Ⓔ	20 Ⓐ Ⓑ Ⓒ Ⓓ Ⓔ
3 Ⓐ Ⓑ Ⓒ Ⓓ Ⓔ	9 Ⓐ Ⓑ Ⓒ Ⓓ Ⓔ	15 Ⓐ Ⓑ Ⓒ Ⓓ Ⓔ	21 Ⓐ Ⓑ Ⓒ Ⓓ Ⓔ
4 Ⓐ Ⓑ Ⓒ Ⓓ Ⓔ	10 Ⓐ Ⓑ Ⓒ Ⓓ Ⓔ	16 Ⓐ Ⓑ Ⓒ Ⓓ Ⓔ	22 Ⓐ Ⓑ Ⓒ Ⓓ Ⓔ
5 Ⓐ Ⓑ Ⓒ Ⓓ Ⓔ	11 Ⓐ Ⓑ Ⓒ Ⓓ Ⓔ	17 Ⓐ Ⓑ Ⓒ Ⓓ Ⓔ	23 Ⓐ Ⓑ Ⓒ Ⓓ Ⓔ
6 Ⓐ Ⓑ Ⓒ Ⓓ Ⓔ	12 Ⓐ Ⓑ Ⓒ Ⓓ Ⓔ	18 Ⓐ Ⓑ Ⓒ Ⓓ Ⓔ	24 Ⓐ Ⓑ Ⓒ Ⓓ Ⓔ

Part D—Following Oral Instructions

1 Ⓐ Ⓑ Ⓒ Ⓓ Ⓔ
2 Ⓐ Ⓑ Ⓒ Ⓓ Ⓔ
3 Ⓐ Ⓑ Ⓒ Ⓓ Ⓔ
4 Ⓐ Ⓑ Ⓒ Ⓓ Ⓔ
5 Ⓐ Ⓑ Ⓒ Ⓓ Ⓔ
6 Ⓐ Ⓑ Ⓒ Ⓓ Ⓔ
7 Ⓐ Ⓑ Ⓒ Ⓓ Ⓔ
8 Ⓐ Ⓑ Ⓒ Ⓓ Ⓔ
9 Ⓐ Ⓑ Ⓒ Ⓓ Ⓔ
10 Ⓐ Ⓑ Ⓒ Ⓓ Ⓔ
11 Ⓐ Ⓑ Ⓒ Ⓓ Ⓔ
12 Ⓐ Ⓑ Ⓒ Ⓓ Ⓔ
13 Ⓐ Ⓑ Ⓒ Ⓓ Ⓔ
14 Ⓐ Ⓑ Ⓒ Ⓓ Ⓔ
15 Ⓐ Ⓑ Ⓒ Ⓓ Ⓔ
16 Ⓐ Ⓑ Ⓒ Ⓓ Ⓔ
17 Ⓐ Ⓑ Ⓒ Ⓓ Ⓔ
18 Ⓐ Ⓑ Ⓒ Ⓓ Ⓔ
19 Ⓐ Ⓑ Ⓒ Ⓓ Ⓔ
20 Ⓐ Ⓑ Ⓒ Ⓓ Ⓔ
21 Ⓐ Ⓑ Ⓒ Ⓓ Ⓔ
22 Ⓐ Ⓑ Ⓒ Ⓓ Ⓔ
23 Ⓐ Ⓑ Ⓒ Ⓓ Ⓔ
24 Ⓐ Ⓑ Ⓒ Ⓓ Ⓔ
25 Ⓐ Ⓑ Ⓒ Ⓓ Ⓔ
26 Ⓐ Ⓑ Ⓒ Ⓓ Ⓔ
27 Ⓐ Ⓑ Ⓒ Ⓓ Ⓔ
28 Ⓐ Ⓑ Ⓒ Ⓓ Ⓔ
29 Ⓐ Ⓑ Ⓒ Ⓓ Ⓔ
30 Ⓐ Ⓑ Ⓒ Ⓓ Ⓔ
31 Ⓐ Ⓑ Ⓒ Ⓓ Ⓔ
32 Ⓐ Ⓑ Ⓒ Ⓓ Ⓔ
33 Ⓐ Ⓑ Ⓒ Ⓓ Ⓔ
34 Ⓐ Ⓑ Ⓒ Ⓓ Ⓔ
35 Ⓐ Ⓑ Ⓒ Ⓓ Ⓔ
36 Ⓐ Ⓑ Ⓒ Ⓓ Ⓔ
37 Ⓐ Ⓑ Ⓒ Ⓓ Ⓔ
38 Ⓐ Ⓑ Ⓒ Ⓓ Ⓔ
39 Ⓐ Ⓑ Ⓒ Ⓓ Ⓔ
40 Ⓐ Ⓑ Ⓒ Ⓓ Ⓔ
41 Ⓐ Ⓑ Ⓒ Ⓓ Ⓔ
42 Ⓐ Ⓑ Ⓒ Ⓓ Ⓔ
43 Ⓐ Ⓑ Ⓒ Ⓓ Ⓔ
44 Ⓐ Ⓑ Ⓒ Ⓓ Ⓔ
45 Ⓐ Ⓑ Ⓒ Ⓓ Ⓔ
46 Ⓐ Ⓑ Ⓒ Ⓓ Ⓔ
47 Ⓐ Ⓑ Ⓒ Ⓓ Ⓔ
48 Ⓐ Ⓑ Ⓒ Ⓓ Ⓔ
49 Ⓐ Ⓑ Ⓒ Ⓓ Ⓔ
50 Ⓐ Ⓑ Ⓒ Ⓓ Ⓔ
51 Ⓐ Ⓑ Ⓒ Ⓓ Ⓔ
52 Ⓐ Ⓑ Ⓒ Ⓓ Ⓔ
53 Ⓐ Ⓑ Ⓒ Ⓓ Ⓔ
54 Ⓐ Ⓑ Ⓒ Ⓓ Ⓔ
55 Ⓐ Ⓑ Ⓒ Ⓓ Ⓔ
56 Ⓐ Ⓑ Ⓒ Ⓓ Ⓔ
57 Ⓐ Ⓑ Ⓒ Ⓓ Ⓔ
58 Ⓐ Ⓑ Ⓒ Ⓓ Ⓔ
59 Ⓐ Ⓑ Ⓒ Ⓓ Ⓔ
60 Ⓐ Ⓑ Ⓒ Ⓓ Ⓔ
61 Ⓐ Ⓑ Ⓒ Ⓓ Ⓔ
62 Ⓐ Ⓑ Ⓒ Ⓓ Ⓔ
63 Ⓐ Ⓑ Ⓒ Ⓓ Ⓔ
64 Ⓐ Ⓑ Ⓒ Ⓓ Ⓔ
65 Ⓐ Ⓑ Ⓒ Ⓓ Ⓔ
66 Ⓐ Ⓑ Ⓒ Ⓓ Ⓔ
67 Ⓐ Ⓑ Ⓒ Ⓓ Ⓔ
68 Ⓐ Ⓑ Ⓒ Ⓓ Ⓔ
69 Ⓐ Ⓑ Ⓒ Ⓓ Ⓔ
70 Ⓐ Ⓑ Ⓒ Ⓓ Ⓔ
71 Ⓐ Ⓑ Ⓒ Ⓓ Ⓔ
72 Ⓐ Ⓑ Ⓒ Ⓓ Ⓔ
73 Ⓐ Ⓑ Ⓒ Ⓓ Ⓔ
74 Ⓐ Ⓑ Ⓒ Ⓓ Ⓔ
75 Ⓐ Ⓑ Ⓒ Ⓓ Ⓔ
76 Ⓐ Ⓑ Ⓒ Ⓓ Ⓔ
77 Ⓐ Ⓑ Ⓒ Ⓓ Ⓔ
78 Ⓐ Ⓑ Ⓒ Ⓓ Ⓔ
79 Ⓐ Ⓑ Ⓒ Ⓓ Ⓔ
80 Ⓐ Ⓑ Ⓒ Ⓓ Ⓔ
81 Ⓐ Ⓑ Ⓒ Ⓓ Ⓔ
82 Ⓐ Ⓑ Ⓒ Ⓓ Ⓔ
83 Ⓐ Ⓑ Ⓒ Ⓓ Ⓔ
84 Ⓐ Ⓑ Ⓒ Ⓓ Ⓔ
85 Ⓐ Ⓑ Ⓒ Ⓓ Ⓔ
86 Ⓐ Ⓑ Ⓒ Ⓓ Ⓔ
87 Ⓐ Ⓑ Ⓒ Ⓓ Ⓔ
88 Ⓐ Ⓑ Ⓒ Ⓓ Ⓔ

TEAR HERE

SCORE SHEET

ADDRESS CHECKING: Your score on the Address Checking part is based upon the number of questions you answered correctly minus the number of questions you answered incorrectly. To determine your score, subtract the number of wrong answers from the number of correct answers.

Number Right – Number Wrong = Raw Score

________ – ________ = ________

MEMORY FOR ADDRESSES: Your score on the Memory for Addresses part is based upon the number of questions you answered correctly minus one-fourth of the questions you answered incorrectly (number wrong divided by 4 =). Calculate this now:

Number wrong ÷ 4 = .

Number Right – Number Wrong ÷ 4 = Raw Score

________ – ________ = ________

NUMBER SERIES: Your score on the Number Series part is based only on the number of questions you answered correctly. Wrong answers do not count against you.

Number Right = Raw Score

________ = ________

FOLLOWING ORAL INSTRUCTIONS: Your score on the Following Oral Instructions part is based only upon the number of questions you marked correctly on the answer sheet. The worksheet is not scored, and wrong answers on the answer sheet do not count against you.

Number Right = Raw Score

________ = ________

TOTAL SCORE: To find your total raw score, add together the raw scores for each section of the exam.

Address Checking Score ________

+

Memory for Addresses Score ________

+

Number Series Score ________

+

Following Oral Instructions Score ________

=

Total Raw Score ________

Self-Evaluation Chart

Calculate your raw score for each test as shown above. Then check to see where your score falls on the scale from Poor to Excellent. Lightly shade in the boxes in which your scores fall.

Part	Excellent	Good	Average	Fair	Poor
Address Checking	80–95	65–79	50–64	35–49	1–34
Memory for Addresses	75–88	60–74	45–59	30–44	1–29
Number Series	21–24	18–20	14–17	11–13	1–10
Following Oral Instructions	27–31	23–26	19–22	14–18	1–13

ADDRESS CHECKING

Time: 6 Minutes. 95 Questions.

Directions: *For each question compare the address in the left column with the address in the right column. If the addresses are ALIKE IN* ***EVERY*** *WAY, blacken space A on your answer sheet. If the two addresses are DIFFERENT IN ANY WAY, blacken space D on your answer sheet. Correct answers for this test are on page 255.*

1 …7399 NW Candleworth Dr	7399 NW Candleworth Dr
2 …New Castle AL 35119	New Castle AL 35119
3 …2098 NE Catalpa Ln	2098 NW Catalpa Ln
4 …17001 NE Rappaix Court	17001 NE Rappaix Court
5 …10091 NE Larryvale Rd	10091 NE Larryville Rd
6 …2896 NE Wallaston Way	2896 NE Walleston Way
7 …Timonium MD 21093	Timanium MD 21093
8 …7749 NW Barracuda Cove Ct	7749 NW Barracuda Cove Ct
9 …6099 NW Atterbury Rd	6099 NW Atterbury Dr
10 …2198 NE Springs St	2198 NW Springs St
11 …6089 SE Flintshire Rd	6089 SW Flintshire Rd
12 …13111 SE Throgmorton Ct	13111 SE Throgmorton Ct
13 …Estacada OR 97023	Estacada OK 97023
14 …5301 NE Monocacy Cir	5301 NE Monocacy Ct
15 …6066 NW Schissler Ave	6606 NW Schissler Ave
16 …1915 NE Chapletowne Cir	1915 NE Chapeltowne Cir
17 …4505 NE Reisterstown Plaza	4505 NE Reisterstown Plaza
18 …3399 NW Ivydene Ter	3399 NW Ivydene Trl
19 …8605 Commanche Ave	8605 Commanche Ave
20 …Winnemucca NV 89445	Winnemocca NV 89445
21 …467 SE Chatterleigh Cir	467 SE Chatterleigh Cir
22 …3300 SE Golupski Rd	3300 SE Golpski Rd
23 …4884 NW Farmvale Ave	4884 NW Farmdale Ave
24 …Kalamazoo MI 49009	Kalamazoo MI 49009
25 …11676 SE Harryweiss Rd	11676 SE Harrywise Rd
26 …4395 Auchentoroly Ter	4395 Auchentoroly Ter
27 …11321 NE Pageland Rd	11321 NE Pageland Rd
28 …2488 Jeannett Ave	2488 Jeannett Ave

29 ...1900 Gilford Ter	1900 Gulford Ter
30 ...5177 NE Bridgehampton Dr	5177 NE Bridgehampton Dr
31 ...7333 Martingale Ave	7333 Martingale Ave
32 ...11577 Delagrange Way	11571 Delagrange Way
33 ...13852 NE 68th Ave	13852 NE 86th Ave
34 ...11736 NE Uffington Rd	17736 NE Uffington Rd
35 ...21199 NW Huntington Ave	21199 NW Huntingdon Ave
36 ...Merriweather NY 11548	Merriweather NY 11548
37 ...11001 NE Cedarcrest Rd	11001 NE Cedarchest Rd
38 ...3569 NE Tazewell Rd	3569 NE Tazewell Rd
39 ...5297 Popperdam Creek	5297 Pepperdam Creek
40 ...2288 Dundawan Rd	2288 Dundawan Rd
41 ...17299 Rhuddlan Rd	17299 Rhuddlan Rd
42 ...37719 Underwood Ct	37719 Underwood Cir
43 ...22700 S Strathdale Rd	22700 S Strathdale Rd
44 ...Homeworth OH 44634	Homeworth OH 46434
45 ...3727 NW Ayleshire Rd	3727 NE Ayleshire Rd
46 ...4585 E Englemeade Ave	4585 E Englemeade Ave
47 ...37741 NE Jacqueline Ln	34771 NE Jacqueline Ln
48 ...3800 N Grinnalds Ave	3800 N Grinnalds St
49 ...10990 NE Kennicott Rd	10990 NE Kenningcott Rd
50 ...Vanderpool TX 78885	Vanderpool TX 78885
51 ...11799 NE Brattel Rd	11799 NE Brattle Rd
52 ...2196 Leadenhall Court	2196 Leadenhall Court
53 ...Albuquerque NM 87109	Albuquerque NM 81709
54 ...3789 Featherstone Ln	8789 Featherstone Ln
55 ...18076 Martinque Rd	18076 Martinque Ct
56 ...60111 Debonair Ct	6011 Debonair Ct
57 ...4131 NE Tussock Rd	4131 NE Tussock Road
58 ...299 Susquehanna Ave E	299 Susquehanna Ave W
59 ...53116 NE T Avenue	53116 NE T Avenue
60 ...16917 Saint Elmo Ave	16917 Saint Almo Ave
61 ...10401 Olde Georgetown Rd SE	10401 Old Georgetown Rd SE
62 ...7550 Wisconsin Ave	7550 Wisconsin St

63 …8054 Aberdeen Rd	8054 Aberdeen Rd
64 …Wheelersburg KY 41473	Wheelersburg KY 41473
65 …3138 Edgemere Ave	3138 Edgemore Ave
66 …11595 Heathcliff Dr	11595 Heathcliff Dr
67 …13531 N Keutel Rd	13531 N Kratel Rd
68 …7585 Breezewick Cir	78575 Breezewick Cir
69 …15530 NE Jimrowe Cir	15530 NE Jimrowe Ct
70 …2001 Quantico Way	2001 Guantico Way
71 …8899 Randolph Springs Pl	8899 Rudolph Spring Pl
72 …4010 Oakleigh Beach Rd	4010 Oakleigh Beach Rd
73 …3977 Mc Teague Ave	3977 Mc Teague Ave
74 …13827 N Lavington Pl	13827 N Lavingston Pl
75 …17390 Youngstown Ave NE	17390 Youngstown Ave SE
76 …15999 Brookview Ave	15999 Brookview Ave
77 …12733 NE 88th Ave	1273 NE 88th Ave
78 …P.O. Box 34001	P.O. Box 34007
79 …Selingsgrove PA 17870	Selingrove PA 17870
80 …3425 Chelmareford Trl	3245 Chelmareford Trl
81 …6080 Knickerbocker Cir	6080 Knickerbocker Dr
82 …1700 Alconbury Rd	1700 Alconbury Rd
83 …2620 Winnettka St	2620 Winnettka St
84 …2367 Essextowne Cir	2367 Essextowne Cir
85 …3588 Investment Pl	3588 Investment Pl
86 …11888 Margarette Ave	11888 Margaretta Ave
87 …4756 Ridervale Rd	4756 Riderview Rd
88 …16491 Zeppelin Ave	16491 Zepperlin Ave
89 …10195 Highway 210 N	10195 Highway 201 N
90 …11811 Vailthorn Ln	11181 Vailthorn Ln
91 …7299 E 41st St	7299 W 41st St
92 …P.O. Box 30399	P.O. Box 30399
93 …4710 Bethesda Ave N	4710 Bethesda Blvd N
94 …Waynesboro MS 39367	Waynesboro MN 39367
95 …99 NW M Street	99 NW M Street

END OF ADDRESS CHECKING

PRACTICE FOR MEMORY FOR ADDRESSES

Directions: *The five boxes below are labelled A, B, C, D, and E. In each box are three sets of number spans with names and two names that are not associated with numbers. In the next THREE MINUTES, you must try to memorize the box location of each name and number span. The position of a name or number span within its box is not important. You need only remember the letter of the box in which the item is to be found. You will use these names and numbers to answer three sets of practice questions that are NOT scored and one actual test that is scored. Correct answers are on pages 256 and 257.*

A	B	C	D	E
2500–2999 Mist Forest 1400–1899 Tank Tarot 3600–3899 Kite	3600–3899 Mist Season 2500–2999 Tank Howard 1900–2499 Kite	1400–1899 Mist Anchor 3600–3899 Tank Bongo 3000–3599 Kite	1900–2499 Mist Cupola 3000–3599 Tank Gibbon 2500–2999 Kite	3000–3599 Mist Jester 1900–2499 Tank Lattice 1400–1899 Kite

Practice I

Directions: *Use the next THREE MINUTES to mark on the answer sheet at the end of Practice I the letter of the box in which each item that follows is to be found. Try to mark each item without looking back at the boxes. If, however, you get stuck, you may refer to the boxes during this practice exercise. If you find that you must look at the boxes, try to memorize as you do so. This test is for practice only. It will not be scored.*

1. 2500–2999 Mist
2. 3000–3599 Tank
3. Season
4. Lattice
5. 1400–1899 Kite
6. 3600–3899 Tank
7. 3000–3599 Mist
8. 1400–1899 Tank
9. Anchor
10. Forest
11. 1900–2499 Mist
12. 2500–2999 Tank
13. 2500–2999 Kite
14. Gibbon
15. 3600–3899 Kite
16. 1900–2499 Tank
17. Cupola
18. Bongo
19. 1400–1899 Mist
20. 1900–2499 Tank
21. 3600–3899 Kite
22. 2500–2999 Tank
23. Tarot
24. Jester
25. 3600–3899 Mist
26. 2500–2999 Kite
27. 3600–3899 Tank
28. Howard
29. Season
30. 1900–2499 Kite
31. 1900–2499 Mist
32. 3000–3599 Kite
33. Forest
34. Lattice
35. 1400–1899 Kite
36. 1400–1899 Tank
37. 2500–2999 Mist
38. 3000–3599 Mist
39. Anchor
40. Gibbon
41. 3000–3599 Tank
42. 3600–3899 Mist
43. 3000–3599 Tank
44. 3600–3899 Kite
45. 1900–2499 Tank
46. 2500–2999 Kite
47. Howard
48. Jester
49. 2500–2999 Mist
50. 3600–3899 Kite
51. 1400–1899 Mist
52. 1400–1899 Kite
53. Cupola
54. Bongo
55. Gibbon
56. 2500–2999 Tank
57. 1900–2499 Tank
58. Tarot
59. 1900–2499 Mist
60. 3600–3899 Tank

61. 3000–3599 Mist
62. Forest
63. Anchor
64. Season
65. 1900–2499 Kite
66. 3000–3599 Kite
67. 3600–3899 Mist
68. 1400–1899 Tank
69. 3000–3599 Tank
70. Lattice
71. 3600–3899 Kite
72. 1900–2499 Mist
73. 2500–2999 Tank
74. 3600–3899 Tank
75. 2500–2999 Mist
76. 1400–1899 Kite
77. Bongo
78. Gibbon
79. 3000–3599 Mist
80. 1400–1899 Kite
81. 3600–3899 Tank
82. Tarot
83. Lattice
84. Howard
85. 1900–2499 Mist
86. 1900–2499 Kite
87. 2500–2999 Tank
88. 3600–3899 Mist

Practice I Answer Sheet

1 Ⓐ Ⓑ Ⓒ Ⓓ Ⓔ	23 Ⓐ Ⓑ Ⓒ Ⓓ Ⓔ	45 Ⓐ Ⓑ Ⓒ Ⓓ Ⓔ	67 Ⓐ Ⓑ Ⓒ Ⓓ Ⓔ
2 Ⓐ Ⓑ Ⓒ Ⓓ Ⓔ	24 Ⓐ Ⓑ Ⓒ Ⓓ Ⓔ	46 Ⓐ Ⓑ Ⓒ Ⓓ Ⓔ	68 Ⓐ Ⓑ Ⓒ Ⓓ Ⓔ
3 Ⓐ Ⓑ Ⓒ Ⓓ Ⓔ	25 Ⓐ Ⓑ Ⓒ Ⓓ Ⓔ	47 Ⓐ Ⓑ Ⓒ Ⓓ Ⓔ	69 Ⓐ Ⓑ Ⓒ Ⓓ Ⓔ
4 Ⓐ Ⓑ Ⓒ Ⓓ Ⓔ	26 Ⓐ Ⓑ Ⓒ Ⓓ Ⓔ	48 Ⓐ Ⓑ Ⓒ Ⓓ Ⓔ	70 Ⓐ Ⓑ Ⓒ Ⓓ Ⓔ
5 Ⓐ Ⓑ Ⓒ Ⓓ Ⓔ	27 Ⓐ Ⓑ Ⓒ Ⓓ Ⓔ	49 Ⓐ Ⓑ Ⓒ Ⓓ Ⓔ	71 Ⓐ Ⓑ Ⓒ Ⓓ Ⓔ
6 Ⓐ Ⓑ Ⓒ Ⓓ Ⓔ	28 Ⓐ Ⓑ Ⓒ Ⓓ Ⓔ	50 Ⓐ Ⓑ Ⓒ Ⓓ Ⓔ	72 Ⓐ Ⓑ Ⓒ Ⓓ Ⓔ
7 Ⓐ Ⓑ Ⓒ Ⓓ Ⓔ	29 Ⓐ Ⓑ Ⓒ Ⓓ Ⓔ	51 Ⓐ Ⓑ Ⓒ Ⓓ Ⓔ	73 Ⓐ Ⓑ Ⓒ Ⓓ Ⓔ
8 Ⓐ Ⓑ Ⓒ Ⓓ Ⓔ	30 Ⓐ Ⓑ Ⓒ Ⓓ Ⓔ	52 Ⓐ Ⓑ Ⓒ Ⓓ Ⓔ	74 Ⓐ Ⓑ Ⓒ Ⓓ Ⓔ
9 Ⓐ Ⓑ Ⓒ Ⓓ Ⓔ	31 Ⓐ Ⓑ Ⓒ Ⓓ Ⓔ	53 Ⓐ Ⓑ Ⓒ Ⓓ Ⓔ	75 Ⓐ Ⓑ Ⓒ Ⓓ Ⓔ
10 Ⓐ Ⓑ Ⓒ Ⓓ Ⓔ	32 Ⓐ Ⓑ Ⓒ Ⓓ Ⓔ	54 Ⓐ Ⓑ Ⓒ Ⓓ Ⓔ	76 Ⓐ Ⓑ Ⓒ Ⓓ Ⓔ
11 Ⓐ Ⓑ Ⓒ Ⓓ Ⓔ	33 Ⓐ Ⓑ Ⓒ Ⓓ Ⓔ	55 Ⓐ Ⓑ Ⓒ Ⓓ Ⓔ	77 Ⓐ Ⓑ Ⓒ Ⓓ Ⓔ
12 Ⓐ Ⓑ Ⓒ Ⓓ Ⓔ	34 Ⓐ Ⓑ Ⓒ Ⓓ Ⓔ	56 Ⓐ Ⓑ Ⓒ Ⓓ Ⓔ	78 Ⓐ Ⓑ Ⓒ Ⓓ Ⓔ
13 Ⓐ Ⓑ Ⓒ Ⓓ Ⓔ	35 Ⓐ Ⓑ Ⓒ Ⓓ Ⓔ	57 Ⓐ Ⓑ Ⓒ Ⓓ Ⓔ	79 Ⓐ Ⓑ Ⓒ Ⓓ Ⓔ
14 Ⓐ Ⓑ Ⓒ Ⓓ Ⓔ	36 Ⓐ Ⓑ Ⓒ Ⓓ Ⓔ	58 Ⓐ Ⓑ Ⓒ Ⓓ Ⓔ	80 Ⓐ Ⓑ Ⓒ Ⓓ Ⓔ
15 Ⓐ Ⓑ Ⓒ Ⓓ Ⓔ	37 Ⓐ Ⓑ Ⓒ Ⓓ Ⓔ	59 Ⓐ Ⓑ Ⓒ Ⓓ Ⓔ	81 Ⓐ Ⓑ Ⓒ Ⓓ Ⓔ
16 Ⓐ Ⓑ Ⓒ Ⓓ Ⓔ	38 Ⓐ Ⓑ Ⓒ Ⓓ Ⓔ	60 Ⓐ Ⓑ Ⓒ Ⓓ Ⓔ	82 Ⓐ Ⓑ Ⓒ Ⓓ Ⓔ
17 Ⓐ Ⓑ Ⓒ Ⓓ Ⓔ	39 Ⓐ Ⓑ Ⓒ Ⓓ Ⓔ	61 Ⓐ Ⓑ Ⓒ Ⓓ Ⓔ	83 Ⓐ Ⓑ Ⓒ Ⓓ Ⓔ
18 Ⓐ Ⓑ Ⓒ Ⓓ Ⓔ	40 Ⓐ Ⓑ Ⓒ Ⓓ Ⓔ	62 Ⓐ Ⓑ Ⓒ Ⓓ Ⓔ	84 Ⓐ Ⓑ Ⓒ Ⓓ Ⓔ
19 Ⓐ Ⓑ Ⓒ Ⓓ Ⓔ	41 Ⓐ Ⓑ Ⓒ Ⓓ Ⓔ	63 Ⓐ Ⓑ Ⓒ Ⓓ Ⓔ	85 Ⓐ Ⓑ Ⓒ Ⓓ Ⓔ
20 Ⓐ Ⓑ Ⓒ Ⓓ Ⓔ	42 Ⓐ Ⓑ Ⓒ Ⓓ Ⓔ	64 Ⓐ Ⓑ Ⓒ Ⓓ Ⓔ	86 Ⓐ Ⓑ Ⓒ Ⓓ Ⓔ
21 Ⓐ Ⓑ Ⓒ Ⓓ Ⓔ	43 Ⓐ Ⓑ Ⓒ Ⓓ Ⓔ	65 Ⓐ Ⓑ Ⓒ Ⓓ Ⓔ	87 Ⓐ Ⓑ Ⓒ Ⓓ Ⓔ
22 Ⓐ Ⓑ Ⓒ Ⓓ Ⓔ	44 Ⓐ Ⓑ Ⓒ Ⓓ Ⓔ	66 Ⓐ Ⓑ Ⓒ Ⓓ Ⓔ	88 Ⓐ Ⓑ Ⓒ Ⓓ Ⓔ

Practice II

Directions: *The next 88 questions constitute another practice exercise. Mark your answers on the Practice II answer sheet. Again, the time limit is THREE MINUTES. This time, however, you must NOT look at the boxes while answering the questions. You must rely on your memory in marking the box location of each item. This practice test will not be scored.*

1. 1400–1899 Mist
2. 3000–3599 Kite
3. 1900–2499 Tank
4. 1400–1899 Tank
5. Howard
6. Gibbon
7. 3600–3899 Mist
8. 2500–2999 Kite
9. 1400–1899 Kite
10. Lattice
11. Jester
12. 2500–2999 Mist
13. 3600–3899 Tank
14. 3000–3599 Mist
15. 3000–3599 Tank
16. Cupola
17. Tarot
18. Bongo
19. 1900–2499 Kite
20. 3600–3899 Kite
21. Anchor
22. Season
23. 1900–2499 Mist
24. 2500–2999 Tank
25. Forest
26. 3000–3599 Mist
27. 3000–3599 Tank
28. 3000–3599 Kite
29. Jester
30. Gibbon
31. 2500–2999 Mist
32. 2500–2999 Tank
33. 1400–1899 Mist
34. Tarot
35. Forest
36. Anchor
37. 1400–1899 Kite
38. 3600–3899 Tank
39. 3600–3899 Kite
40. 1900–2499 Mist
41. 1400–1899 Tank
42. Bongo
43. Cupola
44. Season
45. Howard
46. 1900–2499 Tank
47. 1900–2499 Kite
48. 2500–2999 Kite
49. 3600–3899 Mist
50. 3600–3899 Tank
51. 2500–2999 Kite
52. 3000–3599 Mist
53. 3600–3899 Kite
54. Cupola
55. Lattice
56. Season
57. 1400–1899 Mist
58. 3000–3599 Kite
59. Anchor
60. Gibbon
61. 1900–2499 Tank
62. 1400–1899 Tank
63. 2500–2999 Mist
64. 1400–1899 Kite
65. Forest
66. Tarot
67. 1900–2499 Mist
68. 2500–2999 Tank
69. 3000–3599 Tank
70. Jester
71. Howard
72. Bongo
73. 1900–2499 Kite
74. 3600–3899 Tank
75. 1400–1899 Kite
76. 2500–2999 Mist
77. Cupola
78. Season
79. 1900–2499 Kite
80. 1900–2499 Mist
81. 1900–2499 Tank
82. 1400–1899 Tank
83. Lattice
84. Anchor
85. 3600–3899 Mist
86. 2500–2999 Kite
87. 3000–3599 Kite
88. 3000–3599 Mist

Practice II Answer Sheet

1 Ⓐ Ⓑ Ⓒ Ⓓ Ⓔ	23 Ⓐ Ⓑ Ⓒ Ⓓ Ⓔ	45 Ⓐ Ⓑ Ⓒ Ⓓ Ⓔ	67 Ⓐ Ⓑ Ⓒ Ⓓ Ⓔ
2 Ⓐ Ⓑ Ⓒ Ⓓ Ⓔ	24 Ⓐ Ⓑ Ⓒ Ⓓ Ⓔ	46 Ⓐ Ⓑ Ⓒ Ⓓ Ⓔ	68 Ⓐ Ⓑ Ⓒ Ⓓ Ⓔ
3 Ⓐ Ⓑ Ⓒ Ⓓ Ⓔ	25 Ⓐ Ⓑ Ⓒ Ⓓ Ⓔ	47 Ⓐ Ⓑ Ⓒ Ⓓ Ⓔ	69 Ⓐ Ⓑ Ⓒ Ⓓ Ⓔ
4 Ⓐ Ⓑ Ⓒ Ⓓ Ⓔ	26 Ⓐ Ⓑ Ⓒ Ⓓ Ⓔ	48 Ⓐ Ⓑ Ⓒ Ⓓ Ⓔ	70 Ⓐ Ⓑ Ⓒ Ⓓ Ⓔ
5 Ⓐ Ⓑ Ⓒ Ⓓ Ⓔ	27 Ⓐ Ⓑ Ⓒ Ⓓ Ⓔ	49 Ⓐ Ⓑ Ⓒ Ⓓ Ⓔ	71 Ⓐ Ⓑ Ⓒ Ⓓ Ⓔ
6 Ⓐ Ⓑ Ⓒ Ⓓ Ⓔ	28 Ⓐ Ⓑ Ⓒ Ⓓ Ⓔ	50 Ⓐ Ⓑ Ⓒ Ⓓ Ⓔ	72 Ⓐ Ⓑ Ⓒ Ⓓ Ⓔ
7 Ⓐ Ⓑ Ⓒ Ⓓ Ⓔ	29 Ⓐ Ⓑ Ⓒ Ⓓ Ⓔ	51 Ⓐ Ⓑ Ⓒ Ⓓ Ⓔ	73 Ⓐ Ⓑ Ⓒ Ⓓ Ⓔ
8 Ⓐ Ⓑ Ⓒ Ⓓ Ⓔ	30 Ⓐ Ⓑ Ⓒ Ⓓ Ⓔ	52 Ⓐ Ⓑ Ⓒ Ⓓ Ⓔ	74 Ⓐ Ⓑ Ⓒ Ⓓ Ⓔ
9 Ⓐ Ⓑ Ⓒ Ⓓ Ⓔ	31 Ⓐ Ⓑ Ⓒ Ⓓ Ⓔ	53 Ⓐ Ⓑ Ⓒ Ⓓ Ⓔ	75 Ⓐ Ⓑ Ⓒ Ⓓ Ⓔ
10 Ⓐ Ⓑ Ⓒ Ⓓ Ⓔ	32 Ⓐ Ⓑ Ⓒ Ⓓ Ⓔ	54 Ⓐ Ⓑ Ⓒ Ⓓ Ⓔ	76 Ⓐ Ⓑ Ⓒ Ⓓ Ⓔ
11 Ⓐ Ⓑ Ⓒ Ⓓ Ⓔ	33 Ⓐ Ⓑ Ⓒ Ⓓ Ⓔ	55 Ⓐ Ⓑ Ⓒ Ⓓ Ⓔ	77 Ⓐ Ⓑ Ⓒ Ⓓ Ⓔ
12 Ⓐ Ⓑ Ⓒ Ⓓ Ⓔ	34 Ⓐ Ⓑ Ⓒ Ⓓ Ⓔ	56 Ⓐ Ⓑ Ⓒ Ⓓ Ⓔ	78 Ⓐ Ⓑ Ⓒ Ⓓ Ⓔ
13 Ⓐ Ⓑ Ⓒ Ⓓ Ⓔ	35 Ⓐ Ⓑ Ⓒ Ⓓ Ⓔ	57 Ⓐ Ⓑ Ⓒ Ⓓ Ⓔ	79 Ⓐ Ⓑ Ⓒ Ⓓ Ⓔ
14 Ⓐ Ⓑ Ⓒ Ⓓ Ⓔ	36 Ⓐ Ⓑ Ⓒ Ⓓ Ⓔ	58 Ⓐ Ⓑ Ⓒ Ⓓ Ⓔ	80 Ⓐ Ⓑ Ⓒ Ⓓ Ⓔ
15 Ⓐ Ⓑ Ⓒ Ⓓ Ⓔ	37 Ⓐ Ⓑ Ⓒ Ⓓ Ⓔ	59 Ⓐ Ⓑ Ⓒ Ⓓ Ⓔ	81 Ⓐ Ⓑ Ⓒ Ⓓ Ⓔ
16 Ⓐ Ⓑ Ⓒ Ⓓ Ⓔ	38 Ⓐ Ⓑ Ⓒ Ⓓ Ⓔ	60 Ⓐ Ⓑ Ⓒ Ⓓ Ⓔ	82 Ⓐ Ⓑ Ⓒ Ⓓ Ⓔ
17 Ⓐ Ⓑ Ⓒ Ⓓ Ⓔ	39 Ⓐ Ⓑ Ⓒ Ⓓ Ⓔ	61 Ⓐ Ⓑ Ⓒ Ⓓ Ⓔ	83 Ⓐ Ⓑ Ⓒ Ⓓ Ⓔ
18 Ⓐ Ⓑ Ⓒ Ⓓ Ⓔ	40 Ⓐ Ⓑ Ⓒ Ⓓ Ⓔ	62 Ⓐ Ⓑ Ⓒ Ⓓ Ⓔ	84 Ⓐ Ⓑ Ⓒ Ⓓ Ⓔ
19 Ⓐ Ⓑ Ⓒ Ⓓ Ⓔ	41 Ⓐ Ⓑ Ⓒ Ⓓ Ⓔ	63 Ⓐ Ⓑ Ⓒ Ⓓ Ⓔ	85 Ⓐ Ⓑ Ⓒ Ⓓ Ⓔ
20 Ⓐ Ⓑ Ⓒ Ⓓ Ⓔ	42 Ⓐ Ⓑ Ⓒ Ⓓ Ⓔ	64 Ⓐ Ⓑ Ⓒ Ⓓ Ⓔ	86 Ⓐ Ⓑ Ⓒ Ⓓ Ⓔ
21 Ⓐ Ⓑ Ⓒ Ⓓ Ⓔ	43 Ⓐ Ⓑ Ⓒ Ⓓ Ⓔ	65 Ⓐ Ⓑ Ⓒ Ⓓ Ⓔ	87 Ⓐ Ⓑ Ⓒ Ⓓ Ⓔ
22 Ⓐ Ⓑ Ⓒ Ⓓ Ⓔ	44 Ⓐ Ⓑ Ⓒ Ⓓ Ⓔ	66 Ⓐ Ⓑ Ⓒ Ⓓ Ⓔ	88 Ⓐ Ⓑ Ⓒ Ⓓ Ⓔ

Practice III

Directions: *The names and addresses are repeated for you in the boxes below. Each name and each number span is in the same box in which you found it in the original set. You will now be allowed FIVE MINUTES to study the locations again. Do your best to memorize the letter of the box in which each item is located. This is your last chance to see the boxes.*

A	B	C	D	E
2500–2999 Mist Forest 1400–1899 Tank Tarot 3600–3899 Kite	3600–3899 Mist Season 2500–2999 Tank Howard 1900–2499 Kite	1400–1899 Mist Anchor 3600–3899 Tank Bongo 3000–3599 Kite	1900–2499 Mist Cupola 3000–3599 Tank Gibbon 2500–2999 Kite	3000–3599 Mist Jester 1900–2499 Tank Lattice 1400–1899 Kite

Directions: *This is your last practice test. Mark the location of each of the 88 items on your answer sheet. You will have FIVE MINUTES to answer these questions. Do NOT look back at the boxes. This practice test will not be scored.*

1. 3600–3899 Kite
2. 1400–1899 Mist
3. Season
4. Howard
5. 1900–2499 Tank
6. 1400–1899 Kite
7. 1900–2499 Mist
8. 2500–2999 Tank
9. Gibbon
10. Jester
11. 1400–1899 Tank
12. 3000–3599 Kite
13. 1400–1899 Mist
14. 3000–3599 Tank
15. 2500–2999 Mist
16. 1900–2499 Kite
17. Bongo
18. Anchor
19. 3600–3899 Tank
20. 3600–3899 Mist
21. 2500–2999 Kite
22. 2500–2999 Tank
23. Lattice
24. Cupola
25. Tarot
26. 3000–3599 Kite
27. 3000–3599 Mist
28. 1400–1899 Tank
29. 3000–3599 Mist
30. 3600–3899 Kite
31. 2500–2999 Mist
32. 1400–1899 Kite
33. Season
34. Forest
35. Jester
36. 1400–1899 Tank
37. 1900–2499 Tank
38. 3600–3899 Mist
39. 2500–2999 Kite
40. 2500–2999 Tank
41. Tarot
42. Lattice
43. Bongo
44. Cupola
45. 3600–3899 Tank
46. 3000–3599 Tank
47. 1400–1899 Mist
48. 1900–2499 Kite
49. Gibbon
50. Howard
51. 1900–2499 Mist
52. 3000–3599 Kite
53. Anchor
54. 1900–2499 Tank
55. 2500–2999 Kite
56. 3600–3899 Mist
57. 1400–1899 Tank
58. 2500–2999 Mist
59. 1900–2499 Kite
60. Season
61. Bongo
62. Lattice
63. 2500–2999 Tank
64. 2500–2999 Kite
65. 3600–3899 Tank
66. 3600–3899 Kite
67. Jester
68. Forest
69. 3000–3599 Kite

70. 1900–2499 Tank
71. 3600–3899 Mist
72. 1900–2499 Mist
73. Anchor
74. Cupola
75. 3000–3899 Tank
76. 1400–1899 Mist
77. 1400–1899 Kite
78. Tarot
79. Gibbon
80. 3000–3899 Mist
81. 1400–1899 Tank
82. Howard
83. 3600–3899 Mist
84. 2500–2999 Kite
85. 3600–3899 Kite
86. 2500–2999 Mist
87. Bongo
88. Lattice

Practice III Answer Sheet

1 Ⓐ Ⓑ Ⓒ Ⓓ Ⓔ	23 Ⓐ Ⓑ Ⓒ Ⓓ Ⓔ	45 Ⓐ Ⓑ Ⓒ Ⓓ Ⓔ	67 Ⓐ Ⓑ Ⓒ Ⓓ Ⓔ
2 Ⓐ Ⓑ Ⓒ Ⓓ Ⓔ	24 Ⓐ Ⓑ Ⓒ Ⓓ Ⓔ	46 Ⓐ Ⓑ Ⓒ Ⓓ Ⓔ	68 Ⓐ Ⓑ Ⓒ Ⓓ Ⓔ
3 Ⓐ Ⓑ Ⓒ Ⓓ Ⓔ	25 Ⓐ Ⓑ Ⓒ Ⓓ Ⓔ	47 Ⓐ Ⓑ Ⓒ Ⓓ Ⓔ	69 Ⓐ Ⓑ Ⓒ Ⓓ Ⓔ
4 Ⓐ Ⓑ Ⓒ Ⓓ Ⓔ	26 Ⓐ Ⓑ Ⓒ Ⓓ Ⓔ	48 Ⓐ Ⓑ Ⓒ Ⓓ Ⓔ	70 Ⓐ Ⓑ Ⓒ Ⓓ Ⓔ
5 Ⓐ Ⓑ Ⓒ Ⓓ Ⓔ	27 Ⓐ Ⓑ Ⓒ Ⓓ Ⓔ	49 Ⓐ Ⓑ Ⓒ Ⓓ Ⓔ	71 Ⓐ Ⓑ Ⓒ Ⓓ Ⓔ
6 Ⓐ Ⓑ Ⓒ Ⓓ Ⓔ	28 Ⓐ Ⓑ Ⓒ Ⓓ Ⓔ	50 Ⓐ Ⓑ Ⓒ Ⓓ Ⓔ	72 Ⓐ Ⓑ Ⓒ Ⓓ Ⓔ
7 Ⓐ Ⓑ Ⓒ Ⓓ Ⓔ	29 Ⓐ Ⓑ Ⓒ Ⓓ Ⓔ	51 Ⓐ Ⓑ Ⓒ Ⓓ Ⓔ	73 Ⓐ Ⓑ Ⓒ Ⓓ Ⓔ
8 Ⓐ Ⓑ Ⓒ Ⓓ Ⓔ	30 Ⓐ Ⓑ Ⓒ Ⓓ Ⓔ	52 Ⓐ Ⓑ Ⓒ Ⓓ Ⓔ	74 Ⓐ Ⓑ Ⓒ Ⓓ Ⓔ
9 Ⓐ Ⓑ Ⓒ Ⓓ Ⓔ	31 Ⓐ Ⓑ Ⓒ Ⓓ Ⓔ	53 Ⓐ Ⓑ Ⓒ Ⓓ Ⓔ	75 Ⓐ Ⓑ Ⓒ Ⓓ Ⓔ
10 Ⓐ Ⓑ Ⓒ Ⓓ Ⓔ	32 Ⓐ Ⓑ Ⓒ Ⓓ Ⓔ	54 Ⓐ Ⓑ Ⓒ Ⓓ Ⓔ	76 Ⓐ Ⓑ Ⓒ Ⓓ Ⓔ
11 Ⓐ Ⓑ Ⓒ Ⓓ Ⓔ	33 Ⓐ Ⓑ Ⓒ Ⓓ Ⓔ	55 Ⓐ Ⓑ Ⓒ Ⓓ Ⓔ	77 Ⓐ Ⓑ Ⓒ Ⓓ Ⓔ
12 Ⓐ Ⓑ Ⓒ Ⓓ Ⓔ	34 Ⓐ Ⓑ Ⓒ Ⓓ Ⓔ	56 Ⓐ Ⓑ Ⓒ Ⓓ Ⓔ	78 Ⓐ Ⓑ Ⓒ Ⓓ Ⓔ
13 Ⓐ Ⓑ Ⓒ Ⓓ Ⓔ	35 Ⓐ Ⓑ Ⓒ Ⓓ Ⓔ	57 Ⓐ Ⓑ Ⓒ Ⓓ Ⓔ	79 Ⓐ Ⓑ Ⓒ Ⓓ Ⓔ
14 Ⓐ Ⓑ Ⓒ Ⓓ Ⓔ	36 Ⓐ Ⓑ Ⓒ Ⓓ Ⓔ	58 Ⓐ Ⓑ Ⓒ Ⓓ Ⓔ	80 Ⓐ Ⓑ Ⓒ Ⓓ Ⓔ
15 Ⓐ Ⓑ Ⓒ Ⓓ Ⓔ	37 Ⓐ Ⓑ Ⓒ Ⓓ Ⓔ	59 Ⓐ Ⓑ Ⓒ Ⓓ Ⓔ	81 Ⓐ Ⓑ Ⓒ Ⓓ Ⓔ
16 Ⓐ Ⓑ Ⓒ Ⓓ Ⓔ	38 Ⓐ Ⓑ Ⓒ Ⓓ Ⓔ	60 Ⓐ Ⓑ Ⓒ Ⓓ Ⓔ	82 Ⓐ Ⓑ Ⓒ Ⓓ Ⓔ
17 Ⓐ Ⓑ Ⓒ Ⓓ Ⓔ	39 Ⓐ Ⓑ Ⓒ Ⓓ Ⓔ	61 Ⓐ Ⓑ Ⓒ Ⓓ Ⓔ	83 Ⓐ Ⓑ Ⓒ Ⓓ Ⓔ
18 Ⓐ Ⓑ Ⓒ Ⓓ Ⓔ	40 Ⓐ Ⓑ Ⓒ Ⓓ Ⓔ	62 Ⓐ Ⓑ Ⓒ Ⓓ Ⓔ	84 Ⓐ Ⓑ Ⓒ Ⓓ Ⓔ
19 Ⓐ Ⓑ Ⓒ Ⓓ Ⓔ	41 Ⓐ Ⓑ Ⓒ Ⓓ Ⓔ	63 Ⓐ Ⓑ Ⓒ Ⓓ Ⓔ	85 Ⓐ Ⓑ Ⓒ Ⓓ Ⓔ
20 Ⓐ Ⓑ Ⓒ Ⓓ Ⓔ	42 Ⓐ Ⓑ Ⓒ Ⓓ Ⓔ	64 Ⓐ Ⓑ Ⓒ Ⓓ Ⓔ	86 Ⓐ Ⓑ Ⓒ Ⓓ Ⓔ
21 Ⓐ Ⓑ Ⓒ Ⓓ Ⓔ	43 Ⓐ Ⓑ Ⓒ Ⓓ Ⓔ	65 Ⓐ Ⓑ Ⓒ Ⓓ Ⓔ	87 Ⓐ Ⓑ Ⓒ Ⓓ Ⓔ
22 Ⓐ Ⓑ Ⓒ Ⓓ Ⓔ	44 Ⓐ Ⓑ Ⓒ Ⓓ Ⓔ	66 Ⓐ Ⓑ Ⓒ Ⓓ Ⓔ	88 Ⓐ Ⓑ Ⓒ Ⓓ Ⓔ

MEMORY FOR ADDRESSES

Time: 5 Minutes. 88 Questions.

Directions: *Mark your answers on the answer sheet in the section headed "MEMORY FOR ADDRESSES." This test will be scored. You are NOT permitted to look at the boxes. Work from memory, as quickly and as accurately as you can. Correct answers are on page 257.*

1. 3600–3899 Tank
2. 1900–2499 Kite
3. 1900–2499 Mist
4. Bongo
5. Tarot
6. 2500–2999 Mist
7. 1400–1899 Kite
8. 3000–3599 Tank
9. Jester
10. Anchor
11. Forest
12. 1400–1899 Tank
13. 2500–2999 Kite
14. 2500–2999 Tank
15. 3600–3899 Mist
16. 3000–3599 Mist
17. Lattice
18. Forest
19. Gibbon
20. 1900–2499 Tank
21. 1400–1899 Mist
22. 3000–3599 Kite
23. Howard
24. Season
25. Cupola
26. 2500–2999 Kite
27. 1900–2499 Tank
28. 3600– 3899 Mist
29. Lattice
30. 1900–2499 Kite
31. 1400–1899 Mist
32. 1400–1899 Tank
33. Tarot
34. Bongo
35. 3000–3599 Tank
36. 3600–3899 Kite
37. 2500–2999 Mist
38. 3000–3599 Mist
39. 3600–3899 Tank
40. Howard
41. Anchor
42. Gibbon
43. 1400–1899 Kite
44. 2500–2999 Tank
45. 3000–3599 Kite
46. Season
47. Anchor
48. 1900–2499 Tank
49. 2500–2999 Kite
50. 1900–2499 Kite
51. 3600–3899 Mist
52. Jester
53. Howard
54. 3600–3899 Kite
55. 2500–2999 Tank
56. 1400–1899 Mist
57. 2500–2999 Mist
58. Tarot
59. Lattice
60. Bongo
61. 1400–1899 Tank
62. 3600–3899 Tank
63. 3000–3599 Kite
64. 3000–3599 Mist
65. Gibbon
66. Forest
67. Cupola
68. 3000–3599 Tank
69. 1400–1899 Kite
70. 1900–2499 Mist
71. 3600–3899 Mist
72. 1900–2499 Mist
73. 3000–3599 Kite
74. Bongo
75. Howard
76. 2500–2999 Mist
77. 1400–1899 Kite
78. 3600–3899 Tank
79. 2500–2999 Tank
80. Anchor
81. Jester
82. 3600–3899 Mist
83. 1900–2499 Mist
84. 1900–2499 Tank
85. Lattice
86. 1900–2499 Kite
87. Tarot
88. 3000–3599 Tank

NUMBER SERIES

Time: 20 Minutes. 24 Questions.

***Directions:** Each number series question consists of a series of numbers that follows some definite order. The numbers progress from left to right according to some rule. One lettered pair of numbers comprises the next two numbers in the series. Study each series to try to find a pattern to the series and to figure the rule that governs the progression. Choose the answer pair that continues the series according to the pattern established and mark its letter on your answer sheet. Correct answers are on page 257. Explanations are on page 258.*

1. 10 11 12 10 11 12 10 .... (A) 10 11 (B) 12 10 (C) 11 10 (D) 11 12 (E) 10 12

2. 4 6 7 4 6 7 4 .... (A) 6 7 (B) 4 7 (C) 7 6 (D) 7 4 (E) 6 8

3. 10 10 9 11 11 10 12 ...... (A) 13 14 (B) 12 11 (C) 13 13 (D) 12 12 (E) 12 13

4. 3 4 10 5 6 10 7 .... (A) 10 8 (B) 9 8 (C) 8 14 (D) 8 9 (E) 8 10

5. 6 6 7 7 8 8 9 .... (A) 10 11 (B) 10 10 (C) 9 10 (D) 9 9 (E) 10 9

6. 3 8 9 4 9 10 5 .... (A) 6 10 (B) 10 11 (C) 9 10 (D) 11 6 (E) 10 6

7. 2 4 3 6 4 8 5 .... (A) 6 10 (B) 10 7 (C) 10 6 (D) 9 6 (E) 6 7

8. 11 5 9 7 7 9 5 .... (A) 11 3 (B) 7 9 (C) 7 11 (D) 9 7 (E) 3 7

9. 7 16 9 15 11 14 13 .... (A) 12 14 (B) 13 15 (C) 17 15 (D) 15 12 (E) 13 12

10. 40 42 39 44 38 46 37 .... (A) 48 36 (B) 37 46 (C) 36 48 (D) 43 39 (E) 46 40

11. 1 3 6 10 15 21 28 36 ..... (A) 40 48 (B) 36 45 (C) 38 52 (D) 45 56 (E) 45 55

12. 1 2 3 3 4 7 5 6 11 7 .... (A) 8 12 (B) 9 15 (C) 8 15 (D) 6 12 (E) 8 7

13. 3 18 4 24 5 30 6 .... (A) 7 40 (B) 7 42 (C) 42 7 (D) 36 7 (E) 40 7

14. 3 3 4 8 10 30 33 132 ..... (A) 152 158 (B) 136 680 (C) 165 500 (D) 143 560 (E) 300 900

15. 18 20 22 20 18 20 22 .... (A) 18 20 (B) 20 18 (C) 22 20 (D) 24 20 (E) 18 22

16. 4 8 8 16 16 32 32 .... (A) 32 64 (B) 36 40 (C) 64 64 (D) 64 128 (E) 64 82

17. 1 2 12 3 4 34 5 .... (A) 6 5 (B) 7 12 (C) 5 6 (D) 6 60 (E) 6 56

18. 8 16 24 32 40 48 56 ...... (A) 64 72 (B) 60 64 (C) 70 78 (D) 62 70 (E) 64 68

19. 5 15 18 54 57 171 174 .. (A) 176 528 (B) 522 821 (C) 177 531 (D) 522 525 (E) 525 528

20. 25 20 24 21 23 22 22 .... (A) 24 20 (B) 23 21 (C) 23 24 (D) 24 21 (E) 22 23

21. 99 88 77 66 55 44 33 .... (A) 22 11 (B) 33 22 (C) 44 55 (D) 32 22 (E) 30 20

22. 7 5 9 7 11 9 13 .... (A) 9 11 (B) 11 9 (C) 7 11 (D) 9 15 (E) 11 15

23. 47 44 41 38 35 32 29 .... (A) 28 27 (B) 27 24 (C) 26 23 (D) 25 21 (E) 26 22

24. 99 99 99 33 33 33 11 .... (A) 9 7 (B) 22 33 (C) 11 0 (D) 11 33 (E) 11 11

END OF NUMBER SERIES

FOLLOWING ORAL INSTRUCTIONS

Time: 25 Minutes

Listening to Instructions

Directions: *When you are ready to try this test of the Model Exam, give the following instructions to a friend and have the friend read them aloud to you at the rate of 80 words per minute. Do NOT read them to yourself. Your friend will need a watch with a second hand. Listen carefully and do exactly what your friend tells you to do with the worksheet and with the answer sheet. Your friend will tell you some things to do with each item on the worksheet. After each set of instructions, your friend will give you time to mark your answer by darkening a circle on the answer sheet. Since B and D sound very much alike, your friend will say "B as in baker" when he or she means B and "D as in dog" when he or she means D.*

Before proceeding further, tear out worksheet on page 253. Then hand this book to your friend.

TO THE PERSON WHO IS TO READ THE INSTRUCTIONS: The instructions are to be read at the rate of 80 words per minute. Do not read aloud the material that is in parentheses. Once you have begun the test itself, do not repeat any instructions. The next three paragraphs consist of approximately 120 words. Read these three paragraphs aloud to the candidate in about one and one-half minutes. You may reread these paragraphs as often as necessary to establish an 80-words-per-minute reading speed.

Read Aloud to the Candidate

On the job you will have to listen to directions and then do what you have been told to do. In this test, I will read instructions to you. Try to understand them as I read them; I cannot repeat them. Once we begin, you may not ask any questions until the end of the test.

On the job you won't have to deal with pictures, numbers, and letters like those in the test, but you will have to listen to instructions and follow them. We are using this test to see how well you can follow instructions.

You are to mark your test booklet according to the instructions that I'll read to you. After each set of instructions. I'll give you time to record your answers on the separate answer sheet.

The actual test begins now.

Look at line 1 on your worksheet. (Pause slightly.) Next to the left-hand number write the letter E. (Pause 2 seconds.) Now, on your answer sheet, find the space for the number beside which you wrote and darken space E. (Pause 5 seconds.)

Now look at line 2 on your worksheet. (Pause slightly.) There are 5 boxes. Each box has a letter. (Pause slightly.) In the fifth box write the answer to this question: Which of the following numbers is largest: 18, 9, 15, 19, 13? (Pause 5 seconds.) Now, on your answer sheet, darken the space for the number-letter combination that is in the box you just wrote in. (Pause 5 seconds.) In the fourth box on the same line do nothing. In the third box write 5. (Pause 2 seconds.) Now, on your answer sheet, darken the space for the number-letter combination that is in the box you just wrote in. (Pause 5 seconds.) In the second box, write the answer to this question: How many hours are there in a day? (Pause 2 seconds.) Now, on your answer sheet, darken the space for the number-letter combination that is in the box you just wrote in. (Pause 5 seconds.)

Look at line 3 on your worksheet. (Pause slightly.) Draw a line under every number that is more than 50 but less than 85. (Pause 12 seconds.) Now, on your answer sheet, for each number that you drew a line under, darken space D as in dog. (Pause 25 seconds.)

Look at line 4 on your worksheet. (Pause slightly.) Write a B as in baker in the third circle. (Pause 2 seconds.) Now, on your answer sheet, find the number in that circle and darken space B as in baker for that number. (Pause 5 seconds.)

Look at line 4 again. (Pause slightly.) Write C in the first circle. (Pause 2 seconds.) Now, on your answer sheet, find the number in that circle and darken space C for that number. (Pause 5 seconds.)

Look at line 5 on your worksheet. (Pause slightly.) There are two circles and two boxes of different sizes with numbers in them. (Pause slightly.) If 4 is more than 6 and if 9 is less than 7, write D as in dog in the smaller box. (Pause slightly.) Otherwise write A in the larger circle. (Pause 2 seconds.) Now, on your answer sheet, darken the space for the number-letter combination for the box or circle you just wrote in. (Pause 5 seconds.)

Now look at line 6 on your worksheet. (Pause slightly.) Write an E in the second circle. (Pause 2 seconds.) Now, on your answer sheet, find the number in that circle and darken space E for that number. (Pause 5 seconds.)

Now look at line 6 again. (Pause slightly.) Write a B as in baker in the middle circle. (Pause 2 seconds.) Now, on your answer sheet, find the number in that circle and darken space B as in baker for that number. (Pause 5 seconds.)

Look at the numbers on line 7 on your worksheet. (Pause slightly.) Draw a line under the largest number in the line. (Pause 2 seconds.) Now, on your answer sheet, find the number and darken space C for the number. (Pause 5 seconds.)

Now look at line 7 again. (Pause slightly.) Draw a circle around the smallest number in the line. (Pause 2 seconds.) Now, on your answer sheet, find the number that you just drew a circle around and darken space A for that number. (Pause 5 seconds.)

Now look at line 8 on your worksheet. There are 3 boxes with words and letters in them. (Pause slightly.) Each box represents a station in a large city. Station A delivers mail in the Chestnut Street area, Station B delivers mail in Hyde Park, and Station C delivers mail in the Prudential Plaza. Mr. Adams lives in Hyde Park. Write the number 30 on the line inside the box that represents the station that delivers Mr. Adams' mail. (Pause 2 seconds.) Now, on your answer sheet, find number 30 and darken the space for the letter that is in the box you just wrote in. (Pause 5 seconds.)

Now look at line 9 on your worksheet. (Pause slightly.) Write a D as in dog in the third box. (Pause 2 seconds.) Now, on your answer sheet, find the number that is in the box you just wrote in and darken space D as in dog for that number. (Pause 5 seconds.)

Now look at line 10 on your worksheet. (Pause slightly.) Draw a line under all the even numbers in line 10. (Pause 5 seconds.) Find the second number with a line under it. (Pause 2 seconds.) On your answer sheet blacken space C for that number. (Pause 5 seconds.)

Now look at line 11 on your worksheet. (Pause slightly.) Count the number of C's in line 11 and write the number at the end of the line. (Pause 3 seconds.) On your answer sheet blacken the letter E for that number. (Pause 5 seconds.)

Now look at line 12 on your worksheet. (Pause slightly.) The time written in each circle represents the last pickup of the day from a particular street box. Write the last two numbers of the earliest pickup time on the line next to the letter in that circle. (Pause 2 seconds.) Now, on your answer sheet, blacken the space for the number-letter combination in the circle in which you just wrote. (Pause 5 seconds.)

Look at line 12 on the worksheet again. (Pause slightly.) Find the second earliest pickup time and write the last two numbers of the second earliest pickup time on the line next to the letter in that circle. (Pause 2 seconds.) Now, on your answer sheet, blacken the space for the number-letter combination in the circle in which you just wrote. (Pause 5 seconds.)

Look at line 13 on the worksheet. (Pause slightly.) If there are 365 days in a leap year, write the letter B as in baker in the small circle. (Pause 2 seconds.) If not, write the letter A in the triangle. (Pause 2 seconds.) Now, on your answer sheet, blacken the space for the letter-number combination in the figure in which you just wrote. (Pause 5 seconds.)

Look at line 13 again. (Pause slightly.) Write the letter D as in dog in the box with the lower number. (Pause 2 seconds.) Now, on your answer sheet, blacken the space for the number-letter combination in the box in which you just wrote. (Pause 5 seconds.)

Look at line 14 on the worksheet. (Pause slightly.) Draw two lines under all the numbers that are greater than 12 but less than 41. (Pause 8 seconds.) Count the number of numbers under which you drew two lines and blacken the letter B as in baker for that number on your answer sheet. (Pause 10 seconds.) Still on *line 14* on the worksheet (pause slightly) circle all the even numbers. (Pause 2 seconds.) Count all the numbers that you marked in any way and blacken the letter E for that number on your answer sheet. (Pause 10 seconds.)

Look at line 15 on the worksheet. (Pause slightly.) Circle the fourth letter in the line. (Pause 2 seconds.) Add together the number of hours in a day, the number of months in a year, and the number of days in a week. (Pause 10 seconds.) Now, on your answer sheet, blacken the circled letter for that number. (Pause 5 seconds.)

Look at line 16 on the worksheet. (Pause slightly.) Write the first letter of the third word in the second box. (Pause 5 seconds.) On your answer sheet, mark the number-letter combination in the box in which you just wrote. (Pause 5 seconds.) Look again at line 16. (Pause slightly.) Write the third letter of the second word in the first box. (Pause 5 seconds.) On your answer sheet, mark the number-letter combination in the box in which you just wrote. (Pause 5 seconds.) Look once more at line 16. (Pause slightly.) Write the second letter of the second word in the third box. (Pause 5 seconds.) Now, on your answer sheet, mark the number-letter combination in the box in which you just wrote. (Pause 5 seconds.)

Look at line 17 on the worksheet. (Pause slightly.) Draw a wavy line under the middle letter in the line. (Pause 2 seconds.) On your answer sheet, blacken that letter for answer space 36. (Pause 5 seconds.)

Look at line 18 on the worksheet. (Pause slightly.) Count the number of Y's in the line and write the number at the end of the line. (Pause 2 seconds.) Add 27 to that number (pause 2 seconds) and blacken B as in baker for the space that represents the total of 27 plus the number of Y's. (Pause 5 seconds.)

Look at line 19 on the worksheet. (Pause slightly.) In the last box write the answer to this question: Which of the following numbers is smaller than 20: 41, 82, 1, 36? (Pause 2 seconds.) Now, on your answer sheet, darken the space for the number-letter combination in the box you just wrote in. (Pause 5 seconds.)

TEAR HERE

FOLLOWING ORAL INSTRUCTIONS

Worksheet

Directions: *Listening carefully to each set of instructions, mark each item on this worksheet as directed. Then complete each question by marking the answer sheet as directed. For each answer you will darken the answer for a number-letter combination. Should you fall behind and miss an instruction, don't become excited. Let that one go and listen for the next one. If, when you start to darken a space for a number, you find that you have already darkened another space for that number, either erase the first mark and darken the space for the new combination or let the first mark stay and do not darken a space for the new combination. Write with a pencil that has a clean eraser. When you finish, you should have no more than one space darkened for each number. Correct answers begin on page 259.*

1. 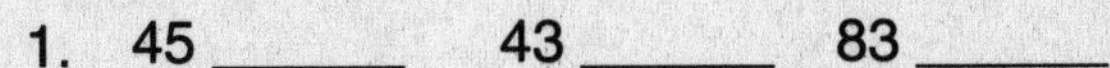

2. 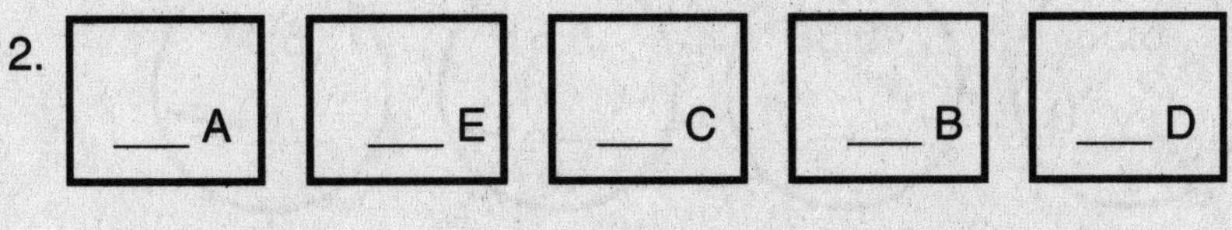

3. 

4. 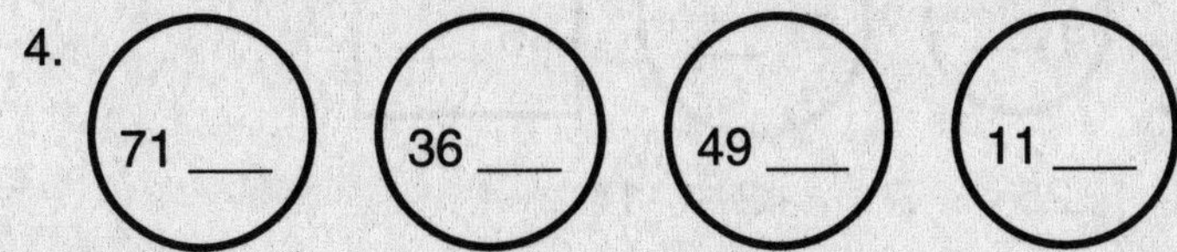

5. 

6. 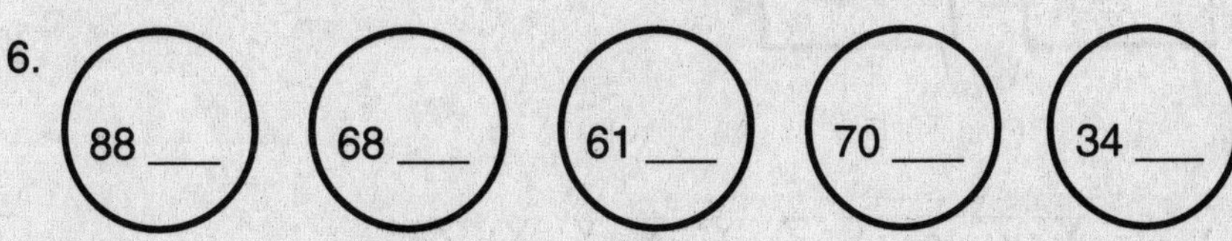

7. 28 67 29 77 26

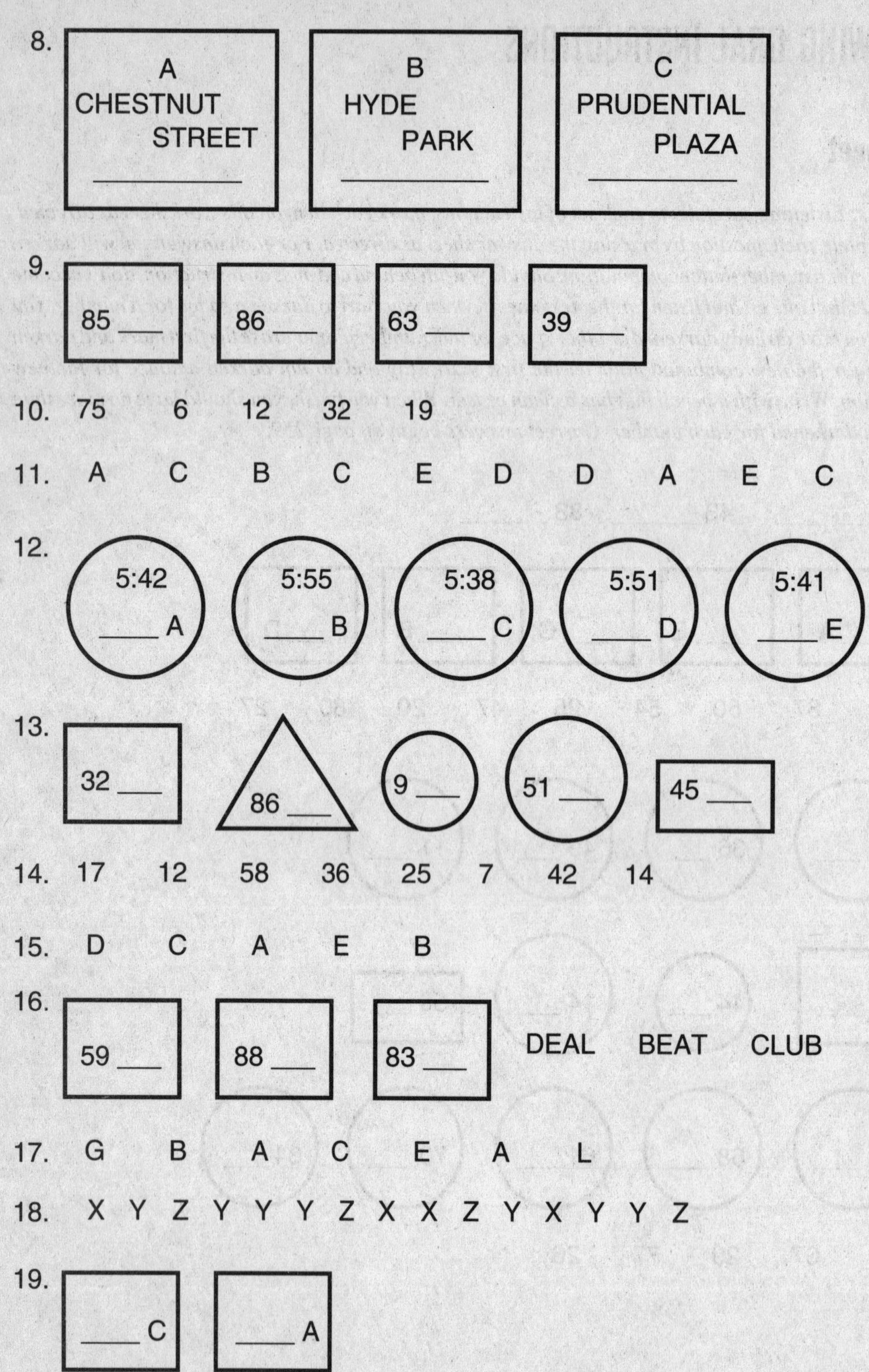

END OF EXAMINATION

CORRECT ANSWERS

PART A—ADDRESS CHECKING

1. A	13. D	25. D	37. D	49. D	61. D	73. A	85. A
2. A	14. D	26. A	38. A	50. A	62. D	74. D	86. D
3. D	15. D	27. A	39. D	51. D	63. A	75. D	87. D
4. A	16. D	28. A	40. A	52. A	64. A	76. A	88. D
5. D	17. A	29. D	41. A	53. D	65. D	77. D	89. D
6. D	18. D	30. A	42. D	54. D	66. A	78. D	90. D
7. D	19. A	31. A	43. A	55. D	67. D	79. D	91. D
8. A	20. D	32. D	44. D	56. D	68. D	80. D	92. A
9. D	21. A	33. D	45. D	57. D	69. D	81. D	93. D
10. D	22. D	34. D	46. A	58. D	70. D	82. A	94. D
11. D	23. D	35. D	47. D	59. A	71. D	83. A	95. A
12. A	24. A	36. A	48. D	60. D	72. A	84. A	

ANALYZING YOUR ERRORS

Type of Difference	Question Numbers	Number of Questions You Missed
Difference in NUMBERS	15, 32, 33, 34, 44, 47, 53, 54, 56, 68, 77, 78, 80, 89, 90	
Difference in ABBREVIATIONS	3, 9, 10, 11, 13, 14, 18, 42, 45, 48, 55, 57, 58, 62, 69, 75, 81, 91, 93, 94	
Difference in NAMES	5, 6, 7, 16, 20, 22, 23, 25, 29, 35, 37, 39, 49, 51, 60, 61, 65, 67, 70, 71, 74, 79, 86, 87, 88	
No Difference	1, 2, 4, 8, 12, 17, 19, 21, 24, 26, 27, 28, 30, 31, 36, 38, 40, 41, 43, 46, 50, 52, 59, 63, 64, 66, 72, 73, 76, 82, 83, 84, 85, 92, 95	

PART B—MEMORY FOR ADDRESSES

Practice I

1. A	12. B	23. A	34. E	45. E	56. B	67. B	78. D
2. D	13. D	24. E	35. E	46. D	57. E	68. A	79. E
3. B	14. D	25. B	36. A	47. B	58. A	69. D	80. E
4. E	15. A	26. D	37. A	48. E	59. D	70. E	81. C
5. E	16. E	27. C	38. E	49. A	60. C	71. A	82. A
6. C	17. D	28. B	39. C	50. A	61. E	72. D	83. E
7. E	18. C	29. B	40. D	51. C	62. A	73. B	84. B
8. A	19. C	30. B	41. D	52. E	63. C	74. C	85. D
9. C	20. E	31. D	42. B	53. D	64. B	75. A	86. B
10. A	21. A	32. C	43. D	54. C	65. B	76. E	87. B
11. D	22. B	33. A	44. A	55. D	66. C	77. C	88. B

Practice II

1. C	12. A	23. D	34. A	45. B	56. B	67. D	78. B
2. C	13. C	24. B	35. A	46. E	57. C	68. B	79. B
3. E	14. E	25. A	36. C	47. B	58. C	69. D	80. D
4. A	15. D	26. E	37. E	48. D	59. C	70. E	81. E
5. B	16. D	27. D	38. C	49. B	60. D	71. B	82. A
6. D	17. A	28. C	39. A	50. C	61. E	72. C	83. E
7. B	18. C	29. E	40. D	51. D	62. A	73. B	84. C
8. D	19. B	30. D	41. A	52. E	63. A	74. C	85. B
9. E	20. A	31. A	42. C	53. A	64. E	75. E	86. D
10. E	21. C	32. B	43. D	54. D	65. A	76. A	87. C
11. E	22. B	33. C	44. B	55. E	66. A	77. D	88. E

Practice III

1. A	12. C	23. E	34. A	45. C	56. B	67. E	78. A
2. C	13. C	24. D	35. E	46. D	57. A	68. A	79. D
3. B	14. D	25. A	36. A	47. C	58. A	69. C	80. E
4. B	15. A	26. C	37. E	48. B	59. B	70. E	81. A
5. E	16. B	27. E	38. B	49. D	60. B	71. B	82. B
6. E	17. C	28. A	39. D	50. B	61. C	72. D	83. B
7. D	18. C	29. E	40. B	51. D	62. E	73. C	84. D
8. B	19. C	30. A	41. A	52. C	63. B	74. D	85. A
9. D	20. B	31. A	42. E	53. C	64. D	75. D	86. A
10. E	21. D	32. E	43. C	54. E	65. C	76. C	87. C
11. A	22. B	33. B	44. D	55. D	66. A	77. E	88. E

Memory for Addresses

1. C	12. A	23. B	34. C	45. C	56. C	67. D	78. C
2. B	13. D	24. B	35. D	46. B	57. A	68. D	79. B
3. D	14. B	25. D	36. A	47. C	58. A	69. E	80. C
4. C	15. B	26. D	37. A	48. E	59. E	70. D	81. E
5. A	16. E	27. E	38. E	49. D	60. C	71. B	82. B
6. A	17. E	28. B	39. C	50. B	61. A	72. D	83. D
7. E	18. A	29. E	40. B	51. B	62. C	73. C	84. E
8. D	19. D	30. B	41. C	52. E	63. C	74. C	85. E
9. E	20. E	31. C	42. D	53. B	64. E	75. B	86. B
10. C	21. C	32. A	43. E	54. A	65. D	76. A	87. A
11. A	22. C	33. A	44. B	55. B	66. A	77. E	88. D

PART C—NUMBER SERIES

1. D	4. E	7. C	10. A	13. D	16. C	19. D	22. E
2. A	5. C	8. A	11. E	14. B	17. E	20. B	23. C
3. B	6. B	9. B	12. C	15. B	18. A	21. A	24. E

Explanations

1. **(D)** The sequence, 10 11 12, repeats itself.
2. **(A)** Another repeating sequence; this one is 4 6 7.
3. **(B)** Two sequences alternate. The first repeats itself, then advances by +1 and repeats again. The alternating sequence proceeds forward one number at a time.
4. **(E)** The sequence consists of numbers proceeding upward from 3, with the number 10 intervening between each set of two numbers in the sequence.
5. **(C)** The numbers proceed upward from 6 by +1, with each number repeating itself.
6. **(B)** One series starts at 3 and proceeds upward by +1. The alternating series consists of two numbers that ascend according to the following rule: +1, repeat; +1, repeat.
7. **(C)** One series proceeds upward by +1. The alternating series proceeds up by +2.
8. **(A)** The first series begins with 11 and descends by –2. The alternating series begins with 5 and ascends by +2.
9. **(B)** There are two alternating series, the first ascending by +2, the other descending one number at a time.
10. **(A)** The first series descends one number at a time while the alternating series ascends at the rate of +2.
11. **(E)** The rule is +2, +3, +4, +5, +6, +7, +8, +9.
12. **(C)** Basically the series ascends 1 2 3 4 5 6 7 8, but there is a twist to this problem. The number which intervenes after each two numbers of the series is the sum of those two numbers. Thus, the series may be read: 1 + 2 = 3; 3 + 4 = 7; 5 + 6 = 11; 7 + 8 = 15.
13. **(D)** Look carefully. This is a × 6 series. 3 × 6 = 18; 4 × 6 = 24; 5 × 6 = 30; 6 × 6 = 36; 7 . . .
14. **(B)** This one is not easy, but if you wrote out the steps between numbers, you should have come up with: ×1, +1; ×2, +2; ×3, +3; ×4, +4; ×5 . . .
15. **(B)** This series is deceptively simple. The sequence 18 20 22 20 is repeated over and over again.
16. **(C)** The series picks up with the second member of a repeat. The pattern is × 2 and repeat, × 2 and repeat . . .
17. **(E)** There is no mathematical formula for this series. By inspection you may see that two successive numbers are brought together to form a larger number. Thus, 1 2 12; 3 4 34; 5 6 56 . . .
18. **(A)** Straightforward +8.
19. **(D)** The pattern is ×3, +3; ×3, +3 . . .
20. **(B)** There are two alternating series. The first begins with 25 and descends, one number at a time. The alternating series begins with 20 and ascends one number at a time.
21. **(A)** A simple descending series of –11.
22. **(E)** You may see this as two alternating series, both ascending in steps of +2. You might also interpret the series as reading –2, +4; –2, +4 . . . With either solution you should reach the correct answer.
23. **(C)** The series is a simple –3 series that begins with an unusual number.
24. **(E)** Repeat, repeat, ÷3, repeat, repeat, ÷3, repeat, repeat, ÷3.

PART D—FOLLOWING ORAL INSTRUCTIONS

Correctly Filled Answer Grid

1 ● Ⓑ Ⓒ Ⓓ Ⓔ
2 Ⓐ Ⓑ Ⓒ Ⓓ Ⓔ
3 Ⓐ Ⓑ Ⓒ Ⓓ ●
4 Ⓐ ● Ⓒ Ⓓ Ⓔ
5 Ⓐ Ⓑ ● Ⓓ Ⓔ
6 Ⓐ Ⓑ Ⓒ Ⓓ Ⓔ
7 Ⓐ Ⓑ Ⓒ Ⓓ ●
8 Ⓐ Ⓑ Ⓒ Ⓓ Ⓔ
9 Ⓐ Ⓑ Ⓒ Ⓓ Ⓔ
10 Ⓐ Ⓑ Ⓒ Ⓓ Ⓔ
11 Ⓐ Ⓑ Ⓒ Ⓓ Ⓔ
12 Ⓐ Ⓑ ● Ⓓ Ⓔ
13 Ⓐ Ⓑ Ⓒ Ⓓ Ⓔ
14 ● Ⓑ Ⓒ Ⓓ Ⓔ
15 Ⓐ Ⓑ Ⓒ Ⓓ Ⓔ
16 Ⓐ Ⓑ Ⓒ Ⓓ Ⓔ
17 Ⓐ Ⓑ Ⓒ Ⓓ Ⓔ
18 Ⓐ Ⓑ Ⓒ Ⓓ Ⓔ
19 Ⓐ Ⓑ Ⓒ ● Ⓔ
20 Ⓐ Ⓑ Ⓒ Ⓓ Ⓔ
21 Ⓐ Ⓑ Ⓒ Ⓓ Ⓔ
22 Ⓐ Ⓑ Ⓒ Ⓓ Ⓔ
23 Ⓐ Ⓑ Ⓒ Ⓓ Ⓔ
24 Ⓐ Ⓑ Ⓒ Ⓓ ●
25 Ⓐ Ⓑ Ⓒ Ⓓ Ⓔ
26 ● Ⓑ Ⓒ Ⓓ Ⓔ
27 Ⓐ Ⓑ Ⓒ Ⓓ Ⓔ
28 Ⓐ Ⓑ Ⓒ Ⓓ Ⓔ
29 Ⓐ Ⓑ Ⓒ Ⓓ Ⓔ
30 Ⓐ ● Ⓒ Ⓓ Ⓔ
31 Ⓐ Ⓑ Ⓒ Ⓓ Ⓔ
32 Ⓐ Ⓑ Ⓒ ● Ⓔ
33 Ⓐ Ⓑ Ⓒ Ⓓ Ⓔ
34 Ⓐ ● Ⓒ Ⓓ Ⓔ
35 Ⓐ Ⓑ Ⓒ Ⓓ Ⓔ
36 Ⓐ Ⓑ ● Ⓓ Ⓔ
37 Ⓐ Ⓑ Ⓒ Ⓓ Ⓔ
38 Ⓐ Ⓑ ● Ⓓ Ⓔ
39 Ⓐ Ⓑ Ⓒ Ⓓ Ⓔ
40 Ⓐ Ⓑ Ⓒ Ⓓ Ⓔ
41 Ⓐ Ⓑ Ⓒ Ⓓ ●
42 Ⓐ Ⓑ Ⓒ Ⓓ Ⓔ
43 Ⓐ Ⓑ Ⓒ Ⓓ ●
44 Ⓐ Ⓑ Ⓒ Ⓓ Ⓔ
45 Ⓐ Ⓑ Ⓒ Ⓓ ●
46 Ⓐ Ⓑ Ⓒ Ⓓ Ⓔ
47 Ⓐ Ⓑ Ⓒ Ⓓ Ⓔ
48 Ⓐ Ⓑ Ⓒ Ⓓ Ⓔ
49 Ⓐ ● Ⓒ Ⓓ Ⓔ
50 Ⓐ Ⓑ Ⓒ Ⓓ Ⓔ
51 Ⓐ Ⓑ Ⓒ Ⓓ Ⓔ
52 Ⓐ Ⓑ Ⓒ Ⓓ Ⓔ
53 Ⓐ Ⓑ Ⓒ Ⓓ Ⓔ
54 Ⓐ Ⓑ Ⓒ ● Ⓔ
55 Ⓐ Ⓑ Ⓒ Ⓓ Ⓔ
56 Ⓐ Ⓑ Ⓒ Ⓓ Ⓔ
57 Ⓐ Ⓑ Ⓒ Ⓓ Ⓔ
58 Ⓐ Ⓑ Ⓒ Ⓓ Ⓔ
59 ● Ⓑ Ⓒ Ⓓ Ⓔ
60 Ⓐ Ⓑ Ⓒ Ⓓ Ⓔ
61 Ⓐ ● Ⓒ Ⓓ Ⓔ
62 Ⓐ Ⓑ Ⓒ Ⓓ Ⓔ
63 Ⓐ Ⓑ Ⓒ ● Ⓔ
64 Ⓐ Ⓑ Ⓒ Ⓓ Ⓔ
65 Ⓐ Ⓑ Ⓒ Ⓓ Ⓔ
66 Ⓐ Ⓑ Ⓒ Ⓓ Ⓔ
67 Ⓐ Ⓑ Ⓒ Ⓓ Ⓔ
68 Ⓐ Ⓑ Ⓒ Ⓓ ●
69 Ⓐ Ⓑ Ⓒ ● Ⓔ
70 Ⓐ Ⓑ Ⓒ Ⓓ Ⓔ
71 Ⓐ Ⓑ ● Ⓓ Ⓔ
72 Ⓐ Ⓑ Ⓒ Ⓓ Ⓔ
73 Ⓐ Ⓑ Ⓒ Ⓓ Ⓔ
74 Ⓐ Ⓑ Ⓒ Ⓓ Ⓔ
75 Ⓐ Ⓑ Ⓒ Ⓓ Ⓔ
76 Ⓐ Ⓑ Ⓒ Ⓓ Ⓔ
77 Ⓐ Ⓑ ● Ⓓ Ⓔ
78 Ⓐ Ⓑ Ⓒ Ⓓ Ⓔ
79 Ⓐ Ⓑ Ⓒ Ⓓ Ⓔ
80 Ⓐ Ⓑ Ⓒ ● Ⓔ
81 Ⓐ Ⓑ Ⓒ Ⓓ Ⓔ
82 Ⓐ Ⓑ Ⓒ Ⓓ Ⓔ
83 Ⓐ Ⓑ Ⓒ Ⓓ ●
84 Ⓐ Ⓑ Ⓒ Ⓓ Ⓔ
85 Ⓐ Ⓑ Ⓒ Ⓓ Ⓔ
86 ● Ⓑ Ⓒ Ⓓ Ⓔ
87 Ⓐ Ⓑ Ⓒ Ⓓ Ⓔ
88 Ⓐ Ⓑ ● Ⓓ Ⓔ

Correctly Filled Worksheet

1. 45 E____ 43 ______ 83 ______

2. [___ A] [24 E] [5 C] [___ B] [19 D]

3. <u>69</u> 87 50 <u>54</u> 25 47 20 <u>80</u> 27

4. (71 C) (36 ___) (49 B) (11 ___)

5. [42 ___] (44 ___) (14 A) [56 ___]

6. (88 ___) (68 E) (61 B) (70 ___) (34 ___)

7. 28 67 29 <u>77</u> (26)

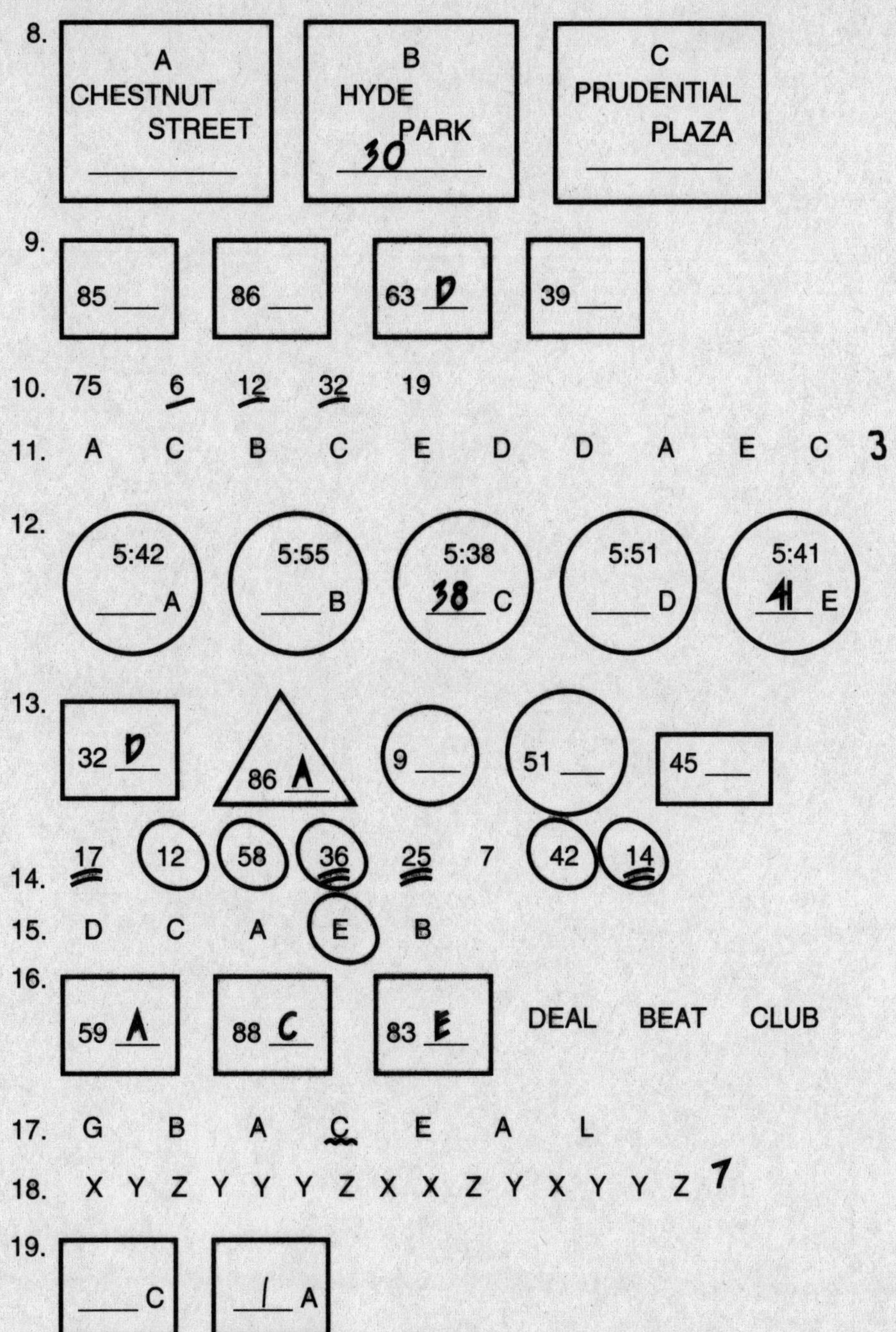

8.
A CHESTNUT STREET
B HYDE PARK 30
C PRUDENTIAL PLAZA
9.
85 ___ 86 ___ 63 D 39 ___
10. 75 6 12 32 19
11. A C B C E D D A E C 3
12.
5:42 ___ A
5:55 ___ B
5:38 38 C
5:51 ___ D
5:41 41 E
13.
32 D
86 A
9 ___
51 ___
45 ___
14. 17 12 58 36 25 7 42 14
15. D C A E B
16.
59 A
88 C
83 E
DEAL BEAT CLUB
17. G B A C E A L
18. X Y Z Y Y Y Z X X Z Y X Y Y Z 7
19.
___ C
1 A

BIOGRAPHICAL/ ACHIEVEMENT INVENTORY

Many federal and state civil service, postal, and military examinations now conclude with a self-descriptive inventory which is designed to resemble a test section. This inventory is set up to look like a multiple-choice test and is timed like a test, but it is not a test at all. There are no right or wrong answers. The examiners are looking for a pattern of achievement, interests, and personality traits that they can compare to the achievement, interests, and personality profile of persons who are currently active and successful in the occupation for which you have applied.

You cannot study for this inventory. The only possible preparation is searching out old school records to refresh your own mind as to subjects that you studied—those in which you did well and those which gave you trouble—attendance record, grades, and extra-curricular activities. If you cannot find your records, just answer to the best of your ability. Some questions allow for a response of "do not recall"; many require you to choose an answer. Aside from high school and college related questions (if you did not attend college at all you are permitted to skip over a whole section of the inventory), you are asked questions about your likes and dislikes and about the impression that you make upon others. There are questions about how you rank yourself with relation to other people, about what your friends think of you, and about the opinions of your supervisors or teachers. Do not try to second guess the test makers to give the "right" answer. There are internal checks for consistency and honesty built into the questions. Your best bet is to answer quickly and candidly. Dwelling over the questions is not likely to help.

The inventories for different positions tend to emphasize different topics, but there is a certain similarity from one to the next. The questions below offer you a sampling of the types of questions that are often asked.

1. My favorite subject in high school was

   (A) math

   (B) English

   (C) physical education

   (D) social studies

   (E) science

2. My GPA upon graduation from high school (on a 4.0 scale) was

   (A) lower than 2.51

   (B) 2.51 to 2.80

   (C) 2.81 to 3.25

   (D) 3.26 to 3.60

   (E) higher than 3.60

3. In my second year of high school, I was absent

   (A) never

   (B) not more than 3 days

   (C) 4 to 10 days

   (D) more often than 10 days

   (E) do not recall

4. While in high school, I participated in

   (A) one sport

   (B) two sports and one other extracurricular activity

   (C) three nonathletic extracurricular activities

   (D) no extracurricular activities

   (E) other than the above

5. During my senior year in high school, I held a paying job
   (A) 0 hours a week
   (B) 1 to 5 hours weekly
   (C) 6 to 10 hours a week
   (D) 11 to 16 hours a week
   (E) more than 16 hours a week

6. In high school, I did volunteer work
   (A) more than 10 hours a week
   (B) 5 to 10 hours a week on a regular basis
   (C) sporadically
   (D) seldom
   (E) not at all

7. My standing in my graduating class was in the
   (A) bottom third
   (B) middle third
   (C) top third
   (D) top quarter
   (E) top 10 percent

8. In comparison to my peers, I cut classes
   (A) much less often than most
   (B) somewhat less often than most
   (C) just about the same as most
   (D) somewhat more often than most
   (E) much more often than most

9. The campus activities in which I participated most were
   (A) social service
   (B) political
   (C) literary
   (D) did not participate in campus activities
   (E) did not participate in any of these activities

10. While a college student, I spent most of my summers
    (A) in summer school
    (B) earning money
    (C) traveling
    (D) in service activities
    (E) resting

11. My college education was financed
    (A) entirely by my parents
    (B) by my parents and my own earnings
    (C) by scholarships, loans, and my own earnings
    (D) by my parents and loans
    (E) by a combination of sources not listed above

12. In the college classroom, I was considered
    (A) a listener
    (B) an occasional contributor
    (C) an average participant
    (D) a frequent contributor
    (E) a leader

13. I made my greatest mark in college through my
    - (A) athletic prowess
    - (B) success in performing arts
    - (C) academic success
    - (D) partying reputation
    - (E) conciliatory skill with my peers

14. My cumulative GPA (on a 4.0 scale) in courses in my major was
    - (A) lower than 3.00
    - (B) 3.00 to 3.25
    - (C) 3.26 to 3.50
    - (D) 3.51 to 3.75
    - (E) higher than 3.75

15. My supervisors (or teachers) would be most likely to describe me as
    - (A) competent
    - (B) gifted
    - (C) intelligent
    - (D) fast-working
    - (E) detail oriented

16. My peers would probably describe me as
    - (A) analytical
    - (B) glib
    - (C) organized
    - (D) funny
    - (E) helpful

17. According to my supervisors (or teachers), my greatest asset is my
    - (A) ability to communicate orally
    - (B) written expression
    - (C) ability to motivate others
    - (D) organization of time
    - (E) friendly personality

18. In the past year, I read strictly for pleasure
    - (A) no books
    - (B) one book
    - (C) two books
    - (D) three to six books
    - (E) more than six books

19. When I read for pleasure, I read mostly
    - (A) history
    - (B) fiction
    - (C) poetry
    - (D) biography
    - (E) current events

20. My supervisors (or teachers) would say that my area of least competence is
    - (A) analytical ability
    - (B) written communication
    - (C) attention to detail
    - (D) public speaking
    - (E) self-control

21. In my opinion, the most important of the following attributes in an employee is
    - (A) discretion
    - (B) loyalty
    - (C) open-mindedness
    - (D) courtesy
    - (E) competence

22. My supervisors (or teachers) would say that I react to criticism with
    - (A) a defensive attitude
    - (B) quick capitulation
    - (C) anger
    - (D) interest
    - (E) shame

23. My attendance record over the past year has been
    (A) not as good as I would like it to be
    (B) not as good as my supervisors (or teachers) would like it to be
    (C) a source of embarrassment
    (D) satisfactory
    (E) a source of pride

24. My peers would say that when I feel challenged my reaction is one of
    (A) determination
    (B) energy
    (C) defiance
    (D) caution
    (E) compromise

There are no "right" answers to these questions, so there is no answer key.